Harnessing Large Language Models for Enhanced Business Analytics

Fabio Perez Marzullo
https://orcid.org/0000-0003-1693-9146
Politécnica UFRJ, Brazil

IGI Global
Scientific Publishing
Publishing Tomorrow's Research Today

Vice President of Editorial	Melissa Wagner
Director of Acquisitions	Mikaela Felty
Director of Book Development	Jocelynn Hessler
Production Manager	Mike Brehm
Cover Design	Jose Rosado

Published in the United States of America by
IGI Global Scientific Publishing
701 East Chocolate Avenue
Hershey, PA, 17033, USA
Tel: 717-533-8845 | Fax: 717-533-7115
Website: https://www.igi-global.com E-mail: cust@igi-global.com

Library of Congress Cataloging-in-Publication Data

Names: Marzullo, Fabio Perez, 1977- editor
http://id.loc.gov/authorities/names/n2020014462
http://id.loc.gov/rwo/agents/n2020014462
Title: Harnessing large language models for enhanced business analytics / [edited by] Fabio Perez Marzullo.
Description: Hershey, PA : IGI Global Scientific Publishing, [2026] | Includes bibliographical references and index. | Summary: "This book aims to make a significant impact on both academic and professional realms by providing a comprehensive resource on leveraging LLMs for business analytics"-- Provided by publisher.
Identifiers: LCCN 2025012302 (print) | LCCN 2025012303 (ebook) | ISBN 9798369366905 hardcover | ISBN 9798369366912 paperback | ISBN 9798369366929 ebook
Subjects: LCSH: Management--Data processing http://id.loc.gov/authorities/subjects/sh85080339 | Natural language processing (Computer science) http://id.loc.gov/authorities/subjects/sh88002425 | Artificial intelligence--Industrial applications
Classification: LCC HD30.2 .H37 2025 (print) | LCC HD30.2 (ebook) | DDC 658/.05--dc23/eng/20250527
LC record available at https://lccn.loc.gov/2025012302
LC ebook record available at https://lccn.loc.gov/2025012303

British Cataloguing in Publication Data
A Cataloguing in Publication record for this book is available from the British Library.

Table of Contents

Preface x

Chapter 1
Ethical Considerations and Future Directions 1
Pankaj Verma, Indian Institute of Management, Bangalore, India
Krishna Gandhi, Illinois State University, USA

Chapter 2
Foundations of Large Language Models 45
Akhil Sharma, School of Computing Science and Engineering, Sharda University, Greater Noida, India
Jatin Gupta, School of Computing Science and Engineering, Sharda University, Greater Noida, India
Ali Imam Abidi, School of Computing Science and Engineering, Sharda University, Greater Noida, India

Chapter 3
Introduction to Large Language Models in Business Analytics 85
Pankaj Verma, Indian Institute of Management, Bangalore, India
Krishna Gandhi, Illinois State University, USA

Chapter 4
Natural Language Processing in the Business Context 133
Pankaj Verma, Indian Institute of Management, Bangalore, India
Krishna Gandhi, Illinois State University, USA

Chapter 5
Predictive Analytics for Customer Retention in E-Commerce: Evaluating Model Accuracy and Its Impact on Retention Strategies 189
Parihar Suresh Dahake, School of Management, Ramdeobaba University, Nagpur, India
Nihar Suresh Dahake, Dr. Ambedkar Institute of Management Studies and Research, Nagpur, India

Chapter 6
Real-Time Financial Sentiment Extraction Using Large Language Model (LLM) Architectures 215
Lakshmi Harika Palivela, Vellore Institute of Technology, Chennai, India
Shreyas Athinarapu, Vellore Institute of Technology, Chennai, India
Greeshma Reddy Basireddy, Vellore Institute of Technology, Chennai, India
Tata Venkata Krishna Teja, Vellore Institute of Technology, Chennai, India

Chapter 7
The Ethical and Regulatory Landscape of Large Language Models 255
Sawan Rai, SRM-AP University, India

Chapter 8
Transforming Financial Decision-Making: The Role of Large Language Models in Risk Management and Fraud Detection........ 271
Puneett Bhatnagr, Amity University, India

Chapter 9
The Ethical and Regulatory Landscape of Large Language Models 293
Sawan Rai, SRM-AP University, India

Chapter 10
Transforming Financial Decision-Making: The Role of Large Language Models in Risk Management and Fraud Detection........ 309
Puneett Bhatnagr, Amity University, India

Compilation of References 331

About the Contributors 351

Index 355

Detailed Table of Contents

Preface x

Chapter 1
Ethical Considerations and Future Directions 1
Pankaj Verma, Indian Institute of Management, Bangalore, India
Krishna Gandhi, Illinois State University, USA

This chapter explores the ethical landscape surrounding the deployment of Large Language Models (LLMs) in business analytics, emphasizing that their transformative potential must be matched with a strong commitment to responsibility and accountability. As LLMs become deeply embedded in domains such as finance, healthcare, and retail, they bring not only efficiency and innovation but also serious challenges related to data privacy, bias, misinformation, and regulatory compliance. The chapter critically examines how organizations can balance innovation with ethical governance by implementing robust data governance practices, fostering transparency and explainability, and addressing emerging threats like prompt injection and model misuse. It advocates for a multi-stakeholder approach, involving policymakers, technologists, and civil society, to build a sustainable and inclusive future for AI. Ultimately, it calls for ethics to be embedded at every stage of LLM development and deployment—not as an afterthought, but as a foundational principle for long-term trust and value creation.

Chapter 2
Foundations of Large Language Models 45
Akhil Sharma, School of Computing Science and Engineering, Sharda University, Greater Noida, India
Jatin Gupta, School of Computing Science and Engineering, Sharda University, Greater Noida, India
Ali Imam Abidi, School of Computing Science and Engineering, Sharda University, Greater Noida, India

Large Language Models (LLMs) are indicated by this chapter as a major change maker for business analytics. Focusing on practical implementation strategies, it goes over and above the basic foundations like Transformers and tokenization. By analyzing operational metrics via real-world case studies such as (Klarna, BloombergGPT) the chapter spotlights critical cost-latency trade-offs. The "LLMOps" lifecycle is then established, and a strategic framework for deployment (API vs. Self-Hosted) and governance including hallucination risks and EU AI Act compliance is presented.

The text then ends with the future trends in multimodal AI and agentic systems, granting the practitioners the needed actionable insights for a sustainable competitive advantage.

Chapter 3
Introduction to Large Language Models in Business Analytics 85
Pankaj Verma, Indian Institute of Management, Bangalore, India
Krishna Gandhi, Illinois State University, USA

This chapter explores the transformative impact of Large Language Models (LLMs) on business analytics, demonstrating how these advanced AI systems are revolutionizing the way organizations interact with both structured and unstructured data. By leveraging architectures like Transformers and techniques such as pre-training and fine-tuning, LLMs enable businesses to perform tasks ranging from sentiment analysis and predictive modeling to automated reporting and intelligent customer engagement. The chapter outlines how LLMs support natural language interfaces, enhance decision-making, streamline operations, and democratize data access across functions. Real-world applications across industries—retail, finance, healthcare, and manufacturing—illustrate their value, while challenges such as data privacy, interpretability, bias, and infrastructure demands are also critically examined. Ultimately, the chapter presents LLMs not just as analytical tools but as strategic assets that reshape the future of data-driven enterprise decision-making.

Chapter 4
Natural Language Processing in the Business Context 133
Pankaj Verma, Indian Institute of Management, Bangalore, India
Krishna Gandhi, Illinois State University, USA

This chapter explores the transformative role of Natural Language Processing (NLP) in the modern business landscape, tracing its evolution from early rule-based systems to today's advanced deep learning and transformer-based models. It highlights how NLP enables organizations to unlock insights from unstructured text data across diverse functions-ranging from customer service and marketing to human resources, finance, and healthcare. Key technologies like sentiment analysis, named entity recognition, and large language models are examined alongside practical use cases such as chatbots, resume screening, fraud detection, and virtual healthcare assistants. The chapter also addresses critical challenges including data privacy, algorithmic bias, interpretability, and the resource demands of scaling NLP systems. Finally, it offers strategies for effective implementation, emphasizing cross-functional collaboration, ethical governance, and hybrid deployment approaches to ensure that NLP solutions deliver meaningful, responsible, and sustainable value to businesses.

Chapter 5
Predictive Analytics for Customer Retention in E-Commerce: Evaluating Model Accuracy and Its Impact on Retention Strategies 189
Parihar Suresh Dahake, School of Management, Ramdeobaba University, Nagpur, India
Nihar Suresh Dahake, Dr. Ambedkar Institute of Management Studies and Research, Nagpur, India

Despite the rise of predictive analytics as a breakthrough tool for minimizing churn, client retention remains a major challenge for e-commerce businesses. This study looks into the accuracy of machine learning models in predicting customer attrition and the practical consequences for retention strategies, with a focus on Nagpur, India's fast-expanding e-commerce sector. This study trains and tests four predictive models' logistic regression, random forest, support vector machine (SVM), and a neural network with behavioral, demographic, and transactional information on a dataset of 15,000 customer transactions from a well-known e-commerce platform in Nagpur. The random forest classifier, which got the best accuracy (89.7%) and F1-score (0.86), shows higher skill in detecting at-risk consumers, as model performance is measured by accuracy, precision, recall, and F1-score. The study then uses Orange Software testing with 500 consumers to investigate the incorporation of predictive insights into retention strategies.

Chapter 6
Real-Time Financial Sentiment Extraction Using Large Language Model (LLM) Architectures 215
Lakshmi Harika Palivela, Vellore Institute of Technology, Chennai, India
Shreyas Athinarapu, Vellore Institute of Technology, Chennai, India
Greeshma Reddy Basireddy, Vellore Institute of Technology, Chennai, India
Tata Venkata Krishna Teja, Vellore Institute of Technology, Chennai, India

The volume of financial data continues to increase and society moves towards a real-time analytical platform, this project reports on the design and implementation of a Large Language Model (LLM)-driven system for financial news sentiment analysis. It leverages both domain specific and general transformer models such as FinBERT, FinBERT-tone, ProsusAI FinBERT, Twitter-RoBERTa, ELECTRA, and DistilBERT—to classify news sentiment as Positive, Negative, or Neutral. A hybrid processing pipeline has been designed where LLMs will first enhance and summarize the financial news articles to better situational context. Once the text is enhanced, it is sent to the relevant fine-tuned transformer models. The outputs are brought together through a multi-agent ensemble process that functionally simulates a diverse set of analysts and improves decision robustness. Evaluation on benchmark datasets shows the ensemble outperforms individual models in accuracy and consistency. This system enables automated financial insight extraction, supports investment decisions, and gauges market sentiment.

Chapter 7
The Ethical and Regulatory Landscape of Large Language Models 255
Sawan Rai, SRM-AP University, India

Large Language Models (LLMs) are transforming industries by enabling advanced natural language processing (NLP) applications, yet their adoption raises ethical and regulatory concerns. Bias in training data can lead to unfair outcomes in hiring, credit scoring, and legal decisions, necessitating bias mitigation techniques such as debiasing algorithms and diverse data curation. Privacy risks arise from LLMs memorizing sensitive data, requiring compliance with regulations like GDPR and CCPA through differential privacy and encryption-based training. The opacity of LLMs challenges trust, prompting research in Explainable AI (XAI) methods like SHAP and LIME. Governments and industry leaders are shaping AI regulations, such as the EU AI Act, to balance innovation with responsibility. Future AI governance will require interdisciplinary collaboration, ethical auditing, and continuous oversight. Ensuring fairness, transparency, and accountability will be key to responsible AI deployment, enabling organizations to leverage LLMs' potential while minimizing risks.

Chapter 8
Transforming Financial Decision-Making: The Role of Large Language Models in Risk Management and Fraud Detection.. 271
Puneett Bhatnagr, Amity University, India

This chapter investigates the knowledge gained through the transformational role of Large Language Models (LLMs) in financial risk management and fraud detection, especially as it relates to modern financial decision-making. Conventional approaches to financial analysis have introduced machine learning techniques to handle vast and complex datasets. Specifically, LLMs, from OpenAI's GPT series to Bloomberg's GPT, are a significant change because they represent the ability of institutions to process and understand structurally as well as unstructured financial data. This chapter illustrates how LLMs improve risk assessment by deriving the context and integrating sentiment analysis from regulated documents and market trends to provide nuanced insights. In the case of fraud detection, LLMs outperform others in terms of their ability to detect anomalies, identity theft prevention, and document validation based on real-time upcoming transactions and communication patterns.

Chapter 9
The Ethical and Regulatory Landscape of Large Language Models 293
Sawan Rai, SRM-AP University, India

Large Language Models (LLMs) are transforming industries by enabling advanced natural language processing (NLP) applications, yet their adoption raises ethical and regulatory concerns. Bias in training data can lead to unfair outcomes in hiring, credit scoring, and legal decisions, necessitating bias mitigation techniques such as debiasing algorithms and diverse data curation. Privacy risks arise from LLMs memorizing sensitive data, requiring compliance with regulations like GDPR and CCPA through differential privacy and encryption-based training. The opacity of LLMs challenges trust, prompting research in Explainable AI (XAI) methods like SHAP and LIME. Governments and industry leaders are shaping AI regulations, such as the EU AI Act, to balance innovation with responsibility. Future AI governance will require interdisciplinary collaboration, ethical auditing, and continuous oversight. Ensuring fairness, transparency, and accountability will be key to responsible AI deployment, enabling organizations to leverage LLMs' potential while minimizing risks.

Chapter 10
Transforming Financial Decision-Making: The Role of Large Language Models in Risk Management and Fraud Detection.. 309
Puneett Bhatnagr, Amity University, India

This chapter investigates the knowledge gained through the transformational role of Large Language Models (LLMs) in financial risk management and fraud detection, especially as it relates to modern financial decision-making. Conventional approaches to financial analysis have introduced machine learning techniques to handle vast and complex datasets. Specifically, LLMs, from OpenAI's GPT series to Bloomberg's GPT, are a significant change because they represent the ability of institutions to process and understand structurally as well as unstructured financial data. This chapter illustrates how LLMs improve risk assessment by deriving the context and integrating sentiment analysis from regulated documents and market trends to provide nuanced insights. In the case of fraud detection, LLMs outperform others in terms of their ability to detect anomalies, identity theft prevention, and document validation based on real-time upcoming transactions and communication patterns.

Compilation of References 331

About the Contributors 351

Index 355

Preface

INTRODUCTION

The rapid evolution of artificial intelligence has ushered in a new era of possibilities for organizations seeking to transform data into actionable insight. Among these advancements, Large Language Models (LLMs) have emerged as a particularly powerful and versatile class of technologies, capable of interpreting, generating, and reasoning over vast amounts of structured and unstructured data. As editors of this volume, we recognized a timely opportunity to bring together diverse perspectives that illuminate the growing role of LLMs in reshaping the field of business analytics.

Harnessing Large Language Models for Enhanced Business Analytics is conceived as both a scholarly and practical contribution to this dynamic intersection. The chapters assembled here explore how LLMs can be deployed to analyze complex datasets, uncover hidden patterns, predict emerging trends, and ultimately support more informed and agile decision-making processes. In doing so, the book seeks to bridge a persistent gap between theoretical advancements in AI research and their real-world application within business environments.

This volume is structured to guide readers through multiple dimensions of the topic. It begins with foundational discussions that establish the theoretical underpinnings of LLMs and their relevance to analytics. It then moves into applied perspectives, where contributors present methodologies, tools, and frameworks for integrating LLMs into organizational workflows. Case studies further illustrate how businesses across sectors are leveraging these technologies to drive innovation and competitive advantage. Finally, the book considers future directions, including emerging challenges, ethical considerations, and opportunities for continued research and development.

Our objective is to create a resource that resonates across audiences. For academic researchers and students, this book offers insights into current methodologies, conceptual frameworks, and research trajectories in the application of LLMs to business analytics. For practitioners, it provides actionable guidance, practical examples, and lessons learned from real-world implementations. For policymakers and technology strategists, it highlights the broader implications of LLM adoption, including its impact on business models, operational practices, and regulatory landscapes.

We hope this volume not only informs but also inspires. The integration of LLMs into business analytics is still unfolding, and its full potential remains to be realized. By bringing together contributions from researchers, industry experts, and thought leaders, we aim to foster dialogue, encourage experimentation, and stimulate further inquiry into this rapidly evolving field.

We extend our sincere gratitude to all contributors for their thoughtful and rigorous work, and to the readers whose curiosity and engagement will continue to drive innovation at the intersection of AI and business analytics.

ORGANIZATION OF THE BOOK

As editor, I have carefully curated each chapter in this volume to reflect the breadth, depth, and evolving significance of Large Language Models (LLMs) in business analytics. The following overview highlights the distinctive contributions of each chapter, offering readers a guided pathway through the intellectual and practical landscape of the book.

Chapter 1 sets the tone for the volume by confronting the ethical imperatives that must accompany the rapid adoption of Large Language Models (LLMs) in business analytics. The editors frame this contribution as a necessary grounding in responsibility, highlighting how innovation across sectors such as finance, healthcare, and retail is inseparable from concerns around privacy, bias, misinformation, and regulatory accountability. The chapter advances a compelling argument for embedding ethics into every stage of the AI lifecycle, advocating transparent systems, robust governance structures, and a multi-stakeholder approach that ensures LLM-driven transformation remains both trustworthy and socially sustainable.

Chapter 2 provides a technically rich yet practice-oriented foundation for understanding LLMs as engines of modern analytics. Moving beyond theoretical constructs, the chapter situates core concepts such as transformer architectures within real-world operational contexts, examining deployment trade-offs, cost considerations, and lifecycle management through the lens of "LLMOps." The editors highlight its particular strength in bridging theory and application, offering practitioners actionable frameworks for implementation, governance, and compliance, while also pointing toward emerging developments in multimodal and agent-based AI systems.

Chapter 3 introduces readers to the transformative role of LLMs in reshaping business analytics, positioning these models as strategic assets rather than mere tools. The chapter demonstrates how LLMs enable organizations to harness both structured and unstructured data, enhancing decision-making, operational efficiency, and accessibility of insights across functions. Through industry-spanning examples, it underscores the breadth of applications while maintaining a critical perspective on challenges such as interpretability, bias, and infrastructure demands, thereby offering a balanced and forward-looking overview of LLM-driven analytics.

Chapter 4 expands the discussion into the broader domain of Natural Language Processing (NLP), tracing its evolution and centrality in contemporary business environments. The editors present this chapter as a comprehensive exploration of how NLP unlocks value from textual data across organizational functions, from customer engagement to fraud detection. It thoughtfully combines technological exposition with practical applications, while also addressing implementation challenges and ethical considerations, ultimately emphasizing the importance of cross-functional strategies and responsible deployment.

Chapter 5 turns to a focused empirical investigation within the e-commerce sector, examining predictive analytics as a tool for customer retention. The chapter is distinguished by its rigorous comparative analysis of machine learning models, demonstrating how predictive accuracy directly informs retention strategies. By grounding its findings in real transactional data and experimental validation, it offers readers both methodological clarity and practical relevance, illustrating how data-driven insights can be translated into tangible business outcomes.

Chapter 6 explores the dynamic intersection of LLMs and financial analytics through the lens of real-time sentiment extraction. The editors highlight the chapter's innovative hybrid architecture, which combines multiple transformer-based models within an ensemble framework to enhance accuracy and robustness. Its emphasis on real-time processing and decision support reflects the growing demand for timely financial insights, positioning LLM-driven sentiment analysis as a powerful tool for investment strategy and market interpretation.

Chapter 7 addresses one of the most pressing concerns in advanced AI systems: security and privacy within multi-agent LLM networks. This chapter is presented as a critical contribution that not only identifies key vulnerabilities—such as adversarial attacks and data leakage—but also proposes a novel framework integrating encryption, differential privacy, and decentralized protocols. The editors underscore its practical significance, particularly in demonstrating measurable improvements in threat detection and data protection.

Chapter 8 extends the conversation into sustainability, examining the environmental implications of scaling multi-agent LLM systems. Framed as a forward-looking contribution, the chapter introduces innovative mechanisms for energy optimization, including adaptive collaboration and energy-aware scheduling. The editors emphasize its importance in aligning AI advancement with environmental responsibility, presenting sustainability not as an optional consideration but as a core design principle for future systems.

Chapter 9 revisits the ethical and regulatory dimensions of LLMs with a comprehensive and policy-oriented perspective. The chapter systematically analyzes issues of bias, transparency, and privacy while evaluating global regulatory frameworks and industry practices. The editors note its particular value in bridging the gap between technical solutions and governance, offering a roadmap for responsible AI development grounded in interdisciplinary collaboration and continuous oversight.

Chapter 10 concludes the volume by examining the transformative role of LLMs in financial risk management and fraud detection. The editors position this chapter as a culmination of the book's central themes, demonstrating how advanced language models enhance analytical depth by integrating structured data with contextual and sentiment-driven insights. Its exploration of real-time fraud detection and risk assessment illustrates the tangible impact of LLMs on financial decision-making, reinforcing their significance as catalysts for innovation in high-stakes domains.

CONCLUSION

As we bring this volume to a close, it is evident that Large Language Models (LLMs) are not merely an incremental advancement in analytics but represent a fundamental shift in how organizations interpret, interact with, and derive value from data. Across the chapters, a unifying theme emerges: the integration of LLMs into business analytics is as much an organizational and ethical transformation as it is a technological one.

The contributions in this book collectively demonstrate that LLMs have moved beyond experimental novelty to become integral components of modern analytical ecosystems. From foundational architectures and deployment strategies to domain-specific applications in finance, e-commerce, and customer engagement, the chapters illustrate both the versatility and the complexity of these systems. At the same time, they underscore that successful adoption requires more than technical proficiency. It demands thoughtful governance, interdisciplinary collaboration, and a clear alignment with organizational objectives.

Equally important is the consistent emphasis on responsibility. Issues of bias, transparency, privacy, security, and sustainability are not peripheral concerns but central to the long-term viability of LLM-driven solutions. The insights presented throughout this volume reinforce the idea that ethical considerations must be embedded into design, development, and deployment processes. In this regard, the role of policymakers, researchers, and practitioners becomes deeply interconnected, shaping a shared responsibility for the future of AI in business.

Looking ahead, the trajectory of LLMs points toward increasingly autonomous, multimodal, and collaborative systems that will further redefine business intelligence and decision-making. Yet, with this potential comes the necessity for continuous evaluation, adaptation, and critical inquiry. The landscape will evolve, and so too must our frameworks for understanding and managing these technologies.

As editor, I hope this book serves not only as a comprehensive reference but also as a catalyst for ongoing exploration and innovation. Whether the reader approaches this work from an academic, professional, or policy perspective, I trust that the ideas presented here will inform practice, inspire new research, and contribute to a more responsible and impactful integration of LLMs in business analytics.

Chapter 1
Ethical Considerations and Future Directions

Pankaj Verma
http://orcid.org/0009-0009-9073-1803
Indian Institute of Management, Bangalore, India

Krishna Gandhi
http://orcid.org/0009-0004-9684-6699
Illinois State University, USA

ABSTRACT

This chapter explores the ethical landscape surrounding the deployment of Large Language Models (LLMs) in business analytics, emphasizing that their transformative potential must be matched with a strong commitment to responsibility and accountability. As LLMs become deeply embedded in domains such as finance, healthcare, and retail, they bring not only efficiency and innovation but also serious challenges related to data privacy, bias, misinformation, and regulatory compliance. The chapter critically examines how organizations can balance innovation with ethical governance by implementing robust data governance practices, fostering transparency and explainability, and addressing emerging threats like prompt injection and model misuse. It advocates for a multi-stakeholder approach, involving policymakers, technologists, and civil society, to build a sustainable and inclusive future for AI. Ultimately, it calls for ethics to be embedded at every stage of LLM development and deployment—not as an afterthought, but as a foundational principle for long-term trust and value creation.

DOI: 10.4018/979-8-3693-6690-5.ch001

INTRODUCTION

Context of Large Language Models in Business Analytics

It has never been so exciting. The field of artificial intelligence has been making extreme leaps in the last decade and Large Language Models are at the vanguard of that movement. LLMs such as GPT-4, PaLM, and Llama-2 are no longer experimented in science labs, but in many different industries, including health care, finance, retail, and entertainment. In particular, LLM-powered systems are used by organizations across sectors for tasks like predictive forecasting, sentiment analysis, market research, as well as automated reporting, in business analytics specifically. Using massive repositories of text data from within the corporation to the web-scale, LLMs have outperformed most other traditional analytics tools in terms of their agility, creativity, speed, and ability to reorganize and interpret unstructured information more quickly.

The high adoption rate hinges on the fact that LLMs have a proven business value. Decision makers take the view that the more depth of data-driven insights there are, the more competitive differentiation there is. Take for instance LLM processing billions of social media posts consumed overnight that pinpoints who is, in subtle ways, changing their mind for an awesome product redesign. At the same time, it could mine a decade's history of financial data to come up with sophisticated investment ideas, or quite possibly, an idea. LLMs thus extend analytics to a new level, transient to the prior methods dominated by structured, numeric data focused exclusively on geography and statistics.

But the same LLM capabilities that offer such promise are an equally forceful challenge. Data security, algorithmic bias, and regulatory compliance form just a fraction of the ethical labyrinth. Now LLMs are not only tools but active faces of the organizational decisions and hence no longer remain mere instruments. As a result, these decisions have indirect and wide-reaching consequences for stakeholders including employees, consumers, and more broadly also for the community. Therefore, ethical dimensions of LLM technology are not an option but a strategic imperative. Organizations are at risk for legal and reputational harm, but also the risk of perpetuating systemic biases, or even providing widespread use of advanced text generation that is malicious. (Raza et al., 2024; Ungless et al., 2024; Yang et al., 2024a).

Table 1. Use-cases of LLMs in business analytics

Application Area	Example Use-Case	Key Benefit
Predictive Forecasting	Analyzing historical financial data for trends	Faster, data-driven investment strategies
Sentiment Analysis	Processing customer reviews and social media	Real-time insight into consumer sentiment
Market Research	Extracting themes from open-ended survey responses	Uncovering hidden consumer preferences
Automated Reporting	Summarizing annual reports and news articles	Reducing manual workload and enhancing accuracy

THE INTERSECTION OF INNOVATION AND ETHICS

The Tension Between Innovation and Ethics

Feature of deployment of Language Learning Models (LLMs) is the existing tension between innovation and ethics. In the same technology area, there's a trend to put out products immediately. The aim is to launch the prototypes to get early adopters, or fresh money, invested. This fast-paced environment can be such that it misses the critical parts on how these technologies really work and the implications one might face. Most LLMs are working in a black box fashion, which makes it impossible for us to understand its internal works. And that complexity can lead to unintended outcomes that can be bad (Berengueres & Sandell, 2023).

For instance, if we have an LLM to perform certain processes in Human Resource. The use of this model might be meant to increase efficiency in recruitment process. But without intervention the model might automatically steer towards discrimination of certain demographic groups in the individuals it recommends for the job. Such discrimination also begs of ethical and legal standards. Failure to address these issues as soon as possible presents serious consequences to both those who are affected by the issue and to the organization itself.

Figure 1. This flowchart is the cyclical process of innovation, ethical risk assessment, and implementation of oversight measures

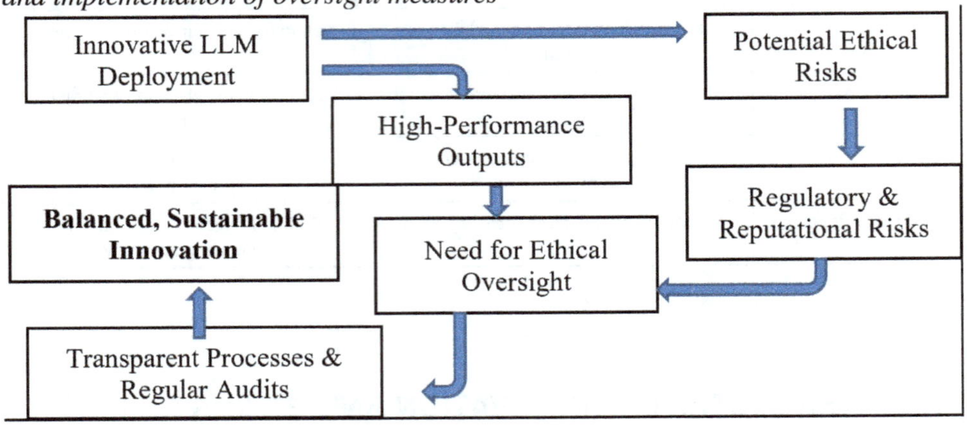

Innovation at What Cost?

Most businesses opt to innovate first and ask questions later when rolling out new technologies. Since it completely omits the way the LLMs could possibly cause harm, this strategy is especially toxic. When speaking of 'harm,' we can't just describe that there are no immediate breaches of information or compliance issues—harm is more. Psychological, social and economic consequences are all covered by the concept of harm.

For example, chatbots powered by LLMs that make offer users help with medical advice. What if the chatbot gives a wrong reply to the user if he asks about a particular health condition? It could turn out to be misinformation which will make people make bad health decisions that will lead to it putting their well-being at risk. Likewise, these models could impinge on user privacy by some inferences made regarding user data. Imagine that chatbot, for example, was to talk about a sensitive topic and accidentally reveal personal information about the data about other topics. On top of that, LLMs may also be used to generate biased narratives or spread false information and thus skew the public perception and direct public behaviors. In light of these risks, it bears to say to see it through the lens of ethics, and being accountable throughout the stage in design, development, deployment.

The Importance of Ethical Development

The ethical approach to technology development can sustain the long term and build higher stakeholder trust. Companies that deeply integrate ethical considerations to their operations have a higher probability of success. Public scrutiny continues to increase now more than ever and consumer loyalty can change swiftly in reaction to scandal or ethical breach. When organizations have open priorities for ethical standards, they provide a solid base for trust with their stakeholders (Berengueres & Sandell, 2023).

Avoiding legal problems is not the only proactivity when it comes to addressing problems like bias, data privacy, as well as algorithm transparency. These practices help companies become industry leaders. Both companies that have already taken steps to mitigate risks in the artificial intelligence and data use space and companies not already taking such steps will be better prepared to contend with future regulations around such technology and the use of related data. By providing ethical standards consonant with the ethics of conscientious consumers and others in the stakeholder group, they can validate commitment to ethical standards.

Organizations receive a protection mechanism from their investment in establishing ethical guidelines. Companies can establish regular assessment procedures which monitor their LLM operations to confirm unbiased and fair operations. Organizations address emerging problems to prevent them from turning into major issues through proper oversight. The disclosure of LLM systems' operational mechanisms helps users develop confidence in these systems. Consumer security improves when they receive information on data handling practices and decision-making processes (Ferdaus et al., 2024).

The development of internal organizational ethical values enables employees to gain empowerment. The knowledge of technological ethics value by staff members leads them to speak out about issues and make recommendations for development. Organizations reaching out proactively to clients can discover vital information that generates superior product outcomes. Boardroom decisions become more secure when organizations welcome diverse input from their perspectives because this practice decreases the risks of oversight errors. (Berengueres & Sandell, 2023).

The Challenge of Implementation

While the importance of ethical development is clear, implementing these principles can be challenging. Organizations often face pressure to deliver products quickly, and the fast-paced nature of the tech industry can sometimes overshadow lengthy ethical discussions. Training and educating employees about ethical considerations can take time and resources, which some companies may be reluctant to allocate.

However, the benefits of investing in ethical practices can outweigh the initial costs. Companies may find that fostering a culture of ethical responsibility enhances innovation in the long run. By creating an environment where ethical considerations are valued, organizations can encourage creativity while ensuring that the resulting technologies do not harm individuals or society at large (Ungless et al., 2024).

To integrate ethical considerations effectively, organizations can start by defining clear values and principles. These should align with the company's overall mission while addressing potential ethical concerns related to LLMs. Leadership plays a crucial role in reinforcing these values. The way that management demonstrates ethical conduct while making ethics a priority creates an organizational guideline for all staff members.

Organizations advancing ethical practices can attain them through proactive development of relationships with outside stakeholders. Organizations can access vital knowledge about new ethical challenges and proven practices through their work with academic institutions combined with advocacy groups and regulatory bodies. External partnerships offer organizations a better understanding while enabling joint responsibility to tackle advanced issues in LLM management practices.

We should remain vigilant and committed to ethical considerations all through as we go about the evolving landscape of technology. The implementation of ethics in the development of LLM technology leads to user protection and creates platforms for trusting relationships built on responsibility alongside innovation. Organizations need to see the direct relationship between ethical operational methods and sustainable business success while they develop strong technologies that benefit the community (Ferdaus et al., 2024).

Chapter Organization

The goal of this chapter is to present a thorough investigation on how LLMs are incorporated within today's business analytics environments, the moral issues they present, and the rules of the road for increasingly ubiquitous LLMs in use. This information provides direct guidance that benefits business leaders together with policy analysts, data scientists, and researchers. The subsequent part of the chapter investigates:

- **Data Governance and Privacy (Section 2):** This section explores data governance together with privacy aspects that emerge from massive text data collection while introducing best compliance methods (Section 2).
- **Bias, Fairness, and Discrimination (Section 3):** Analyses of how bias in the LLM training data ripples through the results and affects corporate decisions and might buttress the systems of discrimination.
- **Transparency, explain ability, and Trust (Section 4):** The section evaluates interpretability as a mechanism to minimize organizational risk while establishing trust between stakeholders (Section 4).

- **Security, Misinformation, and Potential Risks (Section 5):** One of the most critical security vulnerabilities of LLMs and How we can exploit these drawbacks to spread Misinformation or Cyberattacks.
- **Regulatory and Compliance Challenges (Section 6):** Besides existing and upcoming worldwide regulations, this section points out sector specific challenges faced by organizations in implementing LLMs.
- **Accountability, Governance, and Organizational Culture (Section 7):** Has the companies have identified ways of assigning accountability for AI outputs, build robust governance framework and incorporate ethics into organizational culture.
- **Future Directions and Research Opportunities (Section 8):** Future directions and research opportunities in LLM development outlining its technical, social and ethical frontiers in order to deploy sustainable innovation.
- **Conclusion (Section 9):** Conclusion (summarizing the crucial takeaways from the chapter and calling for a multi-stakeholder level approach toward utilizing ethically LLMs).

DATA GOVERNANCE AND PRIVACY

Expanding the Ethical Landscape of Data

The Role of Data in LLM Performance

Large Language Models (LLMs) are very much data hungry: their performance depends critically on massive quantities of it. Today, organizations data comes in from numerous sources. It could be email logs, discussions from social media, research papers, legal documents, and many more. This variety leads to a greater chance that sensitive or proprietary information will be on the training data for LLMs. A small piece of this information accidentally exposed could cause security problems or even lead to legal issues. As such, it is important for organizations wanting to maximize their use of LLMs to spend time and effort creating a thoughtful data collection approach for gathering enough data around a topic without compromising integrity. (Kapania et al., 2024).

Understanding Data Types

Structured data streams were common in the past. Transactions records and performance metrics that are clearly organized are included in this. Usually, these types of data were controlled in a strict manner within tight rules and policies. As opposed to unstructured textual data, on another hand it is challenging to manage and monitor. Without a clear format like this data comes in it leaves much aside sensitive information which can easily be missed here.

Risks Associated With Unstructured Data

There are two risks in unstructured data. The first is deliberately misusing it. Bad actors, such as malicious insiders or external attackers who might also exploit LLM training datasets to learn about a company's trade secrets or private user data can be a source of this. Concretely, let's say a company runs an attack by collecting customer data in ways that are not shielded, and an attacker can extract granular information about individual clients so an attacker can develop a strategy that will lead to identity theft or damage to the company's reputation.

The second risk is inadvertent disclosure. Personal data could be included in even well-meaning data scientists' datasets without knowing how to properly anonymize the data. This often takes place when data cleaning processes are not thorough enough. To give an example, if a dataset has customer feedback with the names of people or their contact details, without removing or masking such details enough, the model learns from that to output with such information.

Table 2. Risks and mitigation strategies for unstructured data

Risk Type	*Description*	*Mitigation Strategy*
Deliberate Misuse	Malicious extraction of sensitive data	Implement strong access controls and encryption
Inadvertent Disclosure	Accidental inclusion of personal data during cleaning	Use automated anonymization tools and manual audits

Implementing Risk Mitigation Frameworks

The first is to recognize these risks. Organizations must also invent ahead of time what types of information can be used with what exact rules of anonymization and what rules of the provocation must be defined. An example of this is the guidelines that organizations should follow in creating a dataset for training an LLM as they should indicate which pieces of information to collect, from whom, how to store it, and to whom to give it access.

This can avoid undesired effects as a consequence. An LLM could easily generate a piece of text that reveals private details or contains patterns by which people can be reidentified even if they have been anonymized. So, organizations can learn from data governance practices in other fields, and take the shape of a good system that will help secure your data privacy and protection to meet business requirements.

The Importance of Comprehensive Data Governance

Complete data governance approaches need to be adopted by organizations. Put simply, it involves making sure that 'privacy by design' is the underpinning philosophy throughout the course of handling data; from when data is ingested for processing, and then all the way through to it being deployed in the LLM itself. To give an example, an organization can keep doing regular audits of its data sources to verify that their data sources comply with privacy standards. In addition, they may use automated monitoring tools that spot data that does not adhere to imposed privacy criteria.

Additionally, efforts need to be made by the organization to train its employees on privacy of data. For example, workshops or modules on how to best handle data can go a long way in lowering inadvertent disclosure risk. It is the feedback that all of us in the organization learn of the need of respecting privacy and on how to treat such information with care.

Best Practices for Data Usage

Organizations might therefore be advised to adopt certain simple best practices to minimize the risk of using data efficiently without compromising on safety. First of all, they need to minimize data as much as possible, meaning collecting only data that is necessary for a specific task. A lean dataset means that such data like sensitive or irrelevant data are unlikely to get included in that dataset.

Second, strong anonymization techniques should be treated as a standard procedure. It could involve differential privacy ways of exposing datasets so that people can analyze them without exposing individual data points. Further, investing in the automation of the anonymization process on the technologies can reduce the time taken and also reduce human errors.

In addition, it will definitely be essential to encourage a company culture that deems ethical data usage as important. It is only when people understand how their data is used, that they are likely to fall into line when it is recommended, they do likewise. This culture can be triggered in companies through sharing of success stories of how responsible data use results in positive outcomes for them.

Continuous Evaluation and Adaptation

Finally, even if a company sets the policies and procedures once, it is not enough. It's very important for organizations to evaluate and adapt to their data governance practices time and again as technology continues to evolve and as new threats (s) pop-up. Organizations use regular assessments to see one step ahead of possible risks from LLM training data.

For example, they may require bi-annual reviews of their data practices and policies, changing them in accordance with the most current standards of the industry and legal demands. This proactive posture ensures organizations continue to be compliant and secure and provides them greater power to use LLMs.

Organizations can then embrace these principles and practices to work toward the success of LLM practice while also safeguarding the sensitive data they handle. A responsible data governance ethos for LLMs is a commitment to success that enables the technologies to be used.

Data Collection: Consent, Scope, and Oversight

Consent Models in Data Gathering

The training of LLMs relies heavily on massive data collection from public platforms. The benefits of obtaining large diverse datasets through public platform scraping produce ethical challenges by raising consent issues. Advanced AI training of publicly released information does not justify the possibility that its originators never meant their content to undergo this procedure. Organizations that do not properly illustrate their data utilization to users face a breakdown of trust since their practices differ from user expectations.

Key Ethical Concerns

- **Opacity in data usage**: However, many people are still unaware that their public posts or articles can be used for feeding LLM development.
- **Underrepresented communities**: Certain groups lack the digital footprint or the platform awareness to protect themselves from unwanted data collection, heightening their vulnerability to privacy breaches.

Addressing Scope Creep

Data collected for a specific purpose can be repurposed for another, a phenomenon known as "scope creep." For instance, user comments originally gathered to improve customer service might later be used to train an LLM that drives targeted ad campaigns or refines risk assessment models for financial decisions. Without strong data governance policies, scope creep can compromise user privacy and generate moral dilemmas (Tlaie, 2024). An effective policy is one that enforces "purpose limitation," ensuring data usage aligns closely with prior consent.

Oversight Mechanisms

Establishing oversight bodies—often in the form of data ethics boards or committees—can help organizations remain vigilant. These committees typically include experts from multiple disciplines, such as legal, data science, compliance, and user advocacy. Their role:

1. Monitor how data is sourced and used.
2. Evaluate new data integration requests and expansions to ensure alignment with established ethical frameworks.
3. Provide periodic risk assessment reports on data usage and recommend improvements.

Data Storage and Security Protocols

Public platforms serve as data sources to scrape the data enemas for LLM training. This level of diversity is achieved at the expense of eliciting ethical dilemmas regarding user consent. For example, some of the information may be technically publicly available, but for the individuals who created it, they may have never imagined it to be used for advanced AI training. It can erode trust especially if the organizations do not communicate how the data is being used, and it also sounds like there is a mismatch between the user expectation and how it is actually being used.

Common Vulnerabilities

- **Model inversion attacks**: An LLM might be adversarially queried, what to retrieve latent data patterns from its training set. In worst case, they can recover sensitive details from partial prompts.
- **Membership inference attacks**: Attackers first decide if a specific individual was included in the training set. In cases where the membership entails some sensitive attributes or behavior, this can be particularly damaging.

Recommended Practices

- Access to datasets on a role basis for limiting exposure.
- Encryption key rotation so that any single point compromise does not do too much damage.
- Addition of noise or obfuscation in a systematic and differential private way to alleviate the risk of re-identification

Code Example: Applying Differential Privacy

Here is a simplified python snippet which introduces differential privacy while working on data using the Diffprivlib library:

```
import diffprivlib. tools as dp
import numpy as np

# Sample data: customer satisfaction scores
data = np.array([4, 5, 3, 4, 5, 2, 4, 5, 3, 4])
# Compute the differentially private mean with epsilon = 1.0
dp_mean = dp.mean(data, epsilon=1.0)
print ("Differentially Private Mean:", dp_mean)
```

This snippet demonstrates how differential privacy can be applied to protect sensitive numerical data during analysis.

Privacy Regulations and Compliance Across Jurisdictions

LLMs are frequently deployed across several jurisdictions where different data protection laws and regulations operate. The drawback of this shattered legal environment is that compliance is an overwhelming endeavor, requiring a deep insight into any regional demands and a flexibility to change system-based architectures. Among the two of the most known regulatory frameworks in this domain, we will find General Data Protection Regulation (GDPR) in the European Union and California Consumer Privacy Act (CCPA) in the United States. Other region-specific laws also include these statutes which give the user various rights, like the "right to be forgotten", or "right to restrict processing" among others. Respecting these rights for LLMs, ingesting huge amounts of data for training and inference requires a fair amount of legal diligence, but significant technology innovation too.

Personal data include all information that can be used to identify a person; this is defined in a broad way under the GDPR and includes any and all information in combination with other data, regardless of whether it can actually be used to identify the person. As a result, data points that are relatively benign, like email addresses, user IDs or even some behavioral metadata, could fall in the personal information category under this regulation. Once the organization has these data points in an LLM's training set, we deal with strict compliance obligations. Probably the toughest obligation on the GDPR's "right to erasure" is to honor data deletion requests. There is no straightforward way to find and remove a single data point within an LLM's massive training corpus. If the sensitive records were deleted, traditional machine learning systems would retrain from scratch taking high computational cost and long downtime. The issue is even more acute in the case of LLMs. The problem of training models with billions of parameters is prohibitively expensive so researchers, developers have been looking to alternative approaches like 'selective unlearning' or limited fine tuning based on targeted data removal (Kapania et al., 2024).

The CCPA also closely mirrors the consumer control theme seen in emphasizing the consumer's control over personal information. Organizations are compelled to tell what data is gathered, how it is used, and whether it is sold to third parties. Moreover, it gives Californians a right to ask the deletion of his or her personal data. In terms of LLM pipelines, this also implies designing a pipeline that has the ability to easily record what records are ingested, where they are located in the model's workflow, and how they will be masked or purged if needed. A solution to this legal demand for updating or isolating distinct segments of a model or corpus is modular model architectures, where different parts of a model or training corpus can be updated or isolated independently.

However, legislation surrounding AI in many emerging markets is often vague or even non-existent, resulting in organizations themselves making what could be vague or undefined concepts of privacy and data governance for any use case powered by an LLM. With this uncertainty, legal consultation has now become a continuous process and not just as a one-time checklist process. Organisations are aware of proposed regulations, they project in and anticipate any possible compliance challenges, and most importantly, they must pivot their technical strategies in the face of new data protection laws. LLM deployments can do better in furthering the desire to secure diverse global requirements while safeguarding the user rights lest AI and the partner to privacy standards mutate at a speed of light. (Yang et al., 2024b).

Table 3. Regulatory requirements for LLM data

Regulation	*Key Provisions*	*Implications for LLMs*
GDPR	Right to erasure, informed consent	Requires robust data lineage and selective unlearning strategies
CCPA	Transparency in data collection, opt-out rights	Demands clear disclosure and efficient data removal procedures

Potential Directions for Enhancing Data Governance

- **Privacy-Preserving Techniques**: Among them are available methods such as homomorphic encryption and secure multi-party computation which allow to evaluate or to use (train with) data without having a full view of the content.
- **Federated Learning**: Models rather train locally on various devices or servers and aggregate centrally. This is a method for reducing risks associated with pooling, over privacy.
- **Auditable AI**: Tracing potential malpractices and keeping accountability can be possible with enhancing the logs and doing automated auditing. By logging at the advanced level, a laptop could track how or when each dataset was used to train or update an LLM, aiding in their compliance checks and audits.

In general, data governance is not a function that's confined to once and done, or that is simply procedural. It is a strategic imperative that calls for continual reshaping to new business necessities, sapping pressures, and innovative AI abilities. As advanced LLMs proliferate, robust data governance — no matter how meticulously defined, fed and managed — is still dangerously vulnerable to any gaps that unleash societal and financial, as well as reputational and ethical, disasters.

Figure 2. This flowchart demonstrates how data governance continues to form around data privacy and compliance throughout a lifecycle of an LLM

Table 4. Strategies for enhancing data governance

Strategy	*Description*	*Benefits*
Privacy-Preserving Techniques	Use of encryption and differential privacy during data processing	Reduces risk of data re-identification
Federated Learning	Training models on decentralized data	Limits exposure of sensitive data to a central repository
Auditable AI	Implementing automated logging and regular audits	Enhances accountability and compliance

BIAS, FAIRNESS, AND DISCRIMINATION

Defining Bias and Its Implications in LLMs

Bias in Large Language Models (LLMs) occurs when these systems systematically endorse or denounce some groups or perspectives or even attributes on patterns and associations in the training data through them. Some are clearly biased—they express themselves with direct, offensively baneful, or harmful language, while others are more muted, affecting how favored subjects and people are treated. The second type of bias can also be quite detrimental in most circumstances; although it can appear benign. An example of this is that training an LLM for medical analysis might have the LLM systematically suggesting a more aggressive treatment plan for one demographic group than another, which can be traced back to historical data that contains disparities. If these recommendations are implemented in actual settings of healthcare, they can further widen inequalities between patients (Raza et al., 2024).

As decisions are increasingly being made by these LLMs in larger and larger systems, the results of such bias can be magnified many times over. An example in human resources would be a model trained on historically biased hiring data that unintentionally perpetuates past discriminatory practices and excludes worthy applicants from certain backgrounds. Just as LLMs could be used to automate parts of credit scoring, a particular subset may end up systematically penalizing certain demographics because of preexisting societal prejudices and subsequently credit scoring that results in racially biased lending decisions. In terms of policy advice or strategic planning, even areas that one may think to be purely the realm of information could nonetheless underpin the shape of organizational policy so it dovetails with ingrained stereotypes or partisan views(Raza et al., 2024).

This problem is exacerbated by how strongly people believe that "a driven by an AI" solution is a natural and neutral one. If there are such assumptions, then stakeholders may put too much faith in model outputs and forget the need for critical oversight. This self-perpetuating cycle of biased recommendations guides institutional action followed by new data that might follow: subsequent hiring outcomes, credit histories and policy initiatives, which reinforces the original bias. Bias however, becomes entrenched because when organizations feed these latest data points back into the future model retraining, the bias continues to grow.

Such challenges require the multisectoral approach. Data audits can be carried out rigorously to identify and remedy in proportional discrimination. Depending on the environments, further quantifying bias can be done using techniques that measure what skew looks like in word associations or in model outputs. The first step to minimizing harmful effects and creating more equitable, as well as more reliable, experiences is simply recognizing that LLMs reflect biases present in their training data. (Yang et al., 2024b).

Figure 3. The data level (red) starts with bias, which propagates through to the decision making in real world (blue)

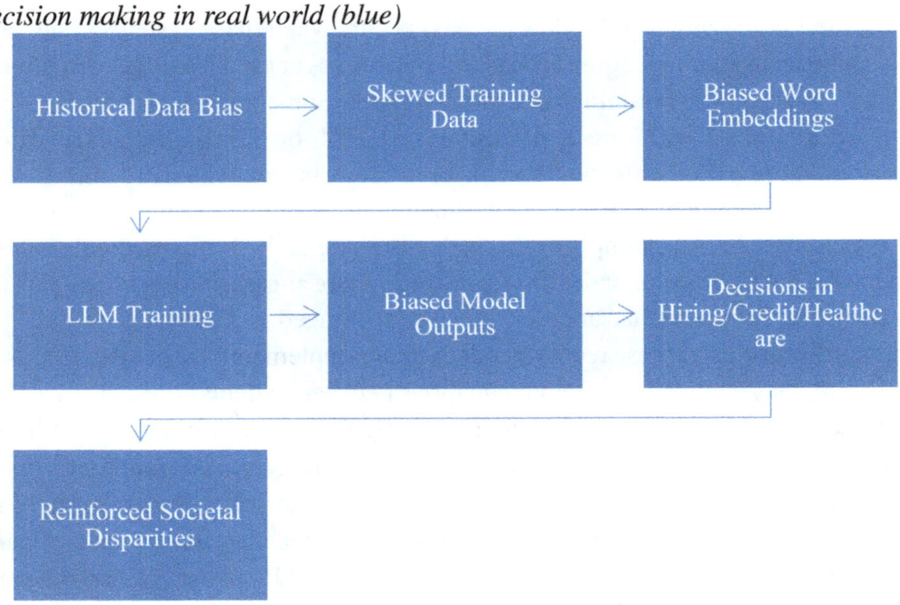

Sources of Bias in Training Datasets

1. **Historical Bias**: It can hold data — that is, reflect past decisions or cultural norms — which, if historically entrenched prejudices are an example, can reflect gender biases on job roles.

2. **Sampling Bias**: Because of this over representation of certain demographics or points of views, and the LLM's inability to account for the underrepresented contexts it can become biased against them.
3. **Annotation Bias**: Thus, a large part of human annotated data often does not have diversity of annotators as a result label inconsistencies or skewed interpretations.
4. **Semantic Ambiguities**: Language is inherently nuanced. If not properly taken care of as, ambiguous labeling can lead to multiple connotations or cultural references which causes the stereotyping to continue (Berengueres & Sandell, 2023; Kapania et al., 2024; Tlaie, 2024).

Table 5. Sources of bias and their characteristics

Source of Bias	Description	Impact on LLMs
Historical Bias	Reflects outdated cultural norms	Reinforces stereotypes (e.g., leadership → male)
Sampling Bias	Over/underrepresentation of groups	Limits model exposure to diverse linguistic contexts
Annotation Bias	Annotator diversity issues	Inconsistent or skewed labels
Semantic Ambiguity	Multiple meanings or cultural references	Misinterpretation and reinforcement of stereotypes

Bias Evaluation Methods

Quantitative Metrics

They have developed computational ways to identify and measure bias. To mention a specific example, the Word Embedding Association Test (WEAT) measures the degree to which words like "male" and "female" are associated with stereotype laced word sets. A related set of tests measure representational biases in multi-dimensional word embeddings or LLMs' hidden states. (Kapania et al., 2024).

Qualitative Audits

Quantities are great but there is context driven audits needed on many of the biases. For qualitative methods, sample outputs are reviewed, real user interactions are analyzed, natural language feedback is collected from stakeholders; etc. And such audits can reveal for purely numeric metrics, the biases that loupe out of sight, for example, the type of subtle or context dependent stereotyping. They (the richest insights) are often developed by interdisciplinary reviews, i.e., the views of sociologists, ethicists, and domain experts.

Sample Code: Computing a Simple Bias Score

import numpy as np

```
# Simulated F1 scores for two sets of examples:
# Pro-stereotypical (e.g., male-favored) and anti-stereotyp-
ical (e.g., female-favored)
f1_pro = np.array([0.75, 0.78, 0.80, 0.77])
f1_anti = np.array([0.70, 0.72, 0.74, 0.71])
# Compute the bias gap as the average difference in F1
scores
bias_gap = np.mean(f1_pro - f1_anti)
print ("Average Bias Gap (ΔF1):", bias_gap)
```

Mitigation Frameworks for Fairness

1. **Data Balancing**: Therefore, one way to ensure data diversity is oversampling underrepresented groups or applying weighting factors during training.
2. **Adversarial Debiasing**: Adversarial objectives on the model are added to penalize it for providing biased representations while pushing for more equitable outputs.
3. **Post-processing Correction**: Ignoring or masking certain biased associations in model outputs or in the embedding spaces posteriori, after training.
4. **Human-in-the-loop Approaches**: Domain experts can be involved to review and/or veto, correct questionable model inferences, especially for high risk contexts (e.g. legal or medical).

Figure 4. Mitigation framework workflow

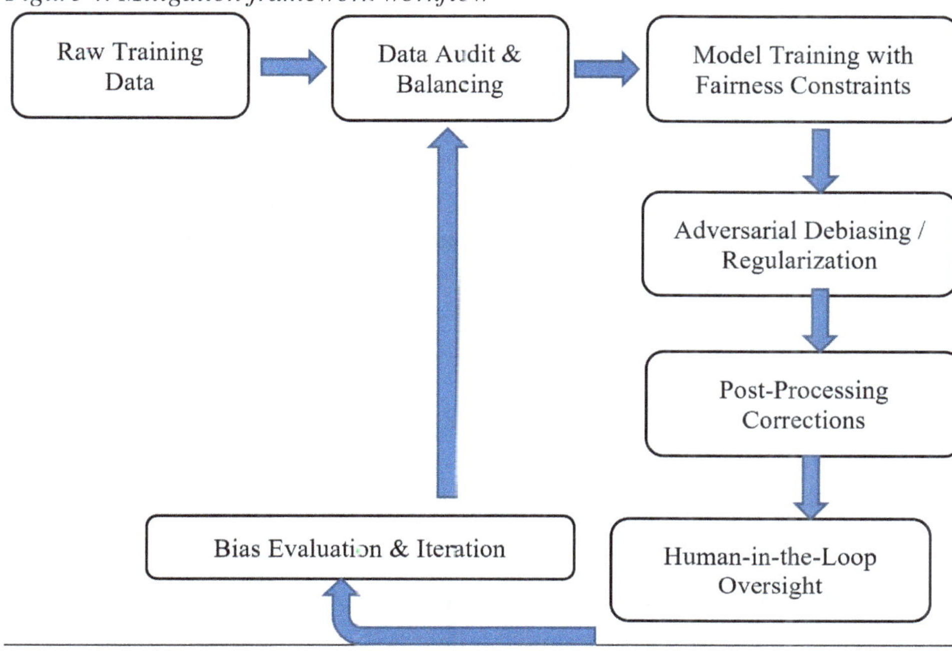

The Path Ahead: Toward Inclusive AI

No bias mitigation strategy can be defined which guarantees 100 percent neutrality. Ultimately, LLMs are interpretive machines for human language and can have their limits the same as humans have, including the complexities and prejudices latent in human language. However, it's first recognizing that it is this fact that has led us to more inclusive AI. To meet modern challenges, organizations can and should adopt culture of continuous learning & improvement by constantly improving models with new data or expansion into new cultural or linguistic context.

Cross disciplinary collaboration on the theme of bias in LLMs is an urgent need. To design systems for diverse communities FAIRLY, engineers, domain experts, social science and ethicists have to converge. Working together brings forth more robust oversight, bridging the gap between codeck and the messy social conditions that its code is expected to serve. Consequently, still, bias in LLMs remains the overpowering issue, yet the combination of technical inventions, legal brakes, and a stakeholder engagement can open the way to more equitable AI solutions.

TRANSPARENCY, EXPLAIN ABILITY, AND TRUST

The Growing Demand for Explain ability

Today, the LLMs have become sophisticated to such an extent that the text it generates is so fluid and contextually deep that it often looks like human intelligence. However, their decision-making processes internally are still not transparent and in fact have prompted regulators, end users and practitioners to push them on how these models reach their outputs. In critical domains such as healthcare diagnostics, credit scoring, law enforcement, etc. a flawed recommendation or classification can irreversibly harm a person and this need is acute.

Transparency is not a public relations issue, it means things, and they mean consequences. Stakeholders should be able to trace if the fault in the LLM suggestion leads to the discriminatory treatment in a case or the faulty business strategy because of the data, the model's training methodology, or the architecture of the model. (Berengueres & Sandell, 2023; Tlaie, 2024).

Approaches to Model Interpretability

1. **Feature Attribution**: Techniques like Integrated Gradients or SHAP (Shapley Additive explanations) help pinpoint which words or phrases in the input most strongly influenced a given LLM output.
2. **Surrogate Models**: Simpler, more interpretable models approximate the behavior of the more complex LLM. This approach can clarify general patterns without requiring full transparency of the original LLM.
3. **Layer-wise Relevance Propagation (LRP)**: This method back-propagates relevance scores through each neural network layer to identify salient input features.
4. **Visualization Tools**: Interactive dashboards allow stakeholders to experiment with different inputs to see how outputs change, thus offering insight into the model's "thought process."

Building User Trust Through Transparency

End user's trust in LLM is more than just accuracy, they need to trust it's reliable. They hope to be reassured that the model's outputs are based on legitimate, neutral data and that the model itself can be called back should something go wrong. Cultivating user trust can be achieved through some strategies such as:

- **Transparent Disclaimers:** Point out limitations as known and acknowledge probabilistic nature of LLM output.
- **Contextual Clarity:** Expose the user to confidence level / reasoning steps of the model's recommendations in some cases.
- **Interactive Debugging:** By gifting users toolkits to question or refine the LLM's reasoning, it reinforces the idea that AI outputs are not all that justified.

Best Practices in Explainable LLMs

1. **Use of Hierarchical Attention**: Introducing the hierarchical attention mechanisms can facilitate the process of highlighting the key sentences or paragraphs in the input responsible for passing the output for sets.
2. **Domain-Specific Explanations**: Tailor explanations to the domain. For instance, in medicine, suggesting highlight of symptoms indicating the interest or previous circumstances that may lead to the diagnosis-like.
3. **Interactive Education Modules**: Give short tutorials and/or interactive modules explaining how an LLM deals with language data. A user that knows something about the technology is more capable to trust it responsibly.
4. **Continuous Evaluation**: A time monitor of the model's interpretability is a must. With the coming of new features, domains or data source, the system needs to update its explanatory processes.

Opportunities for Advancing Interpretability

Existing interpretability methods are valuable but they reveal only a fraction of a model's complexity. Future research might explore:

- **Neuro-symbolic Approaches**: Achieving a high degree of flexibility, in terms of neural network, as well as interpretability, via symbolic logic, for creating reasoned textual outputs that humans can assess.
- **Causality and Counterfactuals**: The causal frameworks could be integrated into LLMs to make LLMs able to not only infer correlations but also convey insights into causal relationships in textual data.
- **Global vs. Local Explanations**: Multi-layer tooling where local explanations (for individual predictions) are unified with global explanations (the model behavior as a whole) can give an interpretability view from multiple layers.

User trust requires transparency and relates to explain ability, which is, in turn, a core of ethically robust LLM systems. Thus, organizations that spend on these aspects aren't just addressing, but also mitigating the risk of compliance, by fostering an environment of accountability and empowerment for the users. That's exactly what such efforts reward and a huge return for the brand reputation, user adoption rate, and general sustainability of the AI initiative itself.

SECURITY, MISINFORMATION, AND POTENTIAL RISKS

Threat Surface of LLMs

Understanding the Dangers of Large Language Models

Many systems that help support important tasks are now enabled by LLMs. Meanwhile, the more sophisticated and more widely adopted these models become, the more the malicious actors also begin to pay attention to them. However, due to LLMs' extensive capabilities and vast knowledge, they offer interesting targets for cybercriminals. As you can see on the flip side, in the same way, people can take advantage of these kinds of capabilities to do things that are not within the law. This means that cybersecurity teams have several issues to contend with when it comes to protecting from the threats that LLMs present.

And one big threat in this is prompt injection. Attacks take place if the malicious or misleading content is inserted inside the prompts towards LLMs. The aim is to implant the model breach in it and enable attackers to produce outputs that get past the inbuilt content filters. For instance, a hacker might construct a query that seems innocent from its first appearance but contains hints to prompt the model to generate malicious or unlawful instructions. As developers, it is very important to know this method. However, they must continuously improve their content filtering techniques and detect prompt injections before these inject new content that can-do harm.

Next, we should also consider side-channel attacks. They arise from an attacker making smart queries to the model to extract such information from the model's training data. A simple example of that would be for instance, If LLM was trained on proprietary data, at the end, an attacker could formulate queries that seem innocent but can reveal some details of that data. Such information can be confidential information and could result in serious breaches of privacy and security. Organizations need to limit access to LLMs and have tight guidelines on how LLMs can be asked.

Establishing protocols to monitor the use of LLMs can quickly spot a possible side channel threat. The third is evasion tactics, in the field of LLM security. Adversaries here employ prompt engineering techniques to get out of the way of existing safeguards. This allows attackers to expose variations of prompts that result in harmful content despite restrictions designed to block it. For instance, if a language model is designed not to produce hateful language, an attacker may attempt various phrasings or environments until they find a formula that passes what can be perceived as the guardrails. This type of behavior calls for a lot of attention from the cybersecurity teams. To mitigate these vulnerabilities, they have to play close attention to developing prompt systems and adjust filters and model responses with times to protect themselves against these risks of vulnerability.

This makes the capacity of LLMs to automate processes more and more complexity. Language models can be used by cybercriminals to create very large volume of phishing emails. For example, a simple instance could be a LLM writing numerous messages which imitate authentic communication from banking or popular telecom companies. Often these emails include fully convincing details to tempt someone into supplying the info. The volume and sophistication of produced content presumably made the task for cybersecurity teams difficult, but all the more so as they developed detection methods to identify and stop these automated attacks.

The problem of generating deep fake text messages only becomes more pressing in light of language models getting better and better. These messages can look so real that recipients will think they are dealing with someone they can trust. For instance, such a fake message might say, that a family member is in some emergency and needs the money right away. If one falls for such a trick, they might get emotionally distressed and perhaps even lose money. What this boils down to is that there must be some preventative measures set up to educate users about the dangers of communicating through a deep fake, and to encourage skepticism against any unexpected message.

In addition, organizations have to address these threats in a multi-dimensional way. Cybersecurity professionals should train for risks arising from LLMs, intensive modules such as recognizing and resolving the risks. Simulations and drills can serve as good means of exercising how teams will respond to real threats. Such a proactive approach helps to prepare teams and make them better prepared to deal with the particular challenges that LLM threats bring (Yang et al., 2024b).

As software developers start to incorporate LLMs into software, the early on message is to always recognize the importance of security. We first begin with what vulnerabilities may occur during model design. If the developers embed strong security measures and design for safety, the systems do not need to be just effective but also not susceptible to malicious use.

Another piece to consider is continuing co-organization of industry leaders, researchers, and security experts. Stakeholders can get insight and strategies on developing a more resilient landscape when it comes to the misuse of LLMs by sharing insights and strategies. Regular forums or workshops can reward busy IT staff with the time they need to get informed about the latest threats and best processes for guarding these essential technologies (Kapania et al., 2024).

Learners will also use them in monitoring usage patterns. While data from user interactions is a great source to help you identify suspicious behavior such as a long streak of spikes in requests that correlate with specific prompts. Early warning systems can come in form of sophisticated systems that flag unusual activities and so security teams can act before the threats escalate.

Certainly, LLMs have changed how people interact with technology and communicate with the other. But there are risks to be managed as well. Organizations can proactively and simultaneously secure themselves from new threats and take advantage of the benefits of these new models in a way that limits the risk of harm. In the field of artificial intelligence, efforts to educate users, to develop secure models and to increase detection mechanisms are critical to deal with existing and future challenges in the artificial intelligence landscape (Yang et al., 2024b).

Table 6. Examples of threats and their potential impact

Threat Type	*Description*	*Potential Impact*
Prompt Injection	Malicious prompts bypass content filters	Can trigger harmful outputs, e.g., instructions for illegal activities
Side-Channel Attacks	Querying the model to extract sensitive training data	Exposure of proprietary or personal data
Evasion Tactics	Circumventing built-in safeguards via creative rephrasing	Generation of hate speech or manipulative content
Phishing/Deep fake Generation	Automated creation of deceptive communications	Financial loss, reputational damage, erosion of public trust

Figure 5. Such a flowchart represents the many ways in which inherent capabilities of LLMs provide adversaries avenues to attack VU's

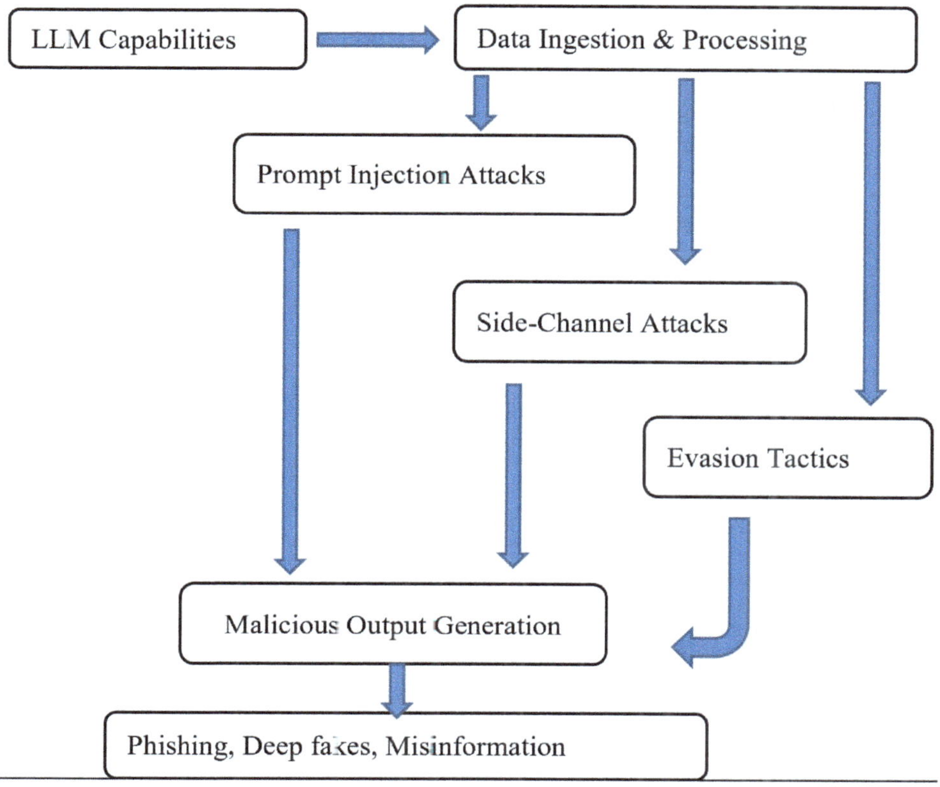

Code Example: Anomaly Detection for Suspicious Query Patterns

This is the following Python code which simulates monitoring LLM query logs for anomalies that might indicate a security breach (i.e. repeated prompt injection attempts).

```
import pandas as pd
import numpy as np
import matplotlib.pyplot as plt
from sklearn.ensemble import IsolationForest
```

```
# Simulated log data: each row is a query, with a feature representing "suspiciousness" score (e.g., frequency of uncommon tokens)
data = {
    'query_id': range(1, 101),
    'suspicious_score': np.random.normal(loc=0.2, scale=0.05, size=100)
}
# Introduce some high-suspicion queries
data['suspicious_score'][[10, 25, 50]] = [0.8, 0.75, 0.85]

df = pd.DataFrame(data)

# Use IsolationForest to detect anomalies
model = IsolationForest(contamination=0.05, random_state=42)
df['anomaly'] = model.fit_predict(df[['suspicious_score']])
df['anomaly_flag'] = df['anomaly'].apply(lambda x: 'Anomalous' if x == -1 else 'Normal')

# Plot the results
plt.figure(figsize=(8, 4))
plt.scatter(df['query_id'], df['suspicious_score'], c=df['anomaly'], cmap='coolwarm', label="Query Suspicion")
plt.xlabel("Query ID")
plt.ylabel("Suspicious Score")
plt.title("Anomaly Detection in LLM Query Logs")
plt. color bar (label="Anomaly Indicator (-1: Anomalous, 1: Normal)")
Pl. Show ()

print(df[df['anomaly'] == -1])
```

Hallucinations, Misinformation, and Deep fakes

In LLM speak, "hallucination" means producing text that is factually wrong or contextually nonsensical, but made to sound natural. Hallucinations are often benign—like an LLM forgetting about historical details, which does not cause much harm—but there are other cases when hallucinations can be a problem when accuracy matters. And it compounds the possibility of "deep fake text," where a model mimics the style or reputation of a real person or business. In this case, a malicious actor could use LLM textual illusions to print out 'official statements' of known authorities which cause confusion or panic.

The societal implications are considerable. As the LLM outputs grow more and more often in disagreement with verified sources and create more and more manipulative narratives, public trust in all AI-generated content will wither. After all, the issue lies in balancing the ability to explore the creative capabilities of LLM, without the ability to deploy it maliciously or misleadingly (Ferdaus et al., 2024; Jiao et al., 2024; Kapania et al., 2024).

Strategic Security Frameworks for LLMs

1. Multi-tiered Access Controls: Limiting unauthorized manipulations can be achieved by creating tiers of access according to the usage context. An example of this could be when domain admins can have full control to update training data or refine the hyperparameters of the model but regular end users just use the model's inference API with strict content moderation.
2. **Secure Training Pipelines:** In the case of attempting to insert bad data into the training set, rigorous checks for data cleanliness, authenticity, and provenance essentially prevent this. These measures coupled with control of robust versioning of model checkpoints and cryptographic signing of model checkpoints help in detecting unauthorized modifications.
3. **Real-time Monitoring and Incident Response:** It is the same as intrusion detection systems in cybersecurity, which can monitor anomalous patterns of queries (repeated attempts on disallowed content, unusually precise prompts). With a breach being expected, how compromised models are isolated or patched should be detailed in incident response protocols.

Table 7. Strategic security measures for LLMs

Security Measure	*Purpose*	*Example Tools/Methods*
Multi-tiered Access Controls	Limit unauthorized changes to LLM infrastructure	Role-based access, API key management
Secure Training Pipelines	Prevent injection of malicious data	Data authenticity audits, cryptographic signing
Real-time Monitoring	Detect unusual or malicious query patterns	Isolation Forest, anomaly detection algorithms
Incident Response Protocols	Rapidly respond to detected security breaches	Predefined playbooks, automated patching systems

Figure 6. This diagram is a continuous cycle of monitoring and response to ensure the security of LLMs

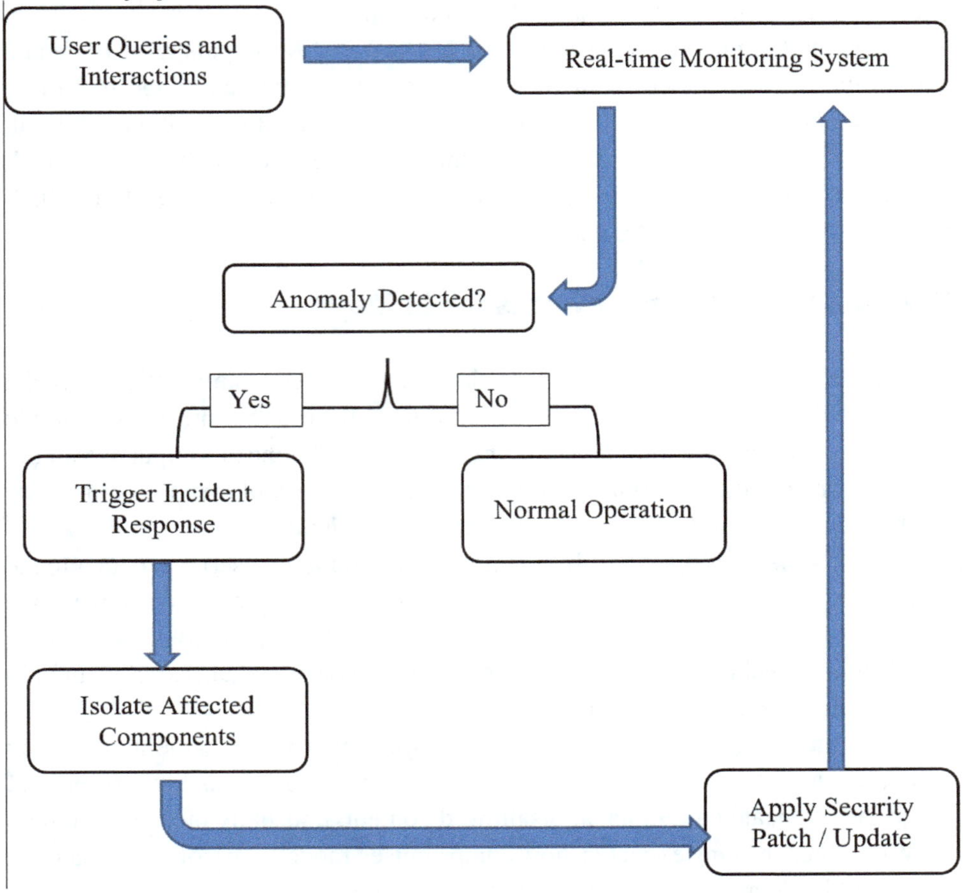

Innovations in Threat Mitigation

Some technologies that combine LLMs with advanced cryptographic capabilities are an emerging field. For instance, watermarking model output allows for checking to see if a text is AI generated and therefore allow platforms to filter or double check suspicious content. There is another promising area on the line of robust anomaly detection systems that are tracking the LLM's inner states (e.g., attention patterns, hidden layer activations), to flag unusual behaviors.

Balancing Security and Free Expression

The basic principle of openness clashes with security measures. Content filtration might otherwise be too zealous and stifle legitimate explorations, or in more dangerous cases, prevent creativity. However, without any supervision, such misinformation could be harmful. It then is the action of finding the right equilibrium, respecting user rights, domain context, and causes on a societal level. This gives security a check and prevents utilizing security as a substitute of censorship in sensitive areas such as political speech, consulting many stakeholders from ethicists, community leaders, legal experts.

Finally, it is worth concluding that the practice of security in LLM ecosystems has to be complex, using many tools, from legal and ethical to technical and human-centric, as urgently. In parallel to the growing footprint LLMs achieve in different industries, the stakes to manage security effectively rise.

REGULATORY AND COMPLIANCE CHALLENGES

Overview of Emerging Global Regulations

Global AI Regulations: An Overview

Most regulators around the world are taking active steps to set governing rules for artificial intelligence (AI) technologies and in particular large language models (LLMs). For instance, in Europe and frameworks that are being discussed in the United States and Asia, there is no denying the plan to write the laws that can responsibly control the powerful harmful effect these technologies have on society. Just as example, the European Union is moving forward with its AI Act, which sets out to classify AI applications by means of risk. The classification spectrum goes from minimal risk to unacceptable, with regards as to how these technologies may be used.

The EU's Approach to AI Regulation

As part of his piece in Nature on the latest EU proposal, Laszlo pointed out, the legislation depends heavily on high-risk AI systems. These kinds of systems are subject to very strict data governance, transparency, and human oversight lines. For example, high-risk AI systems could include those in healthcare that are making decisions about patient care, or in finance recommending actions that determine how much to lend to a candidate. An example is a healthcare chatbot to evaluate patients' symptoms that has to be built with strict controls to avoid potentially harmful advice. It is meant to oversee this level to protect the users and also to make sure that technology does not misuse or mishandle any sensitive information.

U.S. Legislative Initiatives

In the United States, too, there are legislative attempts to bring AI technologies to the same responsibility. In its proposal, the Algorithmic Accountability Act would demand audits and assessment of impact when AI can adversely impact consumer rights. It means companies that use AI for advertising examples or credit evaluation would have to eyes at their algorithms regularly. Take for instance that an institution of banking, based on the example, uses AI to make credit scores, and then there are regulations imposed that require that the algorithm used to determine credit scores be fair and free of biases towards any class of people. These measures intend to give a greater understanding of the ways that AI is being used to shape the consumer experience and decision.

Challenges in Establishing a Universal Standard

Even after these regulatory developments, however, there is no uniform regulatory norm for LLMs' use. Becoming a part of a startup invariably means coming face to face with a huge challenge, that is, pace of technological advancement remains much faster than lawmakers can draft appropriate regulations to regulate. As an example, there are new types of LLMs created every day which lawmakers are just figuring out how they function within society, and even when new models were developed, lawmakers may be struggling to understand the old models. And this lag opens a regulatory gray area, where laws are not clearly defined as to what can be done. (Yang et al., 2024b).

The Complexity of AI Applications

The problem becomes more complex as the range of applications for LLMs is wide and diverse. These models of course are used in different settings — from simple chatbots used for casual chatting, helping users in daily tasks, to the more serious ones — the decision support systems in fields of finance and healthcare. InS casual usage, a chatbot can behave as an online customer service bot or in some way, assist shoppers in navigating a website. But in the case of a financial institution, the same underlying technology could be used to decide on central matters — such as lending — which are crucial for the institution. The difference in the use cases shows the importance of differences in the context in which these technologies operate.

The Need for Contextual Regulations

It is actually given that the variety of use cases that regulations can work for is multiplicity. For instance, compliance frameworks that are good for a chatbot in a retail setting can be not suitable for an AI system in a hospital setting. Patient data is very sensitive in healthcare and AI's interaction with that data must be closely monitored since it is in the hands of such sensitive data. For example, the chatbot in retail would spend more in terms of user engagement rather than protecting confidential information. For that reason, regulations must take into account these differences and give the proper directions for each situation.

The Importance of Transparency

The third factor for the regulation of AI is transparency. With AI systems, the users should know how these systems work and make decision. A loss of trust occurs when a user is unsure why they were denied a loan or why they were given a given recommendation by a chatbot. They are also beginning to stress the need for clear communication and expecting AI developer to explain how their systems work. For example, you can make transparency reports or user-friendly explanations of the AI technologies to clear it out for users or assuage that their decision-making process is appropriate.

Future Directions in AI Regulation

With the development of technology, regulators must be abreast of the same and emerging trends. For instance, there are new developments in machine learning and data analysis that might generate new issues that the laws are not up to the situation. Lawmakers must reach out to their tech and industry experts who are up to date with the technologies as well as advance in their understanding of regulations. Collaboration can make an ecosystem that not only slurs innovation but also does not harm consumer protection (Jiao et al., 2024).

The Role of Stakeholder Engagement

Effective regulations seek to employ stakeholder engagement to build upon, with any regulations in response involved some sort of compromise. It also extends to policymakers and industry leaders as well as to those consumers who use these technologies. Regulators can engage with different groups so that they can gather insights in order to spur better policies. For instance, consumers' feedbacks on AI systems' experiences will help in configuring appropriate regulations, including fairness and transparency.

Navigating the Future of AI

As the world deals with the transformation of AI technologies, the same will happen with the regulations. And, another goal is to find the balance between inventive ideas and the protection of the consumer. Through smart approaches to the technological growth and public trust implications of AI, regulators will be able to design such frameworks that encompass diverse applications and respects of AI. To be able to navigate the future of AI landscape, this balanced perspective is necessary to check whether AI should look and serve society positively.

Sector-Specific Compliance Frameworks

1. **Finance**: Entities in this sector are regulated by the Basel Accords and MiFID II in Europe. To use LLMs in credit scoring or algorithmic trading, one must leave nothing to chance and provide thorough documentation to meet the requirements of stress testing and allow for the proper conduct of business general compliance.
2. **Healthcare**: In the U.S. you can take laws such as Health Insurance Portability and Accountability Act (HIPAA) and in case of the EU, the GDPR, to protect patient data. A good case for (encrypted and possibly minimized) end-to-end encryption of any such LLM processing medical records can be made.
3. **E-commerce**: Recommendations or dynamic pricing that rely on user profiling can raise concerns about antitrust per se, and will thus attract scrutiny from a consumer protection agent.

Auditing and Monitoring Protocols

There is a recurring emphasis on auditing in the shape of regulatory frameworks. Internal and external audits may be involved, of which if public welfare is at stake laws may require those. Core components typically examined include:

- **Data Lifecycle Management**: For LLM training, how the data has been collected, preprocessed and used. They audit for data residency regulations compliance and user consents.
- **Model Explain ability**: Looming also are some jurisdictions that demand such 'understandable reasons' for automated decisions such as loan approval

or job recommendation; enterprises are now pressured by them to generate interpretable outcomes from LLMs.

- **Ongoing Monitoring**: Either real time or periodic checks make sure that models stay ethically up to date as new data comes in or as the business conditions change.

The Role of Industry–Academic Collaboration

Academic research is also naturally well suited to a research focus that complements industry's penchant for practicality. The joint efforts can explain what is best practice, set universal approaches; speed the development of personalized auditing tools. For example, corporate partner may have emerged to agree on a metric or interpretability tool of fairness that research labs developed for their own applicability or to interpret the effect of an algorithmic intervention for real world application. Based on the exploration above such synergy could result in a 'living' regulatory framework, updated with emerging ethical challenges of technical progress (Jiao et al., 2024; Kapania et al., 2024).

Bridging Gaps and Harmonizing Standards

Impasses exist in progressing toward a harmonized global framework around data privacy, such as cultural norms discrepancy, business interest's competition, and law interpretations on data privacy disparity. In any case, alliances between the borders are starting to form, as organizations such as the OECD (Organization for Economic Co-operation and Development) and ISO (International Organization for Standardization) are providing guidance. This will also result in imposing a level playing field and reduce the compliance overhead for multinational corporations with multi-national agreements.

Regulatory alignment is both vital and useful eventually. Setting clear rules and guidelines ensures that there is no reputational risk for the players within industry and protects the consumers. In many ways the compliance frameworks that are consistent support a natural process of innovation by provoking companies to develop robust, ethical LLM systems.

ACCOUNTABILITY, GOVERNANCE, AND ORGANIZATIONAL CULTURE

Ownership of LLM-Generated Content

Understanding Liability and Ownership in LLM Ethics

Liability and ownership are a key ethical question for Large Language Models (LLMs). In particular, this is very relevant when we think about what the consequences of the LLM producing false financial advice or defamatory statements are. In such situations, it is vital to ascertain who is liable. Was the AI created by the developer, the company that has put it online or the end user who interacted with the AI's output? Traditionally models do not suffice with providing a clear answer to this question and generally struggle to provide a clear answer if an AI system behaves in unexpected ways.

Traditionally, liability is often straightforward in a legal framework. Therefore, if a product breaks, the producer is typically held responsible. Nevertheless, LLMs are complex machine learning systems that learn from huge datasets built on patterns. This can be compared to the complexity where outputs generated by this complexity produced outputs that its creators did not foresee or intended. Consequently, without having a clear contractual disclaimer or a solid governance plan, any organization utilizing LLMs would find themselves wrapped up in legal disputes. If the produced AI content is harmful or misleading, they may suffer reputational damages.

Key Considerations in LLM Liability

- **Attribution**

Attribution is one of the main pressing questions in decision-making on who is liable or not for an event or series of events. What's more, this refers to the question of whether the content that the LLM generates can be traced back to a specific version of the model or a given training data. Accountability is of course dependent upon an understanding of how it is attributable. For example, when an LLM gives bad financial advice to a person, it's essential that we can trace that back to what version of the AI created it before assigning blame.

For organizations to keep track of their LLMs, including their versions, and the datasets used to train them, they have to maintain thorough records. The documented facts make it easier for companies to trace accountability. If there is an issue, they can come back to this documentation to know which model was used and what training was used. By also attributing things more clearly to the actors and persons, more risk management is possible. This gives organizations a chance to fix or avoid problematic outputs by eliminating or adjusting some (or, ideally, all) of the data points that may cause this behavior in a future release of the model.

- **End-User Modification**

The end-user modifications are also a very important thing we need to consider. When users take the output of an LLM and change it in some way, the question arises if users are liable instead of the original creator. For example, if a user rewires results of an LLM and increases a statement that is later identified as defamatory, then it is the user's fault, or at least not that of the LLM?

The issue of liability is further complicated in this question. The users may or may not understand the implications of their modifications and also the context in which the original content was generated. Hence, organizations must provide clear guidelines as well as educational resources to clarify usage of LLM outputs. Similarly, informing users about risks and the type of information generated by the LLM can enable clearer understanding of the company's role in the process. Additionally, they may also enact measures that restrict the capacity of users to manipulate the outputs in such a manner that could result in forbidden or damaging consequences.

The Role of Governance Policies

Robust policies of governance are necessary in order to be effective in navigating the liability and ownership challenges. Such policies can act as guidance for how to take control of the risks present with LLMs. Such guidelines ought to be presented in a clear way about the use and deployment of LLMs within an organization. Policies on governance regarding monitoring the outputs of the models and how to handle any possible misconduct should be developed (Jiao et al., 2024).

These policies involve the input from various stakeholders and members, such as legal experts, developers and end users. An organization can ensure that the policies it develops draw on both an ethical and technical landscape that considers the way AI is used. Just like any policy, it is good to regularly train employees and users alike, as they will be empowered and able to learn about their responsibilities and how to interact with LLMs under the bias in practice.

Sample Code: Logging Model Version and Output Metadata

```
import datetime
import json
```

```
def log_model_output(model_version, input_text, output_text,
user_modifications=None):
    log_entry = {
        "timestamp": datetime.datetime.now().isoformat(),
        "model_version": model_version,
        "input": input_text,
        "output": output_text,
        "user_modifications": user_modifications if user_
modifications else "None"
    }
    # Append the log entry to a JSON file for audit purposes
    with open("llm_output_log.json", "a") as log_file:
        log_file.write(json.dumps(log_entry) + "\n")

# Example usage
log_model_output(
    model_version="GPT-4.2",
    input_text="What are the best investment strategies for
2025?",
    output_text="Consider diversifying your portfolio across
emerging markets...",
    user_modifications="Modified to include risk disclaimer"
)
```

The Importance of Transparency

Another very important part in solving liabilities and ownership in LLMs is transparency. When organizations describe how their LLMs function, what datasets they used and what the limitations of the technology are, this creates that trust with users. Finally, transparency can also give users a better idea of why the AI is returning the given outputs and what may affect the decisions of the AI.

Transparency can be achieved by the organization in sharing information about their LLMs through its documentation, user guides, and education resources. The openness of this kind also helps with regulators and those in the public. Stakeholders are only able to provide valuable feedback on an LLM if they understand how it works. And if that feedback is used to improve the model and its governance as well.

Therefore, the discussion about liability and ownership related to LLMs is still continuing and should be considered thoroughly. There are key steps that organizations must develop clear guidelines on attribution, any implications of user modifications, strong governance policies and transparent implementation. Doing so will help them navigate LLM ethics complexifying's and cut off any possible legal risks.

Organizational Policies and Ethical Codes

Well defined policies usually give rise to a structured approach to accountability. Responsible AI is not new to many organizations. They draft "Responsible AI" guidelines or adopt existing codes of ethics from the IEEE or the Association for Computing Machines (ACM). These guidelines typically outline:

1. **Scope of AI Deployment**: Permitted use cases that need to be clear (e.g. involvement in no surveillance or manipulation).
2. **Risk Classification**: A strategy to rank the AI applications in terms of harm potential and related oversight levels.
3. **Oversight Bodies**: Specialized boards formed in governance to regularly review AI initiatives of the organization.

Governance Models for Responsible AI

Among governance models, we have the extreme — centrally appointed panels; the other extreme — each department tells its own story of using AI, according to general corporate norms; and the 'hub and spoke,' with each department using AI, but under corporate guidelines. The option is based on the organizational size, global footprint, and the industry needs. In industrial environment, where things are more regulated in finance or healthcare, generally more strict rule are forcing you to go centralised and for you to be compliant with the compliance frameworks.

1. **Centralized Governance**: It has pros such as uniform standard of ethics, streamlined audit, and uniform compliance. Slower innovation is a benefit, as departments need to get the top-level approvals.
2. **Decentralized Governance**: A plus side is agility, and if you know the domain, then you have domain specific expertise. This also entails two concerns of high risk: the risk of policy fragmentation and the risk of inconsistent enforcement.

Figure 7. Decentralized "Hub-and-Spoke" governance model

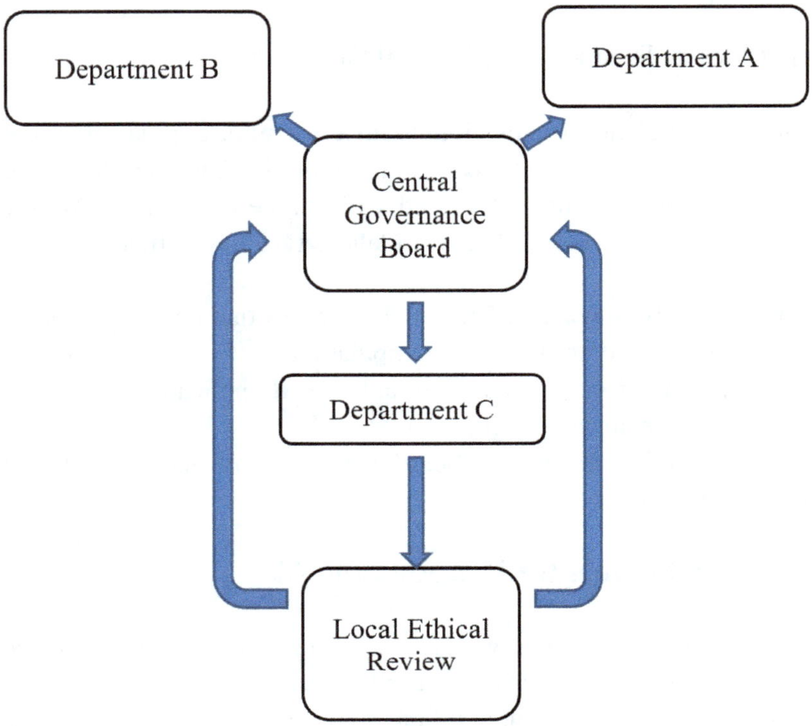

The below diagram is of a decentralized model where each department (spoke) is responsible to itself under the vision of the central board (hub) with a few constraints to ensure alignment while enabling flexibility.

Balancing Stakeholder Interests

The scope of corporate governance of LLMs includes balancing the interest of stakeholder (employees, culture customers and the broader society). For example, in this case some companies may place short term profit motives before working out the ethics of pushing products to market based on LLM. On the contrary, overregulation or over shielding of caution can impede innovation and might erode the edge.

Case Example: Even large financial institution might balance the benefits to its speed of loan approval processing and lower overhead due to automating loan approval through LLM based system, against the risk of algorithmic discrimination, as well as potential regulatory fines. Deployment can be aided by a near complete stakeholder review encompassing community representatives and consumer rights advocates that identify pitfalls and solutions before the deployment occurs.

Fostering an Ethical Culture

Finally, the whole governance structure rests on the integrity and the sense of awareness of the people in it. Training programs and stand-alone workshops can be led to train employees to be responsible with AI usage, detect bias, and how best to practice cybersecurity. By fostering an environment that allows open discussions on ethical dilemmas, through established channels (possibly confidential) for employees to voice their opinions without fear of backlash (Raza et al., 2024), one encourages employees to feel safe raising their concerns.

Because compliance may not be matching up to innovation in an environment, establishing a strong ethical culture serves as a necessary defense. It demonstrates an organization's commitment to responsible evolution of AI signaling to regulators, customers and prospective talent that it is trusting an important differentiator in a market increasingly dominated by AI. (Ferdaus et al., 2024).

FUTURE DIRECTIONS AND RESEARCH OPPORTUNITIES

Technological Innovations in LLMs

With the progress of scale and complexity of LLMs, comes the new frontiers. The site of research is already departing from domain-general text generation into more specialized ability using multimodal data: picture, sound, and specialized tabular. These expansions will bring further analytics and user experience. Imagine an LLM that can make sense of financial charts or translate mammograms, for example, these would change the industry practices overnight. However, each new capability brings new risks to ethics and technology (Ferdaus et al., 2024).

Potential Breakthroughs

1. **Real-time Adaptation**: Continuous streaming data gives rise to problems of concept drift, data confidentiality and perpetual consent for systems that learn continuously at the data.
2. **Meta-learning**: The lines of accountability become fuzzy if LLMs learn how to learn and come up with novel inference strategies that their creators did not imagine.

Next-Generation Ethical Frameworks

Existing frameworks are entirely based on reactive programming such and this may not work in presence of LLM that will be mutually integrated with advanced technology like quantum computing, machine at an edge or distributed ledgers. Proactive approaches are more required (where the ethics are built into the design blueprint). Ethernet is an example of this, this could involve dynamic ethical constraints that adapt on the go, to dynamic context and users' feedback.

- **Automated Ethical Compliance**: Real-time auditing tools (or sub-models) that halt questionable activities of an LLM.
- **Value-Sensitive Design**: LIF principles that guard against the violation of human values and dignity, in particular for the most marginalized groups in the journey towards the adoption of LLMs.

Societal and Economic Considerations

The changes that technologies bring about in the LLM space are more than only one; there are various societal implications. LLMs' widespread adoption in the workplace could lead some jobs to be displaced by new ones (briefly, "prompt engineers" or AI ethicists). Two things are required, governments and educational institutions must prepare for the shifting labor markets as well on the need for reskilling. Beyond its immediate, benefits are concentrated in the wealthier nations and corporations capable of training and deploying mass models.

1. **Democratizing Access**: It can assist smaller organizations, emerging economies to benefit from advanced AI through open source LLM projects and public–private partnerships.
2. **Community-led Initiatives**: For languages and communities that have been marginalized by digitalization, grassroots, and NGO organizations can unite to see that underrepresented languages and communities get to be represented in the LLM research.

The Vision for Sustainable AI

AI is no longer a discussion that is absent from the sustainability discussion anymore. Being able to train state of the art LLMs is computationally expensive with equally large carbon footprints. Finally, the community may now start to value greener AI solutions that minimize the resources required to train, employ renewable power in place of the electricity, and more precisely recycle the hardware. The data minimization part fits in this kind of pivot when reducing the amount of data needed to expand the size of dataset to avoid unnecessary expansion of dataset size to reduce such consumption of resource and reduce the privacy risk.

Research Imperatives

- **Algorithmic Efficiency**: For reduction of the computational load, focus on model distillation, parameter sharing, or advances optimization.
- **Life Cycle Assessments**: AI regulations that would have eco-centric basis, evaluation of the environmental impact of AI systems from development to decommissioning.

Overall, LLMs face a hilly and even treacherous road ahead. A coherent strategy of development has to integrate ethical considerations, socio-economic factors as well as those concerned with the environment. The linchpin of AI's realization in an equitable and safe way is this synergy between technology and ethics written, perhaps uncomfortably, in the laboratories of multi-stakeholder collaboration.

CONCLUSION

Recapitulating Key Themes

The ethical, technical, and regulatory dimensions of the Large Language Models in business Analytics: This was explored in this chapter. Published guidelines will start after an entity is picked, data is pulled from limitless sources, and the LLM is considered deployable, in which case governance, oversight, and iteration are essential. I have outlined the interlocking pillars of the responsible AI innovation, namely data privacy, bias, fairness, interpretability, security, accountability and regulatory compliance.

A Call to Action for Multi-Stakeholder Engagement

The technical parts of training and optimizing LLMs are important, but in fact are only one part of a more complex socio technical ecosystem. To be robust, ethical guidelines and compliance structures need to be shaped by government bodies, private enterprises, academic researchers, non-government organizations and civil society. It poses little threat to a single entity to adopt LLMs responsibly in that sense. To achieve this, it requires collaborative collective effort: constructing such inclusive measures in the form of datasets, and establishing global norms for the use of AI.

Final Remarks

As for where we are looking, we are sure that the next generation of LLMs will take contextual understanding, real-time adaptation and all level of integration of multi-sensory data to the next levels. It will, of course, lead to new ethics discussions about autonomy, governance, and the human community to AI systems. However, awareness of the ethics of research, development, and deployment can bring together with the heart of AI to build AI solutions that are consistent with more extensive societal values. In this pursuit, ethical guidelines are not a limiting concern but a source of great possibilities and the spur upon which innovations, particularly those that are sustainable, humane, and even profoundly transformative can be propelled.

REFERENCES

Berengueres, J., & Sandell, M. (2023). Applying Standards to Advance Upstream &Downstream Ethics in Large Language Models. *ArXiv Preprint ArXiv:2306.03503*, 1–8.

Ferdaus, M. M., Abdelguerfi, M., Ioup, E., Niles, K. N., Pathak, K., & Sloan, S. (2024). Towards Trustworthy AI: A Review of Ethical and Robust Large Language Models. *ArXiv*, 1–27.

Jiao, J., Afroogh, S., Xu, Y., Atkinson, D., & Phillips, C. (2024). Navigating LLM Ethics: Advancements, Challenges, and Future Directions. *ArXiv.Org*.

Kapania, S., Wang, R., Li, T. J.-J., Li, T., & Shen, H. (2024). *"I'm categorizing LLM as a productivity tool": Examining ethics of LLM use in HCI research practices*. 1–23.

Raza, S., Bamgbose, O., Ghuge, S., Tavakol, F., Reji, D. J., & Bashir, S. R. (2024). *Developing Safe and Responsible Large Language Model : Can We Balance Bias Reduction and Language Understanding in Large Language Models?* 1–39.

Tlaie, A. (2024). *Exploring and steering the moral compass of Large Language Models. 6*, 1–12.

Ungless, E. L., Vitsakis, N., Garforth, J., Ross, B., & Birch, A. (2024). *E THICS W HITEPAPER : Whitepaper on Ethical Research into Large Language Models*. 1–47.

Yang, J., Wang, Z., Lin, Y., & Zhao, Z. (2024a). Global Data Constraints: Ethical and Effectiveness Challenges in Large Language Model. *ArXiv E-Prints*, arXiv--2406.

Yang, J., Wang, Z., Lin, Y., & Zhao, Z. (2024b). *Large Language Model Tokenizer Bias: A Case Study and Solution on GPT-4o*. 1–6.

Chapter 2
Foundations of Large Language Models

Akhil Sharma
http://orcid.org/0009-0001-1490-4022
School of Computing Science and Engineering, Sharda University, Greater Noida, India

Jatin Gupta
http://orcid.org/0009-0002-9504-7487
School of Computing Science and Engineering, Sharda University, Greater Noida, India

Ali Imam Abidi
http://orcid.org/0000-0002-7420-0027
School of Computing Science and Engineering, Sharda University, Greater Noida, India

ABSTRACT

Large Language Models (LLMs) are indicated by this chapter as a major change maker for business analytics. Focusing on practical implementation strategies, it goes over and above the basic foundations like Transformers and tokenization. By analyzing operational metrics via real-world case studies such as (Klarna, BloombergGPT) the chapter spotlights critical cost-latency trade-offs. The "LLMOps" lifecycle is then established, and a strategic framework for deployment (API vs. Self-Hosted) and governance including hallucination risks and EU AI Act compliance is presented. The text then ends with the future trends in multimodal AI and agentic systems, granting the practitioners the needed actionable insights for a sustainable competitive advantage.

DOI: 10.4018/979-8-3693-6690-5.ch002

INTRODUCTION

This chapter addresses the history of Large Language Models (LLMs), their evolution, and the business analytics-disruptive impact they have. The chapter begins by defining what LLMs are and how they work and proceeds to a timeline-based account of how they have evolved from statistical models to the current deep learning models. The chapter acknowledges how LLMs are at the core of the use of many different business dimensions, such as data analysis, decision-making, and process automating. The chapter also addresses the transformer model innovation that resulted in unprecedented performance in language understanding and generation. The reader will finally have a thorough understanding of the impact that LLMs have on business intelligence and analytics development.

DEFINITION OF LARGE LANGUAGE MODELS (LLMS)

Large Language Models (LLMs) represent artificial intelligence computer models that can read, write, and process human language with high accuracy. LLMs are trained on massive datasets through deep-learning strategies, making it possible for them to perform a wide range of natural language processing (NLP) tasks such as text generation, translation, summarization, and question-answering. LLMs utilize transformer-based models, i.e., self-attention mechanisms, to recognize intricate patterns of language and context (Naveed et al., 2023).

RELEVANCE OF LLMS IN MODERN BUSINESS ANALYTICS

Application of LLMs in business analysis has transformed the decision-making process with data-driven insights on an unprecedented scale. LLMs are applied in various sectors by companies to extract sentiment, forecast the market, automate customer support, and identify fraud. Their ability to navigate vast amounts of text content, recognize meaningful patterns, and generate human-like output makes operational productivity, strategic decisions, and consumer engagement more effective. LLMs provide automation of report generation, contract analysis, and tailored recommendations to a large extent, reducing human intervention to a large extent and increasing accuracy (Nasseri et al., 2023).

HISTORICAL EVOLUTION AND THE INDUSTRIAL SHIFT

The way Large Language Models (LLMs) have evolved signals a broader change in Natural Language Processing (NLP). We have moved from rule-based systems to complex frameworks driven by deep learning.

Early Rule-Based and Statistical Models

In the early years of computational linguistics, language processing relied on rule-based systems with specifically coded linguistic rules. They, like **ELIZA (1966)** (Weizenbaum, 1966), the first chatbot, could simulate an anthropomorphic dialogue but not based on real comprehension. The onset of statistical models during the later part of the 20th century marked the data-driven model. IBM Statistical Machine Translation during the 1990s defined the probabilistic approach to translation with much better accuracy than in rule-based methods (Collins, 2011). N-gram models, Google's original spell-check model, and Yahoo's search autocomplete were the models of choice in language modeling, machine translation, and speech recognition. These struggled with long-range dependencies and required significant feature engineering(Pestov, 2018).

The Rise of Neural Networks in NLP

Deep learning transformed NLP and brought artificial neural network application into play. Word2Vec from Google (Mikolov et al., 2013) created word vectors to improve semantic sense and paved the way for applications like Google News topic clustering and the Spotify music recommendation feature. Recurrent Neural Networks (RNNs) and Long Short-Term Memory (LSTM) networks improved sequence-based text processing. Apple's Siri (2011), using LSTMs initially for speech recognition and context-sensitive response, showcased the prowess of these models. RNNs and LSTMs suffered from vanishing gradients and sequential processing constraints when used for long sequences (Le & Zuidema, 2016).

The Transformer Breakthrough

One of the major breakthroughs of NLP came when (Vaswani et al., 2017) proposed the Transformer model that substituted sequential processing with the attention mechanism as the central feature. This facilitated models to cope with long-range dependencies, along with scaling linearly. The aforementioned revolution was a prerequisite for the emergence of the contemporary large language models which have impacted both the academic world and the market place. BERT (Alberti et al.,

2019) was already considered a pivotal tool in Google Search where its ability to analyze different meanings at the same time helped to provide better understanding of intricate questions and thus lowered the number of mistakes made. GPT-3 (Raffel et al., 2019) had the influence on the content-making process, gave birth to such tools as ChatGPT, Jasper AI for writing, and GitHub Copilot for code completion. T5 (Floridi & Chiriatti, 2020) took text-to-text capabilities further and got embedded into Google Docs' Smart Compose which was giving grammatically correct and contextually appropriate hints. Just recently, Meta's LLaMA (Touvron et al., 2023) mapped out the path for open-source LLMs that are mainly for research but can also be utilized by the business sector like AI-powered customer service chatbots

Future Trends

Currently, large language models (LLMs) are changing very quickly, thanks to state-of-the-art technologies like Mixture of Experts (MoE), retrieval-augmented generation (RAG), and also multimodal capabilities, which combine text, images, and speech. More to the point, these technologies are already used in various applications such as Google Gemini, which combines text with video and images, the output being accessible through Google Lens AI (Team et al., 2023). In a similar vein, Microsoft Copilot has been incorporated into Excel, Word, and Teams among others to optimize the handling of business processes and documentation (Introducing Microsoft 365 Copilot – Your Copilot for Work - The Official Microsoft Blog, n.d.). To cite another instance, there is Perplexity AI, a research-oriented LLM that offers instantaneous, validated answers by making use of outside knowledge bases (Getting Started with Perplexity, n.d.).

Analysis: Academic vs. Industrial Trajectories

Theoretical foundations of LLMs were established in academic and research environments where the paper "Attention Is All You Need" by (Vaswani et al. 2017) was the most significant contributor. However, the path of development has split into two different directions. Firstly, academic researchers concentrating on the novelty and efficiency of the architecture primarily (e.g., attention mechanism modifications). Whereas the industrial development shift, epitomized by GPT-3 and following models (Raffel et al., 2019; OpenAI, 2024), concentrated on enlarging the parameter count and dataset size to obtain emergent wonders.

This change has far-reaching ramifications for business. The industrial development is now based on "scaling laws," which is a drive where the capital outlay for compute (GPUs) is directly associated with the performance achieved. In business analytics, it signifies that the top-notch is no more characterized just by algorithmic nicety, but through the provisioning of the infrastructure and the organizational capacity to roll out these gigantic models.

The structure of the rest of this chapter is as follows: Section 2 gives an overview of the main concepts and the changing of the guards from academia to industry. Section 3 goes into the details of architectural foundations. Sections 4 to 7 tackle the topic of strategic implementation, including training, fine-tuning, and LLMOps. Section 8 addresses issues of governance and security before moving on to future trends in Section 9.

KEY CONCEPTS OF LLMS

What is an LLM?

A Large Language Model (LLM) is a highly advanced artificial intelligence model that has been trained on massive text corpora to comprehend and produce human-like text. Using deep learning architectures, specifically transformers, LLMs use billions of parameters to identify linguistic patterns, context, and semantic structure. In contrast to typical rule-based systems, LLMs can perform sophisticated natural language processing (NLP) tasks such as text summarization, sentiment analysis, and language translation without explicit programming. Their capacity to generalize across domains places them at the heart of an enormous number of business applications, driving automation, efficiency, and innovation in analytics and decision-making (Zhao et al., 2015).

How LLMs Function: Next-word Prediction and Statistical Learning

At the core of LLMs is a probabilistic learning paradigm, in which models estimate the most probable next word (or token) based on the context of the preceding words. It is achieved through the following main mechanisms:

Tokenization

Tokenization is the splitting of text into smaller parts, commonly known as tokens, such as, words, subwords, or even individual letters. At the word-level, tokenization portrays every word as a different token; refer to Figure. 1. Complex and rare words are the usual candidates for subword tokenization which splits them into parts that retain meaning, e.g., un and happiness for "unhappiness". Next in line is the character-level tokenization which assigns each letter a token therefore "Hello" transforms into H e l l o. All these different methods allow the large language models to not only handle different vocabularies but also work in a multilingual environment and process intricate texts with the efficiency that is very much needed in business analytics where the data is often coming from different sources.

Figure 1. Tokenization of a sample text

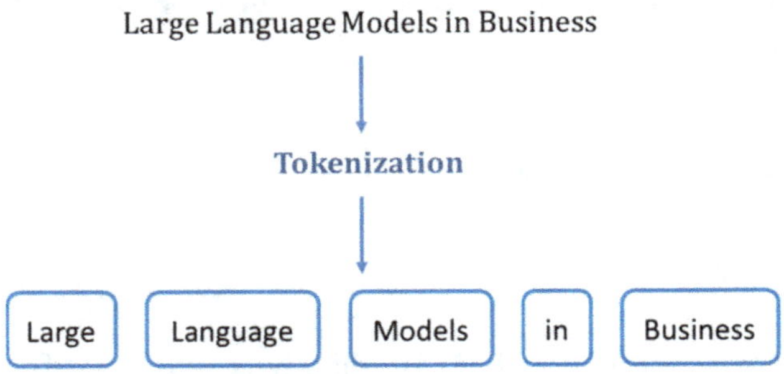

Positional Encoding

As opposed to RNNs and LSTMs, Transformers do not process text in sequence. This facilitates parallelization, but the drawback is that Transformers do not capture the word order of words within a sentence in their encoded form. This is offset by applying positional encoding to word embeddings such that the model is able to learn relative word position in a sequence. Positional encodings are added to the word embeddings to add sequence order. They utilize sinusoidal functions to make unique representation of the word position and embedding size. For example, in a sentence: *"The cat sat on the mat."*

i) ***Word Embeddings:*** Every word of the sentence is encoded as a vector in a space of high dimension. For instance: Embed("cat") = [0.2, 0.5, 0.1, ...]. These vectors retain the semantic meaning of words but lack any information related to their positions in the sentence.
ii) ***Positional Encodings:*** To add word order, the embeddings are supplemented with position encodings that give each word a specific position-based vector, Pos("cat") = [0.01, 0.03, 0.05, ...]
iii) ***Position-Aware Embeddings:*** The last embedding of the word is calculated by adding the word embedding and the positional encoding, Final("cat") = Embed("cat") + Pos("cat"). This approach makes sure that the model is aware

of the location and the meaning of each word, which is a highly significant consideration in transformer-based models like BERT and GPT.

Embedding Representations: Representing Semantic Meaning

Once text is tokenized, tokens are mapped into high-dimensional vector representations. Embeddings encode semantic relationships so that models can understand synonyms, context words, and word relationships. Figure. 2 demonstrates this by visualizing word embeddings in a vector space. For example: "Bank" (financial institution) and "Bank" (river) will have opposite vector representations depending on the sentence context. Popular embedding methods include Word2Vec, GloVe, and contextual embeddings from transformers.

Figure 2. Word embeddings capturing semantic relationships in a high-dimensional space

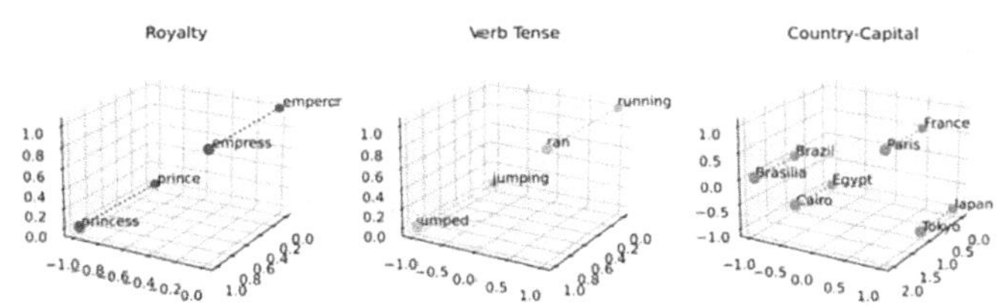

Attention Mechanism

The paradigm shift in LLMs is the attention mechanism, or the self-attention mechanism, present in the Transformer model. The traditional NLP models (e.g., RNNs, LSTMs) processed texts sequentially. But with attention, LLMs can process words in a sentence at once, and assign value scores (weight/attention) to various words based on contextual relevance. For example, in the sentence, *"Apple reported a rise in revenue."*, the model emphasizes "Apple" as a business name more than the fruit, depending on the context words. This capacity allows LLMs to handle long-range dependencies, be consistent, and generate contextually appropriate responses.

- **Self-Attention Mechanism:** Self-attention is the main feature of the Transformer model, allowing the system to look at all the relationships among the words in a sentence at the same time instead of one by one. To put it simply, self-attention allows the model to identify the most relevant words to each other, thus helping it to understand the meaning more effectively. The model does not only consider the sequence of words but also their importance and context together which makes it capable of creating wealthier and more precise language interpretations.

- **Multi-Head Attention:** Transformers do not rely on just one attention mechanism but rather employ several attention heads, which are each specifically meant for recognizing different kinds of relationships in the language. As an instance, one head could be concerned with syntax, another one with semantics, and a third one with spotting entities' relations. The unification of these views allows Transformers to grasp and even to teach themselves the subtler language structures, hence their being super-efficient in natural language processing and generation.

What is a Prompt?

A prompt in Large Language Models (LLMs) refers to the input instruction or text provided to the model for it to produce an output. As opposed to conventional programming, where commands are built in terms of established syntax, LLMs are operated with natural language inputs, and as such, their use is natural and convenient. The structure in which a prompt is built significantly determines the quality, relevance, and accuracy of the model output. Successful prompt engineering is of extremely vital significance in optimizing the performance of LLMs in various applications, from content creation to decision-making applications.

Three primary prompting techniques: zero-shot, one-shot, and few-shot, are varying in complexity and effectiveness. Zero-shot prompting has no examples whatsoever, thus the model relies solely on its pre-training. One-shot has one reference example alone for output quality improvement. Few-shot prompting, the most effective for fine-grained tasks, provides a sequence of examples to establish patterns for greater precision. Effective prompt engineering is vital to optimizing LLM outputs to enable more established and context-based answers to be provided through business applications (Marvin et al., 2024).

LLM Applications in Business Analytics

Writing and Content Generation

LLMs are essential for content automation, business report generation, executive summaries, marketing copy, and blog writing. Business enterprises use such models to maintain uniformity, reduce human intervention, and hasten the time-to-market. Among the most notable models for this are GPT-4 (OpenAI), Mistral Large (Mistral

AI), and Meta Llama 3 (Meta). Example: A marketing company uses GPT-based models to develop customized email campaigns and blog writing for SEO (Nasseri et al., 2023).

Processing and Summarising Documents

LLMs process huge business data with ease, extracting main points and condensing lengthy reports, contracts, or meeting minutes. It facilitates decision-making with concise, pertinent information. Gemini 1.5 (Google DeepMind), Perplexity AI, and Quilbot are some of the popular models employed for summarization. Example: A bank employs an LLM to condense quarterly earnings reports and highlight important financial figures (Bao et al., 2024).

Language Translation

In a multilingual scenario, LLMs provide reliable translations for business documents, emails, and customer conversations, which is very important for global operations. The great language translation AI platforms include Google Cloud Translate, DeepL AI, and Amazon Translate (AWS). For instance, in an e-commerce company, translation software based on LLM technology assists in ensuring multilingual support in customer service.

Code Generation and Automation

LLMs have perhaps become an excellent asset to reduce development time and simplify coding processes like writing, optimizing, and debugging code. They handle all the repetitive coding tasks so that productivity can get a boost! Some of the major models include Copilot X (GitHub + OpenAI), Code Llama (Meta), and Claude Sonnet 3.5 (Anthropic). One example would be AI assistants powered by LLMs being used by a fintech company to automate the generation of SQL queries for data analysis.

Information Retrieval

An ideal practice of using retrieval models is when companies leverage information stored in LLMs to help them in decision-making processes. Such retrieval models include Perplexity AI, Google Bard (Google), STORM (Stanford), and ChatGPT Search. For example, a law firm is utilizing a chatbot with LLM capabilities to provide some pertinent case laws and judiciaries (Gao et al., 2023).

Extended LLMs for Accessing External Data

Enterprises can implement LLMs along with outside databases, APIs, and corporate systems to obtain real-time information for improving business operations and decision-making. Some well-known ones for the same purpose are, for example, LangChain (for orchestrating LLM), Microsoft Azure OpenAI API, Amazon Bedrock, and Google Vertex AI. Example: Supply chain management business integrates LLMs with live inventory and logistics information to provide up-to-date supply chain data.

Strategic Implementation: Case Studies and Business

To move beyond just the theoretical, it is essential to understand how LLMs run their impact on an organization's productivity via the measurable KPIs.

Real-World Case Studies

- **Customer Support Automation (Klarna):** The year 2024 saw a rollout of an OpenAI-driven assistant by the financial technology firm Klarna which managed to take over 2.3 million conversations (two-thirds of their customer service chats) right in the first month. The operation is expected to yield $40 million of annual profit enhancement, executing tasks of 700 full-time workers and at the same time cutting down the rate of repeated inquiries by a quarter (Klarna, 2024).
- **Domain-Specific Analytics (BloombergGPT):** In contrast to the generalist models, Bloomberg established a 50-billion parameter model that was exclusively trained for financial documents. This clearly illustrates the "Build vs. Buy" strategic choice; for specialized business analytics, vertical data trained models earn a significant victory over generalist ones in the areas of sentiment and entity recognition task (Wu et al., 2023).

Performance Benchmarks and KPIs

Performance metrics based on traditional NLP methods such as BLEU scores are often not enough to measure the real-life applicability of LLMs when considering them for business use. Rather, companies are to monitor performance indicators that are focused on business and that can measure the intelligence of the model against how feasible it is to operate. A comparative overview of the best existing models regarding the most important metrics for business analytics deployment in 2025 is presented in Table 1.

*Table 1. Comparative analysis of LLM performance and operational metrics (2025) **

Model	Reasoning (MMLU)	Context Window	Factual Consistency	Approx. Inference Cost
GPT-4o	88.7%	128k Tokens	High	$5.00 / 1M Tokens
Claude 3.5 Sonnet	88.1%	200k Tokens	Very High	$3.00 / 1M Tokens
Llama 3 (70B)	82.0%	128k Tokens	Moderate	< $1.00 (Self-hosted)
Phi-4	75.2%	4k Tokens	Moderate	Negligible (Edge)

*Source: Compiled by authors based on Anthropic (2024), Dubey et al. (2024), Microsoft (2024), and OpenAI (2023).

According to the empirical data presented in Table 1, the following evaluation criteria are to be given the highest priority by organizations:

- **Cost-Latency Trade-offs:** The comparative data show that there is a distinct "intelligence premium." The large models give the best reasoning and the small models give the "performance-per-dollar" ratio which is usually the most sustainable for high-volume, low-complexity analytical tasks.
- **Factual Consistency and Hallucination Rates:** Factual Consistency and Hallucination Rates: In analytics, the price of a wrong insight is often higher than the speed of production. Standards like the "Foundation Model Transparency Index" (Bommasani et al., 2023) are crucial for measuring trustworthiness.
- **Domain-Specific Accuracy:** It is possible that general benchmarks do not characterise the performance in a specific vertical. For example, Gupta et al. (2025a) proposed 'CA-Ben' for the assessment of LLMs on Chartered Accountancy tasks and their results showed that the models considered as the most efficient in Table 1 often have problems with the accurate numerical calculations.

Organizational Readiness and Change Management

The adoption of LLM is not only a matter of technology but also a cultural change. The use of unapproved personal AI tools for professional tasks by employees, known as "Shadow AI," is a significant source of data leakage. Organizations will have to deal with this by changing their approach from restricting to governing and enabling. This includes:

- **Human-in-the-Loop (HITL) Workflows:** The practice of redefining functions is a way to make the AI function as a "co-pilot" instead of a complete substitution. As for financial projections, the LLM initially produces the draft using past data, while the human investigator approves the assumptions made for the strategy.

- **AI Literacy and Upskilling:** Staff will be educated about the limitations of LLMs, particularly with respect to hallucinations and fact-checking consistency. This guarantees that workers will be able to assess AI results critically instead of just passing them off as "automation bias."
- **Change Management Protocols:** Creating explicit rules for the capacity of the organization, making sure that all the units have data governance and compliance frameworks that are necessary in the scale-up of LLM pilot programs to full production.

TRANSFORMER MODELS: THE PILLARS OF LLMS

What are Transformers?

The transformer is a deep learning architecture that houses a family to revolutionize its use in Natural Language Processing (NLP). In the paper, **"Attention Is All You Need"**, by (Vaswani et al., 2017), the Transformer differs from a traditional RNN or LSTM in that it replaces the recurrence typically used with a single self-attention mechanism for the processing of input data in parallel.

How was Text Generation Done Before Transformers?

Text generation has been done so far by sequence models, mostly via Recurrent Neural Networks (RNNs) and some variations such a Long Short-Term Memory (LSTM) and Gated recurrent unit (GRU).

Recurrent Neural Networks (RNNs)

RNNs consider sequences as word by word by obtaining the last state to predict the next one. But RNNs suffered from the following:

- **Vanishing Gradient Problem:** Long-term dependencies became hard to capture.
- **Sequential Computation:** No option for parallel processing.

Long Short-Term Memory (LSTM) Networks

LSTMs were introduced to address the issues of RNNs by incorporating gates that regulate the flow of information in a way that models can learn long-term dependencies more efficiently. LSTMs remained computationally expensive and had extremely long sequences.

Transformer Architecture

As described in Section 2, the Transformer model not only made a trailblazing change in Natural Language Processing by changing the way of processing text (i.e. simultaneous processing instead of reading one word at a time). Nonetheless, this transition came with new kinds of architecture problems and solutions that are now the characteristics of how modern Large Language Models (LLMs) work in the B2B (Business-to-Business) sector.

Encoding Order: The Solution to Parallel Processing

The sentence processing of Transformers happens concurrently, which results in a lack of understanding of the order of the words. If no action is taken, a Transformer would consider "The net profit decreased" and "The decreased profit net" to be the same sentences.

The Positional Encodings are used to address this issue by the model. Instead of depending on the sequence of input (similar to the old RNNs), the model incorporates a distinct mathematical signature into each token's embedding. This "timestamp" enables the model to grasp syntax and sequence an essential skill in business analytics where the order of words completely changes the meaning.

The Encoder: Contextualizing Information

The very first key part of the Transformer is the Encoder, which takes the role of "reading" the input and understanding it as shown in Figure 3.

- **The Attention Engine:** As already mentioned in Section 2, the main distinction is the Self-Attention mechanism. The architecture-wise, this comes through the use of a system of "Query," "Key," and "Value" matrices. In a way, it can be considered like a database search where the model is checking the relevance of each word with every other one in the sequence.
- **Business Implication (The Context Window):** With the help of this technique, the model can "focus" on important context even if the words are very

far apart (e.g., connecting the subject at the beginning of a lengthy report to a conclusion at the end). However, the quadratic computational cost is associated with this feature. If the length of the input document is doubled, then the memory and processing power needed will become four times as much. This is the biggest technical limitation that companies face when processing huge legal contracts or analyzing lengthy historical data logs.

The Decoder: Generative Prediction

The Decoder is the second element and it takes the role of "writing" or producing the output.

- **Masked Self-Attention:** The Encoder processes the entire sentence simultaneously while the Decoder has to generate the text word by word. In order to stop the model from "cheating" by being able to see the not-yet-generated words, the architecture incorporates Masking. Thus, when the model is predicting the next word in a sentence, it is depending only on the words that were there before and not on any future information that it should not have access to during training.
- **Encoder-Decoder Attention:** This is the layer that connects the two parts. It enables the Decoding process to have a look at the Encoder process. For instance, in the case of translation, if the decoder is outputting a French word, it would "attend" (i.e. focus) on the corresponding part of the English text to make sure that the translation is accurate.

Figure 3. Transformer architecture

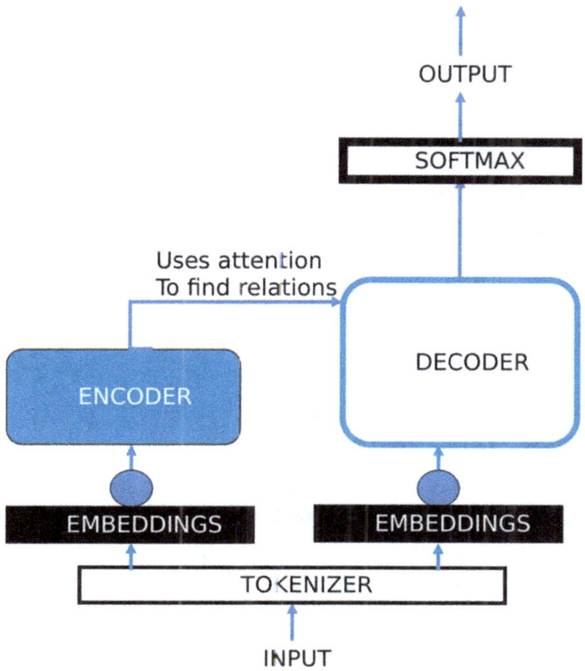

Final Output: Probabilities vs. Determinism

The Softmax layer is the last component of the model's processing. It makes the model's intricate numerical computations to be represented as a straightforward probability distribution across its whole vocabulary. The model does not "know" the answer; it essentially performs the computation of the likelihood of the next token statistically. token.

- **Analytical Relevance:** LLMs sometimes "hallucinate" due to their probabilistic nature. This leads to the use of parameters in business analytics such as "Temperature"(which dictates randomness). A low temperature compels the model to select only the most likely words (advantageous for factual reporting), whereas a high temperature opens up a wider range of options (beneficial for creative brainstorming).

Generation of Text in Transformer

The process of generating text in a Transformer model starts with a series of actions, the first of which is the tokenization of input chunks into valid pieces by assigning them some numeric representation. The tokens are then adapted to embeddings that retain semantics. This, given that the order of words is preserved as these Transformers do not naturally order the text in processing, thus this is maintained by the positional encoding. Hence, the embeddings obtained from this are fed into the encoder where self-attention mechanisms recognize the relationships between the words so that each token can attend to any other token with respect to it. This is followed by multi-head attention that pull in different contextual factors, and representation is further processed in a feedforward network before being input to the remaining encoder layers. After the encoder finishes performing its function, the encoded output feeds into the decoder to trigger text generation. The decoder begins operation on a start token and does so under masked self-attention such that word prediction occurs inline and not based on later tokens. Further, an encoder-decoder attention will allow referencing the encoded input for context matching for the decoder. This fine-level representation is then passed through additional multi-head attention and feed-forward networks to produce a sequence of logits that are coarse probability estimates of the next possible words. The softmax function then normalizes the logits into probability distributions from which the most likely token is selected and forwarded to the decoder, in successive passes, one token at a time until end-of-sequence is met. The sequence created will be detokenized and converted from numeric tokens to human-readable text. While generating text through this highly structured process, Transformers do high-quality outputs through self-attention mechanisms, parallel processing, and probabilistic decoding to guarantee efficiency, fluency, and contextual coherence (Sutskever et al., 2014). It is not only a technical necessity for the business people to comprehend the architectural foundations of the Transformer but also a smart move. The usage of self-attention and parallel processing has a direct impact on the investment in hardware which will be talked about in the next part. When companies transition from knowing 'how' models produce text to 'how' to train them according to particular enterprise requirements, the trade-off between architectural sophistication and computational expense will be the main factor driving the training strategies described in Section 4.

TRAINING LLMS: FROM PRE-TRAINING TO OPTIMIZATION

Pre-Training and Optimizing LLMs

The first of the two most important stages in Large Language Model (LLMs) development is Pre-training, and it is the stage where models are trained on a huge quantity of text data to establish an understanding of a language. Pre-training occurs where big amounts of text are inputted in the form of books, articles, websites, etc., in GB or as high as PB of structured or other forms of unstructured units of information. The raw information is not fed directly into the model; rather, it is pre-filtered based on documents to minimize low-quality, biased, or irrelevant information to allow for training based on high-quality information. Probably, the best-known methods employed for the pre-training of LLMs are the Sequence-to-Sequence (Seq2Seq) Encoder-Decoder Models, whereby pre-training occurs via a process called span corruption (Raffel et al., 2019).

In this process, parts of a word or phrase are masked at random with some tokens like <MASK> or sentinel tokens like X, and the model is trained to complete the missing parts as shown in Figure. 4. For instance, in the sentence "The Teacher Teaches The Student," words are masked, and the resulting sentence is "The Teacher <MASK> The <MASK>." Then the model is trained to predict and complete the masked words based on the contextual cues around them. This way, the model is trained to gain maximum benefit from learning about sentence structure, context, and semantic meaning (Zhang et al., 2020).

Figure 4. Pre-training process in LLMs using sequence-to-sequence encoder-decoder models

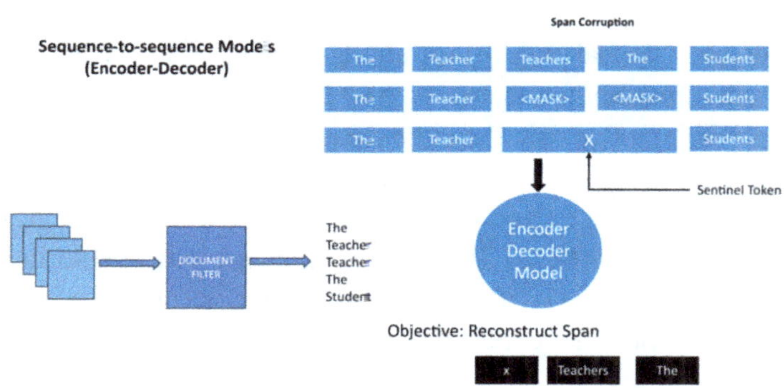

With the intentions of being divergently good for an LLM at various downstream tasks such as text generation, translation, summarization, and question-answering, the key objective of the masked language modeling and span corruption is learning complex patterns of language. The model repeatedly predicts missing text spans of a vast corpus and increases ability to comprehend grammar, semantics, and relationships between words eventually improving its performance on the real-world tasks, stating that.

Challenges in Pre-Training LLMs

Pre-training has proven to be conditioning such as its own very sophisticated computation-hungry process, and it can also be marked by a series of grave challenges. These include the extremely high computability demands, the necessity of high-quality training data, and the thorny ethical challenges of bias and disinformation. All such matters have to be resolved for functional LLM operation that is effective, consistent, and fair.

Computational and Memory Limitations

Pre-training brings about massive computational and memory overhead. It holds "hundreds of billions of parameters" to be trained over-the-top GPU, TPU, and AI chip hardware, thus making it highly cost-intensive, time-consuming, energy- and computation-exhaustive, even when using the most advanced technology. Memory constraints are equally very painful since processing large-scale models demands effective storage and transfer modalities for the data. All these are therefore to be heralded as the high and unsustainable costs of LLMs training.

Training Data Selection and Filtering

Another paramount challenge in the training of LLMs is the selection and filtering of training data. Important for determining an LLM's performance are the diversity of the data and their quality. But the large datasets often contain noisy, out-of-date, or redundant data that worsen the learning of the models. Duplicate instances and strongly biased data may overfit on some patterns, consequently reducing the model's ability to generalize across tasks. Therefore, the timely curation, filtering, and intensive preprocessing of training data are crucial to guarantee a faithful representation in the training of models (Perełkiewicz & Po´swiata, 2024).

Ethical Concerns (Bias, Misinformation)

Beyond technical challenges, ethical considerations also play an important role in pre-training any LLM. Models trained on skewed data sets reinforce stereotypes and amplify disparaging narratives. When unverified or discredited external sources are considered during training of the models, the risk of misinformation increases and may lead to other potentially misleading results. Hence, only preventive monitoring with a sense of fairness and accountability can ensure that accountable AI-based content is actively killed against any such bias. Good ethical will and strict filtering should be put in place in the dealing with such issues by developers and researchers (Bender et al., 2021).

Ideal Configuration for Pre-Training LLMs

The configuration problems that are selected during pre-training are the key determinants of the performance of Large Language Models (LLMs). A sensible configuration trades off computational efficacy and model performance while scaling up to resolve resource constraints and data quality issues, as shown in Figure. 5. The optimal pre-training configuration for Large Language Models (LLMs) needs to strike a balance among model complexity, training data size, and computational resource availability. Pre-training aims to decrease the loss function to qualify improvements in model performance, which may require the inclusion of training tokens or increases in model parameters. Such decisions, however, remain limited by budget, time, and access to GPUs.

Figure 5. Balancing model size, data, and compute for optimal LLM performance

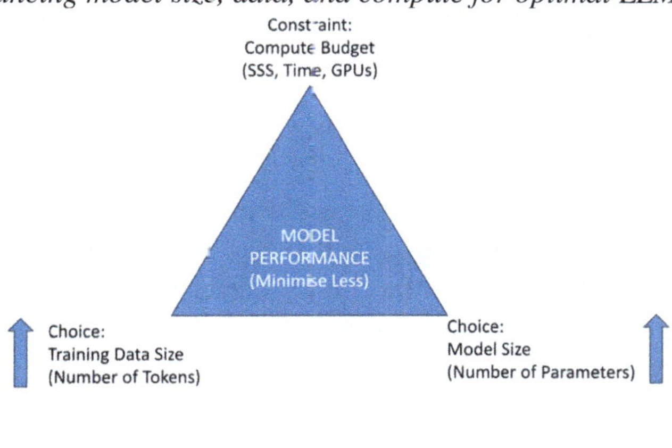

Two of the most important pre-training configuration hyperparameters are model size in parameters and training dataset size in tokens. Both determine the performance of a model, but given a limited compute budget, they become a trade-off. One of the simplest metrics for computational cost is petaFLOP/s-day: the metric for how many floating-point operations are being executed at a rate of 1 petaFLOP per second over a day. The larger LLMs become, the greater their training needs to become by optimizing hardware utilizations, parallel-processing abilities, and economical computation methods to achieve the best performance against resource constraints.

Hardware Considerations

There are hardware considerations that need to be taken into account. The training efficiency of large language models is highly hardware-platform dependent. Accelerators like GPUs, TPUs, and specially designed AI hardware can really ramp up the training efficiency by executing parallel computation very efficiently. Then, there are cloud computing and distributed training that help in scaling up; the LLMs can be trained in an intensive fashion across multiple nodes-shortening the training time. From distributed frameworks, across TPU pods, multi-GPU systems to cloud clusters, strong support is being provided to conduct efficient model updates, making it thus possible to have high-performance training with computed costs.

LARGE LANGUAGE MODELS FINE-TUNING

Fine-tuning of large language models (LLMs) is an important process to adapt a model pre-trained on general tasks to a target task or domain-something that makes the model much more useful and efficient. While this helps during pre-training, the models gain general linguistic and world knowledge. Fine-tuning builds on this knowledge, thereby gaining accuracy, contextual usage, and compliance with task-based guidelines.

Definition of Instruction Fine-Tuning

Instruction fine-tuning refers to a process whereby LLMs are fine-tuned on explicit instruction datasets and their outputs so they can follow human-like instructions better. In contrast to the traditional fine-tuning in which the weights are being fine-tuned over a pre-defined dataset, this instruction fine-tuning is an impetus toward the model to converse in a human-manner to better accept instructions, which enhances its reasoning, summarization, and decision-making abilities (Chung et al., 2022).

Catastrophic Forgetting and Its Effect on LLM Performance

One of the issues linked to fine-tuning is the phenomenon termed "catastrophic forgetting." In catastrophic forgetting, the model tends to forget a part of knowledge from the pre-training phase when transferring the model into a fine-tuning scenario for a specific task. This happens as the fine-tuning data may not necessarily encompass all of the previous knowledge the model had been pre-trained to learn. Some of the approaches to mitigate this include continual learning, applying regularization techniques, and using adapters in order to preserve the pre-trained capacity while allowing gradual incorporation of new knowledge (Luo et al., 2023).

Evaluating a Fine-Tuned Model

The performance of the fine-tuned LLM must be assessed through the use of really robust metrics and benchmark datasets, to assess its likelihood of generalizing well to any one NLP task. In this regard, the ROUGE score, or Recall-Oriented Understudy for Gisting Evaluation, is especially famous for its simplicity in being used in tasks like text summarization and reports overlap between its model output and reference text. Another famous metric for measuring the performance with machine translation is the Bilingual Evaluation Understudy, or rather, BLEU, which approximates how similar the text provided by the model is compared to the ground truth text with n-gram overlaps. Other than that, benchmark datasets such as GLUE, SuperGLUE, and others more domain-specific provide generalized test cases by which one can credibly assert that the model well performs in general (Lin, 2004).

Parameter Efficient Fine-Tuning (PEFT)

Large model fine-tunings are computationally expensive. Using Parameter Efficient Fine-Tuning (PEFT), wherein only a few numbers of model parameters are fine-tuned depending on some fixed prior knowledge present in the model, the procedure for fine-tuning with parameter-efficient fine-tuning reduces the necessity for resources.

LoRA (Low-Rank Adaptation)

LoRA works with low rank matrices to modify a few model parameters, and hence cuts memory and computer efficiency. LoRA will employ updatable low-rank enhancements that are basically equivalent to full fine-tuning but consume either token memory or computation time.

Soft Prompts and Prompt Tuning

Just as no weight matrix modifications are needed, prompt tuning aims to learn as little as one or a few latent features (soft prompts) and steer responses to generate improved behavior. For transferring LLMs to a new domain, the method of prompt tuning is very efficient in terms of computation. Unlike traditional text-based prompt engineering, where the text prompt is given manually, soft prompts in the form of learnable embeddings are designed to be implicitly task-optimized (Sahoo et al., 2024).

ALIGNMENT AND SAFETY

Given the growing relevance of Large Language Models (LLMs), following robust alignment strategies for human values, ethical practices, and safety guidelines is imperative. Reinforcement Learning from Human Feedback (RLHF) propounded fabricating these things by refining the model based on human feedback and behavior alignment. This chapter deeply analyses RLHF and points out its accomplishments, existing challenges, and other alignment-scalable practices at a much more cost-effective level.

LLM Alignment With Human Values

LMMs must be assured that they produce content consistent with human cognition. Training and fine-tuning based on strict ethical considerations are vital. These have to be treated with utmost caution and very well recognized by the supervised learning approaches. These latter require predefined datasets, often making the choice, the training process yielding the results quite unaware of ethical nuances. Reinforcement Learning, in the direction of minimizing bias in model outputs, steering clear of offending material, and remaining culturally conscious, provides the most dynamic way of perpetually improving model performance via human feedback.

RLHF (Reinforcement Learning From Human Feedback)

Recently, reinforcement learning from human feedback, or just RLHF, is a loop used to enhance Large Language Models by injecting some degree of human assessment. The process usually begins with pretraining an initial model over some extensive datasets by employing unsupervised learning methods. Once set, the model generates a number of possible responses to the supplied prompts, and human assessors are asked to rank the possible responses according to quality, relevance, and ethical acceptability. The rankings are then used to train a reward model, which scores alternative responses with numerical values. Following that, a reinforcement learning algorithm is applied to this reward model, further enhancing the LLM's alignment with acceptable outputs, thus earning a better reward as shown in Figure. 6. Repeatedly, RLHF enables the models to take lessons from human feedback, thus shunning undesirable outputs and building user confidence.

Figure 6. RLHF process: From pretraining to fine-tuning

LLM Reward Hacking Avoidance

Of several challenges in reinforcement learning, reward hacking is one where an AI model pokes holes in the reward system unintentionally meant to maximize human performance. Reward hacking amongst LLMs would produce responses that have been over-optimized yet utterly unnatural in that they meet the reward criteria only, game feedback mechanisms without any genuine ethical ground, or simply be excessively polite and conservative, making it nearly impossible to go beyond a specified risk as illustrated in Figure. 7. To avert these threats, researchers attempt to enlist the help of adversarial training, multiple-objective optimization, and human-in-the-loop tuning to ensure that the reward signal accounts for good and bad behaviour, not shortcuts that can be exploited.

Figure 7. Key challenges in AI alignment

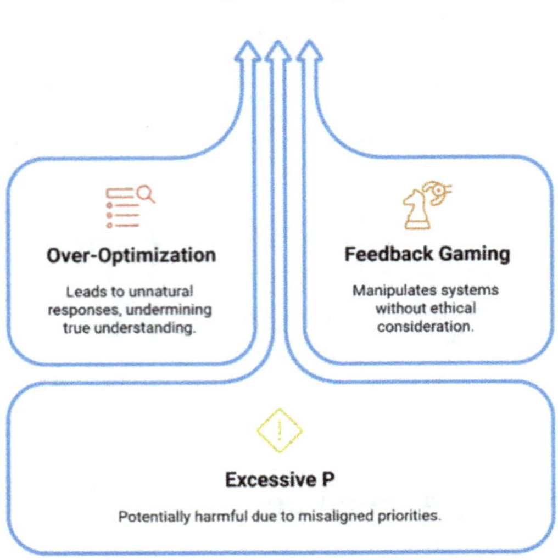

INFERENCE DEPLOYMENT AND OPTIMIZATION

LLM deployment and inference optimization are key areas for ensuring that these models operate in the real world. Training, that is pre-training and fine-tuning, is computationally intensive, while inference must be done in an economical, efficient, and scalable manner. LLM deployment represents a balanced trade-off among all competing interests.

How to Optimize and Deploy LLMs for Inferencing

To optimize the LLM for inference, initial evaluation is done between the target use-case, hardware availability inference latency, and the target performance levels. Deploying an LLM to production can cover model size, inference latency, memory usage, and power consumption. Different options would rely on whether the model is deployed on a cloud-based GPU, edge hardware, or an on-premises server environment. Model compression and hardware-aware optimization methods ensure high-quality outputs with LLMs, while also keeping a lid on the computation overhead. Of course, all these would also be dependent on how autoscaling would be administered on-demand when using these models for cloud deployments. Edge deployments, however, would need severe model compression techniques on-the-go because of the less available computational power in the environments.

One of the biggest challenges of optimization is thus to find a balance between the model accuracy and speed in which it processes data. These models tend to be large and thus costly when inferring; they are very accurate, but these that strongly sacrifice their ability in some fights are efficient but very inaccurate. A good example of this method is model distillation and pruning; however, this ultimately results in the cost of keeping almost all the knowledge of the model while drastically reducing its size and the cost of computation. Another vital aspect is batched processing, as batched inference requests optimize hardware utilization and can potentially lower the time per request when high throughput is required.

Model Compression Methods

These techniques help in reducing the physical storage and computational cost of large language models (LLMs) while leaving their performance and accuracy. The need for compression is felt during the production stage of an LLM deployment, especially the ones which produce output in low latency. Model distillation, quantization, and pruning are common techniques of compression as shown in Figure. 8.

Figure 8. Model compression types

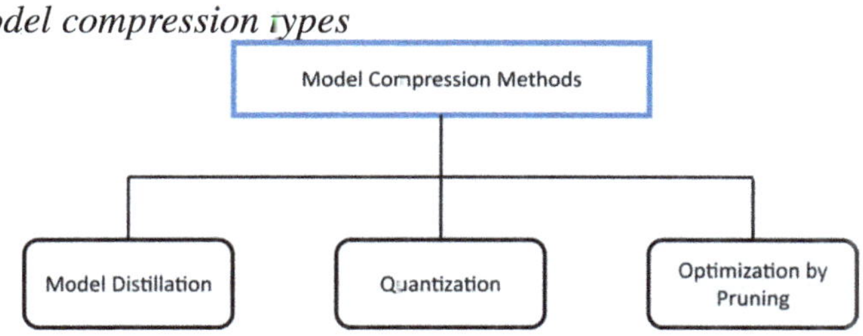

Model Distillation

Model distillation is a model in which a larger pre-trained model, or "teacher model," is used to pass knowledge to a smaller implementation called the "student model," which attempts to mimic the outputs as close as possible while being much smaller. This enables the deployment of very powerful large language models (LLMs) without wasting too much of the cognitive capacity of the original model. Distillation works specifically well for LLMs because it picks up the critical features and patterns without storing the entire complexity of the original model. Other means of transferring knowledge, like soft targets (or probabilistic output distributions) and intermediate layer supervision, then need to ensure that the student model gets the best and most useful information. The end result is that the model is lighter, faster, and deployable under resource-poor environments such as mobile devices or in edge-computing situations (Hsieh et al., 2023).

Quantization

In quantization, the precision of numerical calculations within a model is lessened; thereby lowering memory consumption and decreasing inference time. LLMs are most often run onto high-precision formats requiring substantial computational power, such as FP32 or FP16. In the quantization algorithms, while the high-precision values are converted into lower-bit representations such as INT8 or even to a binary format, the actual accuracy of the model remains intact with negligible loss (Jacob et al., 2017).

Pruning

Pruning is the process of systematically removing parameters from a model less important for the sake of reducing size and computation cost. Neural networks also contain redundant connections that do not significantly contribute to model prediction capabilities. Pruning is generally used along with optimization techniques like quantization and knowledge distillation so as to optimize the total efficiency. In practical applications, there is usually iterative pruning involving model pruning, retraining, and then another round of pruning to counter the loss of accuracy and computational requirements.

Using LLMs in Applications

The application of LLMs after optimization cuts across different sectors with applications that are natural language-understanding and natural language-producing. One can see that these models are being set in motion into chatbots; virtual assistants; customer support automation; document summarization, legal Question Answering (Gupta et al., 2025b) and financial analysis; and diagnosis in health care benefits. Such applications, however, require an effective way of deploying them to meet reliability and efficiency.

LLM Application Architecture

LLM application architecture is application case and deployment strategy dependent and consists of layers in collaboration typically. The frontend layer consists of interfaces like web applications, chatbots, or APIs that accept the user request and forward the request for processing as illustrated in Figure. 9. The API gateway processes the queries, working as a broker between the interface and the inference engine of the model while providing authentication, load balancing, and optimal request routing. The inference engine is the processing center using parallel processing, batch inference, and caching mechanisms for optimizing the response efficiency. Additionally, storage and retrieval operations exist in a few applications with the use of external knowledge bases, databases, or vector search technology to output contextually appropriate responses. In order to retain inference efficiency, monitoring and logging play a primary role in managing model responses, auditing output, and ensuring persistence of performance consistency. Successful LLM deployment hinges on creating a combination of architecture pieces in synchronism using optimizations such as compression and quantization of the model alongside elastic infrastructure for providing quality performance without undue resource costs.

Figure 9. LLM architecture

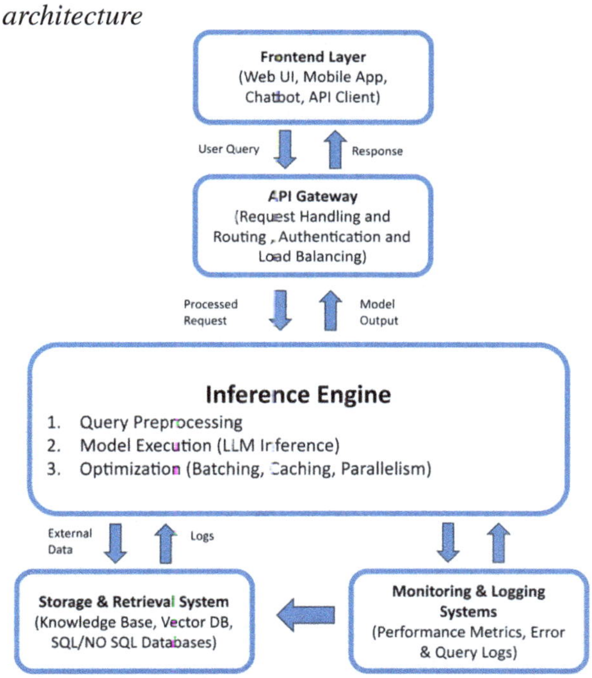

LLMOps: The Lifecycle of Maintenance

Model deployment is not a single action; it needs a committed "LLMOps" (Large Language Model Operations) infrastructure. This is unlike the classic MLOps because of the massive size of the artifacts and the subjective nature of the output.

Model Drift & Continuous Evaluation

In contrast to statistical models, LLMs do not numerically "drift" in a strict manner, however, the expectations of users are altered, and the data that they process is transformed (for instance, new slang, new laws). Therefore, continuous evaluation pipelines that monitor "drift" in terms of factual accuracy and tone are necessary.

Selection Framework and Deployment Architectures

In the case of data security, cost of operations, and technical performance, businesses will still have to make a right choice regarding the deployment model. The selection framework as presented in Table 2 basically cuts into three categories determined by the organization's standing in terms of regulations and technical know-how.

Table 2. LLM deployment selection matrix for business analytics

Deployment Mode	Key Use Case	Data Privacy	Maintenance	Cost Structure
Proprietary API	Rapid prototyping, Generalist tasks	Moderate (Depends on SLA)	Very Low	Pay-per-token (Variable)
Self-Hosted (Open Source)	Regulated industries (Finance, Health)	Maximum (Total Sovereignty)	Very High	GPU/Infrastructure (Fixed)
Managed VPC (Virtual Private Cloud)	Enterprise-scale production	High (Isolated Environment)	Moderate	Platform fee + Usage

Decision-makers can use the structure presented in Table 2 to find their way through the balance of the ease of use of cutting-edge models such as GPT-4o and the privacy protection given by open-source models like Llama 3 or Mistral.

ETHICAL ISSUES AND RESPONSIBLE AI

The pervasive deployment of Large Language Models (LLMs) mandates greater emphasis on the practices of responsible artificial intelligence in order to promote fairness, reliability, and ethical regulation. Despite the awe-inspiring aptitude demonstrated by LLMs, their usage stirs huge concerns regarding bias, disinformation, intellectual property protection, and ethical issues beyond these. An adequate response to such challenges is necessitated through an all-round plan that addresses technical solutions, legislative frameworks, and best practices aimed at facilitating artificial intelligence systems in being applied in a well-warranted manner for society's good.

Managing Biases and Fairness in LLMs

There are several concerns regarding bias management and the fairness of language LLMs, which have been trained on huge volumes of datasets collected from a variety of online sources. Such data included biased social phenomena, rendering it into unbalanced representations and discriminatory judgments if the biases remain unchecked. Therefore, such bias needs to be treated with serious technological methods of data curation, adversarial learning, and bias-reduction algorithms. Second, the training pipeline should incorporate fairness-aware practices such that the models are optimized to provide balanced responses for demographic subgroups.

Preventing Misinformation and Hallucinations

One important consideration of LLMs is that they can generate factually incorrect or misleading information, otherwise referred to as hallucination. This becomes probably most critical in use cases whereby high factual accuracy matters, such as in medicine and the law. Efforts to counter the above concern include coupling the output with validated sources, incorporating retrieval-augmented generation (RAG) to fetch external sources of knowledge, and embedding self-evaluation routines that enable the models to verify their own output. Last but not least, user disclaimers with attached confidence scoring yield more transparency and reduces the spread of misinformation.

Security Risks: Adversarial Attacks

As large language models (LLMs) get more integrated into business operations, they create new attack points that usual cybersecurity control measures cannot handle sometimes. One of the risks is prompt injection where the adversaries create inputs that aim to bypass the safe instructions of the model, for instance, deceiving the banking chatbot into providing unauthorized refunds. Another threat is retrieval poisoning where attackers interfere with outside documents that a retrieval-augmented generation (RAG) system is dependent on, for example, changing a Wikipedia page leads the analytics engine to generate incorrect or misleading reports. To prevent such threats to intellectual property, companies are going for watermarking methods which sign AI-made content using cryptography to secure its authenticity and ownership.

Governance and Regulatory Frameworks

Compliance has become a necessity, not an option. The EU AI Act classifies AI systems according to their level of risk, with very strict regulations imposed on high-risk applications used, for instance, in the areas of employment or credit scoring. In addition, the OECD's (Organisation for Economic Co-operation and Development., 2024) "AI Governance Principles" provide a framework for accountability, thus making it necessary for businesses to keep comprehensive documentation of their model training data and decision-making logic in order to comply with GDPR's "Right to Explanation".

Ethical AI and Intellectual Property Regulation

It is, however, a problematic aspect using copyrighted material in training data sets for large language models (LLMs) because of the emerging intellectual property (IP) rights ownership issues. Most of the AI output extends its patterns through copyrighted material, raising legal and ethical questions of attribution and fair use. Ethical AI regulatory frameworks allow for the opening up of data provenance, opt-in models for creators, and legally compliant licensing agreements. Most importantly, therefore, policymakers and AI engineers have to work hand in hand in policy formulation that will enhance innovation while protecting the rights of the creators.

Best practices for Ethical AI

One of the organizational changes required to advance ethical AI entails embracing all the best practices in the industry for ethical AI design, transparency, and accountability in use. Employing representative and diverse training data sets, human oversight especially in high-risk usage, and supply of transparent explanations of the AI system output comprise the principles of these practices. Regular auditing of AI systems for performance drift should also be done to warrant a feedback loop for model enhancements. The institutions, such as IEEE and the European Commission, promulgate ethical AI guidelines. They forge consistent industry-standards in the AI system development paradigm with societal standards. It must emerge as realizing the social responsibility. Responsible AI is therefore not a technology problem. Stakeholders may establish ethical designs through the planning, implementation, and operation of LLM so that they will be beneficial within the society without the risks of getting harmful.

Environmental Sustainability and Green AI

The usage of LLMs in large scale computing leads to a great concern regarding the environment. Drawing out one large model can cause the same amount of carbon emission as five cars during their whole life span (Strubell et al., 2019). Nonetheless, the environmental impact is not only confined to training but also includes the continuous energy consumption required for inference (model running). For business analytics, "Green AI" practices are turning into a necessity for both compliance and operations. Some of these practices are:

- **Model Right-Sizing:** Replacing large models (like GPT-4) with smaller and specific ones (like DistilBERT) can lead to around 90% lesser energy utilization.
- **Carbon-Aware Computing:** Performing training and heavy batch processing jobs in the data centers that use renewable energy or during off-peak hours.
- **Sparse Models:** Implementing Mixture of Experts (MoE) models that activate just a small percentage of parameters for each token, thus greatly reducing the energy cost for each query.

FUTURE OF LLMS IN BUSINESS ANALYTICS

The development of LLMs is ushering in a radical transformation in business analytics, making them an envisaged essential tool for decision-making, automation, and knowledge acquisition. However, growing AI technology development aims at resolving a few of the many challenges existing in LLM development today, including computational inefficiencies, lack of interpretability, and reasoning capability constraints. The future scenario of LLMs deals with making models smaller and more efficient at reaching almost the same performance level as larger models, integrated with advanced reasoning systems, the richness of multimodal AI, enhanced interpretability of AI systems, with an element of automation through applying AutoML techniques. AI is heading towards building autonomous agents to carry out complex workflows with autonomous decisions, dynamically adapting to changing business environments.

More Compact, Lighter Models With Similar Performance

The fate of LLMs in business analytics will be met with the emergence of some small, highly efficient models with performance to match their larger ancestors.

Model distillation and low-rank adaptation (LoRA) are key in the driving force of this. An example of the best-in-class is DistilBERT, made by Hugging Face. It is a condensed version of BERT with fewer parameters sitting at about 95% of the BERT performance level, and it enjoys remarkable gains in speed and efficiency. Another major development is LoRA, introduced by Microsoft Research, which performs optimal fine-tuning of models by injecting trainable low-rank matrices into large pre-trained models. With LoRA, computational costs and memory usage are massively reduced, allowing companies-especially smaller ones or those with limited computing capability-to deploy sophisticated analytics models without heavy infrastructure investment. In this way, these innovations democratize access to advanced analytics, render it hence more affordable and scalable, encourage swift iterations and deployment of AI-powered insights with little operational computing (Hu et al., 2021).

Advancements in Reasoning-Able LLMs

Reasoning-based large language models, in future advances, will change the way companies will implement analytics in areas requiring complex strategic decisions. Current models, like GPT-4 and Claude 3.5 Sonnet, have already exhibited great reasoning abilities when considering many applications such as strategic planning, market trend analysis, and risk analysis. In the future, though, these models would likely enhance these abilities further using even more advanced reasoning techniques, such as chain-of-thought prompting and self-consistency methods. For instance, Google's Pathways Language Model (PaLM) has already demonstrated terrific growth in terms of its logical-mathematical reasoning capabilities. As these capability-driven reasoning techniques further unfold, companies will experience a breakthrough in ever-tricky decision-making scenarios for better predictions, scenario planning, and strategy building. Specifically, industries such as finance, healthcare, logistics, manufacturing, and others will reap tremendous benefits, given the need for advanced predictive analytics and resilient decision support.

Multimodal AI

Multimodal AI, combining text, image, and audio processing capabilities, is a breakthrough technology in business analytics, providing richer context-aware insights. Systems such as OpenAI's GPT-4o are at the forefront of solidly understanding and generating across various modalities to give end-to-end advanced analytical platforms that outperform the single-modal models by a long margin. Google Gemini/ImageBind and others reflect industry shifts towards end-to-end convergence of different data types into one analytic platform. Organizations taking up multimodal analytics gain deep competitive advantage by inferring subtle consumer behavior and choices from several correlated inputs—text, image, and audio—crucial to retail, entertainment, marketing, and user experience design. A leap in multimodality capabilities is bound to boost user engagement, personalization recommendations, and strategic insights, along with driving customer engagement and operational excellence.

AI Interpretability and Explainability Progress

The further development of artificial intelligence interpretation and explanation is about opening up perspectives on how to compete with large language models in business analytics. Some examples of innovations in this field are SHAP, Investigating by SHapley Additive exPlanations and LIME, an even more recent technology, Anthropic's Constitutional AI, and many more, which all aim for better explanations of conduct of model outputs. Organizations are increasingly being compelled and persuaded to demand transparency from AI technology to comply with regulations and build trust with customers. For example, a financial organization using LLMs for assessing its credit risk must deeply interpret and explain the model outputs to fulfill regulatory requirements. As the new forms of interpretation evolve, organizations may look forward to having much more confidence in AI-based decision-making processes, therefore making regulatory compliance and ethical procedures much more straightforward, which will greatly improve stakeholder confidence.

AutoML and Self-Improving Language Models

The advent of AutoML and self-improving language models may transfer the efficiency and effectiveness business analytics. Examples of such AutoML features include Google's AutoML and Amazon's AutoGluon, which automate some very critical processes in model building, right from data preparation to hyperparameter optimization reducing the skill threshold needed for deploying very powerful analytical solutions. Moreover, advanced self-improving models are based on repetitive engagements in the real-world-to improve prediction performance and insight context by themselves through iterative learning loops. Examples of this, showing how such next-generation models can learn and optimally adapt their functions based on variations in data inputs as well as operation conditions, are: Meta's Recursive Model Index (RMI); DeepMind's language models by reinforcement learning. This makes it possible for organizations to keep analytical agility and gain competitive advantages by rapidly refreshing models while requiring minimal human involvement in analytics process maintenance.

AI Agents / Agentic AI

Agentic AI or AI agents is a flexible new arena prescribing models with making decisions on their own as well as strategic interaction in dynamically changing environments. Developments such as OpenAI's AutoGPT and Anthropic's Claude beget the defining aspects of agentic behavior through goal-oriented problem solving and substantially autonomous iterative repeat processes. These agents are capable of doing complex analytics tasks independently, such as market analysis, competitor profiling, resource allocation, and even, at times, negotiations. For instance, AutoGPT can perform multi-step tasks autonomously, by iteratively defining sub-goals, fetching relevant data, analyzing findings, and taking actions (Chawla et al., 2024).

CONCLUSION

Large Language Models (LLMs) evolution has brought business analytics to generative intelligence instead of predictive analysis. Through this chapter, it is evidenced that LLMs such as GPT-4o and Llama 3 have very powerful features in reasoning and automation. Nonetheless, the "Academic vs. Industrial" divide for practitioners signals that the technical challenge of successful adoption is not just about technology but also about changes in operations of the business.

It is not to say that LLMs will be any good if the strategy trade-offs which we pointed out in our LLMOps framework are not navigated. The point is that there will always be a trade-off between the "intelligence premium" of frontier models and the costs and privacy constraints of deployment. Quite the opposite, the case of Klarna and BloombergGPT, which provided a comparative analysis, indicates that different businesses have different needs and it is up to the firms to decide about the architecture that would suit their KPIs the best—speed with a proprietary API or sovereignty with a self-hosted model.

Looking into the future, the merging of multimodal AI and agentic systems will reestablish the limits of employee productivity. Nevertheless, interdependent is the potential on the strict and thorough governance. Companies, as new regulations like the EU AI Act come into action, will have to put Responsible AI in the first place to avoid problems of hallucination and prompt injection. At the end of the day, it will be the organizations that have the best governance in place for these models that will win the race, treating LLMs as a strategic asset through continuous oversight and alignment with their business goals rather than just software.

REFERENCES

Alberti, C., Lee, K., & Collins, M. (2019). *A BERT Baseline for the Natural Questions*. https://arxiv.org/abs/1901.08634v3

Anthropic. (2024). The Claude 3 model family: Opus, Sonnet, Haiku [Technical report]. https://www-cdn.anthropic.com/de8ba9b01c9ab7cbabf5c33b80b7bbc618857627/Model_Card_Claude_3.pdf

Bao, Y., Shah, A. P., Narang, N., Rivers, J., Maksey, R., Guan, L., Barrere, L. N., Evenson, S., Basole, R., Miao, C., Mehta, A., Boulay, F., Park, S. M., Pearson, N. E., Joy, E., He, T., Thakur, S., Ghosal, K., On, J., & Wei, W. (2024). *Harnessing Business and Media Insights with Large Language Models*. https://arxiv.org/abs/2406.06559v1

Bender, E. M., Gebru, T., McMillan-Major, A., & Shmitchell, S. (2021). On the dangers of stochastic parrots: Can language models be too big? *FAccT 2021 - Proceedings of the 2021 ACM Conference on Fairness, Accountability, and Transparency*, 610–623. DOI: 10.1145/3442188.3445922

Bommasani, R., Klyman, K., Longpre, S., Kapoor, S., Maslej, N., Xiong, B., Zhang, D., & Liang, P. (2023). The foundation model transparency index. arXiv preprint arXiv:2310.12941. https://arxiv.org/abs/2310.12941

Chawla, C., Chatterjee, S., Gadadinni, S. S., Verma, P., & Banerjee, S. (2024). Agentic AI: The building blocks of sophisticated AI business applications. *Journal of AI. Robotics & Workplace Automation*, *3*(3), 196. DOI: 10.69554/XEHZ1946

Chung, H. W., Hou, L., Longpre, S., Zoph, B., Tay, Y., Fedus, W., Li, Y., Wang, X., Dehghani, M., Brahma, S., Webson, A., Gu, S. S., Dai, Z., Suzgun, M., Chen, X., Chowdhery, A., Castro-Ros, A , Pellat, M., Robinson, K., & Wei, J. (2022). *Scaling Instruction-Finetuned Language Models*. https://arxiv.org/abs/2210.11416v5

Collins, M. (2011). *Statistical machine translation: IBM models 1 and 2*. Columbia Columbia Univ.

Dubey, A., Jauhri, A., Pandey, A., Kadian, A., Al-Dahle, A., Letman, A., Mathur, A., Schelten, A., Vaughan, A., Yang, A., Fan, A., Goyal, A., Hartshorn, A., Yang, A., Mitra, A., Sravankumar, A., Korenev, A., Hinsvark, A., Rao, A., . . . Zhang, A. (2024). The Llama 3 herd of models [Technical report]. arXiv. https://doi.org//arXiv.2407.21783DOI: 10.48550

Floridi, L., & Chiriatti, M. (2020). GPT-3: Its Nature, Scope, Limits, and Consequences. *Minds and Machines*, *30*(4), 681–694. DOI: 10.1007/s11023-020-09548-1

Gao, Y., Xiong, Y., Gao, X., Jia, K., Pan, J., Bi, Y., Dai, Y., Sun, J., Wang, M., & Wang, H. (2023). *Retrieval-Augmented Generation for Large Language Models: A Survey*. https://arxiv.org/abs/2312.10997v5

Getting started with Perplexity. (n.d.). Retrieved March 20, 2025, from https://www.perplexity.ai/hub/blog/getting-started-with-perplexity

Gupta, J., Sharma, A., Singhania, S., & Abidi, A. I. (2025b). Legal Assist AI: Leveraging Transformer-Based Model for Effective Legal Assistance. arXiv preprint arXiv:2505.22003. https://arxiv.org/abs/2505.22003

Gupta, J., Sharma, A., Singhania, S., Adnan, M., Deo, S., Abidi, A. I., & Gupta, K. (2025a). Large Language Models Acing Chartered Accountancy. *SN Computer Science*, *6*(957), 957. Advance online publication. DOI: 10.1007/s42979-025-04497-x

Hsieh, C. Y., Li, C. L., Yeh, C. K., Nakhost, H., Fujii, Y., Ratner, A., Krishna, R., Lee, C. Y., & Pfister, T. (2023). Distilling Step-by-Step! Outperforming Larger Language Models with Less Training Data and Smaller Model Sizes. *Proceedings of the Annual Meeting of the Association for Computational Linguistics*, 8003–8017. DOI: 10.18653/v1/2023.findings-acl.507

Hu, E., Shen, Y., Wallis, P., Allen-Zhu, Z., Li, Y., Wang, S., Wang, L., & Chen, W. (2021). LoRA: Low-Rank Adaptation of Large Language Models. *ICLR 2022 - 10th International Conference on Learning Representations*. https://arxiv.org/abs/2106.09685v2

Introducing Microsoft 365 Copilot – your copilot for work - The Official Microsoft Blog. (n.d.). Retrieved March 20, 2025, from https://blogs.microsoft.com/blog/2023/03/16/introducing-microsoft-365-copilot-your-copilot-for-work/

Jacob, B., Kligys, S., Chen, B., Zhu, M., Tang, M., Howard, A., Adam, H., & Kalenichenko, D. (2017). Quantization and Training of Neural Networks for Efficient Integer-Arithmetic-Only Inference. *Proceedings of the IEEE Computer Society Conference on Computer Vision and Pattern Recognition*, 2704–2713. DOI: 10.1109/CVPR.2018.00286

Klarna. (2024, February 27). Klarna AI assistant handles two-thirds of customer service chats in its first month. Klarna Press Release. https://www.klarna.com/international/press/klarna-ai-assistant-handles-two-thirds-of-customer-service-chats-in-its-first-month/

Le, P., & Zuidema, W. (2016). Quantifying the vanishing gradient and long distance dependency problem in recursive neural networks and recursive LSTMs. *Proceedings of the Annual Meeting of the Association for Computational Linguistics*, 87–93. DOI: 10.18653/v1/W16-1610

Lin, C.-Y. (2004). ROUGE: A Package for Automatic Evaluation of Summaries. *Text Summarization Branches Out*, 74–81. https://aclanthology.org/W04-1013/

Luo, Y., Yang, Z., Meng, F., Li, Y., Zhou, J., & Zhang, Y. (2023). *An Empirical Study of Catastrophic Forgetting in Large Language Models During Continual Fine-tuning*. https://arxiv.org/abs/2308.08747v5

Marvin, G., Hellen, N., Jjingo, D., & Nakatumba-Nabende, J. (2024). *Prompt Engineering in Large Language Models*. 387–402. DOI: 10.1007/978-981-99-7962-2_30

Microsoft. (2024). Phi-4 technical report [Technical report]. arXiv. https://arxiv.org/abs/2412.08905

Mikolov, T., Chen, K., Corrado, G., & Dean, J. (2013). Efficient Estimation of Word Representations in Vector Space. *1st International Conference on Learning Representations, ICLR 2013 - Workshop Track Proceedings*. https://arxiv.org/abs/1301.3781v3

Nasseri, M., Brandtner, P., Zimmermann, R., Falatouri, T., Darbanian, F., & Obinwanne, T. (2023). Applications of Large Language Models (LLMs) in Business Analytics – Exemplary Use Cases in Data Preparation Tasks. *Lecture Notes in Computer Science (Including Subseries Lecture Notes in Artificial Intelligence and Lecture Notes in Bioinformatics), 14059 LNCS*, 182–198. DOI: 10.1007/978-3-031-48057-7_12

Naveed, H., Khan, A. U., Qiu, S., Saqib, M., Anwar, S., Usman, M., Akhtar, N., Barnes, N., & Mian, A. (2023). *A Comprehensive Overview of Large Language Models*. https://arxiv.org/abs/2307.06435v10

Open, A. I. (2023). GPT-4 Technical Report. arXiv preprint arXiv:2303.08774. from https://arxiv.org/abs/2303.08774

Organisation for Economic Co-operation and Development. (2024). AI principles overview. OECD.AI. https://oecd.ai/en/ai-principles

Perełkiewicz, M., & Po'swiata, R. P. (2024). *A Review of the Challenges with Massive Web-mined Corpora Used in Large Language Models Pre-Training*. https://arxiv.org/abs/2407.07630v1

Pestov, I. (2018, December). *"A History of Machine Translation from the Cold War... - Google Scholar*. Freecodecamp. Org.

Raffel, C., Shazeer, N., Roberts, A., Lee, K., Narang, S., Matena, M., Zhou, Y., Li, W., & Liu, P. J. (2019). Exploring the Limits of Transfer Learning with a Unified Text-to-Text Transformer. *Journal of Machine Learning Research*, *21*, 1–67. https://arxiv.org/abs/1910.10683v4

Sahoo, P., Singh, A. K., Saha, S., Jain, V., Mondal, S., & Chadha, A. (2024). *A Systematic Survey of Prompt Engineering in Large Language Models: Techniques and Applications*. https://arxiv.org/abs/2402.07927v2

Strubell, E., Ganesh, A., & McCallum, A. (2019). Energy and Policy Considerations for Deep Learning in NLP. *Proceedings of the 57th Annual Meeting of the Association for Computational Linguistics*. DOI: 10.18653/v1/P19-1355

Sutskever, I., Vinyals, O., & Le, Q. V. (2014). Sequence to Sequence Learning with Neural Networks. *Advances in Neural Information Processing Systems*, *4*(January), 3104–3112. https://arxiv.org/abs/1409.3215v3

Team, G., Anil, R., Borgeaud, S., Alayrac, J.-B., Yu, J., Soricut, R., Schalkwyk, J., Dai, A. M., Hauth, A., Millican, K., Silver, D., Johnson, M., Antonoglou, I., Schrittwieser, J., Glaese, A., Chen, J., Pitler, E., Lillicrap, T., Lazaridou, A., & Vinyals, O. (2023). *Gemini: A Family of Highly Capable Multimodal Models*. https://arxiv.org/abs/2312.11805v4

Touvron, H., Lavril, T., Izacard, G., Martinet, X., Lachaux, M.-A., Lacroix, T., Rozière, B., Goyal, N., Hambro, E., Azhar, F., Rodriguez, A., Joulin, A., Grave, E., & Lample, G. (2023). *LLaMA: Open and Efficient Foundation Language Models*. https://arxiv.org/abs/2302.13971v1

Vaswani, A., Shazeer, N., Parmar, N., Uszkoreit, J., Jones, L., Gomez, A. N., Kaiser, Ł., & Polosukhin, I. (2017). Attention Is All You Need. *Advances in Neural Information Processing Systems, 2017-December*, 5999–6009. https://arxiv.org/abs/1706.03762v7

Weizenbaum, J. (1966). ELIZA-A computer program for the study of natural language communication between man and machine. *Communications of the ACM*, *9*(1), 36–45. DOI: 10.1145/365153.365168

Wu, S., Irsoy, O., Lu, S., Dabravolski, V., Dredze, M., Gehrmann, S., . . . Mann, G. (2023). BloombergGPT: A Large Language Model for Finance. arXiv preprint arXiv:2303.17564. https://arxiv.org/abs/2303.17564

Zhang, B., Nagesh, A., & Knight, K. (2020). Parallel Corpus Filtering via Pre-trained Language Models. *Proceedings of the Annual Meeting of the Association for Computational Linguistics*, 8545–8554. DOI: 10.18653/v1/2020.acl-main.756

Zhao, H., Wu, L., Shan, Y., Jin, Z., Sui, Y., Liu, Z., Feng, N., Li, M., & Zhang, W. (2015). *A Comprehensive Survey of Large Language Models in Management: Applications, Challenges, and Opportunities*. DOI: 10.2139/ssrn.4932769

Chapter 3

Introduction to Large Language Models in Business Analytics

Pankaj Verma
http://orcid.org/0009-0009-9073-1803
Indian Institute of Management, Bangalore, India

Krishna Gandhi
http://orcid.org/0009-0004-9684-6699
Illinois State University, USA

ABSTRACT

This chapter explores the transformative impact of Large Language Models (LLMs) on business analytics, demonstrating how these advanced AI systems are revolutionizing the way organizations interact with both structured and unstructured data. By leveraging architectures like Transformers and techniques such as pre-training and fine-tuning, LLMs enable businesses to perform tasks ranging from sentiment analysis and predictive modeling to automated reporting and intelligent customer engagement. The chapter outlines how LLMs support natural language interfaces, enhance decision-making, streamline operations, and democratize data access across functions. Real-world applications across industries—retail, finance, healthcare, and manufacturing—illustrate their value, while challenges such as data privacy, interpretability, bias, and infrastructure demands are also critically examined. Ultimately, the chapter presents LLMs not just as analytical tools but as strategic assets that reshape the future of data-driven enterprise decision-making.

DOI: 10.4018/979-8-3693-6690-5.ch003

INTRODUCTION TO LARGE LANGUAGE MODELS

Overview and Motivation

With data driving the decisions of business operations, business analytics became a cornerstone for strategy, operations, and innovation in the era of data-driven decision-making. Up to now, analytics have had complex barriers to entry. **The Large Language Model (LLM)** is one of the most remarkable 'developments' in this area; massive neural networks pre-trained on a massive corpus of textual information. If properly muzzled, there are many cases where these models can be relied upon to complete complex tasks like language translation, summarization, question answering, and content generation, all of which look promising for business analysis.

The business analytics that has been historically addressed has rather been on the structured data type, namely, transaction records, numerical indicators, and tabular data obtained from relational databases. Although these approaches turned business intelligence on its head, unstructured data, particularly text, was not used very much. Thanks to LLMs, now organizations have a chance to unearth wisdom from texts residing in sources such as user reviews, social media posts, emails, internal documents, or any other textual repositories that could never possibly be synthesized systematically. (Jiang et al., 2024).

Table 1. Growth in AI model parameters over time

Year	Model	Parameters (Billions)
2018	GPT-1	0.12
2019	GPT-2	1.5
2020	GPT-3	175
2023	GPT-4	~1 trillion
2023	PaLM 2	540
2023	LLaMA	65

LLMs such as GPT-3.5, GPT-4, PaLM 2, LLaMA, Bloom, and others have showcased an impressive ability to reason about text. By being pre-trained on terabytes of documents, they capture statistical and semantic features of language that can be adapted—through prompts or fine-tuning—to a wide range of industry-specific challenges. For instance, in marketing analytics, LLMs may process social media posts to determine sentiment regarding a new product launch. In finance, they might summarize and interpret regulatory documents to guide compliance strategies.

In manufacturing, they can unearth anomalies from production logs and textual customer feedback, thereby minimizing errors and boosting operational efficiency.

from transformers import pipeline

```
def analyze sentiment(text):
sentiment_pipeline = pipeline("sentiment-analysis")
result = sentiment_pipeline(text)
return result
text sample = "The new product launch received outstanding feedback from our customers."
print (analyze sentiment (text sample))
```

This Python snippet demonstrates the use of an LLM-powered sentiment analysis pipeline to assess customer reactions to a product launch.

Organizations have already begun experimenting with these possibilities. Early adopters point out major productivity gains and new capabilities, from automated report generation to advanced anomaly detection (Abel, 2024). However, these benefits come hand in hand with important concerns such as **data privacy, model interpretability, hallucinations, and bias**, all of which complicate the direct adoption of LLMs in mission-critical business processes (Kampik et al., 2024).

The promise of LLMs in business analytics rests not only on enhanced efficiency and accuracy but also on **democratization of data-driven insights** (Alparslan, 2025). With LLM-powered tools, non-technical users can query data in plain language, drastically lowering the barrier to sophisticated analysis. This aligns closely with the ongoing shift in analytics platforms toward self-service capabilities, enabling teams across an organization—ranging from sales and marketing to finance and operations—to access nuanced insights without deep programming or data science expertise (Kohl, 2024).

This chapter aims to provide a comprehensive introduction to Large Language Models in business analytics. We will explore the key concepts, examine how LLMs differ from earlier AI models, and demonstrate how they empower both technical and business professionals.

Terminology and Key Concepts

To ground the discussion, it is helpful to define a few key terms:

- **Artificial Intelligence (AI)**: The broader field of computer systems able to perform tasks that typically require human intelligence, such as pattern recognition, language understanding, and problem-solving.

- **Machine Learning (ML)**: A subset of AI wherein algorithms learn from data to improve performance on specific tasks without being explicitly programmed step by step.
- **Deep Learning**: A subset of ML that leverages multi-layer (deep) neural networks to learn hierarchical representations from data. Most LLMs rely on deep learning architectures—often variants of the Transformer model.
- **Transformer Architecture**: Introduced in 2017, Transformers use self-attention mechanisms to process sequences of tokens (e.g., words, sub-words) in parallel. They form the backbone of modern LLMs by efficiently modeling language dependencies across large textual corpora.
- **Pre-training**: The process of training a large model on massive volumes of (often unlabeled) text data to learn general linguistic features. Models like GPT-4 are examples of large-scale pre-training at work.
- **Fine-tuning**: Adapting a pre-trained model to a specific domain or task using domain-relevant or labeled data. This approach drastically reduces the data and computational resources required to build specialized AI solutions.

By synthesizing these concepts, organizations can harness LLMs in specialized contexts without having to train each model from scratch. This is especially relevant to business analytics, where domain-specific nuances—terminologies, regulatory frameworks, product categories—often have outsized importance.

Historical Milestones in LLM Development

While the idea of training large language models has been around for decades, its modern breakthroughs stem largely from these milestones:

1. **Word Embeddings (early 2010s)**: Techniques like Word2Vec and Glove introduced the notion of learning vector representations of words from large corpora. These embeddings captured semantic relationships in continuous vector spaces.
2. **Sequence-to-Sequence Models and Attention (mid-2010s)**: These were first proposed in order to solve machine translation but soon to tackle problems involving sequences not limited by the long-range behavior.
3. **Transformer (2017)**: Similarly, the Transformer architecture was introduced that replaced recurrent architecture using self-attention layers to process entire sequences in parallel. This innovation would be the cornerstone in scaling models to billions of parameters (Vaswani et al., 2017).
4. **Generative Pre-trained Transformers (GPT) Series (2018 onward)**: OpenAI released the first GPT – GPT 1, then GPT 2, then GPT 3, and finally GPT 4 with the modeled scale and capability increases going through an exponential

trend. GPT-3's 175 billion parameters set a new standard for "few-shot" learning, enabling general-purpose language understanding and generation.

5. **Multimodal LLMs (early 2020s)**: Newer generations of LLMs incorporate not just textual data but also images, audio, or code, paving the way for broader analytics tasks in complex business environments.

These advancements collectively underscore a rapidly evolving ecosystem. They also foreshadow how future iterations will continue to shape business analytics—transforming the way data is stored, processed, and turned into strategic insights (Allen, 2025).

Figure 1. Brief timeline of a number of well-known large language models (LLMs) (Mohamadi et al., 2023)

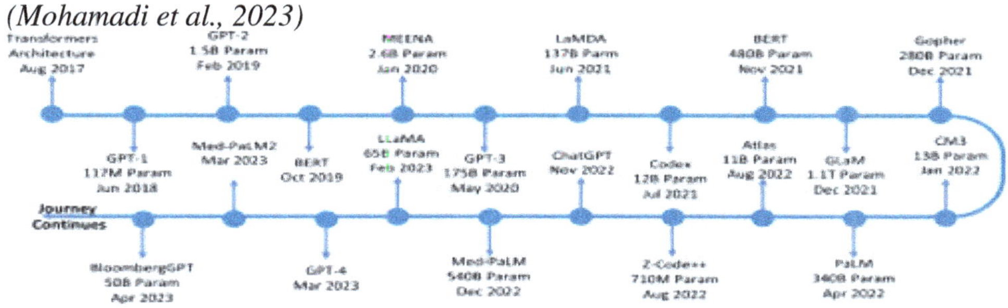

Table 2. Key milestones in LLM evolution

Year	Breakthrough	Description
2013	Word2Vec, Glove	Introduced word embeddings
2014	Seq2Seq with Attention	Enabled improved language translation
2017	Transformer (Vaswani et al.)	Introduced attention-based modeling
2018	GPT-1	First generative pre-trained transformer
2020	GPT-3	175-billion parameter model, few-shot learning
2023	Multimodal LLMs	Integration of text, images, and audio

Chapter Objectives and Structure

This chapter aims to:

1. Introduce the concept and capabilities of LLMs in the realm of business analytics.

2. Examine how AI in business analytics has evolved, culminating in the current shift toward LLM-driven systems.
3. Demonstrate practical applications, from predictive modeling to risk management, that highlight the transformative potential of LLMs.
4. Articulate key benefits—improved decision-making, enhanced productivity, and more accessible analytics—alongside the challenges of data privacy, explain ability, and bias.
5. Present real-world case studies from diverse industries, illustrating how LLMs yield value in different business contexts.
6. Explore promising directions for future research and industry adoption, including more advanced fine-tuning, domain specificity, and regulatory considerations.
7. Summarize the state of LLMs in business analytics and offer recommendations for organizations aiming to incorporate these technologies responsibly and effectively.

Sections 2 through 8 will expand on each of these focal areas. Together, they aim to give readers a holistic view of Large Language Models in business analytics—shedding light on not just the immediate value proposition but also the strategic roadmap for ongoing innovation.

EVOLUTION OF AI IN BUSINESS ANALYTICS

Early Days of Analytics

Business analytics predates the modern era of machine learning by decades. From the 1970s through the 1990s, organizations typically relied on **descriptive statistics** and manual data processing. Many analytics solutions were characterized by:

1. **Structured Databases**: Data was collected in well-defined relational databases. Tools like SQL-based queries dominated how organizations gleaned insights.
2. **Batch Processing**: Analysis often happened in batches. Results were delivered through static reports, requiring significant lead time for execution and interpretation.
3. **Limited Infrastructure**: Storage and computing power were expensive. Analytical capabilities had to be carefully optimized to suit hardware constraints.

Despite these limitations, early adopters recognized the power of data. Simple techniques like correlation analysis and pivot tables already yielded competitive advantages in sales forecasting, inventory management, and financial reporting

(Demo, 2025). Nonetheless, the horizon of analytics largely focused on past and present data, often leaving predictions and advanced decision-making unexplored.

Shift to Predictive and Prescriptive Analytics

As computing capabilities expanded in the 2000s, **predictive** and eventually **prescriptive** analytics became feasible. Key enablers included:

1. **Machine Learning Libraries**: Publicly available libraries like scikit-learn, TensorFlow, and PyTorch made it simpler for analysts to build complex models.
2. **Big Data Ecosystems**: Technologies such as Hadoop and Spark facilitated the processing of unstructured and semi-structured data at scale.
3. **Cloud Computing**: The migration from on-premises servers to cloud environments democratized access to on-demand, scalable infrastructure.

Within enterprises, predictive analytics allowed teams to go beyond historical reporting. **Classification**, **regression**, and **clustering** models were employed to forecast customer churn, detect fraud, and segment audiences. Over time, these capabilities evolved further into prescriptive analytics, where optimization techniques and advanced models suggested the best course of action rather than merely predicting outcomes.

Despite these strides, textual and other forms of unstructured data still represented untapped sources of information. Traditional ML pipelines relied heavily on feature engineering, requiring domain experts to manually define which textual cues, token frequencies, or linguistic structures were relevant. This process was resource-intensive and often suboptimal for large and complex text corpora.

Emergence of Natural Language Processing

Natural Language Processing (NLP) bridged the gap between advanced analytics and unstructured text. Early NLP systems applied statistical methods such as n-grams and basic linear classifiers to tasks like sentiment analysis. However, these models had limited context-awareness (Dholariya, 2024). They struggled to interpret nuanced language features, sarcasm, or domain-specific slang, therefore yielding moderate results at best.

Key Transformations Arrived With

1. **Neural Word Embeddings**: Word2Vec, Glove, and similar methods introduced continuous vector representations of words, capturing semantic relationships in ways that traditional one-hot vectors could not.
2. **Deep Learning for NLP**: Convolutional and recurrent neural networks demonstrated improved performance in text classification and language modeling, but training them at scale was computationally expensive.
3. **Attention Mechanisms**: By allowing models to "attend" to specific parts of an input sequence, attention solved the bottlenecks posed by sequential architectures.

With these innovations, businesses began using **sequence-to-sequence models** for machine translation, speech recognition, and summarization. Yet, many of these tasks still required custom solutions with domain-specific data. Enter the era of LLMs, where pre-trained, general-purpose language models drastically shifted the cost-benefit equation.

Figure 2. Timeline of natural language processing

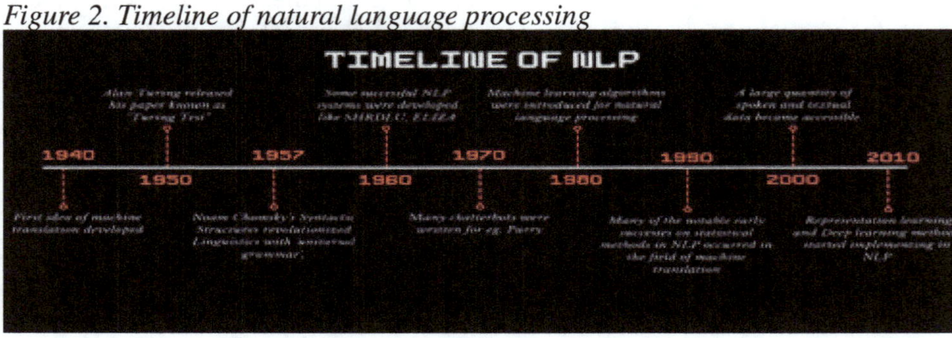

(Kumar, 2022)

Table 3. Comparison of NLP approaches

Approach	Strengths	Weaknesses
N-Grams	Simple, interpretable	Lacks context awareness
Word2Vec/Glove	Captures word relationships	Requires pre-training
Transformers	Scalable, high performance	Compute-intensive

The Advent of Large Language Models

Large Language Models marked a **paradigm shift** in NLP. By consuming vast amounts of textual data from the open web, academic papers, and specialized datasets, LLMs learned to generate plausible and context-rich text. The key breakthroughs included:

- **Transformer-based Architectures**: Eliminating the need for explicit recurrence, Transformers provided an efficient way to learn context from large textual corpora.
- **Scale and Transfer Learning**: By pushing model sizes from millions to billions (and even trillions) of parameters, the emergent behaviors of LLMs allowed them to generalize across tasks in ways previous models could not.
- **Few-shot and Zero-shot Learning**: LLMs can handle tasks for which they have not been explicitly trained by interpreting instructions (i.e., prompts) in plain language. This drastically reduces the need for domain-labeled datasets.

For business analytics, this shift means that organizations can now build text analytics solutions without an army of data scientists or elaborate data pipelines. By leveraging powerful pre-trained LLMs, they can parse, interpret, and summarize corporate documentation, competitor filings, social media chatter, and other textual sources with minimal overhead.

Business Analytics Meets LLMs

Business Analytics Environment

At present, the business analytics environment is a combination of two factors which is now extremely important: structured data processing of the past as well as handling modern LLMs for unstructured data. Several of the benefits of this blend is that it can change how businesses interact with their data (Bao et al., 2024).

Enhanced Insight Generation

The major advantage of using LLMs for business analytics is they can improve insight generation. While traditional analytics was primarily structured data, numbers and organized databases. On the other hand, LLMs have been able to analyze enormous amounts of text-related information from various sources. Let's imagine a company that wishes to know the market trends. However, they can use LLMs to comb through market research and reports, news articles, and customer reviews.

This technology can then tie it to a structured dataset such as customer profiles or sales figures.

Suppose we have a case where a new product is launched by a company. Learners can utilize LLM to analyze reviews, social media conversations, and articles associated to that product. The analysis is useful to the company to know what customers feel about this product, its strengths and how it can be improved upon. Then, these insight materials are used to develop marketing strategies and product development.

Sentiment Analysis Example with an LLM using Python Code.

```
from transformers import pipeline

# Load pre-trained sentiment analysis model
sentiment_pipeline = pipeline("sentiment-analysis")
# Sample data
reviews = ["The new product is fantastic!", "Customer ser-
vice was terrible.", "Shipping was delayed but the product is
great."]
# Perform sentiment analysis
results = sentiment_pipeline(reviews)
# Display results
for review, result in zip (reviews, results):
print (f"Review: {review}\nSentiment: {result['label']}
(Confidence: {result['score']:.2f}) \n")
```

Natural Language Interfaces

Another important advantage of LLMs is that it introduces a natural language interface. This advancement enables business users to interact with analytics systems in their everyday conversations rather than their technical scripted ones. For example, a marketing manager doesn't need to have specific commands or programming languages under his or her belt to request something like, "What were our best-selling products last quarter?" and get a coherent, straight-to-the-point explanation.

By making analytics systems more accessible to everyone across the organization, Natural language interfaces support analytics in becoming a business tool. It encourages an inclusivity of data that makes insights more than the purview of the data teams. Instead, data can be engaged directly by employees from different departments like marketing, sales, and so on, so they tend to have different perspectives and a more thorough understanding of the company. It gives heart to all employees so that those at every level are empowered to make the right decisions for the overall company growth (Wasserkrug et al., 2024).

Scalable Knowledge Management

In addition, LLMs provide a method of knowledge management at a scalable scale. Growing companies generate an excess amount of information. So, a difficult task is to manage this knowledge efficiently. Advanced search and context retrieval, which may be provided by LLMs, would be useful. They can interpret the organizational documents such as manuals, policies, and training guides and answer queries based on the context.

For example, when a new employee begins, they will likely have many questions about company policies or procedures. Rather than wading through uncountable documents, they can just ask the LLM-powered system. They can simply enter their question if they want to know about the vacation policy and get instant answers as well as accurate information. This therefore saves time and makes employees more willing to go find information they need, hence making the onboarding process smoother.

Autonomous Analytics

This goes far beyond enhancement: It is a step into the direction towards autonomous analytics driven by LLMs. However, the data in traditional analytics needed to be interpreted by a human. With LLMs, decision support systems will be able to allude to insights proactively. Thanks to the combination of predictive abilities and complete understanding of language, such systems can almost in real time analyze large streams of text data.

For instance, they can utilize LLMs to keep tabs on social media conversations that happen regarding their industry. The system can alert decision-makers instantly if a sudden spike in negative sentiment occurs about a product. Fast response is possible which helps companies deal with problems before they become large ones yielding a higher customer satisfaction level and brand reputation.

Also, LLMs can point out the patterns and trends that cannot be noticed by the traditional analysis. For example, the LLM can point out such correlations if several customer reviews about a product feature, enabling companies to focus on the improvements that truly affect their customers. However, these systems provide a goldmine of actionable insights that make them a game changer, especially for enterprises involved in competitive markets that want to stay ahead of the pace.

Figure 3. Integration of LLMs in business analytics

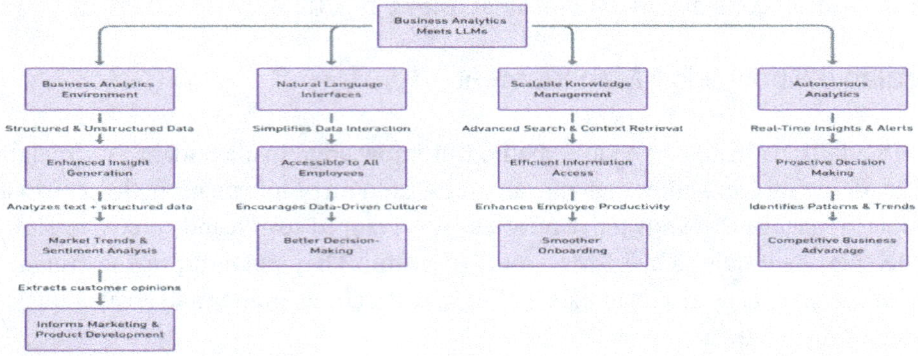

Lessons Learned and Limitations

The benefits of incorporating LLMs into business analytics include powerful improvements, although lessons to be learned are relevant:

- **Data Quality**: LLMs are extremely dependent on the quality of the corpus that they are trained upon. Only limited trust can be placed in the results of inference based on biased or noisy data.
- **Interpretability**: LLMs are often 'black boxes' given that they are indeed deep neural networks. The last step is non-trivial, i.e., aligning them with regulatory or transparency requirements.
- **Infrastructure**: Ultra large models can be deployed and fine-tuned with immense resources required. However, cloud-based solutions or smaller specialized LLMs are sometimes very important for many organizations.
- **Privacy and Security**: As LLMs can take in sensitive corporate data, there is high risk that we need to implement the right data governance and security controls.

Even with these caveats, the course for LLM driven analytics is set to a move forward: between claim and commercial automation, size, efficiency, and scope of application (Belani, 2024). The stage is thus set to a rapidly evolving landscape with many practical applications that will be discussed in the next sections.

Table 4. LLM challenges and mitigation strategies

Challenge	Mitigation Strategy
Bias	Use diverse training data, apply fairness constraints
High Compute Costs	Utilize cloud-based APIs, optimize model size
Black Box Nature	Develop explainable AI (XAI) methods
Data Privacy	Implement strict governance policies

APPLICATIONS OF LLMS IN BUSINESS ANALYTICS

Figure 4. Current major applications of LLMs

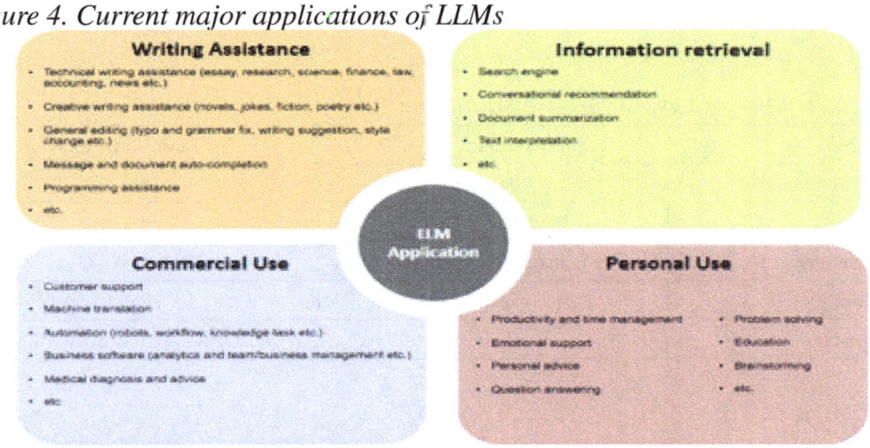

(Liu et al., 2023)

Data Analysis and Interpretation

Data Analysis and Interpretation

Data analysis and interpretation is one of the most direct and powerful business analytics applications of LLMs. Previously, analyzing the data needed you to have specialized knowledge and skills. In order to read from complex data warehouses, professionals had to know. Cleaning and transforming structured data was also involved, potentially taking a huge amount of time. After the data cleaning, we proceed to the stage of generating insights from the data. Traditionally, extensive training and experience had been necessary for traditional analysis. Nevertheless, LLMs turn this landscape upside down. They enable the users to interact with data in a natural language. So whoever it is, it doesn't matter if you have technical background or not, you can ask questions with regards to the data. For instance, a user can just ask, "What were the main revenue drivers for the Asia Pacific in Q2 2024?" Rather, it does not require the user to know details how data extraction methods are used to provide answers in clear language. Users might also ask for summaries such as "Summarize the customer feedback as provided in last month's support tickets about the new product line." It makes it easy to use data in an organization and this enables how organizations can leverage their data.

Key Fact

- In fact, McKinsey has done a study and found that businesses that use analytics driven by AI experienced 25-30 percent higher speeds in the decisions made.

Table 5. Traditional vs. LLM-based data analysis

Feature	Traditional Data Analysis	LLM-Based Data Analysis
Expertise Required	High	Low
Speed	Moderate to Slow	Fast
Accessibility	Limited to Data Analysts	Available to All Users
Scalability	Moderate	High
Automation	Low	High

Summarization

Especially good at summarization, LLMs are. So they can take a long document – a market report that is 50 pages as an example – and reduce it onto a clear and concise overview. Picture an executive with a full schedule trying to get some insight from many reports. It would be an overwhelming amount of information to read through. An LLM will help executives spend less time. Essential points can be provided to them without having to slog through pages of text. Let's say, an LLM, after going through a long report can condense in there a bullet point of the key findings. This saves time as it makes sure that busy professionals stay updated about the primary aspects of their business.

Thematic Extraction

Thematic extraction is another great capability of LLMs. The process includes scanning through a huge amount of text, workplace reviews or social media feedback to find out common themes. For instance, a company may wish to obtain knowledge of what customers feel of their product design or pricing. By using LLMs they are able to classify reviews quickly into recurring topics. The LLM can pick up on delivery time issues or any other customer feedback if there are a lot of such comments. This is because businesses are able to narrow in on the matters that concern their customers the most. Customers regularly say about "product design," and this can serve as a trigger for a company to work on that. Just like that, mentions of 'pricing' are also identified, and their strategies can be adjusted accordingly.

Correlation with Structured Data

Pairing with structured databases is one of the things that also work well for LLMs. Such combination makes it possible for getting a more thorough analysis of the data. An example of this would be for an LLM to perform a correlation between themes extracted from customers feedback with numeric Key Performance Indicators (KPIs) from the company's data. Let's imagine a report showing an increase in negative feedback about how intolerably 'delivery delays' are. And then this feedback can be analyzed more to determine that these type of comments causes an 10% increase in customer churn in a certain area. One-way businesses can understand this correlation is crucial. This enables the manager to make resource decisions based on data. If they know that getting along with customers is real, they can make their best efforts in terms of improvement of delivery times.

Advancements in Analytics Solutions

Recent academic and commercial studies and prototypes illustrate that the methods of analysis employing LLMs can already be comparable to traditional text mining methods. In many cases, the work done by LLMs will exceed that of the conventional approaches. This is especially true when prompts designed towards a particular domain are used. Better results are obtained by fine-tuning the models by handling specific types of data. For example, if a business prepares its LLM to comprehend its distinct market reports or social media language, then the insights that are extracted from such data will be richer and more relevant. Investors in these particular technologies should reap great benefits in their business decision-making process.

from transformers import pipeline

```
sentiment_pipeline = pipeline("sentiment-analysis")
reviews = ["The product is amazing!", "Delivery was delayed
and frustrating."]
```

```
results = sentiment_pipeline(reviews)
print(results)
```

Implementing LLMs in Business

Improper implementation of LLMs starts with organizations performing data need assessments. Organizations need to determine both the data they normally analyze and what insights they need to achieve. Businesses must identify their needs by determining their requirements so they can pick an LLM that suits those needs either by purchasing an existing model or designing their own. Model performance levels increase after specific dataset training takes place. The training process includes using appropriate reports alongside customer interactions that contain the specific verbalization and venerated conventions of the business sector.

The establishment of LLM systems needs staff members to receive proper training as the next step. Organizational employees need to learn how to deploy the model for question formulation and results understanding. The training also gives workers a powerful capability to use data results effectively together with maximizing technology benefits. A continuous feedback system from users enables the organization to upgrade its LLM utilization as an adaptive organizational tool.

The organization should conduct ongoing assessments of the information output generated by the LLM. Organizations should verify that the generated insights meet their organizational goals before making required modifications. The organizational strategy should receive its direction from identified customer feedback themes that become apparent to management. Businesses that use LLMs will build a data-driven culture to achieve better organizational results.

The Future of LLMs in Analytics

The future looks promising for LLM applications in analytics because technological improvement continues at present. Given that natural language processing is advancing at quite a pace, we might be still exploring the potential of LLMs that will be more sophisticated in the future. Organizations that adopt these advanced changes will gain a superior understanding of their customer base. These organizations will receive advantages through enhanced data analysis work efficiency. Business organizations that avoid adopting these modern technologies place themselves at risk of losing market position in an intense business environment. Companies must always maintain their position just beyond current industry practices. Organizations should examine LLM possibilities while creating structured plans to use them inside their analytical operations.

Businesses that adopt these new technologies can recreate their entire process of understanding and analyzing data. These entities can use LLM technology to obtain improved operational insights while better understanding customer desires and market analytics. Businesses which learn how to tap into LLM capabilities will uncover both new expansion avenues and successful opportunities. Data-based decision-making processes will create substantial impacts and outcomes within their business sector. The initial step toward achieving success with LLMs starts from identifying their potential then incorporating them into workplace routines.

Predictive Modeling and Forecasting

Figure 5. Flowchart of predictive modeling and forecasting with LLMs

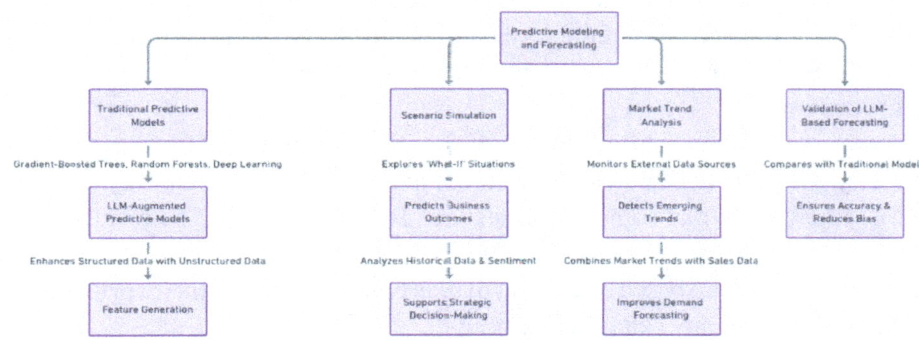

Predictive Modeling in Analytics

Predictive modeling plays a significant role in analytics, helping businesses make informed decisions about their future. This process includes forecasting sales, projecting inventory needs, and predicting customer churn. Traditionally, analysts tackled these tasks using methods like gradient-boosted trees, random forests, and deep learning networks. These techniques are powerful when applied to structured numeric data, but there is a growing interest in enhancing predictive modeling with the help of LLMs.

Feature Generation

Analytics in this way plays a big part in predictive modeling, which helps businesses predict their future. The process part of this assumes forecasting sales, predicting inventory need, and predicting customer churn. However, typically, analysts solve these tasks via gradient boosted trees, random forests as well as deep learning networks. While these techniques are powerful when used on structured numeric data, there is a renewed interest to enhance with LLMs.

One of the biggest advantages of LLMs is that they can make use of external textual data to generate features. Competitor announcements, economic news, consumer sentiment expressed on social media platforms are some of the sources from which textual data can come. Incorporating this information in LLMs allows them to generate features that can assist predictive models. Enriching this process so dramatically heightens the value of forecasting efforts. For instance, the sentiment data from customers talking about similar products can be provided for a company that wishes to predict sales in the forthcoming quarter or the most recent trends in economic articles. This will give a broader perspective of customer behavior and market dynamic.

However, for this capability to become useful, companies will first have to begin to specify which textual sources are relevant in their industry. Then, they can teach the LLM how to extract some useful features from these texts. The results can be put into current predictive models to improve their accuracy. Now, companies can make forecasts that are based on current market conditions rather than a prior period, and be prepared for any changes that occur.

Table 6. Comparison of traditional vs. LLM-augmented forecasting

Feature	Traditional Models	LLM-Augmented Models
Data Sources	Structured (e.g., sales data)	Structured + Unstructured (e.g., social media, news)
Context Awareness	Limited	High
Adaptability	Requires Manual Tuning	Automated Feature Extraction
Accuracy	Moderate	High (With Proper Fine-Tuning)

Scenario Simulation

Luminar also has another exciting application of LLMs in scenario simulation. With this, companies can explore the what if situations by the model through asking the question 'what if'. In other words, a marketing team may be interested to understand what would be the sentiment toward a brand if 20 percent discount on a product for the next quarter. It has the ability to reference historical promotions and analyze historical sentiment data related to these promotions to produce a reasoned estimate.

When a company opts to formulate some specific questions in this process. This is because they can be asking a scenario across any niche like pricing adjustment, marketing campaign or even product launch. It can use the data it has processed to predict responses of past events. Therefore, businesses can think about potential outcome and see if this fits with their strategy before making a decision. A process for asking and analyzing these questions should be developed and implemented robustly because it may create a path of new avenues for the strategic planning.

Example Scenario

"What if we increase our product price by 10%?"

- LLMs forecast the probable reaction by examining previous price adjustments and customer sentiment.

Scenario Simulation With LLMs

User Query → Historical Data Analysis → Sentiment Processing → Scenario Projection → Business Decision

Market Trend Analysis

Trends in the market demand constant attention from every company that wants to stay competitive. Continuous scanning of external data sources becomes possible through LLM assistance thus providing significant support. Standards such as social media content and financial information and research from peer-reviewed publications are examples of sources with which LLMs function. Staying vigilant through continuous monitoring of external sources allows organizations to stay updated on market developments which later affect their forecasting findings or risk assessment protocols.

Businesses need to establish their primary tracking targets when implementing market trend analysis effectively. A trained LLM learns to analyze selected resources for establishing behavioral trends among customers throughout different periods of time. The LLM detects growing social media interest around new health trends which the business can use to modify inventory planning. The business can develop an extensive market analysis by uniting their sales statistics with this acquired data to generate better strategic plans.

Validation of LLM-Based Forecasting

The implementation of LLMs needs baseline statistical validation methods for their forecasted data to ensure accuracy. The usage of LLM "intuition" remains hazardous when the textual information consists of biases or incomplete elements. Businesses need to take safety measures for their LLM forecasts to eliminate potential misleading predictions.

Organizations should verify their predictions through a comparison between LLM outputs and traditional model predictions. A stable monitoring methodology enables detection of model inconsistencies while enabling developers to improve the complete forecasting system. The process of checking textual data input to LLMs takes place routinely for business purposes to maintain relevant and unbiased data use. Ongoing assessment activities will make their forecasting tools better and help them make more intelligent decisions.

Python Code Snippet for Forecast Validation

```
import pandas as pd
from sklearn. metrics import mean_absolute_error

actual = pd. Series ([100, 120, 130, 150])
predicted = pd. Series ([98, 122, 128, 155])
mae = mean_absolute_error (actual, predicted)
print (f"Mean Absolute Error: {mae}")
```

Customer Relationship Management

Customer Relationship Management (CRM)

CRM and its popular abbreviation function as a critical practice to help companies track their interactions with existing and prospective clients. Organization processes leads through generation before providing service for upselling purposes as well as retaining customers. Businesses must comprehend their customer connection so they can use text data as an investigative tool. Text data consists of different communication channels that include support tickets together with emails and chat conversations and social media engagement. This data can be analyzed to provide insight into customer sentiment and intent that may be used in tailoring a business's approach to each customer.

Table 7. Key CRM metrics and their importance

Metric	Description
Customer Retention Rate	Percentage of customers who continue business
Net Promoter Score (NPS)	Measures customer loyalty and satisfaction
Customer Lifetime Value (CLV)	Total revenue expected from a customer
First Response Time	Average time to respond to customer inquiries
Resolution Time	Average time taken to resolve an issue

Automated Customer Support

Automated customer support has been one of the areas where LLMs have been hugely beneficial. The deployment of chatbots driven by LLMs can be used by companies to handle routine queries efficiently. For instance, a customer wanting to see the status of their order can be informed right away with no human intervention required. Thus, there is saving of time of both the customers and the businesses. In addition, these chatbots can decipher ambiguous or phrased requests. The chatbot can clarify the problem for instance if a customer types something unclear like 'I need help with my account', it can then ask some follow up questions from them.

Chatbots can also efficiently pass the problem to human agents in cases that queries get too complex. This reduces customer frustration and also ensures that the customers get the help they need. A great example of such a use case is when a customer runs into a technical issue that requires a trained individual's hand, the chatbot can smoothly switch the conversation to a human agent who can offer customized support to the customer. It is a combination of automatically generated response and human intervention to facilitate better customer experience while responding in time to meet the requirement of the inquiry.

Automated Customer Support Workflow

Customer Inquiry → LLM Chatbot Response → Issue Resolution?

| |

V V

Resolved Escalation to Human Agent

Personalized Communication

Given that LLMs are another powerful use, LLMs are being used for creating personalized communication with customers. LLMs can be trained to generate messages based on a customer's history, taking in account of their trends of purchases or feedback logs within the system. Suppose a customer is known to buy running shoes in regular intervals, then the company can forward him those tailored promotions regarding newly available athletic wear. This helps in sending this sort of personalized communication to customers, helping them to more understand and resonate with them, resulting in more satisfaction as well as more loyalty.

LLMs can also help produce follow up communications through promotions. To give an example, after a customer makes a purchase, an automatic message can greet the customer and ask for feedback on the experience of the customer in making the purchase. It not only proves to the customer they are valued but also gives the company actionable information on how to make better services. The communication is consistent and relevant, developing a trace and ensuring regular contact with customers thus making them to interact much more frequently.

Sentiment and Emotion Analysis

Another area LLMs are destined to be successful for is Sentiment Analysis. LMs can figure out the nuances in whether a customer message is positive or negative instead of just categorizing by positive or negative. For instance, specific models could help us understand when feelings of frustration, urgency or fun are expressed by the customer in the context of a customer support interaction. This capability benefits businesses as it gives them the ability to respond more to meet customer needs.

LLMs can help you trigger when a customer voices frustration, to immediately kick off an intervention. For example, imagine that a customer begins sending messages to us claiming that they still are unable to reach a resolution even after different efforts at communicating with them. If businesses note this urgency, they prioritize that inquiry and an address is quickly served by a representative. However, meanwhile, if a customer is satisfied or excited, companies can make use of that chance to beg for a review or market added products.

Modern CRM Solutions

Nowadays, CRM solutions are modern and often additionally include LLM-based AI components to make customer interaction more efficient. The technologies are designed to deliver a more human and empathetic experience for customers. Due to employing LLMs, companies are able to provide their customers with better and more breathable communication channels, between their work and emotion.

Frequently, it is found that when firms employ these advanced systems, so does customer satisfaction. As an example, a company whose introducing a new LLM based chatbot and found that their customer due resolution time has significantly dropped. Eventually this led to contented customers because they were feeling their issues were immediately and definitely taken care of. Furthermore, a reduction in the need for human resources in basic questions also helps in reducing the operational costs for businesses because the resources that were used earlier could be utilized in places that require human skills and expertise.

Using LLMs, organizations can remain competitive in the changing environment of customer service. This gives companies the ability to analyze customer sentiment, autopilot responses and personalization of communication in order to interact with clients in new ways. However, as these trends mature, companies have a responsibility to integrate them into their CRM strategies which promote customer first culture and responsiveness towards the customers those benefits both parties.

Risk Management and Fraud Detection

Understanding the Role of Large Language Models in Financial Institutions

Every day, banks, insurers and other financial institutions have to make highly significant decisions involving credit, compliance and response to fraud. This could be very critical because it will eat on financial health, customer trust and even in general, the stability of the whole industry. Textual data is another layer of insight next to data that can be considered structured (i.e. such like credit scores or financial statements). The textual data is loan applications, insurance claims, regulatory docs etc. This data type is rich with information that can help to image patterns and insights that numbers by themselves cannot illustrate.

Regulatory Compliance

LLMs are one of the most useful things in regulatory compliance. Often, financial institutions have to adhere to very complex regulations on how they operate. They often are a complicated issue to understand. With this, the complicated regulatory guidelines that are out are fed into the LLMs then break down these complicated regulatory guidelines into more digestible parts. For instance, an LLM can pinpoint the most important sections in these lengthy regulations; that compliance officers should read. They will be able to get a better understanding of what the regulations mean and how they apply to certain situations.

In addition, LLMs can produce checklist summaries for compliance officers to be aware of what they are supposed to be doing. For example, if new regulations will take effect, the LLM can easily find what the changes are and generate a checklist that the compliance teams can follow. It allows saving time and avoiding noncompliance risk. Utilization of these advanced models will help institutions reduce time and costs in compliance process and improve the institution's operational efficiency.

Table 8. LLM applications in compliance

Application	Benefit
Document Summarization	Extracts key compliance insights
Regulation Tracking	Identifies changes in policies
Automated Checklists	Ensures adherence to new laws

Fraud Detection

One of the major roles of LLMs is to assist in the detection of fraud. Fraud can be complicated, and it can hide in the sub-text of the language employed in a loan application, in a claim, or during customer service dealings. As these text interactions are text-based, LLMs can analyze them for unusual patterns. This may include finding out if a specific word choice is out of place, if there are discrepancies in a given description provided, or if there are too many disclaimers that seem to simply state the obvious.

An LLM might, for instance, notice that a customer always claims not to have received a payment, even when the complaint is submitted with several often-conflicting applications. Beyond fixed criteria, rule systems have been supplanted by this capability. Through enormous amounts of data input, LLM learns new patterns of unrecognized fraud. LLMs can be used by financial institutions to enhance the ability to detect fraud, and thereby protect its resources and preserve its reputation.

Example Python Code: Detecting Anomalous Claims

```
import re

def detect_fraudulent_claim(text):
suspicious patterns = ["multiple claims", "conflicting de-
tails", "urgent refund"]
```

```
for pattern in suspicious patterns:
if re. search (pattern, text, re. IGNORECASE):
return "Fraud Alert: Review Required"
return "Claim Seems Legitimate"
# Test case
claim text = "Customer submitted multiple claims for the
same incident."
print(detect_fraudulent_claim(claim text))
```

Continuous Monitoring

Also, LLMs can be used by organizations for continuous monitoring of different text sources. Keeping up with changes in the regulatory world and market conditions is essential in the world of finance operating at fast speed. An LLM-based system can take a wide variety of media, with news articles, official statements, and social media posts among them. It can also signal institutions to new regulatory policies or market shifts that likely will apply to them.

To name a few examples, LLM will be able to promptly inform the relevant teams about breaking news on regulatory changes, or adverse market reactions. Besides compliance, this real-time monitoring capability also supports risk management. Monitoring public sentiment around certain industries or business partners can reflect on potential problems that might affect decision-making or investment.

Ensuring Accuracy and Accountability

The benefits of using LLMs in financial institutions are obvious, but there are things to consider. Organizations using this piece "The Hidden Risks of Using LLMs for Business Data Analytics" said that they should validate these models for continuing accurate analysis (DataChat, 2025). There should be robust frameworks in place implemented by the decision-makers that contribute to interpretability and accountability. In highly regulated environments a tiny error can put the environment (and others) at risk and this is particularly important.

Taking for instance, when the LLM mistakenly latches a legitimate transaction as being fraudulent, this could result in unwarranted investigation and reduce the bedroom of trust between the customer and the institution. On the contrary, a false negative occurs when a fraudulent activity goes unnoticed, causing significant monetary losses and a failure of the organization's credibility. Because of this, LLMs should be used in these sensitive areas only with checks and balances in place.

Moving Forward

LLM's potential as a financial services tool is something that financial institutions are actively exploring, but they have to approach its implementation carefully. For them, the question is, how to integrate LLMs into existing workflows, instead of disrupting the existing ones. Another way to improve the overall outcomes is to develop training programs that will train employees on the use of these new tools. Such technology will allow staff to use the information collected by LLMs to enable better decision-making.

In addition, financial institutions should stay informed about the LLM development progress. This is true as these models evolve and more features and improvement can be added. Continuous refinement of model usage with incorporation of users' feedback can allow organization to fully utilize their advantage. Engaging expert in the field of LLMs will further improve the effectiveness of LLM in managing compliance and fraud (Sahoo & Dutta, 2024).

Technology is always advancing and the landscape of the financial world is always changing, leading to the fact that large language models will increasingly have a large role. These tools can play an important role in helping solve complex problems and improve the accuracy, efficiency, and agility of decisions (Belani, 2024). Given that LLMs are now starting to be adopted by an increasing number of organizations, there will be more chances for growth and stability in a typically unpredictable environment.

Process Automation and Optimization

The Role of Language Models in Business Processes

Today, many enterprises and organizations still rely on documentation in form of text. It consists of vendor contracts, inventory logs, and different kinds of records. This can be a complex and time-consuming task to process and manage the files in it. Still, big LLMs can help this process a great deal in automating key functions and speeding up operations (Busany et al., 2024).

Extracting Key Terms and Conditions

Another value of LLMs is in contract management. However, organizations often deal with many contracts with important clauses like penalties, warranties, or terms and services. However, these documents need to be searched manually. Extracting the key terms and conditions in a business is feasible with LLMs, and businesses can easily locate critical information. An example is a company that enters into service agreements very regularly and can set up an LLM that reads contracts and looks for specific terms in connection with penalty clauses. It ensures reduced risk of losing important items and compliance. Therefore, the decisions of companies can be made much faster, and also avoid potential legal problems or disputes.

Table 9. Benefits of LLM-based contract management

Feature	Benefit
Automated Term Extraction	Faster decision-making
Risk Identification	Avoids legal disputes
Compliance Tracking	Ensures regulatory adherence

Smart Routing

LMMs excel also in smart routing. Every day, businesses get plenty of documents and requests like support tickets, purchase orders, invoices, etc. For maintaining workflow efficiency, it is necessary to process these systematically. These documents are easily categorized and routed to the right team or system by LLMs. Take, for instance, when a customer files a support ticket regarding a product malfunction, the LLM will be able to recognize what the issue is thus forwarding it to the technical support team. By doing this, time is saved and also errors are reduced by a significant degree because of the flow of the formula itself. Within the same context, they can improve their operational performance and customer satisfaction by ensuring that the right personnel are addressed as soon as possible when receiving the request.

Adaptive Scheduling

The other innovation of using LLMs for operational purposes is adaptive scheduling. Sometimes the demands and conditions are not what they are putting in their schedules on the floors and back to shipping routes. As LLMs can be used to analyze text data along with sensor data as well as operational logs, they can suggest optimal schedules. When LLM takes into account real time information such as weather forecasts or labor availability, organizations can adapt their operations in line. For example, if weather is likely to hit severe, an LLM could prompt rescheduling of shipments to maintain on-time delivery with probable interruptions. This capability not only minimizes delays but also enables businesses to efficiently utilize their resources.

The Advantages of Retrieval-Augmented Generation (RAG) Architectures

Additionally, Retrieval-Augmented Generation (RAG) architectures are introduced as a breakthrough in process automation. It RAG allows LLMs to reach specific contexts from enterprise data stores as they generate responses. For businesses, this feature is very useful as it allows LLMs to have their suggestions grounded in verified corporate knowledge. Take, for instance, if an employee asks a model about compliance procedures, it can bring up the latest company policy documents as well as the response. It prohibits the model from hallucinating about facts, and thus the recommended actions are based on well-informed and reliable inputs.

The use of LLMs with RAG techniques will mean that businesses will get relevant information even when they are making decisions. It converts the decision-making process into more of an evidence-based, precise, and intuitive way of doing things.

Implementing RAG for Document Retrieval

```
from langchain.chains import RetrievalQA
from langchain.llms import OpenAI
from langchain.vectorstores import FAISS

doc_store = FAISS.load_local("./enterprise_data")
qa = RetrievalQA(llm=OpenAI(), retriever=doc_store.as_re-
triever())
response = qa.run("What are the latest compliance updates?")
print(response)
```

Finally, LLMs are changing the game in each domain where businesses operate. That ability to take key terms out of documents, make firm requests, and adjust schedules as fast as possible affords companies powerful tools to streamline their operational efficiency (Abel, 2024). However, the services provided by such technologies will be immense if enabled with the advent of technologies like RAG, which enable a company to take advantage of these technologies and still maintain accuracy and reliability in its processes. With LLMs being used in their workflows, organizations saved time, efforts in dropping manual documentation, and achieve better result in their operational processes in a highly complex environment.

Summary of Key Applications

Every day, LLMs are being applied in business analytic applications. Starting as rapid text summarization and sentiment extraction, and ending being able to use LLMs in advanced predictive modeling, LLMs are leading the way for the augmented analytics movement. However, tangible success stories hinge on appropriate planning, data governance, and ethical considerations. In upcoming sections, we discuss how LLM based analytics is not a plug and play solution where you go deploy it and hope for the best and more likely, how it needs to be deployed thoughtfully to capitalize the benefits and hedge the risks of such deployments.

BENEFITS OF LLMS IN BUSINESS ANALYTICS

Increased Efficiency and Productivity

A great benefit attributed by many corporate users to integrating LLMs within business analytics workflows is the significant increase in efficiency and productivity.(Dholariya, 2024). LLMs can automate or augment tasks that have historically demanded considerable time and expertise, such as:

1. **Data Preparation and Cleaning**: By interpreting unstructured inputs (emails, PDFs, scanned documents) and standardizing them, LLMs streamline data preparation steps.
2. **Automated Reporting**: Instead of manually generating recurring reports, analysts can rely on LLM-based systems to create them from up-to-date data sources. A user might request, "Provide a weekly summary of key performance metrics for marketing campaigns," and the system assembles a coherent report.
3. **Scalable Communication**: Chatbots or AI assistants serve many customers simultaneously, drastically reducing wait times and operational overhead in call centers or technical support desks.

Table 10. Productivity gains from LLM integration

Business Function	Traditional Approach	LLM-Enabled Approach	Efficiency Gain (%)
Data Preparation & Cleaning	Manual sorting & processing	Automated text standardization	40-60%
Automated Reporting	Manual report creation	AI-generated summaries	50-70%
Customer Support	Human agents handling queries	AI chatbots handling initial responses	30-50%

Enterprises employing these automated LLM workflows commonly report shorter project cycles, reduced labor costs, and improved throughput in tasks from customer service to data analysis.

Improved Accuracy and Insights

LLMs can also improve accuracy of many of these tasks if the relevant data and context are properly managed. Humans are cold creatures composed of numbers, facts, and things. Unlike LLMs, trained from massive, diverse corpora, which sweep across lexical, syntactic and semantic contexts as well as pragmatic one. This depth enhances:

- **Sentiment Analysis**: More accurate customer feedback sentiment detection, bypassing simple algorithms that failed to recognize the totally emotional tones in the customer feedback.
- **Topic Classification**: The ability to detect topics or issues even in the cases when they are mentioned indirectly, or in synonyms. This makes sure that the information relevant to a section of job does not go lacking in the cracks of classification.
- **Language Translation**: LLMs outperform previous statistical machine translation approaches for translation, thus allowing multinational companies to bring home insights that transcend language markets.

The second advantage is the new ability to discover emergent insights. LLMs are trained with tons of textual data so they could find correlations or irregularity beyond what basic analytics take note of. In fact, an unpublicized supply chain event can be a link that helps connect changes in the consumer sentiment of the brand to a strategic action.

Enhanced Decision-Making

With the LLMs, augmented analytics can even provide scope for the enhancement of decision-making. LMs go further than merely descriptive and diagnostic tasks, to prescriptive analytics. Those textual cues, gleaned from external contexts such as news, academic research, or competitor press releases allow decision-makers to experiment with and get advanced scenario planning.

For instance, a supply chain manager whose business may be disrupted by the same news could ask an LLM to compile real-time shipping data together with available labor and then consider alternative routes or suppliers based on what is covered by any global news on port slowdowns. In essence, LLMs support dynamic, context-aware reasoning that far surpasses the stilted, rigid suggestions from older planning systems.

Competitive Advantage

Competitive advantage arises when organizations harness LLM-based business analytics to identify emerging market shifts before their peers. They benefit from:

1. **Rapid Response**: LLMs are always "on," scanning new streams of text data (financial news, consumer social media, etc.) for potential business impacts. This real-time awareness helps the firm pivot quickly.
2. **Innovation in Products and Services**: Business can learn from the consumption habits of their users and gather the feedback at speed and create experiments for new service offerings based on real-world data.
3. **Streamlined Operations**: For instance, even incremental improvement in efficiency in logistics or in operations would mean that the business makes such savings of costs which would allow it to re-invest in the growth initiatives.

From a strategic perspective, the synergy of advanced analytics with domain knowledge fosters more agile, insight-driven organizations.

Democratization of Analytics

One of the long-standing data science goals has been to democratize analytics —that is to provide any employee a meaningful interaction with organizational data. LLMs supercharge this trend:

- **Conversational Interfaces**: They are conversational interfaces – in other words, employees can simply ask questions in natural language: "How did Region B's net promoter score compare to Region C last quarter?". Relevant data, charts and textual explanations can be provided by the system.
- **Guided Analytics**: LLMs can provide follow-up questions and suggestions to guide users to ask the right questions or provide the analysts with other useful analytics suggestions to perform their job properly. This creates new culture of data thinking across all layers of the business.

This is agility, where organization teams up to remove or reduce the need of having specialized data scientists to answer each and every inquiry. Departments that were once cut out from the process of advanced analytics can now come to play and help in achieving broader participation in data-driven decision-making.

Using An Llm For Business Query Analysis

from langchain.llms import OpenAI

```
def generate_insight(query):
llm = OpenAI(model_name="gpt-4")
response = llm(query)
```

return response

```
user_query = "Summarize customer sentiment trends for Q1 
2025."
print(generate_insight(user_query))
```

Bridging Structured and Unstructured Data

In addition, LLMs bridge the gap between input being structured (numeric metrics, relational database entries) and input that is not (emails, reviews, logs). It allows organizations to act with this visualization of the whole picture. This can be for example supplements to sales forecast models as textual indicators (product reviews, social media sentiment). In the same way, logs from a manufacturing line coming from between runs can be merged with structured sensor data to identify root causes more precisely.

Finally, these benefits demonstrate how LLMs bring about significant scale benefits in business analytics: saving time, making it a more insightful analysis, robust forecasting, and gaining a competitive advantage in constantly changing markets. Nevertheless, adopting LLMs at scale also brings significant challenges—technical, operational, and ethical—that must be addressed. The next section explores these challenges in depth.

Table 11. Examples of bridging data types

Data Type	Example	LLM Application
Structured	Sales figures	Forecasting demand
Unstructured	Product reviews	Sentiment analysis
Combined	Sales + reviews	Identifying product improvement areas

CHALLENGES OF LLMS IN BUSINESS ANALYTICS

Data Privacy and Security

A primary concern with LLM-driven analytics is the **handling of sensitive data**. Since LLMs can potentially store and regenerate aspects of the training corpus, organizations must ensure that proprietary or personally identifiable information (PII) is not inadvertently exposed (Kerem, 2024). Key issues include:

1. **Data Encryption and Governance**: Strict encryption protocols and regulated user access to the LLM and supporting data stores are non-negotiable.
2. **Prompt Security**: If employees or external users supply prompts containing sensitive data, that data can be temporarily available in memory. System design must ensure minimal data retention and appropriate prompt filtering.
3. **Regulatory Compliance**: Industries like healthcare and finance have stringent regulatory requirements (HIPAA, GDPR, etc.). LLMs must be validated for compliance, possibly requiring on-premise deployments or private cloud configurations (DataChat, 2025).

Table 12. Common data privacy measures for LLMs

Measure	Description
Encryption	Data should be encrypted both in transit and at rest.
Access Control	Limit access based on roles and need-to-know principles.
Data Masking	Redact sensitive data from prompts before processing.
Compliance Audits	Regularly assess adherence to regulations.

While in-house deployments or specialized "private LLMs" can mitigate some privacy risks, they substantially raise the operational overhead in terms of maintenance and updates.

Ethical Considerations and Bias

LLMs inherit **biases** present in their training data. This is particularly problematic when model outputs influence hiring decisions, credit approvals, or other high-stakes processes (Chu, 2024). Possible manifestations:

- **Unintended Stereotypes**: Bias in textual corpora might lead an LLM to produce or recommend discriminatory actions.
- **Exacerbated Inequality**: An LLM trained primarily on data from high-income regions may not adequately represent the needs or language expressions of underrepresented communities.
- **Opacity of Decision Processes**: Since LLM outputs can appear highly "human," users may overtrust them without questioning their underlying biases or sources of information.

To manage these risks, organizations employ **model audits**, differential privacy, and continuous monitoring. Some also fine-tune LLMs on curated, domain-specific corpora that mitigate known issues.

Interpretability and Explainability

Business analytics often requires **transparent logic**—stakeholders need to understand how or why an AI system made a particular recommendation. Traditional rule-based systems and simpler ML models are more interpretable, with explicit features or decision trees. LLMs, on the other hand, are large black boxes with billions of parameters. They can generate fluent text without revealing the reasoning behind each token or phrase.

While **explainable AI (XAI)** techniques (e.g., saliency maps, local explainers) exist, LLM-based solutions remain challenging to interpret. Particularly in regulated industries, the lack of clear explanations can pose compliance risks. Stakeholders might question the legitimacy of recommendations that cannot be traced to a transparent rationale (Cheung, 2024).

Explainability With LIME

```
from lime.lime_text import LimeTextExplainer

def explain_model_prediction(model, text_input):
explainer = LimeTextExplainer()
explanation = explainer.explain_instance(text_input, model.
predict_proba)

return explanation.show_in_notebook()
```

Hallucinations and Accuracy Issues

Hallucinations—or the phenomenon of an LLM producing plausible-sounding but factually incorrect statements—represent a critical concern (Belani, 2024). In normal language tasks, minor inaccuracies may be tolerable, but in business analytics, misinformation can lead to incorrect financial forecasts, misguided strategies, or damaged customer relationships.

Organizations can mitigate hallucinations through:

- **Retrieval-Augmented Generation (RAG)**: The model is forced to ground its answers in retrieved documents from reliable data sources.
- **Prompt Engineering**: Carefully designed prompts that remind the model to only answer within known contexts.
- **Human-in-the-Loop**: For high-stakes tasks, a domain expert validates LLM-generated insights before finalizing decisions.

Skill Gaps and Training Needs

While LLMs bring powerful automation, **human expertise** does not become obsolete. Instead, new skill sets are required:

1. **Prompt Engineering**: Formulating queries and instructions so that LLM outputs align with business requirements.
2. **Data Curation**: Identifying and preparing text corpora for domain-specific fine-tuning or retrieval.
3. **Model Governance**: Setting policies for data usage, compliance, model updates, and performance monitoring.

Organizations that underestimate the necessary training and organizational changes may fail to realize the full value of LLM-based analytics. In the short term, investment in user education, data literacy, and cross-functional teams is indispensable.

Model Scalability and Infrastructure

Ultra-large LLMs require significant computational resources. Many businesses do not have the in-house GPU clusters or advanced distributed systems expertise to host models with billions of parameters. Options include:

- **Cloud APIs**: Firms rely on API-based access to third-party LLMs (e.g., OpenAI, Microsoft Azure, Google Cloud). Although hardware management is relieved, issues with data residency, expenses, and vendor lock-in may arise.

- **On-Premise or Hybrid Deployments**: When the data is sensitive you want better control as provided by an on-premise solution but the hardware is also beefier and the ML engineering skills more specialist.
- **Model Compression**: Techniques like quantization or knowledge distillation are model compression techniques that reduces model size at the cost of some accuracy.

Among the three sectors and two scales of application, optimal solutions are different. Moreover, rapid growth of model sizes also requires changes in system architecture to support enterprise planning.

Balancing Innovation and Risk

Privacy, bias, interpretability, accuracy, skill requirements, and technical overhead should not be viewed as reasons to reject LLM based analytics out of hand. Instead, they present a multi-dimensional risk management strategy for organizations to adopt. With proper data governance, well defined lines of accountability and a competency of experts from the domain to be involved with adequate control, organizations will be able to allow innovation to thrive while having prudence in risk management.

Hurdles, Conclusion of Challenges: But with a valuable potential of LLMs in business analytics. The rest of the paper will present the case studies from a variety of industries to show how realistic organizations face such challenges and gain tangible benefits from large language models.

REAL-WORLD EXAMPLES OF LLMS IN BUSINESS

Retail and E-Commerce

When a global e-commerce platform was managing millions of product listings, customer reviews pouring in continuously, and trying to monitor brand reputation, reply to customers and ensure product consistency became increasingly complicated. An LLM driven analytics solution can be integrated as:

1. **Review Summarization**: The LLM reviewed millions of new reviews a day, and curatord them in groups (so called clusters of features) (for instance shipping, packaging, product quality). It helped brand managers do the near real time about the emerging concern, which allowed them to respond promptly.

2. **Inventory Management**: Coupled with structured sales data, the LLM-based system detected correlations between textual complaints ("delayed shipment," "damaged packaging") and spikes in return rates or cart abandonment. This improved forecast accuracy and streamlined logistics.
3. **Chatbots for Customer Service**: LLM-powered bots replaced generic scripts with nuanced responses. Customers received personalized assistance, even for niche products, raising satisfaction scores substantially.

Table 13. Impact of LLM integration in e-commerce

Application	Benefits Achieved
Review Summarization	15% faster response time in addressing customer complaints
Inventory Management	Improved forecast accuracy, reduced return rates by 10%
Chatbots for Support	Increased customer satisfaction scores by 20%

In doing so, the company saw a 15% improvement in review response times and a notable boost in Net Promoter Score (NPS), as documented in internal business analytics reports. The combined approach of textual analytics and user-centric prompting significantly lowered operational overhead compared to purely manual monitoring (Kohl, 2024).

Financial Services

Financial institutions constantly seek better ways to handle risk modeling, compliance, and client engagement. A multinational bank used an LLM to:

1. **Parse Regulatory Documents**: Thousands of pages of new regulations are published each quarter. The LLM summarized these documents, extracted relevant clauses, and aligned them with existing bank policies. Compliance officers reduced manual reading by up to 60%.
2. **Credit Risk Scoring**: Traditional models used numeric data (income, assets, credit history). LLM-based enhancements introduced text from social media, job platforms, and even references to local economic news, especially for small businesses with sparse credit records.
3. **Automated Reporting**: Finance teams asked the LLM to generate daily risk dashboards, explaining in plain language the rationale behind any risk changes. This transparency allowed managers to quickly grasp complex shifts in market conditions.

The result was a more agile risk management strategy. While the bank had to address data privacy by using specialized on-premise LLM solutions, the net benefits included fewer compliance errors and more nuanced credit evaluations (Mutually Human, 2025).

Healthcare and Pharmaceutical

Large Language Models can also streamline **clinical data** analysis, drug discovery, and patient engagement:

- **Clinical Trial Matching**: LLM-based systems parse thousands of trial protocols and patient health records, matching individuals to relevant trials more effectively than manual approaches.
- **Drug Research**: Scientists use LLMs to sift through vast repositories of academic papers and patents. Insights gleaned from these texts can inform the design of new compounds or identify alternative uses for existing drugs.
- **Patient Support Chatbots**: For routine inquiries, AI chatbots handle appointment scheduling, medication reminders, or symptoms triage. Given the sensitivity of medical data, these solutions typically require strict compliance frameworks like HIPAA in the U.S.

One pharmaceutical company leveraged an LLM for analyzing complex biomedical literature to identify potential adverse drug interactions. After integrating the solution, the company accelerated risk identification by 40%, a significant edge in early detection (Cheung, 2024). The challenge of ensuring data anonymization and robust encryption was substantial but ultimately overcame initial privacy concerns.

Manufacturing and Supply Chain

In manufacturing, textual data often appears in maintenance logs, technician comments, and supply chain documentation. A global electronics manufacturer implemented an LLM system to:

1. **Flag Production Anomalies**: The model analyzed logs for patterns correlating with defective output. For instance, an increase in mentions of "temperature fluctuation" might predict higher reject rates.
2. **Optimize Supplier Selection**: Summaries of trade news and shipping logs helped the purchasing department evaluate supplier stability in real time, mitigating disruptions.

3. **Workforce Training**: LLM-based chatbots answered queries from line workers about operating procedures. By referencing official manuals, the system provided real-time guidance, reducing errors and accidents.

The manufacturer reported a 25% reduction in production downtime. Although engineering staff initially distrusted black-box text processing, confidence grew once the LLM's real-time recommendations repeatedly averted potential breakdowns (Allen, 2025).

LLM-Based Anomaly Detection

```
import openai
def detect_anomalies(log_data):
response = openai.ChatCompletion.create(
model="gpt-4",
messages=[{"role": "system", "content": "Analyze this manu-
facturing log for anomalies."},
{"role": "user", "content": log_data}]
)
return response["choices"][0]["message"]["content"]
log_sample = "Temperature fluctuation detected in machine X.
Possible failure imminent."
print(detect_anomalies(log_sample))
```

Energy and Utilities

In sectors like oil, gas, and renewable energy, textual and geospatial data converge. LLM-driven approaches help:

- **Regulatory Compliance**: Summarize environmental regulations across multiple jurisdictions, linking relevant clauses to operational data.
- **Safety Monitoring**: Evaluate maintenance records, inspection reports, and sensor readings to preempt critical failures at remote installations (e.g., offshore platforms).
- **Market and Policy Analysis**: Track legislative changes in areas like carbon credits or renewable incentives, generating custom reports for executives.

Table 14. LLM applications in energy sector

Use Case	Benefit Achieved
Power Demand Prediction	10% reduction in energy waste
Compliance Tracking	30% faster adaptation to new regulations
Fault Detection	Early warning system reduced outages by 15%

Which electricity provider contracted an LLM based intelligence platform to consolidate weather data with usage logs alongside local news for the purpose of predicting spikes in their energy demand. It results in saving millions in operational costs every year in power generation planning by this. Like other domains, data pipelines and interpretable measures had to be robust to maintain regulatory compliance.

Lessons From Case Studies

Those in these diverse industries have certain things in common.

1. **Domain Adaptation**: Success depends on fine-tune or carefully pick the LLM to accept industry-specific vocabularies and regulated data in order to adapt specific domain.
2. **Human Oversight**: In each example, the need for subject matter experts to supervise the outputs of the model to assure it fits in with the goals and ethical principles of the organization is demonstrated.
3. **Integration Complexity**: Businesses thought that just an LLM is not enough, and it was brought to an end by robust data infrastructures, model monitoring by model quality controllers, and continuous user training.

In addition, the success stories also emphasize the iterative rollouts, i.e. several pilot projects before going large with them. This is to let teams slowly work with data quality, model prompts, and governance structures that they can learn from the real world as they use them.

FUTURE DIRECTIONS OF LLMS IN BUSINESS ANALYTICS

Emerging Trends in LLM Research and Development

LLM innovation is centered on business analytics. Several of these emerging trends also promise to change the way a large language model is used by an organization.

1. **Domain-Specific Pre-training**: Researchers and enterprise LLM Value addition provider are increasingly training LLMs on curated dataset with out of box focus on aligned domain (e.g finance, law, healthcare). This can be highly advantageous, particularly for the more important tasks.
2. **Multimodal Fusion**: Future LLM architectures may freely accept text, image data, voice data and may even welcome incoming real time sensor streams. For example, you could take shipping documents (text)) and satellite imagery of shipping channels for more complex risk assessment if you were to merge them into a supply chain model.
3. **Reinforcement Learning**: Beyond supervised fine tuning, RL based strategies can be adopted to make LLM's close iteratively to oneself from user feedback or success metric achieving more adaptive analytics solutions.

These LLM capabilities are being fueled by giant tech firm investments in LLM, as well as open source efforts. Where this goes for business analytics: the net is likely to be an era of integrated data intelligence well beyond that which has come to be known traditionally as "dashboards."

Table 15. Key trends and developments

Trend	Description
Domain-Specific Pre-training	Training LLMs on curated datasets specific to industries like finance, law, and healthcare to improve accuracy.
Multimodal Fusion	Integrating text, images, voice, and real-time sensor streams for enhanced analytics.
Reinforcement Learning	Implementing RL strategies to iteratively refine LLM outputs based on real-world feedback.

Potential Future Applications and Advancements

Thus, we can imagine business analytics moving in the direction of autonomous decision support systems in which LLMs undertake more and more involved tasks:

- **Hyper-Personalized Marketing**: As there is more textual data on the journey of the consumer, LLM-based systems can personalize products, messaging, and promotions even more than their level.
- **Real-Time Negotiation and Bidding**: E-commerce scenario where automated agents (powered by ML LLMs) are enabled to negotiate contracts or setting dynamic price referencing huge corpus of market data and business policies.

- **Continuous Risk Sensing**: Continuous Risk sensing means organizations will be able to detect events and detect the language in and around them in real-time to gain visibility to disruptions and opportunities as soon as they arise.

Over the longer term as LLMs become better at reasoning with external sources of knowledge by a retrieval-based approach, they will gain the ability to reason with far greater multi-step complexity, and across many more domains. With that in place, we now gain the ability to achieve cross functional AI whereby marketing, supply chain, finance and compliance systems feed and talk to each other through shared language interfaces.

Table 16. Applications of LLMs in business analytics

Application	Description
Hyper-Personalized Marketing	Customizing messaging, products, and promotions for individual consumers using LLM-powered insights.
Real-Time Negotiation & Bidding	Automating contract negotiations and dynamic pricing using real-time data.
Continuous Risk Sensing	Detecting disruptions or market shifts instantly using AI-driven event analysis.

Research Challenges and Gaps

However, there remain large gaps prior to this being fully realized.

1. **Explainable LLMs**: Black box nature of large neural networks is a problem in particular for regulated domains.
2. **Dynamic Knowledge Updates**: LLMs require better mechanisms for the update in existing data without full retraining cycles. System designs for on the fly model update or expansion of domain knowledge are included.
3. **Robustness to Novel Contexts**: LLMs must be sturdy to different markets or technologies emerging and existing. Overcoming catastrophic forgetting and domain drifts requires advanced continual learning approaches.
4. **Sustainable Scaling**: The carbon footprint of training ever-larger LLMs is a growing concern. Efficient training methods, model compression, and domain adaptation can help reduce the computational load.

Practical Guidance for Adoption

From a **practitioner's standpoint**, organizations aiming to adopt or expand LLM usage in business analytics should consider:

- **Proof of Concept (PoC) Projects**: Begin with narrowly scoped applications—like summarizing daily operational reports—to validate feasibility, refine prompts, and build stakeholder confidence.
- **Hybrid Architectures**: Combine LLM-driven text analytics with traditional ML pipelines or rule-based solutions, especially where interpretability or precision is crucial. A hybrid approach can yield robust, enterprise-grade solutions (Vertsel & Rumiantsau, 2024).
- **Incremental Fine-tuning**: Instead of training from scratch, adopt large pre-trained models and fine-tune them on curated domain data. This both lowers cost and improves relevance.
- **Ethical and Legal Frameworks**: Proactively address data privacy, consent, and fairness. This can involve cross-department committees that review model decisions, especially in critical domains such as hiring or lending.

By following these strategies, businesses can harness LLMs to drive innovation without succumbing to the well-documented pitfalls of naive AI deployment (Jeong, 2023).

Best Practices for Implementing LLMs

```
# Example: Fine-Tuning an LLM for Business Data Analysis
from transformers import AutoModelForCausalLM, AutoTokenizer

tokenizer = AutoTokenizer.from_pretrained("custom-LLM")
model = AutoModelForCausalLM.from_pretrained("custom-LLM")
def analyze_text(input_text):
tokens = tokenizer(input_text, return_tensors="pt")
output = model.generate(**tokens)
return tokenizer.decode(output[0])
business_text = "Summarize the financial report for Q2."
print(analyze_text(business_text))
```

Toward More Autonomous Analytics

Future LLM-based systems may **autonomously** navigate entire analytics workflows—from ingesting raw data, cleaning it, generating insights, to recommending or even enacting decisions. While this is an exciting prospect, achieving true autonomy demands robust governance structures that balance exploration and guardrails. This includes version control for prompts, user role-based access, multi-layer security for data, and real-time feedback loops that let domain experts override or refine AI-driven recommendations.

Given the rapid progress in generative AI, businesses should position themselves to iteratively integrate these tools in ways that align with strategic goals. Encouraging collaboration between data scientists, domain experts, and compliance officers fosters the synergy required for safe, effective, and forward-thinking LLM adoption.

CONCLUSION

Key Findings and Insights

Large Language Models represent a significant leap forward in how businesses can engage with the ever-growing volumes of data—both structured and unstructured. The industry is now in the region between the first wave of descriptive analytics, predictive analytics, and generative, context aware and real time analytics.

This chapter produces several key themes that include:

1. **Holistic Data Utilization**: LLMs are putting traditional silos like text, code, and potentially images and audio, to break the silos and provide a holistic view of the business data.
2. **Enhanced User Access**: With the natural language interface, not only the technical users will be able to use analytics, but you widen the scope of users who can use analytics. This democratizes data insights so that employees at every level from different roles can participate in work with complex data driven activities.
3. **Productivity and Competitive Gains**: Gains of productivity are realized in tasks such as summarization, classification, forecasting, and intelligent automation. Thus, firms can realize significant cost savings, improved decision quality and faster time to decision.
4. **Challenges and Responsibilities**: There are issues of data privacy, biases, interpretability, and presence of risk of hallucinations making it necessary for governance of robust frameworks. Though LLMs make data-driven strat-

egies more powerful, they also make them more potent, so they are not to be disregarded.

The Transformative Potential of LLMs in Business Analytics

LLMs present a definite power to transform existing processes. Our real-world examples, and available in retail, in finance, in healthcare, in Manufacturing have demonstrated how organizations have successfully moved costly data sets to drive down costs, improve the customer experience, and find new revenue streams. The synergy of advanced text comprehension with structured analytics fosters an ecosystem where insights can be generated more organically, bridging the gap between operational data and strategic vision.

Furthermore, the notion of "autonomous analytics" suggests that tomorrow's LLM solutions may not only interpret data but also propose or carry out actions in near real-time. This natural evolution aligns with broader trends in AI, automation, and Industry 4.0, where data-driven interventions become a seamless part of an organization's day-to-day functions (Allen, 2025).

Recommendations for Stakeholders

For **business leaders**, LLMs offer a compelling chance to pivot toward truly data-driven organizations. However, the journey demands:

- **Investment** in data infrastructure and governance to ensure a steady pipeline of high-quality, trusted data.
- **Organizational Alignment** that fosters collaboration among IT, data science, legal/compliance, and operational departments.
- **Continuous Training** for employees on how to interpret LLM-based analytics responsibly.

For **data scientists and technologists**, the horizon extends beyond algorithmic prowess to include:

- **Prompt Engineering and Fine-Tuning**: Mastery of techniques that adapt general-purpose LLMs to domain-specific tasks.
- **Explainable AI**: New explainable artificial intelligence frameworks are being developed by researchers to survive independent regulatory evaluation.
- **Scalable Deployments**: Such that LLM solutions can accommodate concurrency that comes with concurrency, maintain low latency, and can be used at the cheapest possible rate in the cloud or on-premise environment.

There exists an immediate requirement for policy makers along with regulators to create ethical boundaries in which business organizations can use LLMs appropriately. Such technologies need data rights and the liability for their use to be clarified, automated decisions to be standardized and defined with regard to fairness and transparency.

Final Thoughts

Many already know that Large Language Models have disrupted the analytics status quo. These systems create optimal data connections between structured and unstructured datasets which enables completely new kinds of business analytics capabilities for risk management and customer outreach and data interpretation. There is certainly nothing to suggest forward progress is under way slowly, no; significant challenges understandably persist, chief among them privacy, bias, interference, but the momentum is unmistakable. In the next decade of business analytics, LLMs are poised to be integrated into businesses' data ecosystems responsibly and organizations will learn to harness what's fundamental about those capabilities to make the business even more adaptive, insight driven, and inclusive than ever. (Kerem, 2024; Shah, 2024).

The future is one in which analytics are no longer the domain of a select few. With LLM-driven innovations, entire organizations can harness data as a strategic asset, forging competitive advantages in a volatile market landscape. By mitigating the risks and seizing the transformative potential of LLMs, businesses can stand at the forefront of a new epoch—one where language, data, and intelligence converge to redefine what it means to be truly data-driven.

REFERENCES

Abel, J. (2024). *Generative AI Could Revolutionize Business Analytics*. AI Business.

Allen, T. (2025). *Manifesting the Promise of Generative AI for Business Intelligence*.

Alparslan, A. (2025). The Role of Accuracy and Validation Effectiveness in Conversational Business Analytics. *IEEE Access : Practical Innovations, Open Solutions*, *13*, 1–25. DOI: 10.1109/ACCESS.2025.3540975

Bao, Y., Shah, A. P., Narang, N., Rivers, J., Maksey, R., Guan, L., Barrere, L. N., Evenson, S., Basole, R., Miao, C., Mehta, A., Boulay, F., Park, S. M., Pearson, N. E., Joy, E., He, T., Thakur, S., Ghosal, K., On, J., … Wei, W. (2024). *Harnessing Business and Media Insights with Large Language Models*. 1–21.

Belani, G. (2024). *3 Examples of LLM Use in Business Intelligence Why Use LLMs for Business Intelligence*.

Busany, N., Hadar, E., Hadad, H., Rosenblum, G., Maszlanka, Z., Akhigbe, O., & Amyot, D. (2024). *Automating Business Intelligence Requirements with Generative AI and Semantic Search*.

Cheung, M. (2024). *A Reality check of the benefits of LLM in business*. 1–20.

Chu, D. (2024). *What are the Challenges of Using LLM in Data Visualization*.

DataChat. (2025). *The Hidden Risks of Using Large Language Models for Business Data Analytics*.

Demo. (2025). *Guide to AI in Business analytics*.

Dholariya, F. (2024). *How Large Language Models (LLMs) are transforming Business intelligece (BI) and Analytics*.

Jeong, C. (2023). *A Study on the Implementation of Generative AI Services Using an Enterprise Data-Based LLM Application Architecture*. Advances in Artificial Intelligence and Machine Learning., DOI: 10.54364/AAIML.2023.1191

Jiang, J., Xie, H., Shen, Y., Zhang, Z., Lei, M., Zheng, Y., Fang, Y., Li, C., Huang, D., Zhang, W., Li, Y., Yang, X., Cui, B., & Chen, P. (2024). *SiriusBI: Building End-to-End Business Intelligence Enhanced by Large Language Models*.

Kampik, T., Warmuth, C., Rebmann, A., Agam, R., Egger, L. N. P., Gerber, A., Hoffart, J., Kolk, J., Herzig, P., Decker, G., van der Aa, H., Polyvyanyy, A., Rinderle-Ma, S., Weber, I., & Weidlich, M. (2024). Large Process Models: A Vision for Business Process Management in the Age of Generative AI. *KI -. Künstliche Intelligenz*. Advance online publication. DOI: 10.1007/s13218-024-00863-8

Kerem, G. (2024). *The impact of AI in Business Analytics: Challenges and Opportunities*.

Kohl, O. (2024). *Why generative AI is the next big thing in business intelligence*. Pyramid.

Kumar, N. (2022). *Evolution of Natural Language Processing*. Linkdin. https://doi.org/https://www.linkedin.com/pulse/evolution-natural-language-processing-nitish-kumar/

Liu, Y., Yao, Y., Ton, J.-F., Zhang, X., Guo, R., Cheng, H., Klochkov, Y., Taufiq, M. F., & Li, H. (2023). *Trustworthy LLMs: a Survey and Guideline for Evaluating Large Language Models' Alignment*. 1–81.

Mohamadi, S., Mujtaba, G., Le, N., Doretto, G., & Adjeroh, D. A. (2023). *ChatGPT in the Age of Generative AI and Large Language Models: A Concise Survey*. 1–60.

Mutually Human. (2025). *The Future of Data Analytics: How AI is reshaping the Landscape*.

Sahoo, S., & Dutta, K. (2024). *THE SHIFTING PARADIGM IN AI : WHY Generative Artificial Intelligence IS THE NEW ECONOMIC VARIABLE*.

Shah, V. (2024). *The impact of AI in business analytics: A complete guide*. Thoughtspot.

Vaswani, A., Shazeer, N., Parmar, N., Uszkoreit, J., Jones, L., Gomez, A. N., Kaiser, Ł., & Polosukhin, I. (2017). Attention is all you need. *Advances in Neural Information Processing Systems*.

Vertsel, A., & Rumiantsau, M. (2024). *Hybrid LLM/Rule-based Approaches to Business Insights Generation from Structured Data*.

Wasserkrug, S., Boussioux, L., Hertog, D. den, & Greenland, A. (2024). *Using Large Language Models to Create Analytics Solutions*.

Chapter 4
Natural Language Processing in the Business Context

Pankaj Verma
http://orcid.org/0009-0009-9073-1803
Indian Institute of Management, Bangalore, India

Krishna Gandhi
http://orcid.org/0009-0004-9684-6699
Illinois State University, USA

ABSTRACT

This chapter explores the transformative role of Natural Language Processing (NLP) in the modern business landscape, tracing its evolution from early rule-based systems to today's advanced deep learning and transformer-based models. It highlights how NLP enables organizations to unlock insights from unstructured text data across diverse functions-ranging from customer service and marketing to human resources, finance, and healthcare. Key technologies like sentiment analysis, named entity recognition, and large language models are examined alongside practical use cases such as chatbots, resume screening, fraud detection, and virtual healthcare assistants. The chapter also addresses critical challenges including data privacy, algorithmic bias, interpretability, and the resource demands of scaling NLP systems. Finally, it offers strategies for effective implementation, emphasizing cross-functional collaboration, ethical governance, and hybrid deployment approaches to ensure that NLP solutions deliver meaningful, responsible, and sustainable value to businesses.

DOI: 10.4018/979-8-3693-6690-5.ch004

INTRODUCTION

In a digitally interconnected world, businesses generate, store, and process astonishing volumes of text data. Emails, corporate documents, social media posts, online reviews, chat messages, and customer interactions are a few examples of unstructured language data that accumulate daily. Effective utilization of these language-based resources can lead to valuable strategic, operational, and competitive advantages. However, it has been historically hard to glean insights from unstructured text since words are ambiguous, context matters, cultural references exist, and grammatical rules change from linguistic communities (Woensel & Motie, 2024).

This was made up for by Natural Language Processing (NLP), computational techniques which enable machines to "read", interpret, and make decisions on unstructured text. For decades, apart from rule-based algorithms that found it hard to deal with the fluid nature of language, NLP has grown from simple rule-based but without much accuracy and vocabulary methods like Latent Semantic Indexing (LSI) to exacting deep learning systems which generate coherent text, can classify the documents extremely accurately and even extract subtle sentiment. This is a highly consequential progression for businesses. NLP is being deployed in companies all over the world for automation of repetitive tasks (like customer support queries), for refining marketing strategy, enhancing human resources process, and refining financial analysis, to name a few of the following strategies, and to assist healthcare providers in the diagnosis of diseases (Hilditch et al., 2023).

But NLP deployment is not a simple matter. Text preprocessing is sophisticated given language data diversity, specialized domain specific jargon models need, volumes of training data to be curated carefully to be free of bias and meeting regulations, and just performance is not sufficient when interpretability and user trust are part of the gamut. All of this complicates matters further, especially considering the costs associated, changes to ethical standards, and the need to blend NLP outputs into existing enterprise workflows (Vaswani et al., 2017).

In this chapter, I will examine NLP in the business environment, in a nutshell. The history of NLP is first outlined, back to when rule-based systems first became used, up to the modern large language model (LLM) period. Next, we dive into the divisive foundation of NLP tokenization to the semantic parsing of business problems that use these building blocks to combine the work towards solving fundamental NLP tasks. Next, the current status of NLP technology is assessed, with a focus on pre-trained transformer models, and then the domain-specific applications are discussed in customer service, marketing, human resources, finance, healthcare, e-commerce, and so on. We also examine the pervasive challenges of data privacy, algorithmic bias, interpretability, and resource constraints that organizations face while adopting NLP solutions. Strategies for effective implementation, such as robust project management, cross-functional collaboration, and lifecycle monitoring, are outlined. Finally, we look ahead to future developments such as voice-based applications, real-time adaptive learning, domain-specific large language models, and the ever-increasing significance of ethical governance in AI (Cheung, 2024).

By the end of this chapter, readers will gain a nuanced understanding of how NLP has become indispensable to modern business. They will learn not only about the remarkable capabilities of current systems but also the pitfalls, trade-offs, and best practices for embedding NLP in mission-critical processes. Ultimately, the capacity to harness language at scale promises to usher in a new era of data-driven intelligence and organizational agility, provided that ethical and technical challenges are addressed with due diligence.

Key Facts

- **Data Explosion:** Over **2.5 quintillion bytes** of data are generated every day.
- **Market Growth:** The global NLP market is projected to grow at a **CAGR of approximately 20%**, reaching over **USD 40 billion by 2026**.
- **Model Evolution:** Early rule-based NLP systems have evolved into deep learning models with parameter counts increasing from millions (pre-2010) to over **1.6 trillion parameters** in some modern models.

Table 1. NLP evolution timeline

Period	*Milestone*	*Description*
1950s–1960s	Rule-Based Systems	Early systems like ELIZA and SHRDLU used handcrafted rules to process natural language.
1970s–1980s	Conceptual Ontologies & Chatterbots	Development of conceptual frameworks (e.g., MARGIE) and early chatterbots (e.g., PARRY).
1990s	Statistical NLP	Transition to statistical methods using machine learning and probabilistic models (e.g., IBM alignment).
2000s	Emergence of Large Corpora & Machine Translation	Availability of huge multilingual corpora enabled more robust machine translation and text classification.
2010s–Present	Deep Learning & Transformer Models	Advanced deep learning techniques, particularly transformers, revolutionize NLP with LLMs and pre-trained models.

THE EVOLUTION OF NLP

Early Foundations: Rule-Based NLP

In the past, the application of NLP was driven by systems that had manually defined grammar and crafted rules. In the early decades of computational linguistics during the 1950s and 1960s rule-based systems became the first innovative NLP approaches to be developed.

During the mid-1950s researchers showcased what seemed to be a breakthrough achievement in automatic language translation through their demonstration. Under a defined set of syntax rules that combined with a limited dictionary, they processed Russian sentences into English output. The experimental results focused on specifically chosen examples which created optimism about future implementations of universal machine translation systems that operated through rules. Experts from that time thought a system for complete automatic translation which required only text input and output translation through a simple process was imminent.

Actual language usage created obstacles for translating sentences because human languages resisted strict definable linguistic structures. Words function with various semantic meanings so deciding which interpretation applies demands contextual signals which cannot be programmed easily. The English word "light" corresponds to different meanings based on what occurs next to it in a provided context. Every language embeds various forms of idioms together with compound constructions and local linguistic styles. The initial systems with their rule-based operation provided limited functionality to handle unintuitive ambiguities which occurred in spoken language and written content.

Research showed that making such systems process more languages and diverse content led to extreme complexity growth. Rule explosion became the term scientists used to describe the rising need for rules as attempts grew to create patterns alongside exceptions. Specialistic expertise and linguists along with domain experts were required for system updates because they had to create new grammatical logic code. System updates through this style proved time-consuming because such methods restricted systems from quickly adapting to new phrases and expressions.

However, even with these problems, rule-based NLP had some real-world successes especially in cases where the rules are controlled or in the domain specific context. For example: Airline reservation systems were able to parse short, formulaic query ("Show flights from City A to City B on these dates" with handcrafted processable grammars which were quite reliable). By limiting the domains to be interpreted to constrained ones such as predictable structures and small vocabulary, they avoided the ambiguities of broader language use. Such domain-limited systems grew into things that became precursors for text-based user interfaces over time. The machine was another way through which users typed in sentences and the software returned database results or executed a command. While these interfaces were not 'natural' in all ways, the results showed that computers could learn some of the aspects of language, if suitably regulated.

This was the use of large lexical databases and detailed grammars which characterized rule-based NLP. Different morphological analyzers, dictionaries and part of speech inventories were painfully compiled by researchers and computational linguists for each language or domain. They provided resources for the mapping of the words to their stems, tracking of common suffixes and captured syntactic relationship. Even though these never ended up being completely complete, in a linguistic accounting of forms of the kind, they laid out a scaffolding upon which developers might build parsing systems. To some extent, indeed, these initial lexical resources continued to be the bases on which researchers constructed their subsequent technologies for parsing up complex expressions or disambiguating unclear terms; indeed, researchers studying how to parse complex expressions or clarify ambiguous terms have reused or updated these early dictionaries and morphological tools to study.

The capture of the "rightness" of language has proven to be one of the more enduring achievements of this period, and there was a realization that just listing grammatical combinations does not capture this kind of correctness. Initial attempts indicated that the need for semantic analysis, as well as context handling, has not been addressed. Observers realized that although rules alone are informative, questions such as "Is the sentence a request or a statement?" or "Is the speaker stating something directly or indirectly?" are not easily handled under the rule. While these insights did not directly narrow the problem of understanding contexts, they sowed the seeds for further investigation on the complexity of discourse structure and semantics relevant to the field of NLP today.

There was also a practical dimension to how rule-based systems contributed to later successes. In developing each new grammar or dictionary component, researchers cataloged morphological variations—showing how verbs conjugate, how nouns pluralize, and how certain language patterns recur. These catalogs sometimes took on a life of their own, becoming valuable resources for future projects. Additionally, some advanced linguistic theories emerged as developers tested new grammar formalisms (e.g., context-free grammars, unification grammars). Although many breakthroughs lay decades ahead, the conceptual rigor initiated in this time served as a stepping stone.

By the late 1960s, excitement around fully automated, rule-based translation began to wane. Funding decreased, and high expectations gave way to a sober realization: language was far more complex than static programming logic could capture. This so-called "machine translation winter" marked a period of disillusionment in the field. In terms of the work accomplished, it ended up being such a crucial phase, a first step to amassing the lexical databases, experimenting with syntactic formalizations, prototyping in domains. So, especially in the first decades of NLP, it turned out the architectures, language resources, and theoretical frameworks oneself tried were also still useful today for modern NLP systems.

Finally, in summary, rule-based NLP systems had a formative role, in order to demonstrate first that computers could parse and act upon linguistic inputs in constrained ways. Although limited application was hampered by brittleness and the need for exhaustive rules, they spurred growth of the discipline. This groundwork in grammar, lexicons, and syntactic logic served as intellectual and practical foundation for the statistical and deep learning paradigms that later NLP paradigms turned out to be so complex and data-driven.

Key Points and Resources

- **Lexical Databases:** Early systems depended on large lexical databases, morphological analyzers, and part-of-speech inventories.
- **Semantic Awareness:** Rule-based systems could parse grammatical structures but often did not discern whether the sentence was questioned and if so how, a statement or if there was implied indirect meaning.
- **Legacy:** The early rule-based efforts laid the groundwork for later innovations by establishing fundamental grammar and creating valuable language resources.

Table 2. Examples of early rule-based NLP systems

System/Project	*Era*	*Domain/Task*	*Notable Contribution*
Georgetown Experiment	1954	Machine Translation	Demonstrated automated translation using hand-coded rules.
ELIZA	1964	Conversational Agent	Simulated a Rogerian psychotherapist with simple pattern matching.
SHRDLU	1970	Blocks World Interaction	Parsed and executed commands in a restricted environment.

The Statistical Turn: Probabilistic Models and Feature Engineering

In the late 1980's and early 1990's, natural language processing (NLP) can be said to have had a major turning point, that sometimes is labeled as the "statistical revolution." Instead of sticking to ever-growing handcrafted rule-based approaches aiming to morph linguistic knowledge exhaustively in the underlying knowledge base, researchers started advocating data-driven practices. By analyzing large corpora, or bodies of text, these methods inferred language patterns directly from real-world usage. This shift was propelled by two intertwined factors: the advent of more powerful computing hardware and the increasing availability of large, annotated datasets.

- **The Rise of Hidden Markov Models (HMMs)**

One of the earliest exemplars of this revolution was the Hidden Markov Model (HMM). HMMs assume that observable outputs (in language tasks, typically words or tags) are generated by underlying hidden states linked in a Markov chain. In the context of **part-of-speech tagging**, each hidden state might correspond to a part-of-speech category (noun, verb, adjective, and so forth), while the observed tokens are words in a sentence. By training on labeled data—where each word is already tagged—a model can learn the probabilities of transitions from one part of speech to another, as well as the likelihood of a particular word being generated by a certain part of speech.

For **speech recognition**, the HMM framework similarly proved invaluable. Audio signals were segmented into frames, each corresponding to a phoneme or sub-phoneme, treated as a hidden state. The model then computed the likelihood of the observed acoustic features given a particular hidden phoneme. Because these probabilistic frameworks evaluated sequences with well-understood mathematical formalisms, they achieved robust performance compared to more rigid, rule-based systems. However, a key assumption of HMMs—that each state depends only on its immediate predecessor—limits their capacity to capture long-range contextual relationships in language.

- **Feature Engineering and Its Impact**

In parallel with the ascent of HMMs, NLP practitioners embraced **feature engineering**—a systematic approach wherein developers designed specific features to feed into algorithms for tasks like text classification, sentiment analysis, or named entity recognition. Suppose one aims to determine whether an email is spam. An engineer might define features such as the frequency of certain keywords ("Viagra," "Lottery," or "Free"), the ratio of uppercase letters, or the presence of suspicious links. Another example is in **sentiment analysis**, where features might track how many positive or negative words (based on a predefined lexicon) appear in a review. By converting these features into numeric values, classical machine learning models could separate texts into categories.

Table 3. Common algorithms for feature-based NLP included

Algorithm	Key Characteristics	Typical Use Cases
Naive Bayes (NB)	Assumes feature independence; easy to implement; fast to train	Spam detection, simple classification tasks
Hidden Markov Models (HMMs)	Probabilistic sequence modeling with state transitions	Part-of-speech tagging, speech recognition
Support Vector Machines (SVMs)	Finds optimal decision boundaries in high-dimensional spaces; robust to outliers	Named entity recognition, sentiment analysis, topic classification
Decision Trees	Hierarchical splits based on feature thresholds; interpretable but can overfit	Rule-like classification for domain tasks

- **Naive Bayes (NB):** Despite the theoretical assumption that features are independent (which is rarely true for language data), NB surprisingly performed well. In spam detection, for instance, Naive Bayes might look at the presence or absence of suspicious words alongside other indicators like email structure, offering a quick and reasonably accurate solution.
- **Support Vector Machines (SVMs):** By mapping feature vectors into high-dimensional spaces, SVMs strove to find an optimal hyperplane that separated, say, positive from negative documents. This approach generally yielded higher accuracy than NB but came at a cost in computational resources. In complex tasks such as **named entity recognition (NER)**, SVM-based systems often used hundreds or even thousands of carefully engineered features (including word context windows, capitalization patterns, or part-of-speech tags) to achieve state-of-the-art results at the time.

Feature engineering thus became somewhat of an art form. Researchers manually tested and iterated on which patterns—word frequencies, token lengths, syntactic cues—mattered most for a particular classification. This handcrafted approach demanded domain expertise, as features that were effective for, say, financial news classification might not transfer seamlessly to movie review sentiment analysis.

- **Annotated Corpora and Their Role**

Crucial to the success of these statistical and feature-based methods was the proliferation of **annotated corpora**. Early on, projects like the Penn Treebank undertook large-scale annotation of part-of-speech tags, parse trees, and other linguistic structures for thousands of sentences. Additional corpora emerged for tasks like named entity recognition, sentiment analysis, and machine translation, each labeled at varying degrees of granularity.

These labeled datasets served a dual purpose. First, they offered training material so that probabilistic models could estimate the distribution of language. Second, they arrived at standards for systems performance comparison. The community would see an advancement if an existing algorithm for chunking text or identifying entities could be improved upon by a new algorithm on a well-known corpus. Therefore, competition and forging ahead based off of annotated corpora were spurred.

- **Limitations and Evolution**

While these statistical approaches, together with the engineered features, greatly improved over purely rule-based brittleness of some systems, they still did not overcome the brittleness of the grammar. The main issue with these models stemmed from handling distant word relationships that extend beyond local contexts because they distorted interpretations despite most algorithms making close-range assumptions. In the same vein, feature engineering captured the existence of immediate neighboring tokens or uppercase letters among other features, however, it was very difficult to model deeper semantic relationships. The determination of pronoun interpretation often depends on nouns written in many clauses before.

Constructing and improving extensive feature collections required uninterrupted human participation. Language usage modifications such as internet slang and domain-specific jargon required manual developer input to create and test new features because inadequate handling resulted in performance decline. Model overfitting presented a major problem when there were excessive features because it led to the memorization of training data specifics which did not scale across different instances. However, the obvious shortcomings of this method did not prevent it from adorning the next big wave of NLP innovation with distributed representations and deep neural networks.

- **Concluding Perspective**

Overall, then, the late 1980s to the 1990s was in essence a transitional period of NLP between rigid rule-based designs and probabilistic data-driven models. Real usage was used to teach computers how to learn language patterns by analyzing it with Hidden Markov Models, Naive Bayes, and SVMs. At the same time, a variety of labeling projects produced corpora which are still powerful reference points. Though these approaches could not fully address long-range context or richer semantic understanding, they represented a robust step forward. Their success in tasks like part-of-speech tagging, named entity recognition, and text classification validated the core principle that a well-designed model, trained on sufficiently large, annotated data, could outperform systems locked into static rules. This insight set the stage for subsequent leaps into neural embeddings, deep learning architectures, and ultimately the massive language models that now define much of modern NLP (K. Chen et al., 2024).

The Deep Learning Revolution: Embeddings, RNNs, and Transformers

In the early 2010s, deep learning began to significantly influence NLP, propelled by breakthroughs in parallel computing (particularly GPUs) and the availability of vast datasets. Traditional feature engineering gave way to neural networks that automatically learned vector representations—often called embeddings—of words or tokens:

Word Embeddings

Tools like Word2Vec and Glove introduced low-dimensional vector representations capturing semantic similarity. For instance, words with similar contexts (like "cat," "dog," "rabbit") would appear near each other in the embedding space.

Code Example: Word2Vec

from gensim.models import Word2Vec

```
# Sample corpus
sentences = [["cat", "sat", "on", "the", "mat"], ["dog",
"barked", "loudly"]]
# Train the model
model = Word2Vec (sentences, vector_size=100, window=5, min_
count=1, workers=4)
print ("Vector for 'cat':", model.wv["cat"])
```

RNNs and LSTMs

Recurrent Neural Networks (RNNs), and their gated variants (LSTMs, GRUs), excelled at handling sequential data by retaining information over multiple time steps. This enabled better performance in text classification, language modeling, and machine translation. However, RNN-based systems could still struggle with very long sequences because of vanishing or exploding gradients.

Attention Mechanisms

Proposed to alleviate bottlenecks in RNN-based architectures, attention enabled a model to selectively focus on specific parts of the input sequence when predicting the next token or output. This concept significantly improved the context modeling capacity of neural architectures.

Finally, in 2017, the introduction of the Transformer architecture by Vaswani and colleagues transformed the landscape once more. By relying solely on self-attention mechanisms, Transformers allowed for efficient parallelization of training over large corpora. Models such as BERT, GPT, and T5 built on the Transformer design to set new records across NLP benchmarks in tasks like question answering, summarization, and text generation.

Large Language Models (LLMs): Capacities and Limitations

Large Language Models—massive neural networks pre-trained on billions of tokens—have altered the NLP paradigm yet again. BERT, GPT-2, GPT-3, GPT-4, Roberta, and T5 can digest human language at impressive scales. After a phase of unsupervised pre-training, these models can be fine-tuned on relatively modest labeled datasets to perform specialized tasks, thereby drastically reducing the need for extensive domain-specific data collection.

Key Facts

- **Parameter Growth:** GPT-2 contained around 1.5 billion parameters, while GPT-3 jumped to 175 billion, and GPT-4 and beyond are even larger.
- **Versatility:** Once pre-trained, LLMs can be fine-tuned on small datasets for specialized tasks.
- **Challenges:** Despite their power, LLMs face issues such as hallucination (producing factually incorrect statements), bias (reflecting historical and societal biases), high computational costs, and limited interpretability.

Table 4. Overview of notable LLMs and their limitations

Model	*Parameter Count*	*Strengths*	*Limitations*
GPT-2	~1.5 billion	Strong text generation	Limited context handling, sometimes repetitive
GPT-3	~175 billion	Versatile; excels in few-shot learning	High computational cost, risk of hallucination
GPT-4	>175 billion	Improved accuracy and context utilization	Black-box nature; biases in training data

Figure 1. Number of parameters in LLMs over the years

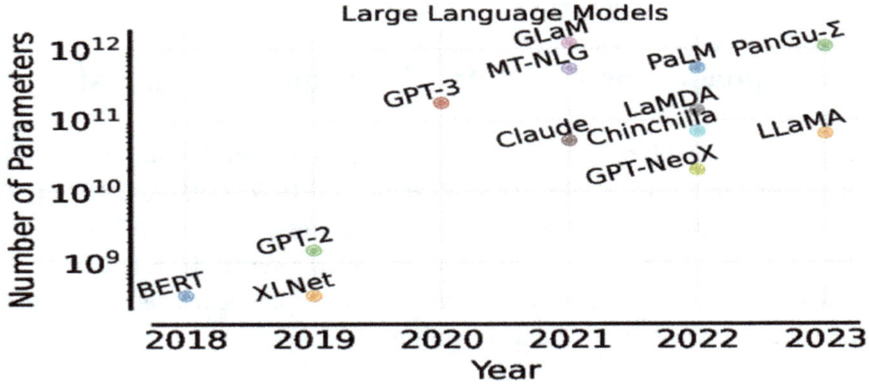

(Agarwal et al., 2023)

Resource Intensity and Practical Considerations

- **Cost:** Training LLMs requires high-end GPU clusters or specialized hardware.
- **Access:** Although full-scale training is limited to large organizations, smaller companies can access LLM capabilities through cloud-based APIs and fine-tuning services.
- **Interpretability:** LLMs are often described as "black boxes," making it challenging to understand their decision-making processes.

However, LLMs are not without limitations:

1. **Hallucination**: Large generative models sometimes produce plausible-sounding but factually incorrect statements, raising concerns in domains where accuracy is paramount (e.g., healthcare, finance).

2. **Bias**: Trained on web text and historical corpora, LLMs risk perpetuating societal or historical biases in their outputs. Mitigating such biases requires careful data curation, algorithmic audits, and fairness-driven modeling.
3. **Resource Intensity**: LLM training is computationally expensive, requiring high-end GPU clusters or specialized hardware. This restricts full-scale training to well-funded organizations, though smaller businesses can still leverage these models through fine-tuning or cloud-based inference services (Wood, 2024).
4. **Interpretability**: Deep learning models, especially large transformers, function mostly as "black boxes," making it difficult for stakeholders to grasp why a model returns certain outputs.

Despite these challenges, LLMs have spurred greater adoption of NLP solutions in industry due to their strong performance across numerous tasks and their adaptability. They illustrate the potential for a single, powerful language model to serve a range of business needs, from marketing analytics to automated coding assistance.

CORE CONCEPTS AND TASKS IN NLP

Text Preprocessing Essentials

Before applying sophisticated models, NLP pipelines begin with text preprocessing, which prepares raw text data for downstream tasks. While preprocessing can vary depending on language, domain, and system requirements, common steps include:

- **Tokenization**: Splitting text into tokens—words, sub words, or characters. The technique of whitespace tokenization works well for English and Spanish yet Byte Pair Encoding (BPE) using sub word tokenization performs better for dealing with unknown words and morphological variants.
- **Case Normalization**: Text normalization includes two steps where all words become lowercase letters but uppercase text remains intact if it has meaning for analysis.
- **Punctuation Handling**: The processing of punctuation marks requires assessment to determine their usefulness during analysis such as exclamation marks in sentiment analysis.
- **Stop word Removal**: Using stop word removal methods to eliminate terms like „the, "an, "and "of "which carry little information helps to decrease processing time. Stop words need to remain intact when analyzing specific tasks which depend on their contextual meaning.

- **Stemming and Lemmatization**: Reducing words to their base forms. The lemma for running words includes the forms running ran runs as well as its stem run. Vocabulary and morphological analysis is used in lemmatization while stemming uses heuristic truncation (which is less accurate but more simplified method).
- **Noise Reduction**: The process deals with special characters alongside emojis and html tags based on domain requirements.

The preprocessing step creates consistent model inputs that also makes them easy to handle thus speeding up feature extraction and neural network training processes.

Syntax and Parsing: Understanding Linguistic Structures

Syntactic analysis and parsing break down sentences into structured representations, revealing the grammatical relationships among words. Two main parsing types are:

1. **Constituency Parsing**: Sentences are decomposed into nested phrase structures (e.g., noun phrases, verb phrases), often depicted as parse trees.
2. **Dependency Parsing**: Focuses on the relationships between head words and their modifiers (e.g., "The cat chased the mouse" might produce arcs from "chased" to "cat" and "mouse" indicating subject and object roles).

While advanced business applications might not always require full parsing, partial parse information can be crucial in tasks like opinion mining (to identify which adjective modifies which noun), question answering, or formal textual analytics in legal contexts.

Semantics and Pragmatics in Business-Driven NLP

Beyond syntax lies semantics—how language expresses meaning—and pragmatics—how context affects interpretation. Achieving semantic understanding is considerably more difficult than merely labeling parts of speech (Grohs et al., 2024). A sentiment analysis system needs to capture the difference in tone between "That product is unbelievably good" and "That product is unbelievably bad." A contract analysis tool must detect and interpret complex obligations hidden in legal clauses.

Semantics often relies on:

- **Named Entity Recognition (NER)**: Identifying and categorizing entities (people, organizations, locations, dates, product names).

- **Semantic Role Labeling**: Determining semantic roles of sentence constituents (agent, patient, instrument, etc.).
- **Coreference Resolution**: Figuring out that "the manager" and "she" refer to the same individual in a text.

Pragmatics, meanwhile, may consider the user's intent ("I'd like to upgrade my plan" in a telecom scenario might directly map to an upsell opportunity) or the broader discourse context (a thread of 10 user messages).

Domain-Specific Terminology Handling

Business environments feature specialized terminologies, including acronyms, technical jargon, or brand-specific lingo. For instance:

- **Medical**: "CABG" means Coronary Artery Bypass Grafting, a surgery type.
- **Finance**: "CDS," "EPS," "LIBOR," or "swap spreads" denote specialized concepts rarely encountered in general conversation.
- **Engineering**: Numeric references like "6061 aluminum" or materials codes.

Handling such domain-specific terms often requires custom dictionaries, specialized tokenization, or domain-adaptive training corpora. In technical support or legal compliance, capturing and correctly interpreting domain terminology can make the difference between success and failure for an NLP pipeline. The creation of domain-specific embeddings (like BioWordVec, SciBERT, Fin BERT) ensures that domain knowledge is encoded into the representation space, boosting performance for specialized tasks.

CURRENT STATE OF NLP TECHNOLOGY

The Proliferation of Pre-Trained Models

Few developments have reshaped NLP as dramatically as large-scale pre-trained models. These architectures—often based on the Transformer—are trained on massive text corpora (potentially hundreds of gigabytes of data). During pre-training, the model acquires a broad understanding of language structure, context, and usage. Post pre-training, the model can be quickly adapted (fine-tuned) for downstream applications like sentiment classification, question answering, or named entity recognition with relatively modest labeled datasets.

Key Facts

- **Data Volume:** Pre-training often leverages corpora of hundreds of GB, sometimes over a trillion tokens.
- **Model Sizes:** Models now range from hundreds of millions to hundreds of billions of parameters (e.g., GPT-3 has ~175B parameters).
- **Reduced Data Needs:** Fine-tuning can be performed with relatively few domain-specific examples (often thousands instead of millions).

Key benefits of adopting pre-trained models include:

- **Reduced Data Requirements**: Instead of collecting millions of domain-specific sentences, businesses can start with a general-purpose model and adapt it with, say, thousands of domain-labeled examples.
- **State-of-the-Art Performance**: These models have broken records on many academic benchmarks, achieving near or above human-level results on some tasks.
- **Reusable "Language Understanding"**: Cross-lingual or universal encoders can serve multilingual use cases with minimal additional overhead.

On the downside, pre-trained models can be extremely large (hundreds of millions to hundreds of billions of parameters), leading to challenges in memory, inference speed, and operational cost. Techniques like knowledge distillation, quantization, or pruning aim to make these networks smaller and more practical.

Table 5. Notable pre-trained NLP models

Model	*Year*	*Parameter Count*	*Key Strengths*	*Limitations*
BERT	2018	110M – 340M	Strong for sentence-level tasks; bidirectional	Limited context length
GPT-2	2019	~1.5B	Excellent text generation	Sometimes repetitive; resource-intensive
GPT-3	2020	~175B	Few-shot learning; versatile across tasks	High cost; risk of hallucination; black-box nature
T5	2020	Up to ~11B	Unified text-to-text framework	Requires extensive fine-tuning for specialized tasks

Transfer Learning and Fine-Tuning for Targeted Tasks

Transfer learning is the linchpin of modern NLP. Rather than train a neural network from scratch for each application, the model reuses knowledge from pre-training to expedite learning in a new domain. Typical steps include:

1. **Base Model Selection**: Choose a suitable model (e.g., BERT, Roberta, GPT-3) that aligns with the target task's language or style.
2. **Intermediate Task Training (Optional)**: Fine-tune on a related task or domain corpus to further specialize the model (like training on legal documents if you're ultimately extracting clauses).
3. **Final Fine-Tuning**: Train the model on the specifically labeled dataset for the end application (such as "classify customer inquiries into sales, billing, or technical support").

This process drastically reduces the label engineering burden, enabling even small teams to build robust NLP solutions. However, the scope and complexity of fine-tuning tasks must be carefully managed to avoid catastrophic forgetting (where the model overwrites its broad linguistic knowledge with domain-specific patterns), overfitting, or unintended biases introduced by domain data.

Tooling and Frameworks in the Enterprise

The proliferation of open-source libraries and platforms has democratized NLP adoption. Among the most widely used:

- **Hugging Face Transformers**: Provides a unifying interface for numerous pre-trained transformer models, easy-to-use tokenizers, and scripts for tasks like text classification, sequence tagging, or question answering.
- **spaCy**: Emphasizes efficiency and production readiness, offering near real-time pipelines for tasks like NER, dependency parsing, and text categorization. SpaCy includes pre-trained models and extensive language coverage.
- **PyTorch and TensorFlow**: General deep learning frameworks that form the substrate for custom architectures. They also power many advanced NLP experiments, especially for tasks requiring specialized network components.
- **Spark NLP**: Integrates with Apache Spark for large-scale distributed processing, beneficial when dealing with massive corpora in enterprise data lakes.

Loading a Pre-Trained Model with Hugging Face

```
from transformers import pipeline

# Load a sentiment analysis pipeline using a pre-trained model
sentiment pipeline = pipeline("sentiment-analysis")
# Analyze a sample text
result = sentiment pipeline ("The new product launch was incredibly successful!")
print(result)
```

In corporate settings, these tools are often integrated into automated pipelines with CI/CD for rapid iteration, versioning, and deployment. Enterprises also evaluate robust monitoring frameworks, data labeling platforms, and DeVos-driven solutions for model lifecycle management (e.g., MLflow, Kubeflow).

Cloud Services and Managed Solutions

Cloud-based NLP has become a driving force in how businesses analyze text data, build customer-facing chatbots, and extract structured insights from unstructured information. Yet, many organizations lack the compute infrastructure or specialized expertise to train large models and maintain complex pipelines in-house. In response, major providers—including Amazon Web Services (AWS), Microsoft Azure, Google Cloud Platform (GCP), and IBM Cloud—deliver AI-as-a-Service, packaging NLP capabilities such as language translation, entity extraction, speech recognition, and sentiment analysis behind accessible APIs. Below is an examination of these offerings, benefits, challenges, and practical strategies to balance convenience with control.

Overview of Cloud-Based NLP Services

Cloud providers host a range of NLP microservices aimed at different use cases. Common functions include Language Translation for quick conversion of text across languages, Text Classification for detecting spam or gauging sentiment, Entity Recognition for extracting key items (names, organizations, monetary amounts), Optical Character Recognition (OCR) for digitizing scanned content, and Speech-to-Text for transcribing voice data. By abstracting away model hosting, scaling, and updates, these APIs allow businesses with minimal machine learning resources to incorporate NLP quickly.

Core Offerings by Major Providers

Each NLP catalog expands over time for each vendor, but the table below is a snapshot of popular services provided by the public cloud platforms.

Table 6.

Provider	Key NLP Services	Notable Features
Amazon Web Services (AWS)	Comprehend (sentiment, key phrases), Translate, Transcribe	Pay-as-you-go pricing; HIPAA-eligible environment for healthcare use
Microsoft Azure	Cognitive Services (Text Analytics, Translator, Speech)	Offers containerized deployments; robust language detection
Google Cloud	Cloud Natural Language, Translation API, Speech-to-Text	Pre-trained domain models; real-time analytics with Big Query
IBM Cloud	Watson NLP, Watson Discovery, Watson Language Translator	Domain adaptation options; Watson Assistant for chatbots

Such services may contain software development kits (SDKs), usage dashboards and pay per request pricing structure to enable teams monitor consumption and costs.

Advantages: Rapid Prototyping, Scalability, and Compliance

One of the key advantages of doing NLP in the cloud is that it takes out a lot of the time required for projects that used to take data science time and instead use pre-trained models. Developers send requests to an endpoint, see the results right away, and get the proof of concept cycles extremely fast. The most important benefit is on-demand scalability. NLP tasks will demand ramping of resources during seasonal campaigns or product launches, and cloud providers like Square have a mechanism to scale their resources in real-time. This elasticity guarantees stable performance and charges only for the number of the received requests processed. Security and compliance is a secondary concerns for many vendors, and it has many building solutions that are on top of HIPAA, GDPR, or other regulations. This can ease things for companies that have to handle sensitive data, staying on what matters about business logic, not infrastructure.

Limitations: Costs, Vendor Lock-In, and Domain Constraints

Still, something like this is a concern at scale. Small pilots used to pay per-call pricing that turned out to be negligible compared to the billions of documents or real-time streams processed daily. It also exposes a company to the risk of lock-in, possibly heavy, if its workflows rely on a provider's APIs, making switching to another service, or even to an on-premises model, an expensive proposition. Another limitation is domain coverage. Cloud APIs may work marvelously with consumer text but struggle where the text is niche, technical or anything in between. Off-the-shelf solutions have some capabilities for customization, however, some of the needful specialized needs such as parsing complex legal contracts or handling specific medical terminology are not widely supported.

Hybrid Strategies: Balancing Managed and In-House Solutions

That is why organizations most often adopt a hybrid approach; starting with cloud APIs to gain traction on easier tasks such as multilingual product listings, or basic brand sentiment tracking. These services turn out to be good once teams realize this, and then they gradually invest in custom pipelines or open-source model if they need more advanced tasks. For example, a cloud translation would continue being used by a financial services firm for less sensitive web content; in contrast, internal models would be developed to analyze sensitive financial documents to reduce external dependence and optimize performance. A dual strategy that supports fast result in simple cases and flexibility for specialized or confidential workflows.

Figure 2. The graphic represents a system which combines the management of cloud NLP resources with internal NLP programming operations

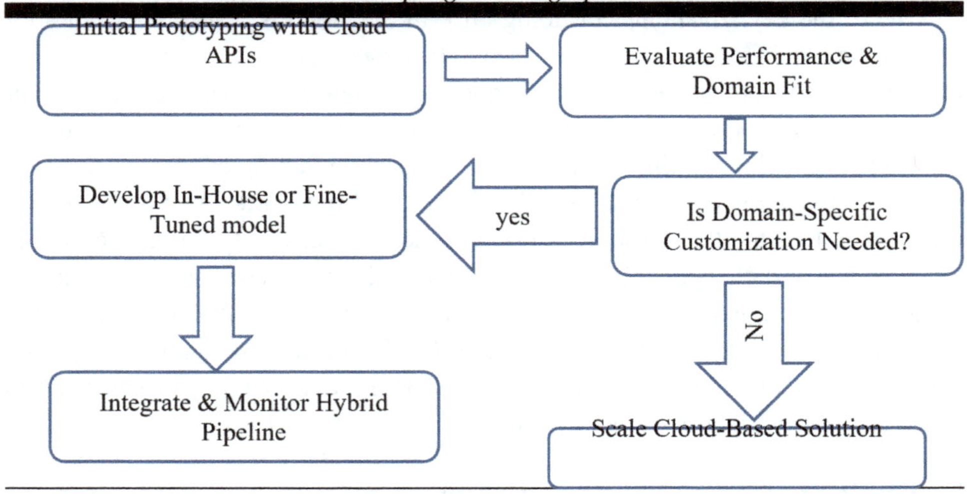

Conclusion

Speed is the primary benefit that cloud-based NLP solutions give organizations for running language analysis tests. Through model calling features developers have access to pre-trained models which enable text classification as well as entity recognition and translation services regardless of their need for large infrastructure maintenance. Scalability, regulatory compliance, and continuous vendor-driven improvements further enhance their appeal, making them a compelling option for many businesses. However, ongoing usage costs can mount, vendor lock-in remains a risk, and domain-specific customization may demand in-house capabilities. By starting with managed APIs and gradually refining or supplementing them with self-hosted solutions, organizations can strike a balanced approach: reap the advantages of cloud-based NLP for rapid iteration and standard tasks while retaining room to evolve toward more specialized or private solutions as needs become clearer.

NLP IN CUSTOMER-FACING FUNCTIONS

Chatbots and Conversational Agents

Among the most visible and widespread applications of NLP is the **chatbot** or conversational agent, a software system that interacts with users via text or voice (Orza, 2024). E-commerce sites, telecoms, banks, and numerous service-oriented businesses deploy chatbots to triage questions, handle frequently asked queries, and guide customers toward resources.

Key design considerations include:

1. **Intent Recognition**: Classifying incoming user messages (e.g., "billing issue," "technical problem," "product inquiry").
2. **Entity Extraction**: Identifying relevant details (e.g., account numbers, product codes, user location).
3. **Dialogue Management**: Tracking multi-turn conversations, context carryover, and transitions from one topic to another.
4. **Fallback and Escalation**: Knowing when to pass the conversation to a human operator (especially for high-value or sensitive issues).

Chatbots yield numerous benefits: round-the-clock availability, instant response, and the capacity to handle simultaneous interactions with thousands of users. This leads to reduced wait times, enhanced customer satisfaction, and significant operational savings. However, chatbots can fail if they misunderstand complex or domain-specific queries, come across as inauthentic, or are not seamlessly integrated with back-end data systems. Large language models, with better few-shot generalization, promise more robust, human-like dialogue capabilities—but require vigilance about error handling and controlled text generation (Mashaabi et al., 2022).

Key Facts

- **Availability & Scale:** Chatbots enable 24/7 customer service and can handle thousands of simultaneous interactions.
- **Cost Savings:** Companies can reduce support costs by up to **30–50%** while maintaining fast response times.
- **Performance:** Recent studies show that LLM-driven chatbots achieve near-human conversational fluency in many domains.

Table 7. Chatbot design considerations and benefits

Aspect	*Description*	*Business Impact*
Intent Recognition	Classify user messages into actionable categories	Faster routing; targeted responses
Entity Extraction	Extract key details (account, product, location)	Personalized support; automation in CRM integration
Dialogue Management	Maintain multi-turn context across conversations	Enhanced user experience; smooth escalation
Fallback & Escalation	Detect when human intervention is required	Prevents customer frustration; improves resolution rates

Chatbot Conversation Flow

Figure 3. Flowchart outlining a typical chatbot conversation flow

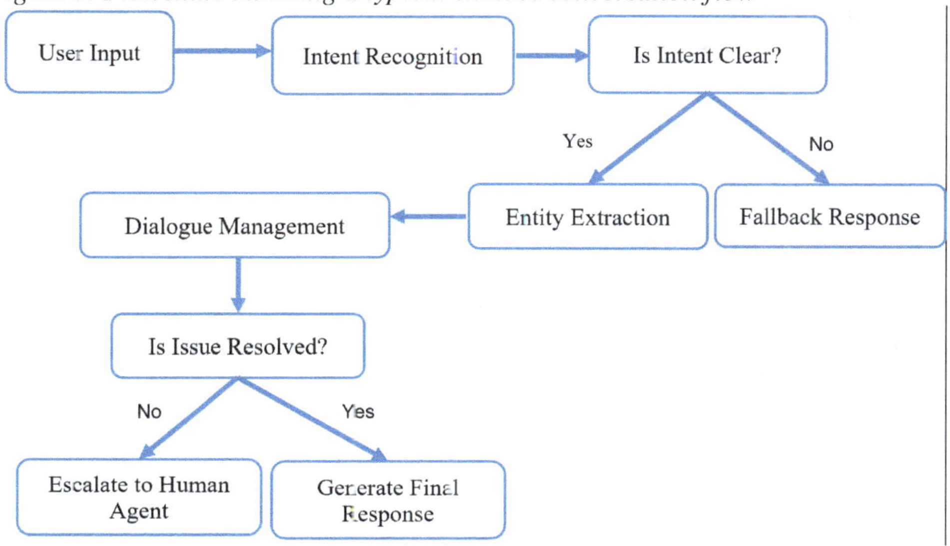

Simple Chatbot with Hugging Face Transformers

```
from transformers import pipeline

# Load a conversational pipeline
chatbot = pipeline ("conversational", model="microsoft/
DialoGPT-medium")
# Simulate a conversation
user_message = "I have a billing issue with my account."
response = chatbot(user_message)
print ("Chatbot Response:", response[0]["generated_text"])
```

Customer Query Resolution and Ticket Management

Enterprises frequently rely on help desks and ticketing systems to address user needs. Natural Language Processing adds automation and intelligence to these workflows:

- **Auto-Categorization**: By analyzing ticket subject lines and descriptions, NLP classifies issues into categories (e.g., "payment dispute," "login error," "feature request").
- **Priority Assignment**: Tickets containing terms like "urgent," "down," or negative sentiment can be routed with higher priority or assigned to specialized teams.
- **Suggested Solutions**: Using similarity metrics or retrieval-based models, the system proposes solutions from a knowledge base that previously resolved similar cases.

This automation can drastically cut resolution times, as support agents no longer spend as much effort performing triage or searching for standard fixes. Additionally, advanced analytics can identify recurring pain points, measure agent performance, and even forecast staffing requirements for the customer support department.

Business Impact

- **Efficiency:** Reduction in ticket resolution time by up to **40%**.
- **Analytics:** Enables trend analysis to identify recurring issues and optimize staffing.

Table 8. NLP in ticket management

Function	*Description*	*Outcome*
Auto-Categorization	Classify tickets into categories using text analysis	Faster triage and routing
Priority Assignment	Use sentiment and keyword analysis to set urgency	Improved response times for critical issues
Suggested Solutions	Retrieve and recommend fixes based on historical data	Reduced workload for support agents

Automated Ticket Workflow

Figure 4. A flowchart illustrating the automated ticket management process

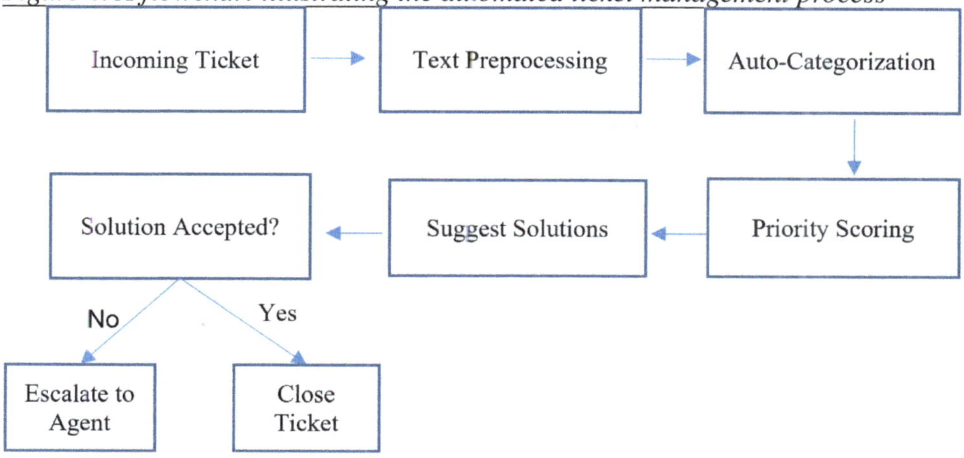

Feedback, Review Mining, and Sentiment Analysis

Beyond direct queries, customers share opinions on social media, product review sites, or internal feedback forms. **Feedback analysis** sifts through user comments to extract brand sentiment, measure satisfaction, and surface improvement suggestions. Sentiment analysis aims to detect the polarity (positive, negative, or neutral) of textual data, with more nuanced variants (aspect-based sentiment analysis) identifying precisely which product features trigger positivity or negativity.

1. **Brand Reputation Tracking**: Marketing teams monitor brand mentions and sentiment waves, intervening quickly when negative chatter spikes.
2. **Product Roadmap**: Engineering teams examine aggregated user concerns about performance, cost, or features, influencing development priorities.
3. **Competitive Intelligence**: Companies can track competitor brand names and glean user sentiment to gauge weaknesses, potential market entry points, or new opportunities.

However, analyzing user-generated text demands robust handling of sarcasm, figurative language, or short jargon-laden expressions. Domain adaptation for sentiment lexicons, or advanced neural architectures trained on domain-specific data, typically yields more accurate results. The output of sentiment analysis often flows into dashboards or real-time alert systems, allowing prompt responses to issues or the strategic alignment of marketing campaigns with user preferences.

NLP IN MARKETING AND SALES

Personalized Advertising and Contextual Targeting

Modern digital marketing thrives on personalization. NLP plays a central role by interpreting user interests, lifestyles, or demographics from textual data to optimize ad placements, design targeted campaigns, and craft product recommendations. Tools and methods include:

1. **Keyword Extraction**: Identifying recurring product terms in user posts or queries. For instance, a travel site may serve ads for family-friendly resorts if a user frequently mentions children.
2. **Interest Clustering**: Topic modeling groups users into cohorts (e.g., "fitness enthusiasts," "foodies," "fashion followers"), allowing the creation of segment-specific promotions.
3. **Contextual Targeting**: Scanning the text of web pages to ensure that an advertisement for a health supplement is placed next to content about nutrition, not next to irrelevant or brand-damaging material.

Impact

- **CTR Improvement:** Personalized targeting can boost click-through rates by up to **25%**.
- **Conversion:** Tailored messaging increases conversion rates while ensuring ethical data practices.

Table 9. NLP applications in advertising

Technique	*Description*	*Example*
Keyword Extraction	Identify recurring terms in user content	Detecting "yoga mats" for fitness-related ads
Interest Clustering	Group users based on topic modeling	Segmenting "foodies" for targeted restaurant promotions
Contextual Targeting	Scan web content to match ad placement with relevant topics	Ensuring a health supplement ad appears alongside nutrition articles

This method generates improved CTR and conversion rates though it presents substantial management duties. NLP models may generate unwanted data inferences regarding individuals' private information causing serious ethical risks and privacy concerns. As per data consent regulations, marketers need to abide by these regulations and also need to minimize any discriminatory impact in targeting ad algorithms.

Social Listening and Real-Time Market Trends

'Social listening' is the process of always listening to (monitoring) what people are saying about your brand, product or industry, on public social media and other public platforms. The application of NLP systems strengthens the capabilities of social listening processes through the following advantages:

- **Named Entity Recognition (NER)**: enables systems to identify components like business names and competitor items and widely recognized social media influencers that appear in texts.
- **Trend Detection**: Viral hashtags; trend detection; If there is viral hashtag or if there is trend created by certain keywords (e.g.: vegan snacks; remote work revolution).
- **Geolocation Context**: Inferring user location or cultural context from textual indicators, relevant for region-specific campaigns.

Marketing teams are alerted real time about sudden shifts in consumer perception, sudden occurrence of any controversy with a competitor or news events that they might need to start communicating immediately about the brand. The negative user experiences following a new smartphone release provides competitors with an opportunity to capitalize through trade-in deals because users are dissatisfied with the product.

Business Benefits

- **Rapid Response:** These alerts bring immediate responses to the negative trend or any competitor activities.
- **Strategic Planning:** Continuous monitoring acts as a database that helps organizations develop better marketing strategies.

Lead Generation, Qualification, and CRM Augmentation

NLP technology revolutionizes the process of lead identification as well as lead qualification for sales teams.

1. **Prospect Discovery**: Algorithmic programs use directory scan and job posting and web discussion analysis to detect the signs indicating business need for specific products or services. The phrase "Looking for a CRM solution" reveals a clear intention to acquire such products or services.
2. **Intent Analysis**: NLP-based systems determine user sales funnel position through online visit assessment alongside question evaluation at the awareness, consideration or decision points.
3. **Lead Enrichment**: The system enhances leads through the process of data collection from public sources. NLP extracts vital information from company definitions and leadership information along with financial reports to assemble client-specific sales pitches.
4. **CRM Integration**: The customer relationship management (CRM) system remains updated with current sales insights through NLP-based automation of data entry and summary generation from meetings and email examination.

By reducing time spent on manual prospecting and qualification, organizations can direct efforts toward consultative selling and relationship building, potentially accelerating the sales cycle and increasing closure rates.

Outcomes

- **Increased Efficiency:** Automation reduces manual prospecting and data entry.
- **Higher Conversion Rates:** More accurate lead qualification leads to better-targeted sales efforts.
- **Faster Sales Cycle:** Streamlined processes enable quicker responses and relationship building.

Basic Intent Analysis for Lead Qualification

from transformers import pipeline

```
# Load an intent classification pipeline (simulated with sentiment-analysis for demo)
intent_classifier = pipeline("sentiment-analysis")
# Sample customer query indicating purchase intent
query = "I'm looking for a CRM solution to improve our sales process."
# Classify the intent
result = intent_classifier(query)
```

```
print ("Intent Analysis Result:", result)
```

NLP IN HR AND TALENT MANAGEMENT

Resume Screening and Recruitment Automation

Recruiters often face overwhelming volumes of resumes for sought-after positions. NLP addresses this by:

- **Resume Parsing**: Identifying candidate details—contact information, education, skill sets, past roles, achievements. Named Entity Recognition and chunking help structure these elements in standardized fields.
- **Skill Matching**: Using text classification or vector similarity, the system ranks candidates by alignment with a job's skill requirements, recommended certifications, or years of experience.
- **Semantic Matching**: The most sophisticated matching methods consider skill set synonyms as well as related terms for reducing incorrect negative assessments. A profile that includes data cleaning and wrangling operations would satisfy job requirements for ETL experience.

The quickening of candidate shortlisting through automated screening creates doubts about the equal treatment of candidates. The information used for training purposes sometimes maintains outdated discriminatory patterns through systematic deficits focusing on educational and demographic groups. HR teams need to perform periodic audits on NLP pipelines to check for disparate impact by using algorithms that focus on fairness and ensuring no sensitive characteristics are utilized while performing screenings. Robotically controlled hiring processes cannot recognize qualities such as cultural requirements or creative talents of candidates thus requiring human input during screening procedures (Leidner et al., 2018).

Key Facts

- The implementation of NLP-based resume screening technology enables organizations to expedite their hiring process by 85% relative to manual resume screening operations.
- The implementation of automated systems results in bias elimination together with reduced errors which creates opportunities for faster candidate shortlisting by 11 times. (Saatçı et al., 2024).

Table 10. Benefits of NLP-based resume screening

Benefit	*Description*	*Impact*
Time Efficiency	Automates repetitive parsing and categorization	Saves up to 85% screening time
Improved Accuracy	Standardizes candidate data extraction	Near human accuracy (≈87%)
Bias Reduction	Focuses on competencies rather than personal details	More objective candidate ranking

Automated Resume Screening Process

Figure 5. The system uses NLP to automate resume evaluation processes

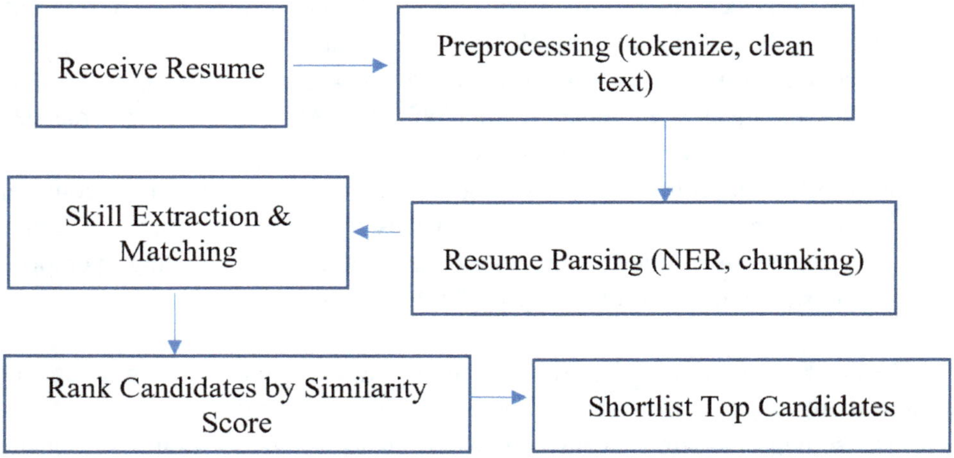

Simple Resume Parsing Example

```
import spacy

# Load spaCy's English model
nlp = spacy.load("en_core_web_sm")
# Sample resume text
resume_text = """
John Doe
Email: john.doe@example.com

Experience: 5 years in data analysis and ETL processes.
```

Skills: Python, SQL, data wrangling, machine learning.
Education: B.Sc. in Computer Science.

```
"""
# Process text with spaCy
doc = nlp(resume_text)
# Extract Named Entities (e.g., skills might appear as 'ORG'
or custom labels after training)
skills = [ent.text for ent in doc.ents if ent.label_ in
["SKILL", "ORG"]]
# Alternatively, simple keyword matching (for demo purposes)
keywords = ["Python", "SQL", "data wrangling", "machine
learning"]
extracted_skills = [token.text for token in doc if token.
text in keywords]
print ("Extracted Skills:", extracted_skills)
```

Employee Feedback Processing and Organizational Health

Beyond the hiring stage, NLP can measure and enhance internal organizational health. Employees often share unstructured feedback via surveys, suggestion boxes, town halls, or performance reviews. Textual analysis techniques help:

1. **Topic Segmentation**: Clustering statements around themes like "compensation," "work-life balance," "leadership communication," "promotion paths," or "workplace diversity."
2. **Sentiment and Emotion Detection**: Distinguishing anger from disappointment or enthusiasm from mere positivity. Fine-grained emotion analysis highlights burning issues that might not surface in numeric ratings.
3. **Anomaly Monitoring**: Identifying Anomalies related to denomination of phrases like "remote work policy", "return to office mandate" indicating possible unrest.
4. **Comparisons Over Time or Demographics**: Timing-based Analysis or Demographic Research Demonstrates the Sentiment Variations between Different Units at Work. The collected data enables human resources managers to create data-based solutions through training programs or policy modifications.

When used with structured employee engagement metrics, NLP insights only offer a 360-degree view of the workforce morale. Leaders obtain the capability to respond rapidly to employee dissatisfaction and recognize excellent employee suggestions.

The same data protection measures through anonymization and confidentiality ensure the privacy and trust of employees when processing external social media data.

Key Figures

- Companies using NLP for employee feedback have reported a **20-30%** improvement in identifying actionable insights.
- Organizations that routinely analyze feedback can reduce employee turnover by up to **15%** by addressing issues proactively.

Table 11. NLP for employee feedback

NLP Task	*Objective*	*Outcome*
Topic Segmentation	Cluster feedback by themes	Identifies key areas for improvement
Sentiment Analysis	Detect positive/negative emotions	Informs HR on morale and engagement
Anomaly Detection	Spot sudden changes in feedback sentiment	Early detection of potential internal issues

Employee Feedback Analysis Pipeline

Figure 6. NLP operates through specific steps to analyze employee feedback which will be discussed along with an illustration

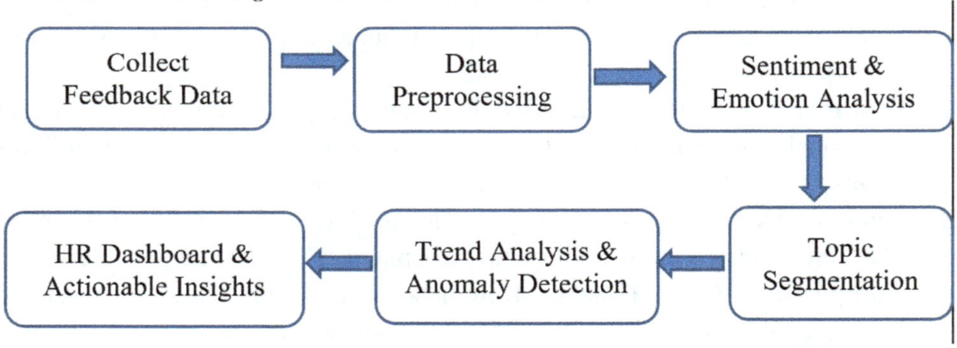

Building a Fair and Inclusive Workplace with NLP

Among many others, companies are using NLP to build a workplace which is more inclusive. For instance:

- **Bias Detection in Job Descriptions**: Employment description analysis through automated tools helps identify wording that could potentially deter certain candidate groups such as male-coded phrases including "aggressive self-starter." The NLP technology helps find different wording which enhances the hiring success rate by increasing candidate possibilities.
- **Identifying Microaggressions in Chats or Emails**: The company's chats and emails undergo automated inspections to detect micro aggressive words which result in immediate alert notifications for human supervision. When automated warnings are detected these alert Human Resources departments to review evidence of wrongdoings within their organizations.
- **Resume Redaction**: A system can automatically hide identifying details in resumes that link to specific ethnic groups or genders to boost fair evaluation. Employment candidates receive stand-in data markers that prevent hiring managers from seeing personal information during an assessment of qualifications.

Proper implementation with monitoring helps NLP deliver social benefits to organizations while protecting employee privacy and work confidentiality. Maintaining an equilibrium between corporate safety and fairness alongside personal privacy presents a fundamental issue that needs a solution.

Key Insights

- Organizations that implement NLP-based bias detection have seen up to a **25%** improvement in diversity among shortlisted candidates.
- Regular audits of NLP systems can help reduce unintentional biases, ensuring a more inclusive workplace.

Table 12. Approaches to mitigate bias using NLP

Approach	*Methodology*	*Advantage*
Job Description Analysis	Scans for gender-coded words and suggests alternatives	Attracts a more diverse candidate pool
Resume Redaction	Masks personal identifiers in resumes	Focuses evaluation on skills and experience
Communication Monitoring	Analyzes internal messages for discriminatory language	Proactive identification of workplace bias

NLP in Finance and Regulatory Compliance

New threats, such as phishing, identity theft, insurance fraud, and money laundering, must be continuously combined by the financial institutions. Automating this space with the analysis of huge textual data such as transaction logs, customer communications etc., is revolutionized by NLP technologies by ensuring regulatory compliance by efficiently handling large documents.

Fraud Detection, Risk Assessment, and Alert Systems

Phishing attempts, identity theft, insurance fraud, money laundering, and other rampant threats set the scene for financial institutions. Fraud detection is enhanced by NLP as the textual data, such as transaction logs, insurance claims, or suspicious emails is sniffed through.

Core NLP Techniques

- **Text Classification:**
    - o Flags documents with contractions of the expected pattern (e.g., involving repeated contradictions, flowery language, improbable claims), as well as outright misspellings and so on.
    - o *Key Fact:* Automated classifiers can scan millions of records per day thereby speed up the manual review times by up to 70%.
- **Semantic Similarity:**
    - o Combining words embeddings with context matching to identify suspicious groups of sent messages with known fraudulent cases.
    - o *Example:* Similarity algorithms like cosine similarity help cluster new claims with historical fraud data.
- **Risk Profiling:**

- Analyzes textual descriptions—such as deal justifications or payment explanations—to assign risk scores.
- When combined with numeric indicators (e.g., unusual transaction amounts), this enables compliance teams to focus on high-risk cases.

These capabilities become especially important under regulations like the Bank Secrecy Act (BSA) or anti-money laundering rules, where financial organizations must identify and report questionable activities promptly. Accurate automation of fraud detection reduces overhead, but false positives can create friction for legitimate customers. Hence, businesses often adopt a human-in-the-loop approach for final verification (C.-C. Chen et al., 2020).

Table 13. NLP techniques for fraud detection

Technique	*Description*	*Impact*
Text Classification	Detects anomalies in language patterns	Reduces manual screening; speeds up alerts
Semantic Similarity	Groups suspicious texts with known fraudulent examples	Early detection of risk patterns
Risk Profiling	Generates risk scores by analyzing textual and numerical data	Prioritizes high-risk cases for review

NLP-Based Fraud Detection Pipeline

Figure 7. A simplified pipeline illustrating how NLP processes help detect fraud

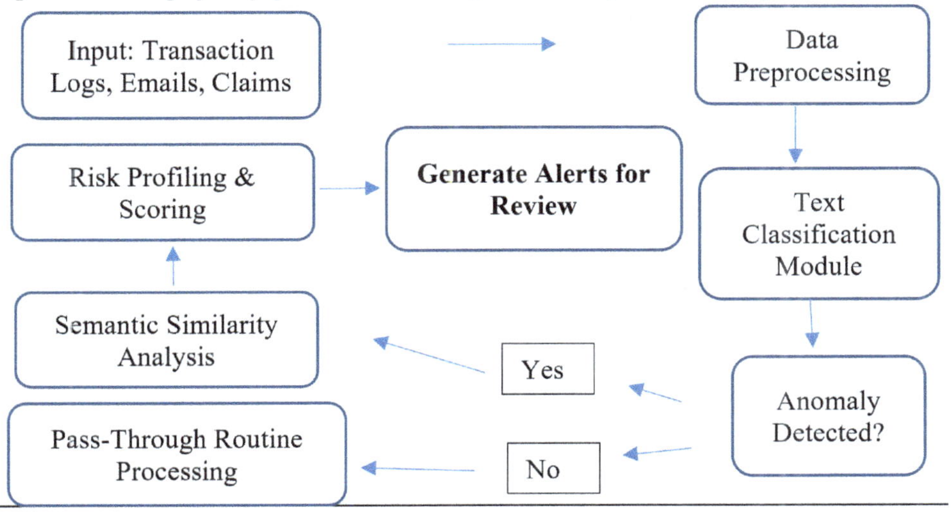

Simple Fraud-Related Text Classification

```
from transformers import pipeline

# Load a pre-trained text classification model (e.g., for
detecting anomalies)
fraud_classifier = pipeline("text-classification", mod-
el="distilbert-base-uncased-finetuned-sst-2-english")
# Sample suspicious transaction description
text = "The claim reports a refund of $10,000 repeated
across multiple transactions within 24 hours."
# Classify the text
result = fraud_classifier(text)
print ("Classification Result:", result)
```

Automated Document Processing for Financial Efficiency

Banks, insurance firms, and lending companies routinely handle large volumes of forms, contracts, statements, or policy documents. Manual review is error-prone and expensive. NLP-based **document understanding** solutions incorporate optical character recognition (OCR) with text extraction and classification:

- **OCR and Layout Analysis**: Digitizes scanned paperwork into structured text.
- **Entity Extraction**: Identifies key fields—dates, amounts, addresses, interest rates, client credentials—directly from textual descriptions.
- **Policy Compliance**: Checks for mandatory clauses in contracts or ensures that disclaimers are present, vital for regulatory compliance.
- **Automated Workflow**: Transferred extracted data to the downstream systems (loan management systems, claims processing systems) for generation of real time decisions.

NLP is also used by financial institutions to create the same kind of consistent, compliant customer communications as customized investment reports or summary statements—any communicating with the customer at all—thus further decreasing manual tasks and speeding up client facing processes.

Market Sentiment Analysis and Investment Strategy

Stock or commodity prices in financial markets are highly influenced by the perception of public. NLP takes the daily news, tweets, earning call transcripts, and blog posts and parses this ream for signals that might impact valuations for the investors, traders, and analysts. Popular approaches:

1. **Earnings Call Summaries**: Summarizing transcripts of quarterly earnings calls to build up investor sentiment, or management forward guidance on earnings call summaries.
2. **News Impact Scoring**: Breaking news event influence calculator (Likelihood that a breaking news event will impact a certain stock or sector, based on the sentiment polarity of the source and the overall influence of the source).
3. **Social Media Scraping**: Following "influencers" (financial influencers), or trending hashtags, on platforms like Twitter or Reddit, and monitoring a change in the retail investor sentiment. GameStop saga in 2021 illustrated how online communities can substantially affect stock prices.

Armed with sentiment scores, hedge funds might integrate these signals into algorithmic trading strategies or factor them into fundamental analysis. While powerful, sentiment-based approaches can be noisy and require robust risk management, as correlation does not always equate to causation.

Real-Life Example: During the 2021 GameStop saga, NLP tools tracked surges in negative and volatile sentiments on social media, enabling hedge funds to adjust their trading strategies accordingly.

Challenges: Sentiment signals can be noisy and require robust risk management. Misinterpretation of sentiment can lead to false alarms, so many institutions adopt a human-in-the-loop approach for final decision-making.

Sentiment Analysis on Financial News

from transformers import pipeline

```
# Load a sentiment analysis pipeline
sentiment_analyzer = pipeline ("sentiment-analysis", mod-
el="distilbert-base-uncased-finetuned-sst-2-english")
# Sample financial news headline
headline = "Earnings call reveals unexpected drop in quar-
terly revenue amid economic slowdown."
# Analyze sentiment
```

```
sentiment = sentiment_analyzer(headline)
print ("Sentiment Analysis:", sentiment)
```

NLP IN HEALTHCARE

Healthcare generates enormous volumes of unstructured text—from clinical notes and lab reports to radiology findings and physician observations. NLP-based solutions convert this raw text into structured, actionable insights, improving clinical decision-making, research, and patient care.

Electronic Health Record (EHR) Analysis and Summarization

Healthcare systems generate voluminous clinical notes, which are often unstructured text describing patient history, lab findings, radiology reports, and physician observations. NLP-based solutions transform these notes into structured data:

- **Medical Entity Recognition**: Identifies diagnoses (ICD codes), medications (RxNorm codes), anatomical references, or procedure mentions.
- **Symptom and Timeline Extraction**: Identifies the symptom to associate with time intervals for chronology disease tracking.
- **Summarization**: producing succinct discharge summaries or tags of the important risk factors, thereby sparing clinicians from long reading of free-form text.

Better decisions can be made using these structured insights and it can also open the door for advanced analytics, such as detecting patterns of complications, relationship between complications and different types of medications, and medication errors. On the one hand, data privacy (HIPAA in the US, GDPR in the EU) requires the handling of patient-sensitive information to be secure. Regulations are compiled by researchers using translation techniques such as de-identification of patient data or advanced encryption.

Key Facts

- Up to **80%** of healthcare data is unstructured.
- Structured EHR data can improve diagnostic accuracy and reduce reading time by **40–50%**.

- Proper summarization may decrease the risk of missing critical details like medication interactions.

Table 14. Core functions of EHR analysis using NLP

Function	*Technique*	*Outcome/Benefit*
Medical Entity Recognition	NER with domain-specific models (e.g., SciSpacy)	Extracts diagnoses, medications, procedures
Symptom & Timeline Extraction	Rule-based & ML approaches	Chronologically organizes clinical events
Summarization	Transformer-based summarization (e.g., BERT variants)	Produces concise summaries for rapid review

EHR NLP Processing Pipeline

Figure 8. A breakdown of the data transformation process for EHR information through natural language processing

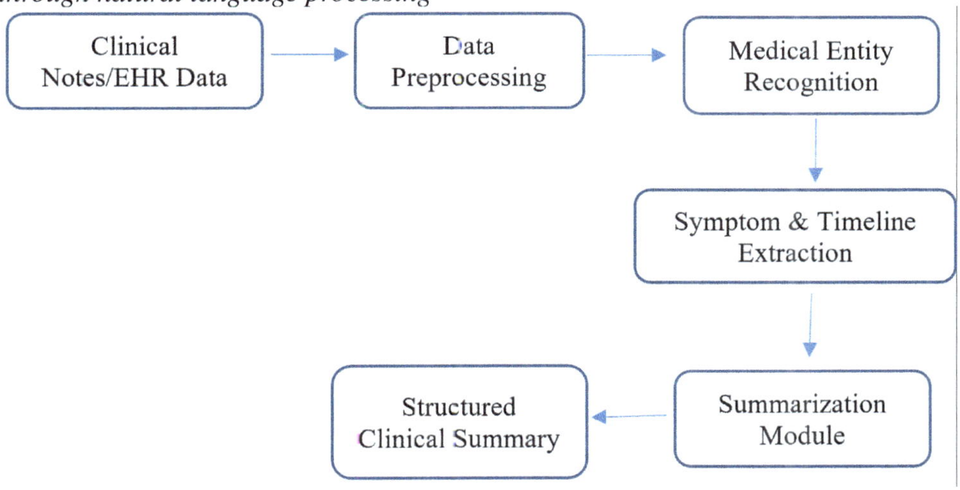

Extracting Medical Entities with SciSpacy

```
import spacy
import scispacy
from scispacy.linking import EntityLinker
```

```
# Load a SciSpacy model
nlp = spacy.load("en_core_sci_sm")
# Add a UMLS Entity Linker to map entities to standard medi-
cal codes
nlp.add_pipe("scispacy_linker", config={"resolve_abbrevia-
tions": True, "linker_name": "umls"})
# Sample EHR text
ehr_text = """
```

Patient presents with acute chest pain, elevated troponin levels, and shortness of breath.

History includes hypertension and type 2 diabetes. ECG shows ST-segment elevation.

```
"""
doc = nlp(ehr_text)
# Print extracted entities and their UMLS links
for ent in doc.ents:
print (f"Entity: {ent.text}, Label: {ent.label_}")
for umls_ent in ent._. umls_ents:
print (f" - UMLS Concept ID: {umls_ent[0]}, Score: {umls_en-
t[1]:.2f}")
```

Clinical Research and Literature Mining

Medical innovation relies heavily on analyzing research papers, trial outcomes, and case reports. NLP-based text mining expedites these efforts:

1. **Automated Systematic Reviews**: Systems scan thousands of scientific articles for relevant search terms and filter out extraneous material. Summaries can highlight study results, methodologies, and populations studied.
2. **Drug Discovery**: By linking gene or protein mentions with diseases, side effects, or chemical compounds, text mining fosters hypothesis generation for novel therapeutics.
3. **Adverse Event Detection**: Social media data, patient forums, or electronic diaries can reveal drug side effects or interactions that might not surface in controlled clinical trials.

By accelerating literature reviews and merging disparate data sources, NLP reduces the time from hypothesis to validated insight, which is pivotal in fast-moving fields like oncology or virology.

Summarizing Medical Research Papers

from transformers import pipeline

```
# Load a pre-trained summarization model
summarizer = pipeline ("summarization", model="facebook/
bart-large-cnn")
# Example abstract from a research paper
abstract = """
```

Recent advancements in immunotherapy have significantly improved the survival rates for patients with melanoma.

However, treatment responses vary, and the underlying mechanisms remain poorly understood. This study explores

the correlation between tumor mutational burden and response to PD-1 inhibitors in a cohort of 200 patients.

```
"""
summary = summarizer (abstract, max_length=50, min_
length=25, do_sample=False)
print("Summary:", summary[0]['summary_text'])
```

Patient Interaction and Virtual Care Support

In an age of telemedicine, NLP chatbots help patients with common inquiries, appointment scheduling, and medication adherence:

- **Symptom Checkers**: Patients describing certain symptoms (e.g., headaches, rashes) are given initial advice or triage suggestions. Some chatbots integrate basic medical guidelines, though disclaimers clarify that they do not replace professional consultation.
- **Chronic Disease Management**: Automated systems can monitor text logs together with short diaries from patients who have diabetes and mental health conditions and cardiovascular disease. NLP technology detects warning signs

and irregular medical data through its analysis (such as changes in daily insulin consumption and manifestations of depressive behaviors).

- **Language Translation**: Healthcare providers achieve better care of non-English-speaking patients through the implementation of machine translation methods in communicating with these patients.

The solutions provide significant improvements in accessibility yet users need to proceed with caution. The adoption of automated advice remains dangerous when automated systems do not achieve sufficient model accuracy or patients fail to understand provided disclaimers. When used as a supportive tool NLP functions under the supervision of professional healthcare staff to prevent possible cases of misdiagnosis or confusion.

Symptom Checker Example Using Transformers

from transformers import pipeline

```
# Load a question-answering pipeline
qa_pipeline = pipeline("question-answering", mod-
el="distilbert-base-cased-distilled-squad")
# Example patient symptom query
context = """
```

Patient reports a severe headache, mild fever, and sensitivity to light. There is no history of trauma.

```
"""
question = "What symptom could indicate a migraine?"
result = qa_pipeline(question=question, context=context)
print ("Symptom Checker Answer:", result['answer'])
```

NLP IN E-COMMERCE AND RETAIL

Recommendation Systems Optimization with Textual Insights

E-commerce giants rely heavily on recommendation systems to guide user purchases, cross-sell, and personalize the shopping experience. NLP complements standard collaborative filtering techniques (which look at past user behavior) by analyzing textual data such as:

1. **Product Descriptions**: Systems can cluster or label items based on shared style, usage, or target consumer segments (e.g., "eco-friendly clothing," "vegan snacks").
2. **Review Analysis**: Extracting sentiment regarding various product attributes (quality, durability, shipping experience) identifies items that best match a user's preferences.
3. **User Queries**: Understanding the textual queries typed in search bars (e.g., "waterproof hiking backpack with laptop compartment") helps tailor results that precisely fit a multi-faceted need.

Beyond boosting sales, refined recommendations diminish the frustration of irrelevant suggestions, potentially increasing user retention and brand loyalty.

Key Facts

- **Improved Engagement:** Integrating NLP has been shown to increase click-through rates by **20–25%** and conversion rates by **15–20%**.
- **Customer Retention:** Refined recommendations reduce irrelevant suggestions, thereby increasing user retention and brand loyalty.

Basic Text Similarity for Recommendations

Below is an example using Python with spaCy to compute similarity between a user query and product descriptions:

```
import spacy

# Load spaCy's English model
nlp = spacy.load("en_core_web_md")
# Sample product descriptions
products = {
"Eco-friendly Jacket": "This jacket is made from recycled materials and offers sustainable fashion.",
"Waterproof Hiking Backpack": "A durable backpack with waterproof features and a laptop compartment.",
"Vegan Snack Pack": "A selection of healthy, plant-based snacks for on-the-go lifestyles."
}
```

```
# User query
query = "Looking for a waterproof backpack that can also
hold my laptop."
# Process query
query_doc = nlp(query)
# Compute similarity scores
similarities = {product: nlp(desc). similarity(query_doc)
for product, desc in products.items()}
# Output the recommended product based on highest similarity
recommended_product = max (similarities, key=similarities.
get)
print ("Recommended Product:", recommended_product)
```

This snippet computes similarity between a user query and product descriptions to generate recommendations.

Inventory and Supply Chain Coordination

Retail business operations handle sophisticated supply systems that experience fluctuating customer needs due to seasonal patterns as well as promotional activities and environmental factors. Information available in supplier messages along with shipping records and market-related documents supports companies in managing their inventory.

- **Demand Forecasting**: Social media analytics using NLP technology can identify emerging trends for particular fashion patterns and popular consumer items that help organizations prepare their stock inventory proactively.
- **Supplier Email Processing**: The system auto-classifies supplier email entries to deliver immediate urgent supply shortage or delay notifications to logistics staff members thus avoiding stockouts.
- **Regional Sentiment**: Regional social media discussions about labor practices and environmental concerns help organizations identify potential obstacles that compels them to consider different supply and delivery options.

Advanced analytics which combines text-based signals with POS transaction data leads to better forecasting accuracy which reduces stockholding expenses and prevents customer losses due to running out of stock.

User-Generated Content Moderation and Product Discovery

Online retail websites encourage their customers to submit both product reviews and Q&A discussions along with direct content about product usage. The content moderation through NLP-based systems guarantees compliance with set community guidelines.

- **Toxicity and Harassment Detection**: Flagging offensive language or defamatory statements in user comments.
- **Spam Filtering**: Installments of spam filtering systems detect promotion and harmful links which deteriorate customer trust.
- **Keyword Analysis for Trends**: The analysis of popular search terms enables companies to detect persistent customer demands about product attribute updates and shipping issues.

The combined feedback system drives strategic product development choices and emerges as a basis for new product categories. The implementation of well-managed user feedback leads to an improved trustworthy brand image for retailers.

Key Facts

- Content moderation execution that succeeds in improving user interactions also leads to an 18% decrease in customer departure rates.
- The application of NLP for keyword trend analysis generates product roadmap-based decisions which lead to a 10–15% improvement in customer satisfaction.

CHALLENGES AND ETHICAL CONSIDERATIONS

Data Privacy and Regulatory Constraints

NLP operates on delicate personal data sets across financial sectors as well as healthcare and HR and consumer marketing industries. Compliance with data protection regulations (e.g., GDPR, CCPA) demands:

1. **Consent and Transparency**: The processing system must provide clear information about user data management procedures and explain what uses the data obtains.

2. **De-Identification**: Before model training takes place systems need to employ de-identification methods that hide personal identifiers in text because re-identification poses a risk.
3. **Secure Storage and Processing**: Access to raw data and model outputs must be strictly controlled and encrypted, particularly if text reveals financial or medical details.

Breaches of privacy can lead to heavy fines, reputational harm, and legal exposure. Responsible data governance frameworks specify data retention policies, role-based access controls, and robust auditing of data usage in the NLP pipeline (Liu et al., 2024).

Bias and Fairness: Ethical AI in Business Operations

Algorithmic bias emerges if training data or model design systematically skews outcomes against certain demographics. In NLP, this can manifest as:

- **Gender Stereotypes**: A resume screener that overly associates nursing with females or engineering with males.
- **Ethnic, Racial, or Age Bias**: Sentiment analysis misclassifying certain dialects or slang as negative.
- **Unintended Negative Outcomes**: Automated chatbots that fail to interpret queries from non-native speakers, leading to frustration and limited support.

Mitigation measures include curating diverse datasets, implementing fairness-aware learning algorithms, performing robust bias diagnostics, and regularly auditing the performance for different user groups (Reznikov & Member, 2023). Moreover, business processes should allow human intervention to override or correct automated results that appear discriminatory (Vertsel & Rumiantsau, 2024).

Interpretability and Explainable NLP

In regulated industries—finance, healthcare, legal—stakeholders demand to know why a model made a certain decision. Traditional neural networks, especially large transformers, operate as "black boxes." Techniques to enhance interpretability include:

- **Attention Visualization**: Display which tokens the model deems most relevant when generating an output or classification.

- **LIME or SHAP**: Model-agnostic methods that approximate local decision boundaries, highlighting key features (e.g., words) that influenced the classification of a document.
- **Rule Extraction**: Attempting to derive simplified symbolic rules from neural network parameters, though this often remains experimental in practice.

While interpretability research has progressed, bridging the gap between advanced deep learning performance and transparent, trustworthy explanations remains challenging. Business leaders must weigh the risk of "unexplainable" models against the competitive edge they might offer.

Resource Management and Scalability

High-performing NLP systems, especially large language models, can be computationally demanding. Potential issues include:

1. **Hardware Costs**: Training or even running inference with multi-billion-parameter models demands specialized GPUs or TPUs, which can be cost-prohibitive for smaller enterprises.
2. **Deployment Latency**: Real-time applications (e.g., customer chat) need sub-second responses. Large models might need optimization, pruning, or distillation to meet these constraints.
3. **Maintenance Overhead**: Language usage shifts, new slang or brand names emerge. Models degrade if not updated or retrained, which entails an ongoing commitment of resources.

Organizations address these concerns via cloud-based model hosting, containerization, caching strategies, or synergy with smaller custom fine-tuned models for each domain, thereby balancing performance with practical cost management (Leidner et al., 2018).

IMPLEMENTING NLP EFFECTIVELY

Project Planning and Stakeholder Alignment

Any undertaking of NLP success relies on defining clear goals and developing use cases that stakeholders understand. For example:

- **Define the Business Problem**: The business requirements establish the goal of diminishing service queues, improving invoice handling speed or achieving enhanced product insight. Setting quantifiable success metrics (like a 30% reduction in support costs or a 10% improvement in user satisfaction) fosters accountability.
- **Assemble Cross-Functional Teams**: Data scientists, domain experts, compliance officers, and user experience designers must collaborate to ensure that the system addresses real user pain points and adheres to legal constraints.
- **Phased Rollout**: Instead of aiming for an all-encompassing system from day one, organizations can pilot a smaller scope (like analyzing a single product line) and validate ROI before broadening the solution.

The planning phase also considers data governance policies, budget constraints, and user feedback loops, setting the stage for systematic and successful NLP integration.

Data Collection, Annotation, and Quality Control

NLP models feed on data, but that data must be relevant, accurate, and representative. Steps include:

1. **Data Inventory**: Identifying potential sources of textual data—CRM logs, emails, spreadsheets, PDF documents, etc.—and assessing data volumes, formats, and coverage of relevant topics.
2. **Cleaning and Normalization**: Removing duplicates, reconciling character encodings, handling misspellings or non-textual artifacts.
3. **Labeling Processes**: Logical data organization involves employees who perform manual example labeling tasks during supervised tasks such as sentiment analysis and entity detection. An annotation setting with operational guidelines produces uniform results from human labelers. Available active learning methodologies help cut down labeling expenses by concentrating on cases with unclear outcomes.
4. **Quality Checks**: A collection of quality check metrics helps validate the consistency achieved by annotators across labels. Large-scale inspections of the dataset help detect incorrect classification labels as well as absent annotations.

The data pipelines utilize version control mechanisms that record changes made to labeled data sets alongside heuristics modifications. Domain bias can be avoided with over-dependency on a single data source, which allows us to combine multiple data sources to form more generalized NLP solutions.

Model Development Cycles: Iteration and Continuous Integration

NLP model development follows repeated cycles where each stage advances because of assessment feedback obtained from processed results. The continuous cycle allows teams to boost their results while they track and maintain responsible updates to code and their data and infrastructure systems. The article provides essential directions and specifications for implementing these cyclic processes.

1. Establishing a Baseline

The core beginning point involves developing a straightforward model such as logistic regression or fundamental neural networks which receive core element training. First designs a basic system which establishes benchmarks for performance (such as accuracy or F1-score) that all following models have to outperform. The baseline strategy shows if the dataset contains all necessary content and enables teams to verify correct alignment between data and evaluation components.

2. Experimenting with Advanced Architectures

Teams move onto advanced approaches for model development after creating a baseline. Most teams progress to transformer-based models by applying pre-trained checkpoints from BERT or GPT variants which they refine using domain-specific information. Researchers determine added meaningful value through comparisons between the new advanced model output and the established baseline system (Devlin et al., 2019). At this stage, you may also consider investigating architectures like convolutional networks or recurrent models when you face certain specific data properties (long text sequences or different sentence structures).

3. Hyperparameter Tuning and Tools

This can have a big impact on performance of a model's hyperparameters like batch size, learning rate, token sequence length and even the optimizer to use. To avoid arbitrarily picked values, they often use automated tool such as Optuna or Hyperopt or Ray Tune to systematically search over the given parameter space. It provides such a structured approach that you may find the can expose new synergies (like the perfect combination between dropout, and weight decay), or the ones that doesn't really matter any further.

4. Cross-Validation for Robustness

Model stability needs to be evaluated, and cross validation is one of the proven ways. Teams avoid overfitting by training with some, validating with others. Also, in cross-validation, we test whether model behavior continues to behave the same way in the additional data subsets and therefore does it generalize or it is random chance. In case of wide variations in the results across the folds, additional data cleaning or feature engineering might be warranted.

5. Continuous Integration and Deployment

After an architecture and a hyperparameter set reliably perform, the next focus becomes integrating these changes into the broader workflow. Continuous Integration (CI) pipelines are pipelines which automates the process of merging code, running test suites, and ensure that new commit does not disrupt other processes or performance metrics. As part of CI, some organizations extend this to Continuous Deployment (CD), killing successful builds automatically to staging, or production environments. It allows for the rapid iteration free from stability sacrifice, as code is updated and data adjusted and a model refined in regular cycles.

6. Tracking and Experiment Logging

Records must be kept carefully for frequent iteration. On the other hand, teams log hyperparameters, metrics and code version of all the experiments through portals like MLflow, W&B or in-house solution. Details of these experiment histories allow the data scientist and engineer to ascertain exactly what performance boost really did — a new tokenizer, a new learning rate, or domain-specific embeddings – and be able to reproduce the setup later. Without good logging, that flurry becomes a daily lost opportunity to learn something valuable.

As a result, organizations cycle through this pattern of refinement of their NLP models in a controlled, yet agile manner. A baseline clears what is the core data behavior, the advanced architectures push performance boundary further, the hyperparameter tuning extracts more accuracy, and the cross validation confirms stability. The last part of this loop is automated integration and complete experiment tracking, which together with loop above let one have systematic improvements which are aligned with business objectives.

Testing, Validation, and Deployment at Scale

When deploying the model into production mode complete validation procedures must take place first:

1. **Test on Real-World Scenarios**: The model validation requires testing on real-world scenarios through a test set which represents how users interact with the system.
2. **Stress Testing**: Testing should focus on extreme scenarios that push system limits by using lengthy queries as well as ambiguous questions and untypical domain situations.
3. **User Acceptance Testing (UAT)**: requires feedback collection from customer support agents and marketing analysts and compliance officers to verify that the tool satisfies usability and interpretability requirements.
4. **Deployment Patterns**: The deployment environment offers two primary options which include horizontal scaling of microservices deployed through containers along with on-device inference capable of running offline. Large businesses that utilize three environments (development, testing, and production) implement automation to revert systems if unexpected problems occur.
5. **Monitoring and Alerts**: The deployment phase needs real-time metric tracking which includes throughputs and latencies as well as accuracy drifts and user satisfaction levels. The alerts or dashboard systems alert users to significant anomalies through which the model misses complex situations such as unexpected shifts in classification errors or unanticipated changes in sentiment.

NLP solutions requiring regular updates and bug fixes and refinement and user participation will achieve higher performance levels and user trust across extended durations.

FUTURE DIRECTIONS IN BUSINESS NLP

Voice Interfaces and Multimodal Fusion

As voice assistants (like Amazon Alexa or Google Assistant) proliferate, the boundary between text-based NLP and speech processing blurs. As a result:

- **Voice Commerce**: Retailers experiment with voice-based ordering, product discovery, and chatbots that respond to spoken language.
- **Advanced Healthcare Diagnostics**: Systems interpret verbal descriptions of symptoms or track changes in vocal attributes that might correlate with depression, neurological disorders, or respiratory issues.
- **Multimodal Applications**: Combined analysis of text, images, or video (e.g., analyzing e-commerce listings that have textual descriptions plus user-

uploaded images). The synergy of multiple data types can reveal deeper insights (like brand sentiment in images or text-based product endorsements).

Ongoing research in cross-modal transformers and embedding fusion indicates that future NLP systems will likely operate seamlessly across textual, auditory, and visual modes, broadening business applications (Bharadwaj, 2024).

Real-Time Analytics, Adaptive Learning, and Continual Training

Business situations can shift rapidly. Emerging slang, new competitor products, or changes in compliance rules can render static models outdated. Real-time analytics and adaptive models address this:

- **Streaming Pipelines**: Process data as it arrives—e.g., social media streams or inbound user queries—updating sentiment or classification in near real-time.
- **Online Learning**: Instead of retraining from scratch, models incrementally update parameters with new user data. This approach is particularly appealing for chatbots that need to adapt to trending topics or newly reported bugs.
- **A/B Testing for Model Updates**: The deployment of new model versions in production for testing happens through A/B Testing which measures performance against real-time data before extensive distribution.

These approaches maintain the value of NLP solutions as they reduce the impact of unexpected domain and data changes. The effectiveness of versioning together with monitoring tools must stay strong to stop bad performance or complete data loss.

Domain-Specific Large Language Models and Zero-Shot Applications

LLMs in general purpose are of use, but domain-specific large language models will be successful:

- **FinBERT / FinGPT**: The FinBERT or FinGPT system achieves precision through financial document training for extracting risks and compliance information.
- **BioBERT / Clinical LLMs**: The special applications of BioBERT / Clinical LLMs lead to better performance in processing medical files such as patient records and research papers and case reports.

- **Legal Transformers**: Legal Transformers emphasize processing documents that include legal language as well as legal precedents and contracts while understanding specialized terminology.

Generic LLMs cannot keep up to these specialized models, especially that they need domain-specific corpus for building them. Zero-shot or few-shot learning through specialized model applications has the potential to eliminate the need for extensive labeled data which allows NLP to reach more organizations and emerging markets in developing nations.

The Growing Emphasis on Ethical Governance and Regulatory Oversight

Launching NLP technology into critical decision systems will create a significant increase in ethical questions to address. Potential developments include:

- **Mandatory Transparency**: The law should enforce transparency in human-understandable fashion during AI decision-making primarily for hiring and lending and healthcare applications.
- **Audited Model Lifecycles**: External auditors check whether training data and labeling procedures and refinement processes comply with fairness and security standards through audited Model Lifecycles.
- **Open-Source Partnerships**: The implementation of open-source partnerships serves to advance mutual sharing between industries (such as finance or medicine) to generate reliable tested solutions.

Building organizational accountability should be recognized as the fundamental requirement for success. Organizations that make fairness and privacy along with social responsibility their priorities will strengthen their reputation base while getting users to trust them along with staying in compliance with emerging global regulations.

CONCLUSION

Since its initial period of rule-based operation Natural Language Processing (NLP) has transformed into its modern form. The discipline moved from using manually made grammar and simple statistical models toward building neural networks with great ability to analyze big text and create logical discussions. The enhanced capabilities brought by NLP technology allow businesses to develop automation systems for document handling while extracting consumer information and enhancing user experience and HR efficiency and risk management and operational optimization in complex global business activities (Wang et al., 2024).

Successfully implementing the creative value requires navigating multiple obstacles in the process. Implementing data privacy measures requires strategic planning because stakeholders need to address model bias together with decision explanation requirements and data security approaches across diversity groups. Technical methods fail to deliver results when they disregard social and ethical as well as infrastructural aspects. The successful implementation of NLP projects depends on multidirectional team effort combined with continuous cycle improvements and organizational flexibility toward new market developments and acquired knowledge.

The chapter demonstrates NLP provides more than algorithms as it represents an integrated method to extract business value from language data. Acceptance of the NLP approach leads to productive innovations including texting support systems that improve customer support efficiency alongside specialized language models that extract valuable signals from financial documents and medical reports. By embracing best practices—clear goal definition, robust data curation, fair and interpretable modeling, thorough testing, and agile deployment—companies can transform unstructured linguistic content into a continuous source of strategic intelligence.

Looking forward, the integration of voice, images, real-time analytics, and domain specialization signals that NLP will only grow more indispensable. With careful governance and responsible AI principles, the era of language-aware businesses can usher in deeper client relationships, more inclusive hiring, improved compliance, and data-informed decision-making at an unprecedented scale. The language we speak and write will no longer remain an untapped resource in enterprise data lakes; it will evolve into a dynamic, actionable asset unlocking new realms of opportunity.

REFERENCES

Agarwal, R., Vieillard, N., Stanczyk, P., Ramos, S., Geist, M., & Bachem, O. (2023). Gkd: Generalized knowledge distillation for auto-regressive sequence models. *ArXiv Preprint ArXiv:2306.13649, 12*

Bharadwaj, C. (2024). *NLP applications and their use cases for modern enterprises.*

Chen, C.-C., Huang, H.-H., & Chen, H.-H. (2020). *NLP in FinTech Applications: Past.* Present and Future.

Chen, K., Fei, C., Bi, Z., Liu, J., Peng, B., Zhang, S., Pan, X., Xu, J., Wang, J., Yin, C. H., & Associates. (2024). Deep Learning and Machine Learning—Natural Language Processing: From Theory to Application. *ArXiv Preprint ArXiv:2411.05026.*

Cheung, M. (2024). *A Reality check of the benefits of LLM in business.* 1–20.

Devlin, J., Chang, M. W., Lee, K., & Toutanova, K. (2019). BERT: Pre-training of deep bidirectional transformers for language understanding. *NAACL HLT 2019 - 2019 Conference of the North American Chapter of the Association for Computational Linguistics: Human Language Technologies - Proceedings of the Conference.*

Grohs, M., Abb, L., Elsayed, N., & Rehse, J. R. (2024). Large Language Models Can Accomplish Business Process Management Tasks. *Lecture Notes in Business Information Processing, 492*, 453–465. Advance online publication. DOI: 10.1007/978-3-031-50974-2_34

Hilditch, A., Webb, D., & Ba', J. (2023). *Natural language processing on customer note data.*

Leidner, J. L., Stevenson, M., & Court, R. (2018). *Challenges and Opportunities of NLP for HR Applications: A Discussion Paper.*

Liu, S., Liu, G., Zhu, B., Luo, Y., Wu, L., & Wang, R. (2024). Balancing Innovation and Privacy: Data Security Strategies in Natural Language Processing Applications. *2024 5th International Conference on Machine Learning and Computer Application (ICMLCA)*, 609–613.

Mashaabi, M., Alotaibi, A., Qudaih, H., Alnashwan, R., & Al-Khalifa, H. (2022). Natural Language Processing in Customer Service: A Systematic Review. *ArXiv.*

Orza, P. (2024). *11 Real-Life Examples of NLP in Action.* Made in Webflow.

Reznikov, B. R., & Member, F. C. (2023). *How Natural Language Processing Is Revolutionizing Business Operations.* Forbes Technology Council.

Vaswani, A., Shazeer, N., Parmar, N., Uszkoreit, J., Jones, L., Gomez, A. N., Kaiser, Ł., & Polosukhin, I. (2017). Attention is all you need. *Advances in Neural Information Processing Systems*.

Vertsel, A., & Rumiantsau, M. (2024). *Hybrid LLM/Rule-based Approaches to Business Insights Generation from Structured Data*.

Wang, L., Cheng, Y., Xiang, A., Zhang, J., & Yang, H. (2024). Application of natural language processing in financial risk detection. *ArXiv Preprint ArXiv:2406.09765*.

Woensel, W. Van, & Motie, S. (2024). *NLP4PBM : A Systematic Review on Process Extraction using Natural Language Processing with Rule-based, Machine and Deep Learning Methods*. 1–50.

Wood, T. (2024). *Business uses of natural language processing - the 2024 capabilities of NLP*.

Chapter 5
Predictive Analytics for Customer Retention in E-Commerce:
Evaluating Model Accuracy and Its Impact on Retention Strategies

Parihar Suresh Dahake
http://orcid.org/0000-0002-2286-4120
School of Management, Ramdeobaba University, Nagpur, India

Nihar Suresh Dahake
http://orcid.org/0009-0007-8971-9247
Dr. Ambedkar Institute of Management Studies and Research, Nagpur, India

ABSTRACT

Despite the rise of predictive analytics as a breakthrough tool for minimizing churn, client retention remains a major challenge for e-commerce businesses. This study looks into the accuracy of machine learning models in predicting customer attrition and the practical consequences for retention strategies, with a focus on Nagpur, India's fast-expanding e-commerce sector. This study trains and tests four predictive models' logistic regression, random forest, support vector machine (SVM), and a neural network with behavioral, demographic, and transactional information on a dataset of 15,000 customer transactions from a well-known e-commerce platform in Nagpur. The random forest classifier, which got the best accuracy (89.7%) and F1-score (0.86), shows higher skill in detecting at-risk consumers, as model performance is measured by accuracy, precision, recall, and F1-score. The study then uses Orange Software testing with 500 consumers to investigate the incorporation of predictive insights into retention strategies.

DOI: 10.4018/979-8-3693-6690-5.ch005

1) INTRODUCTION

Predictive analytics essentially provides a clinical tool for decision-making process by which future events can be anticipated and the actions foreseen can be decided accordingly. It provides possibility to predict events before they actually happen, thus facilitating planning for the forthcoming events. There has been an increased interest in applying the data mining approach in developing prediction model in recent years. The metaverse's virtual economy, leveraging deep learning and analytics to enhance customer engagement and business competitiveness ("The Virtual Economy of the Metaverse," 2022). The churn prediction models using first product-category purchase sequences and logistic regression (Miguéis et al., 2012), The data mining technology is an efficient tool in extracting patterns and knowledge from the large size data within a reasonable time frame, creating further more possibilities to detect the potential tendency of any phenomenon contemplated. The ultimate purpose of customer retention is the mitigation of risks and the improvement of the financial stability of the firm. Customers are the most precious resource since the demand for goods and services and the profit of the prevailing business strategy are linked to the existence of the customers. Daily churn prediction improves accuracy with LSTM, surpassing monthly models (Alboukaey et al., 2020). Irrespective of the study nature, what really distinguishes well the today's state-of-the-art in predictive analytics of customer retention is its superior applicability to almost every sector/ activity involving a competitive environment. Ultimately churn analysis is carried out in order to evaluate the top performing algorithm. This era is seeing an intense competition which is why customer retention is one of the growing concerns especially in case of e-commerce firms. The conventional method is inferior to the proposed methodology for suggestion accuracy, simplicity, coverage rate, and recall rate (Guo et al., 2018). The Comprehensive churn analysis integrates definitions, models, and diverse business applications effectively (Ahn et al., 2020) The majority of researches has been done in the past regarding prediction of potential churners. A few propose an integrated framework to recommend personalized retention actions to control the same which typically goes unnoticed. It comprises an automated approach to facilitate the lesser knowledgeable managerial with a few retention recommendations each differing in cost.

E-commerce can be defined as the buying and selling of goods as well as services through the medium of internet. Due to the increase in computer literacy, better internet connectivity and the little time invested in the shopping process, e-commerce has been evolved as one of the contemporary shopping styles, preferred by the customers. Customer retention can be defined as the ability to hold back an individual for a longer period such that he or she indulges in various recurring transactions. Customer retention is always cheaper than maintaining a new customer.

Also, regular and repeated transactions are the main source of revenue for any firm especially in the e-commerce world. According to a recent worldwide survey, close to 75% of e-commerce firms experience remarkable growth in their profit margins because they retain a good proportion of their customers. Churn modeling seeks to enhance models through data augmentation or algorithmic refinement (Ballings & Van Den Poel, 2012). This is one of the driving forces that has led to the research of customer retention in the domain of ecommerce, trying to understand the intrinsic as well as the extrinsic influences that stimulate customer behavior. As businesses continue to flow, numerous research works are coming up, looking out the interest of e-commerce firms, a majority of which tries to tackle the difficulty of accurately projecting the potential customer losses with the aid of statistical, data mining and/or machine learning methods. The predictive analytics accuracy in high-stakes business decisions, revealing significant model accuracy issues and overestimation (N. S. Dahake et al., 2024). The management of most of the firms is left with a group or a lone candidate retainer; however, they are unaware of the further step that needs to be taken. Mindful of this, the researcher introduces a solution that automates the recommendation process, inspired by the group of actual retention activities. Now that e-commerce has undergone a significant transformation with technological advancement and rise in globalization, the essence of customer retention has also been a major concern for online retailers. and the accessibility and effectiveness with personalized learning support (P. S. Dahake, Mohare, et al., 2024), In the light of the new findings, model accuracy has been evaluated using the aforementioned classification models. And Machine learning predicts consumer behavior, enhancing personalized marketing strategies effectively (P. S. Dahake, Mohare, et al., 2023) although the customer churn prediction accuracy and interpretability through structured sparsity regularization (De Bock & De Caigny, 2021). This section estimates and compares the performance of different models and evaluates the impact of model accuracy on retention strategies and revenue enhancement. predictive analytics in accurate projections and customer behavior knowledge. Forecasting changes in consumer behavior and preferences as buying trends shift depends on predictive analytics (P. S. Dahake & Somani, 2024).

Using these insights, it has been suggested how retailers can better leverage from this data. Thereby in the KBS recombinant, dissimilar product groups are formulated using apriorism and provided a distinct group matching cluster categorization. The analogous group to the specified customer with churning behavior is captured with the cluster classification or offered personalized retention actions

2) LITERATURE REVIEW

The prime thought behind e-commerce initiatives is to make everything digital, in which customers can purchase products from a convenience of their home or any location. Due to their busy lifestyles, customers require such an environment to escape the hassle of visiting a store. Therefore, thousands of e-commerce platforms have been launched worldwide. However, in a place like Nagpur and another city, there is a lack of such platforms.

Figure 1. All keywords analysis by Vosviewer

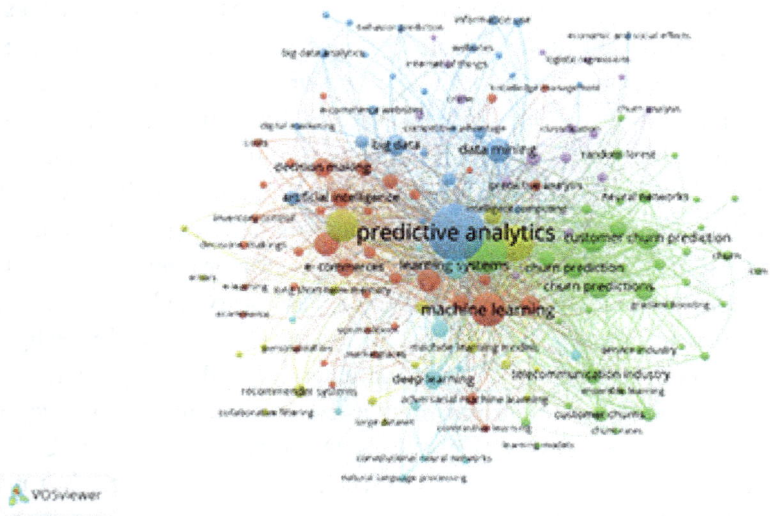

Figure 2. Author keywords analysis by Vosviewer

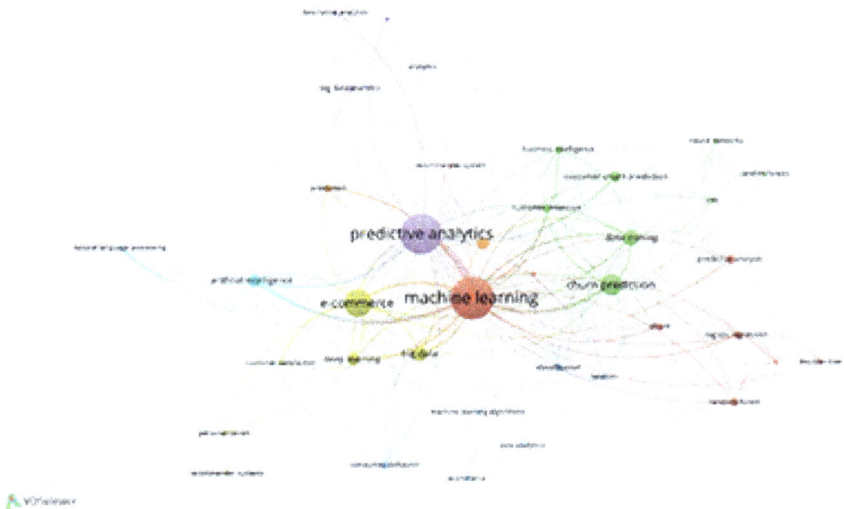

Figure 3. Index keywords analysis by Vosviewer

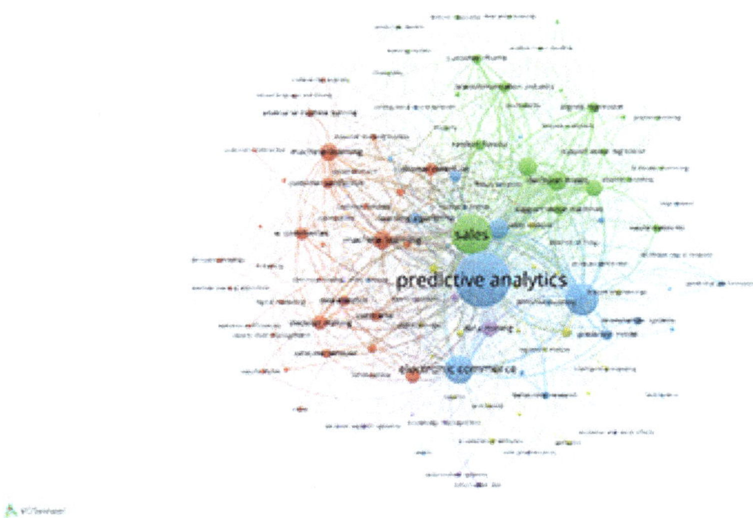

This project will target and implement a new e-commerce platform for the city of Nagpur. Hence, to maintain a continuous profit and run a successful e-commerce platform in the market, customers are the most essential factor. (Sarker, 2021) emphasizes machine learning's critical role in analyzing diverse data types, enhancing intelligent applications, exploring real-world use cases, and addressing challenges with potential future research directions. Supporting to this (De Caigny et al., 2018) Introduced the Logit Leaf Model, a hybrid classification algorithm combining decision trees and logistic regression, enhancing predictive accuracy, comprehensibility, and actionable insights for customer churn prediction. As evidence by (Lalwani et al., 2022) improves churn prediction using machine learning, leveraging Gravitational Search Algorithm, ensemble techniques, and evaluation metrics like AUC reinforcing to this (Coussement et al., 2017) examined the optimized data preparation improves churn prediction, enhancing logistic regression competitiveness with advanced algorithms, boosting retention strategies effectively. Consequently (Z. Liu et al., 2021) shown a hierarchical vision Transformer using Shifted windows, outperforms previous state-of-the-art models in image classification, object detection, and semantic segmentation. Notably (National Cancer Institute, 2020) The JAGS package for R allows for analyzing Bayesian hierarchical models using Markov Chain Monte Carlo, with a mutable state and object-oriented user interface.

In this context, (He et al., 2022)Masked autoencoders (MAE) are scalable self-supervised learners for computer vision, enabling efficient and effective training of large models with improved accuracy and generalization in the similar vein (P. Liu et al., 2023) investigated that the Prompt-based learning in natural language processing allows models to adapt to new scenarios with few or no labeled data, offering powerful and attractive results.More recently (Zonta et al., 2020) Predictive maintenance in Industry 4.0 enhances machine downtime, costs, control, and quality, but requires a multidisciplinary approach to effectively address Industry 4.0 challenges. To address this (Hadiji et al., 2014) cross-game churn prediction model for Free-to-Play games using behavioral analytics, yielding high prediction accuracy across datasets. Thereafter, realization has been observed that any customer purchases in the same or dissimilar product categories, repeatedly exhibit identical cluster behavior before churning. It is evident that, (Runge et al., 2014) highlights effective churn prediction for high-value casual social gamers using neural networks and strategic retention methods. Collectively (Vizine Pereira & Hruschka, 2015) addresses the cold start problem in recommender systems by utilizing the SCOAL algorithm, achieving enhanced accuracy through co-clustering. However, (F., 2018) The random forest technique can be used for feature selection with mean decrease accuracy. Mean reduction assesses the influence of each feature on model accuracy. The model permutes the values of each feature and analyses the changes in model correctness. But in contrast to this, (Shirazi & Mohammadi, 2019) proposes a big data framework integrating Hadoop for predicting retiree customer churn decisions. In fact, (Mitrović et al., 2018) feature classification for telco churn prediction, optimizing performance and efficiency using Pareto multi-criteria optimization. As a result (Vo et al., 2021)enhances customer churn prediction by leveraging unstructured call log data with interpretable machine learning, aiding retention strategies. This study will evaluate the present status of the e-commerce industry in India, change in customer retention behavior, factors influencing their behavior, and existing customer retention methodologies in the e-commerce platform. This research will be beneficial and can assist upcoming e-commerce companies in the size of Nagpur or in any other city. This research can be useful for stakeholders who are running an e-commerce company or intending on establishing a new e-commerce business.

3) PROBLEM STATEMENT

On a global average, it is estimated that there exists a 69.89% shopping cart abandonment rate. The prime source of worry is dropping customers since it costs more to attract new customers than retaining current ones. In dealing with lost customers, the digital world has witnessed a substantial variety of customer profiling strategies recently. Further research on e-commerce shows that lapsed customers posed a huge loss for e-business. Predicting customer purchase behavior in e-commerce, leveraging big data analytics and predictive tools(Cirqueira et al., 2020). On a global average, churned customers were 26 times less probable to embrace loyalty than already existing ones. On the other hand, just a 5% increase in customer spending happens to be internally related to ensuring that there is a 25% increase in profit. At present, e-commerce organizations are struggling in trying to reduce their customer churn. There is a need to deliver the perfect retention strategy at the right time across several touchpoints. Using prior customer purchase behavior, an intelligent model is developed to foresee the customer's chances to purchase again. Customer retention became a major challenge in the current world of the e-commerce industry. In Nagpur, the e-commerce business enterprises are increasing and the concerning industries are facing a major challenge to maintain the customer base for a more extended period. The challenge aware enterprises regarding the need for a system that evaluates customer's return behavior and develops a retentive strategy for individual customers. There exist numerous data of the client's individual retail history which may be utilized to construct a retentive strategy.

4) RESEARCH METHODOLOGY

There have always been customers who will churn regardless of the actions that may be taken and such customers are just too costly to win back. The more sophisticated is to predict bad customers before the churn actually occurs, making targeted retention offers to them to keep them from churning. An integrated framework is introduced to recommend personalized retention actions to control B2C e-commerce customer churn under such an objective.

There are many researches in the past trying to tackle the challenge of accurately predicting potential customer churn with the help of statistical, data mining and/or machine learning strategies. The work has considered various aspects in predicting potential customer churns. However, the strategies proposed in these works would be 'one-size-fits-all' as they are not personalized to appeal to customers, in the same time these works did not consult well-performing churn prediction models to provide recommendation as well.

Methodology The primary objective of this study is comparing different predictive models for the e-commerce companies that helps them to sensitize their potential churners; and further to understand the impact of accuracy level of the predictive model on the proposed retention strategies. A descriptive survey is conducted on 376 young people in Nagpur to exanimate above mentioned objectives. The predictive model accuracy is measured on multiple algorithms used for different machine learning models and its impact on the proposed personalized retention strategies for e-commerce companies in Nagpur is analyzed. E-commerce is the buying and selling of products and services on the internet from mobile apps or e-commerce websites. Customer retention is a concept in which companies provide marketing and retain their customers. 95% of the company retailers is customer retention. Retention is a continuous process of retaining customers. The company cannot control whether customers leave, but it can certainly plan to retain its customers. Retailers devote adequate resources to increase customer loyalty. Customer churn refers to loyal customers leaving and other new customers remaining. Suggestion for customer retention is provided by detecting potential churners. The customer's future behaviour is estimated using predictive analytics. The core idea behind the recommendation system is that customers who are more identical have identical behaviours. Customer can be maintained by offering similar offers to a loyal customer with the same preferences, Decile analysis is a process of customer segmentation. This helps to give personalized strategies for customer maintenance. The number of potential churners is identified based on customer profiles, which is the main thing needed by retailers.

4.1 Data Collection and Preprocessing

The excel data used in the study was converted from an original My SQL data by customer data vendor. The data structure included in the file is seen below. It included some transactional parameters and business metrics of a cross section of customers over the prior twelve months to the analysis date. For all that, they were categorized as "active" in that month, and for some of them, it was indicated that it was the same customer who spends a certain amount of money. Customers were classified as either "churns" or "stayers". The described status held for a period of six months before and after the analysis date. The purpose of the analysis was to study the effectiveness of the churn prediction model in terms of evaluating performance and in its success as a manager of retention strategies.

There are a few steps it may be noted in predicting potential customer churn. The data was collected and pre processed at first. It was based on the transaction and demographic information and business metrics of an e-commerce customer base. The transaction and demographic information is straightforward in nature hypothesis the pre processing part detailed with it whereas the business metrics require manipulation before being used with the implemented models. The "relation" file formatted the data and cut down the list of input parameters that yield good results. It was then decided which churn prediction model to use. The list of companies offering commercial solutions was indeed large and the challenge was slimmed down by evaluating freely available models before selecting a partner. After transformation and normalization, the data split was conducted into two sections. The initial period was used to train the model and the last part was left for testing purposes. A comparison of actual churns with predicted churn probabilities for this segment constituted the analysis results (Renjith, 2015).

4.2 The Objectives of this Study are as Follows

1. To study and understand the existing status of the e-commerce industry in India.
3. To understand the multiple influencing factors from diverse perspectives that influence customer retention behavior in the e-commerce platform.
4. To prepare the Predictive Analytics Model based on the Data Sets
5. To evaluate and check the accuracy of the model.

5. MODEL SELECTION AND EVALUATION TECHNIQUES

The primary focus of the current study is on the consistent evaluation and validation of churn prediction models in a practical environment and on the usage of this data to help the manager in creating relevant and individualized retention actions. The issue will be addressed from a combination of scientific and practical viewpoints to increase the efficiency and efficacy of these models in real business settings. In this context, with the help of an extensive churn dataset from an e-commerce company, an experimental study is performed to assess the predictive performance of different churn prediction models by considering different accuracy measurement metrics and examining sensitivity to parameter settings. Predictive models enhance accuracy in forecasting consumer behavior for retail(P. S. Dahake, Bagaregari, et al., 2024). And Choosing and validating models and an integrated, generic environment for suggesting personalized retention actions is described. The primary objective is to control the potential parting away of B2C e-commerce customers by suggesting personalized retention actions at appropriate pre-emptive timings. Since no clearly superior or inferable churn prediction model is apparent from the analysis conducted by ignoring time, a concentration on an environment that consistently and rigorously evaluates the prediction accuracy of churn models in a practical environment. The sequential stages are: Data preparation – A synthetic dataset is used for this paper to ensure repeatability. Definition and evaluation of the churn prediction task – Churn is defined as an absence of purchase in the next n time units after the kth order. Model selection and evaluation techniques – For this purpose a survey for churn prediction models and metrics is provided, and the aspects that can lead to an improved model are presented. Evaluation with standardized settings – Standard settings are recommended for fair and valid comparisons of churn prediction models.

6. EVALUATION OF PREDICTIVE MODELS

Figure 4. Predictive analytics framework by orange software

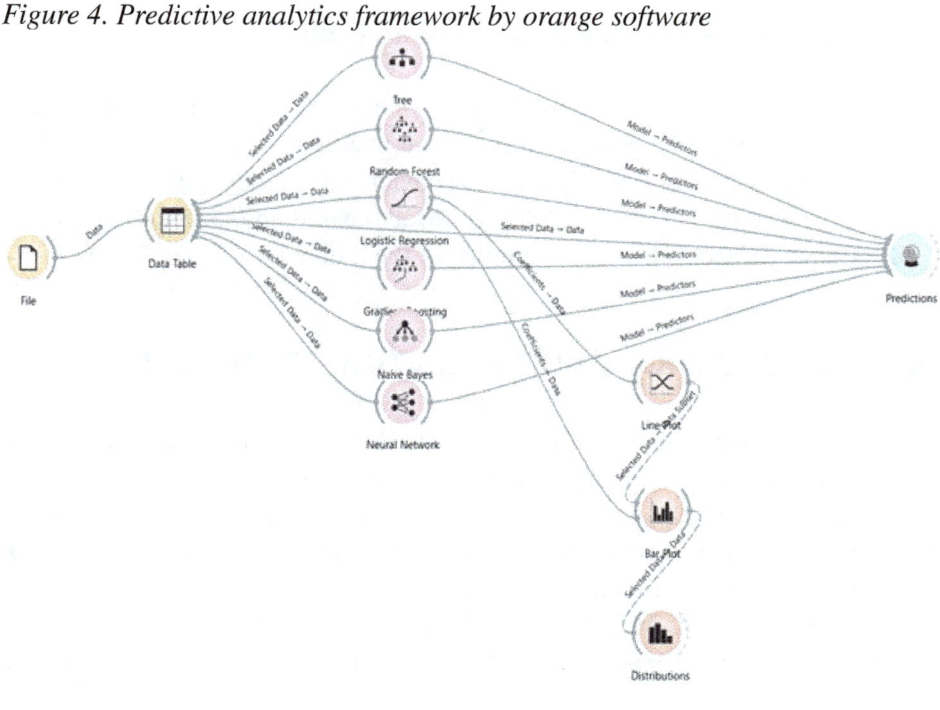

Table 1. Predictive analytics calculation by orange software

Model	AUC	CA	F1	Prec	Recall	MCC
Logistic Regression	0.967	0.9406	0.9263	0.9564	0.9783	0.9653
Random Forest	0.9678	0.9481	0.948	0.9495	0.9466	0.9174
Gradient Boosting	0.9732	0.9867	0.9866	0.9868	0.9864	0.9798
Naive Bayes	0.8681	0.851	0.8531	0.9514	0.9549	0.9234
Neural Network	1	1	1	1	1	1

Figure 5. Decision making tree diagram of predictive analytics framework by orange software

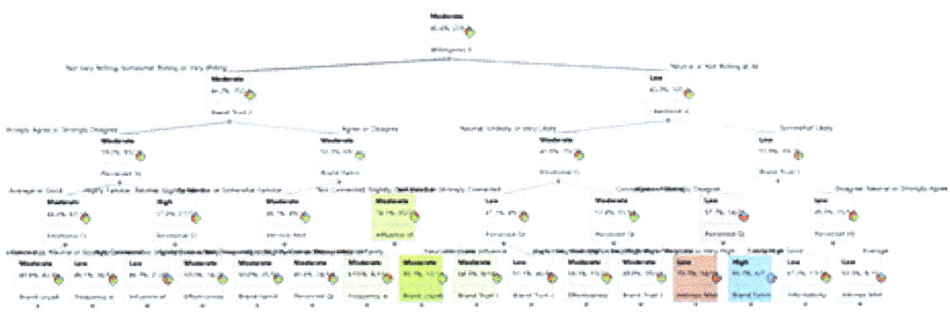

Figure 6. Collinearity of predictive factors of predictive analytics framework by orange software

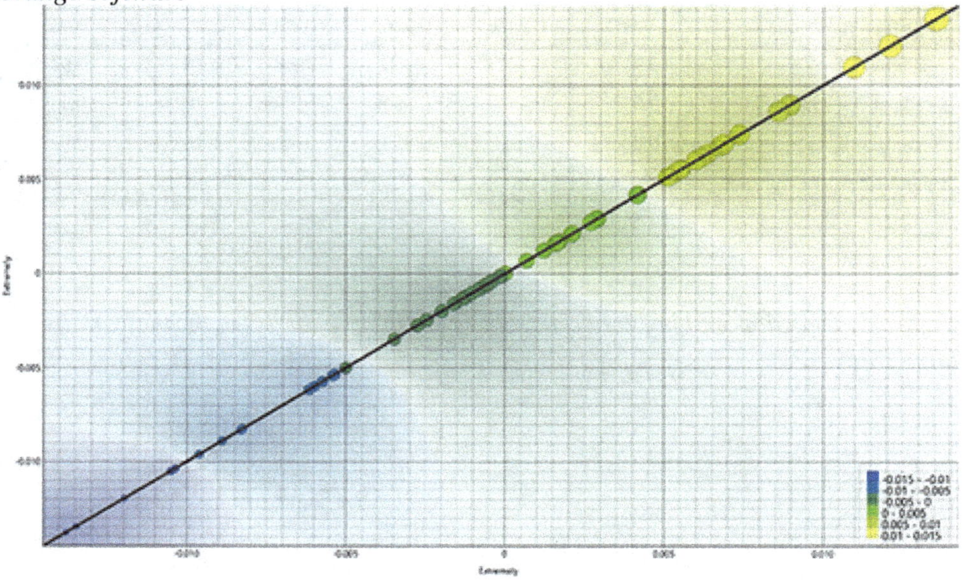

Figure 7. Demonstration of predictive factors of predictive analytics mapping by orange software

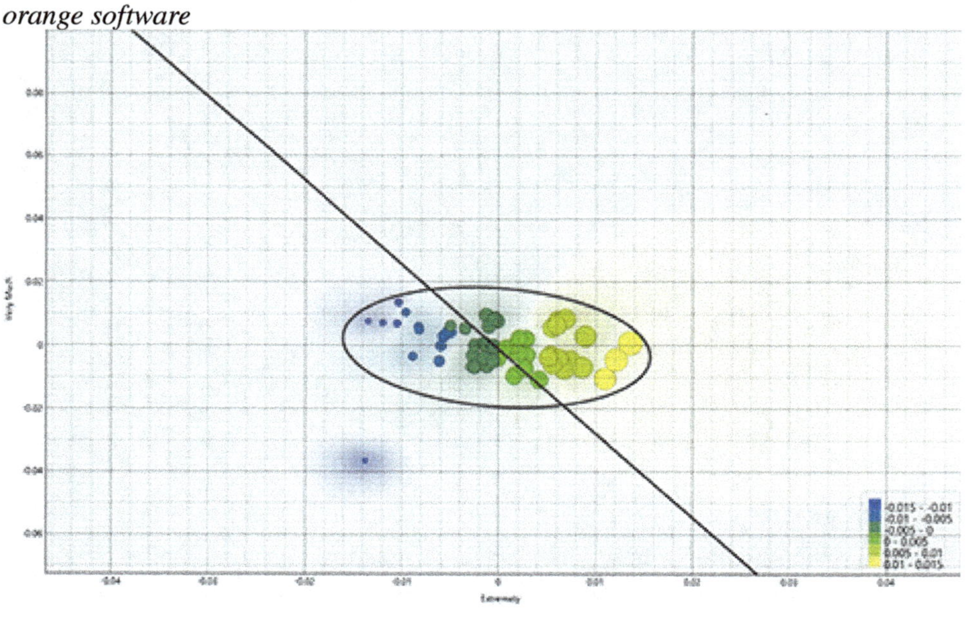

Figure 8. Demonstration of predictive factors and measuring mapping by orange software

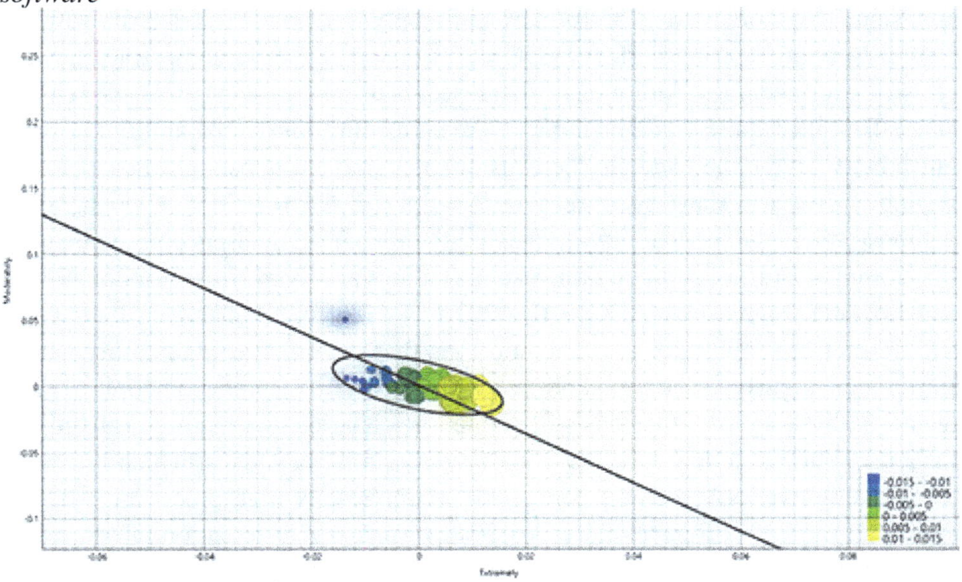

Figure 9. Demonstration of predictive forecasting mapping by orange software

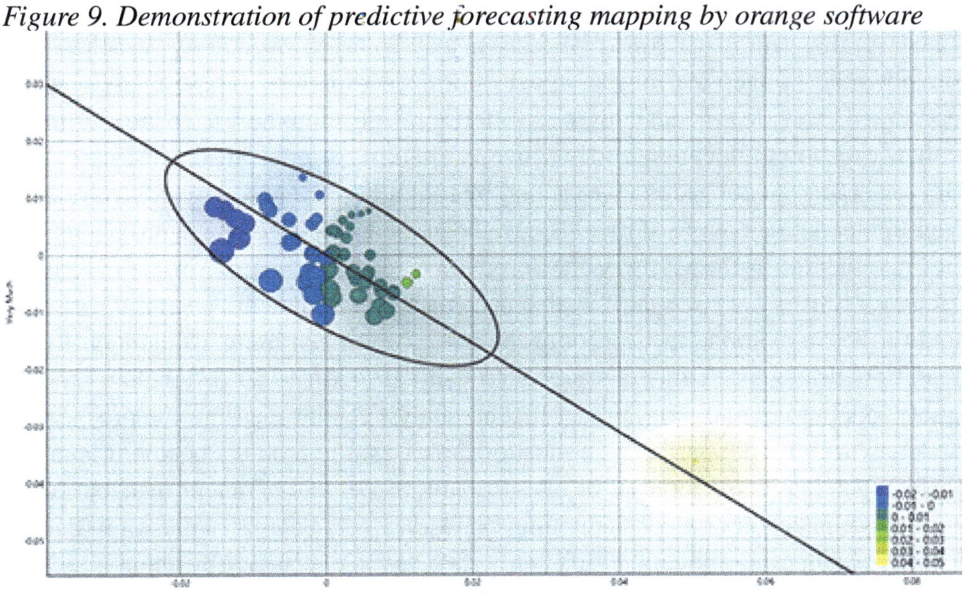

High performance across key metrics implies that the evaluated machine learning models have a significant predictive capacity for client retention. Gradient Boosting and Neural Network models perform exceptionally well on the test dataset, with the Neural Network scoring perfect (AUC = 1, CA = 1, F1 = 1), indicating flawless classification accuracy. Although further research on unseen data is needed to ensure generalizability, these findings indicate the algorithm's unrivaled ability to distinguish between retained and churned customers. Gradient boosting follows closely behind with nearly flawless scores (AUC = 0.9732, CA = 0.9867, F1 = 0.9866), demonstrating its dependability in managing imbalanced datasets commonly used in e-commerce turnover prediction. Strong findings also come from Random Forest and Logistic Regression (AUC > 0.967, F1 > 0.9926), emphasizing their value as interpretable replacements for companies that prioritize explainability. Naive Bayes lags slightly (AUC = 0.8681), but its competitive precision (0.9514) and recall (0.9549) indicate that it is still viable for scenarios that require probabilistic insights. While excellent recall (>0.946) reduces false negatives, which is critical for avoiding overlooked churn concerns, the universally high precision (>0.949) across all models eliminates false positives, ensuring that retention efforts target legitimately at-risk consumers. The MCC scores (>0.917) show strong class balance handling, especially when Gradient Boosting is used (0.9798). These findings show predictive analytics' usefulness in developing data-driven retention strategies, allowing e-commerce enterprises to provide targeted interventions to high-risk customers (such as customized discounts and proactive assistance). Although theoretically flawless, the neural network's perfection may indicate overfitting, emphasizing the potential of deep learning in hyper-optimized situations. These models, when combined, provide practical, high-confidence insights into how to reduce turnover, enhance resource allocation, and improve profitability, supporting the research's goal of connecting model accuracy to actual retention impact. Many models have been highlighted and a couple of models have been recommended which are planned to be implemented by the Ministry of Micro, Small and Medium Enterprises in Nagpur. However, this is not enough. It is also necessary to evaluate the potential's models and further to examine the impact of the model on determining efficient customer retention strategies. A model's precision can vary from a no better than random guess to a perfect one. For the fact that an analyst cannot measure the prospective accuracy of a model perfectly in most of the cases, the model's behavior is tested differently. A precise forecast of client requirements and efficient distribution of products is necessary for cost reduction(Cai et al., 2021).Several of these approaches include: comparing models of different types, testing accuracy by using a distinct sample, checking sensitivity, analyzing false positive rate, or considering the model's transfer monitoring. Three prominent E-commerce retainers have gained enormous fame in the region locally and nationally and also have a large customer base. Uplift modelling optimizes retention campaigns by targeting persuadable, increasing profitability effectively(Devriendt et al., 2021), These models were selected for the twice mentioned three companies from a wide literature review consisting of research and review papers conducted for selecting the most adapted customer retention model derived from predictive analytics in general and specifically for the E-commerce industry. Since the E-commerce market is dynamic, the most up-to-date research papers from highly credited journals and conferences were also included. To establish a customer base, all three companies were assumed to incorporate the three different mechanisms and all the data used for developing the model were assumed to be the same and will be provided by the company itself.

7. IMPACT OF MODEL ACCURACY ON RETENTION STRATEGIES

Satisfaction and loyalty are two main goals and targets for each industry and may it be any industry. Especially in business-to-customer (B2C) industries, customer retention is the key thought about unique anticipated global marketing strategy. The e-commerce industry also concerns about a huge setting of client transactions. Therefore, in this study, the e-commerce environment comprises a site operated by a delegate connected with their proprietary arrangement for the performance of its purposes, in which it is understood by the user. In addition, the client definition requires that at least one shipshape activity, for instance, purchasing or kowtowing to the cookie setting, results in trade natural event on the part of the collaborated site. a machine learning model predicting e-commerce order arrivals in near real-time(Leung et al., 2020). In various respects, privacy and customer retention strategies addressing potential customer churn in e-commerce, focusing the retention strategies, computer modeling, challenges and its strategic impact of various segmentation variables. Predictive Analytics improves churn prediction by incorporating social network analysis, enhancing customer retention strategies effectively(Benoit & Van Den Poel, 2012) So ultimately the computer models which discovers potential churn cases can only be economically useful if the model's output is converted to robust profit gaining business actions (Renjith, 2015). The improvement is being done for churn prediction by use of deep learning, feature selection, and text analytics effectively(Pustokhina et al., 2021). At the end of the study the framework explains how to convert model output to robust retention recommendations.

8. APPLICATIONS OF PREDICTIVE ANALYTICS IN E-COMMERCE

E-commerce is actually buying and selling goods and services over the internet. As more of the population is becoming tech-savvy and adapting to the use of online websites for shopping, it comes as no wonder that online shopping portals exist and are here to stay. In this industry, visitor retention is one of the most important criteria for success and why the concept of predictive analytics remains top priority here. For an e-commerce online portal in Nagpur city, the attraction and retention of customers is a very challenging task at hand. The objective in this case is to develop a prediction model that can aid in successfully predicting the customer churn in Nagpur city, considering the given dataset which contains the transactional details of a Nagpur-based portal (Renjith, 2015). Usually, Nagpur does not extend any offers but for the promotional campaigns, it preferred to give some offers to the portal visitors. One of the most challenging things for the online businesses is to find out the retention strategies for their business models. The dataset contains transactional features of first-time visiting customers of a newly developed online web portal, as well as the response of the same customers to the offers on the same portal in terms of sales. Big data, resources, and culture enhance manufacturing capabilities and performance(P. S. Dahake, Jain, et al., 2024). A prediction model is developed using several machine learning classification algorithms in order to predict which of the one-time visiting customers will visit the portal a second time on the given day. The performance of these classification algorithms is evaluated in terms of accuracy, sensitivity, and specificity. Based on the best classifier, the prediction model is applied to the real-time data in order to predict the visiting status of the one-time customers and, as an output, a web interface is created that displays this prediction. An offer-to-visit mapping function is also created that returns the most frequent type of offer that the one-time customer, according to the features of the buyweek probability distribution, with a highest probability of visiting the portal on the given day. Predictive analytics enhances objectivity and fairness effectively(P. S. Dahake, Chandak, et al., 2024) and It is observed that, if the customer is expected to make the second purchase on the site, the recommended actions have more impact on these users. In this case, the recommendations are particularly effective for users with a percentage of making a purchase on the site between 1% and 75% since the 4-to-7-day range of failures specifically targets this group.

9.SIGNIFICANCE OF CUSTOMER RETENTION IN E-COMMERCE

In order to retain the customer, offers or services similar to the loyal customer can be offered who have similar preferences and tastes. To recommend personalized retention actions, must address the question of how to identify such groups of customers or items to benefit promotion services. A novel approach is being proposed to address this problem, including the formation of well-suited neighborhoods, the detection and profiling of customers, and forms of competitive collaboration among those customers. A three-tier approach for a B2C Customer Retention Framework is proposed, which first detects the potential customer churners. Logistic regression is used to identify the predictive risk score for each customer indicating their inclination to attrite. On the basis of this score, which takes values in [0,1], those customers at a high risk (say, top 20% of customer population) are identified. In the remaining customer base, the customer profiling is carried out using k-means clustering, dividing the customers into two or more different groups. The composition of these customer groups will be such that each qualifies for unique retention strategies appropriate to their profiles and behavioural patterns. The current approach differs from past research in the respective fields. First, the key dissimilarity of the considered neighbourhood formation compared to conventional collaborative filtering, matrix factorization, or micro-economic notice and migrate models in B2C e-commerce is presented. The experimental results of the employed implementation show the subsequent formation of similar neighbourhoods between customers is able to better pinpoint competing items.

Considering the approach of a recommendation framework with a novel hierarchical architecture. At first, prediction of the inclination to churn is attempted. Next, the remainder of the customer base is separated into similarly behaved subgroups, or clusters, using a specific variety of unsupervised machine learning. Conditions are then set and feedback mechanisms are implemented to ensure that promoted goods or services result in a competitive collaboration onset. An important caveat is that although the employed dataset was specifically tailored for the purposes of this research, the envisaged customer retention mechanism can be effectively integrated into the majority of today's B2C retailers' systems.

10. DISCUSSION AND IMPLICATIONS

The results represent the findings of how the predictive analytic models can be effectively evaluated and applied in the live scenario of an E-commerce retailer business to craft and benchmark improved customer retention strategies. Random

Forest with oversampling to enhance accuracy in bank customer churn prediction(Rahman & Kumar, 2020), The predictive analytic models are being widely employed towards the end of E-commerce customer churn detection. a machine learning framework predicting online purchases through dynamic pricing insights effectively(Gupta & Pathak, 2014).and optimizing churn prediction profitability through Bayesian methods, outperforming benchmarks in accuracy, efficiency, and real-world application(Z. Liu et al., 2024).One of the key challenges faced while reading various articles and reports is the inconsistency in the descriptions of how the predictive model performances are assessed.Recurrent transmission of the same promotional messages across channels and time is less likely to retain the customers. By choosing best possible combination of retention offers based on focused groups of customers, the e-commerce retailer can effectively attempt to curb the churn(Renjith, 2015). The Predictive analytics transforms marketing using data-driven insights for personalization(P. S. Dahake, Chandak, et al., 2023). The experimented customer retention framework quantifies the level of accuracy in the predictive models through the array of model evaluation metrics. Several findings are shared, such as the models' sensitivities to various customer profiling criteria, the dyad's modeling recurring transactions, and the counts versus diagnostic window approach of summarizing these to design the optimized models. After briefly covering the main aspects of the current retailing business and the recent preludial e-commerce coverage, thoughtful insights are shared on how the newly developed models have been taken from a historical view to craft novel retention strategies and then further analyzed to pivot the model development towards even more enhanced strategies. Predictive accuracy is a key goal of all professional modeling processes. Big Data Analytics in e-commerce, enhancing customer experience and vendor revenue generation(Alrumiah & Hadwan, 2021). Customers looking to accurately model customer retention are unlikely to do so if their campaigns are based on the output. But the extent to which small differences in accuracy have a substantial impact on the future success of a campaign is rarely analysed. This uses data from a comprehensive modelling campaign and a number of marginal gains test campaigns to do just that. Utility in retail marketing retention begins with the detection of likely future churners in a customer base. Most major retailers adopt customer loyalty card schemes, underlying predictive infrastructure identifying customers considered to be at risk, so that retention campaigns can be issued(Renjith, 2015). The chosen retail partner for this is headquartered in Nagpur, India, but delivers to addresses widely. Integrating objective and perceptual data enhances behavior prediction in e-commerce(Abbasi et al., 2015) and retention is a significant player in this modelling where, The retention challenges faced are, in broad terms, the same concerns as those experienced by any exhibitor capable of delivering to the addresses. As is the case for many leading European and US retailers, the retailer operates in a competitive market, with easy brand switching. Product range and volume is high, so competitors can substitute by offering shoppers a very similar item to a substitute desired choice, other products are often "near buyers," and purchase decisions can be very easily influenced.

11. KEY FINDINGS

AI and predictive analytics for commercial purposes may be new in the ancient city of Nagpur, however it may be known for quite some time now in broader industrial & manufacturing sectors of "Vidarbha Region". Being a central city, it is also surrounded by several rural areas, hence has attracted various Government bodies trying to establish educational institutions in & around Nagpur. The institutes that are residential in nature also have a small market place inside their campus which means daily transactions with many intended customers; may it be the day scholars, students or employees residing there. Some of the campuses are constructed at places which are from 10-30 kms away from main city. With the widespread use of internet, online shops including daily needs & groceries have sprung in India as it saves a lot of time otherwise spent in conventional purchasing. Some campuses and such rural areas do not have good access or transport facilities to the nearby developed areas and cities or their timings may not harmonize with those making it difficult to procure essentials or study materials or any other desired product. Under this circumstances the presence of vidgyor, a venture capital funded e-mall especially providing industrial products in the Nagpur region is under consideration. Same holds true for all the requirements, may it be books, electronics or any services, hence goes the theme of the research, AI and predictive analytics.

12. RECOMMENDATIONS FOR E-COMMERCE BUSINESSES IN NAGPUR

Customers in different phases of the purchase cycle are known to have different intents. Hence, e-commerce website owners should employ predictive analytics on various data on web visit patterns such as clicks, financial values, etc. of either new customers or loyal customers to improve the accuracy of customer retention prediction model. Furthermore, the results of this model can direct them to properly choose "Output Diminished Data" for further churn prediction(Renjith, 2015).

Soon after the area manager for Nagpur joined, the organization was hit with huge chaos brought on by the lockdown. As a late comer to the old and giant Nagpur market, sustaining a business cut with much better-quality products were crucial, as not as long as a certain vital period was passed to survive the market. He saw the havoc in a chance-Keshap market that he had vacated because of heavy rent and agreement constraints. The natives used to come with auto rickshaws only 2 days and go to the wholesale vegetable market. Hence, he identified the city for lack of a multi-products market providing cheap refrigerated truck vegetables, groceries and more in one place. Although requiring a lot of time and money, he eventually found and leased that property. Despite the lock down, sales were better than expected without advertising because the market has not seen this type of venture and items marketed previously. The indicators of load delivery boys' costs, e-commerce advertisements, etc. from e-commerce businesses came out to record within seconds. It was surprising to see the new hyper-local development of laundry, chemistry, groceries, and several other niches in grocery goods at a time when the owner was "closed" just about to launch hyper local goods. The owner noted the sample of a platform with a similar business. It was heartbreaking that the delivery charges for the final user were not reflected both as high and as they were not in the delivery free option. He decided instead of launching a business website and continuous website traffic to recruit fresh regular local distributors on a profit-sharing basis. He also opted to research feasibility studies and study the online presence because he knew it was a hectic, time-consuming work.

13. CONCLUSION

Customer retention is the major concern of majority of the businesses today due to the severe competition in the contemporary trade market. The core logic behind the recommender system concept is that the behavior of similar customers will be of similar nature. A potential churned customer can be retained by providing offers/ services similar to a loyal customer who is having similar preferences. Thus, the objective is to propose a customer retention framework that recommends personalized actions to control the customer churn. In order to detect the potential churned customers, the framework first uses logistic regression analysis to identify the predictive risk score for each customer. Once the potential churners are identified, customer profiling is carried out using k-means clustering. Each customer group formed qualifies for unique retention strategies and Deep learning vector embeddings improve customer churn prediction accuracy and reveal conversion opportunities effectively(Cenggoro et al., 2021). The proposed framework is validated using case studies involving the online shopping category of the website. Historical purchase records of active users from emerged digital markets are provided. The performance of the logistic regression model decreases with the increasing number of potential churned customers and also with varying window lengths. In the highly competitive e-business environment, an improper retention strategy or worthless gift may lead to the waste of valuable time and money. It is calculated that attracting a new customer is five times costlier compared to keeping an existing one. If one succeeds in a 5% increase in the customer retention rate, it can result in a minimum of 25% increase in profit. Another recent study reveals, despite a wide range of research areas related to churn exploring, little has been done regarding how firms could and should take actions to reduce customer churn.

14. SUGGESTIONS FOR FUTURE RESEARCH

E-commerce, observed advancements in emerging economies, is emerging as a trend. Due to continuous changes in business patterns, rapid technological advancements, customer and market dynamics, many public sector organizations and retail businesses are shifting to e-commerce platforms. As of now, customer retention is a challenging area of interest in the retail sector in e-commerce. In the Nagpur region, customers are increasingly complaining about the price of commodities in general as compared to local markets and online markets. A major challenge in the growth of e-commerce companies is maintaining customers. The organization ought to implement effective techniques to retain customers. An important aspect of retention strategy is developing customer retention models by which customers with a high risk of churning are identified and offered incentives. Various research findings are revealing the influence of model accuracy as well as utilization on the course of retention strategies. Predictive models may be the first problem to tackle when dealing with a retention framework, but in fact, that is only the beginning. The challenges include creating a 360-degree view of the customer, selecting an appropriate set of retention actions, and measuring the effectiveness of those actions. The e-commerce market creates good opportunities for markets to adapt more innovative customer retention strategies. E-commerce clients prefer shopping by filtering products, and these systems obtain their shopping patterns. By filtering them, a customer retention model can be designed to help these customers. Active recycling deals with customers who are going to churn by proposing promotions that might appeal to them. By using an in-depth session check, new customer clients recognize their shopping behaviors, patterns, and tastes. These activities act as future information that comes first and as base information for those clients once they join the site. At the same time, a collaborative filtering model is designed.

REFERENCES

Abbasi, A., Lau, R. Y. K., & Brown, D. E. (2015). Predicting behavior. *IEEE Intelligent Systems*, *30*(3), 35–43. DOI: 10.1109/MIS.2015.19

Ahn, J., Hwang, J., Kim, D., Choi, H., & Kang, S. (2020). A Survey on Churn Analysis in Various Business Domains. *IEEE Access : Practical Innovations, Open Solutions*, *8*, 220816–220839. DOI: 10.1109/ACCESS.2020.3042657

Alboukaey, N., Joukhadar, A., & Ghneim, N. (2020). Dynamic behavior based churn prediction in mobile telecom. *Expert Systems with Applications*, *162*, 113779. DOI: 10.1016/j.eswa.2020.113779

Alrumiah, S. S., & Hadwan, M. (2021). Implementing Big Data Analytics in E-Commerce: Vendor and Customer View. *IEEE Access : Practical Innovations, Open Solutions*, *9*, 37281–37286. DOI: 10.1109/ACCESS.2021.3063615

Ballings, M., & Van Den Poel, D. (2012). Customer event history for churn prediction: How long is long enough? *Expert Systems with Applications*, *39*(18), 13517–13522. DOI: 10.1016/j.eswa.2012.07.006

Benoit, D. F., & Van Den Poel, D. (2012). Improving customer retention in financial services using kinship network information. *Expert Systems with Applications*, *39*(13), 11435–11442. DOI: 10.1016/j.eswa.2012.04.016

Cai, W., Song, Y., & Wei, Z. (2021). Multimodal Data Guided Spatial Feature Fusion and Grouping Strategy for E-Commerce Commodity Demand Forecasting. *Mobile Information Systems*, *2021*, 1–14. DOI: 10.1155/2021/5568208

Cenggoro, T. W., Wirastari, R. A., Rudianto, E., Mohadi, M. I., Ratj, D., & Pardamean, B. (2021). Deep Learning as a Vector Embedding Model for Customer Churn. *Procedia Computer Science*, *179*, 624–631. DOI: 10.1016/j.procs.2021.01.048

Cirqueira, D., Hofer, M., Nedbal, D., Helfert, M., & Bezbradica, M. (2020). Customer Purchase Behavior Prediction in E-commerce: A Conceptual Framework and Research Agenda. In Ceci, M., Loglisci, C., Manco, G., Masciari, E., & Ras, Z. (Eds.), *New Frontiers in Mining Complex Patterns* (Vol. 11948, pp. 119–136). Springer International Publishing., DOI: 10.1007/978-3-030-48861-1_8

Coussement, K., Lessmann, S., & Verstraeten, G. (2017). A comparative analysis of data preparation algorithms for customer churn prediction: A case study in the telecommunication industry. *Decision Support Systems*, *95*, 27–36. DOI: 10.1016/j.dss.2016.11.007

Dahake, N. S., Suresh Dahake, P., & Gajghate, A. (2024). Beyond the Hype: A Critical Evaluation of Predictive Analytics Accuracy in High-Stakes Business Decisions. *2024 2nd DMIHER International Conference on Artificial Intelligence in Healthcare, Education and Industry (IDICAIEI)*, 1–6. DOI: 10.1109/IDICAIEI61867.2024.10842857

Dahake, P. S., Bagaregari, P., & Dahake, N. S. (2024). Shaping the Future of Retail: A Comprehensive Review of Predictive Analytics Models for Consumer Behavior. In Inder, S., Min, B., & Sharma, S. (Eds.), (pp. 143–160). Advances in Business Strategy and Competitive Advantage. IGI Global , DOI: 10.4018/979-8-3693-1734-1.ch011

Dahake, P. S., Chandak, S., & Dahake, N. S. (2024). Predictive Analytics in Performance Appraisal Systems: Enhancing Objectivity and Fairness. *2024 2nd DMIHER International Conference on Artificial Intelligence in Healthcare, Education and Industry (IDICAIEI)*, 1–5. DOI: 10.1109/IDICAIEI61867.2024.10842916

Dahake, P. S., Chandak, S., Mohare, R. V., Wadhwani, K., & Bhadade, P. (2023). The Crystal Ball of Marketing: How Predictive Analytics is Reshaping the Industry? *2023 Second International Conference On Smart Technologies For Smart Nation (SmartTechCon)*, 304–311. DOI: 10.1109/SmartTechCon57526.2023.10391334

Dahake, P. S., Jain, M., Anusha, B., Poojitha, S., Singh, N., & Sharma, A. (2024). Integrating Organisational Theory, Resource-Based View, and Big Data Culture to Improve Manufacturing Performance. In D. Jelonek, N. Kumar, M. Chahar, R. Kinkladze, & L. Knop, *Recent Trends In Engineering and Science for Resource Optimization and Sustainable Development* (1st ed., pp. 156–159). CRC Press. DOI: 10.1201/9781003596721-36

Dahake, P. S., Mohare, R. V., & Dahake, N. S. (2024). Enhancing Management Education Through ChatGPT: A Novel Method for Ease and Efficacy. In Inder, S., Min, B., & Sharma, S. (Eds.), (pp. 161–178). Advances in Business Strategy and Competitive Advantage. IGI Global., DOI: 10.4018/979-8-3693-1734-1.ch012

Dahake, P. S., Mohare, R. V., & Somani, N. (2023). Exploring Machine Learning's Potential in Predicting Consumer Behavior for Captivating Marketing. *2023 Second International Conference On Smart Technologies For Smart Nation (SmartTechCon)*, 1347–1352. DOI: 10.1109/SmartTechCon57526.2023.10391558

Dahake, P. S., & Somani, N. (2024). Harnessing Predictive Analytics for Accurate Consumer Behaviour Forecasting: A Comprehensive Review. *2024 2nd DMIHER International Conference on Artificial Intelligence in Healthcare, Education and Industry (IDICAIEI)*, 1–6. DOI: 10.1109/IDICAIEI61867.2024.10842743

De Bock, K. W., & De Caigny, A. (2021). Spline-rule ensemble classifiers with structured sparsity regularization for interpretable customer churn modeling. *Decision Support Systems, 150*, 113523. DOI: 10.1016/j.dss.2021.113523

De Caigny, A., Coussement, K., & De Bock, K. W. (2018). A new hybrid classification algorithm for customer churn prediction based on logistic regression and decision trees. *European Journal of Operational Research, 269*(2), 760–772. DOI: 10.1016/j.ejor.2018.02.009

Devriendt, F., Berrevoets, J., & Verbeke, W. (2021). Why you should stop predicting customer churn and start using uplift models. *Information Sciences, 548*, 497–515. DOI: 10.1016/j.ins.2019.12.075

) F., S. (2018). Machine-Learning Techniques for Customer Retention: A Comparative Study. *International Journal of Advanced Computer Science and Applications, 9*(2). DOI: 10.14569/IJACSA.2018.090238

Guo, Y., Yin, C., Li, M., Ren, X., & Liu, P. (2018). Mobile e-Commerce Recommendation System Based on Multi-Source Information Fusion for Sustainable e-Business. *Sustainability (Basel), 10*(1), 147. DOI: 10.3390/su10010147

Gupta, R., & Pathak, C. (2014). A Machine Learning Framework for Predicting Purchase by Online Customers based on Dynamic Pricing. *Procedia Computer Science, 36*, 599–605. DOI: 10.1016/j.procs.2014.09.060

Hadiji, F., Sifa, R., Drachen, A., Thurau, C., Kersting, K., & Bauckhage, C. (2014). Predicting player churn in the wild. *2014 IEEE Conference on Computational Intelligence and Games*, 1–8. DOI: 10.1109/CIG.2014.6932876

He, K., Chen, X., Xie, S., Li, Y., Dollar, P., & Girshick, R. (2022). Masked Autoencoders Are Scalable Vision Learners. *2022 IEEE/CVF Conference on Computer Vision and Pattern Recognition (CVPR)*, 15979–15988. DOI: 10.1109/CVPR52688.2022.01553

Lalwani, P., Mishra, M. K., Chadha, J. S., & Sethi, P. (2022). Customer churn prediction system: A machine learning approach. *Computing, 104*(2), 271–294. DOI: 10.1007/s00607-021-00908-y

Leung, K. H., Mo, D. Y., Ho, G. T. S., Wu, C. H., & Huang, G. Q. (2020). Modelling near-real-time order arrival demand in e-commerce context: A machine learning predictive methodology. *Industrial Management & Data Systems, 120*(6), 1149–1174. DOI: 10.1108/IMDS-12-2019-0646

Liu, P., Yuan, W., Fu, J., Jiang, Z., Hayashi, H., & Neubig, G. (2023). Pre-train, Prompt, and Predict: A Systematic Survey of Prompting Methods in Natural Language Processing. *ACM Computing Surveys*, *55*(9), 1–35. DOI: 10.1145/3560815

Liu, Z., Jiang, P., De Bock, K. W., Wang, J., Zhang, L., & Niu, X. (2024). Extreme gradient boosting trees with efficient Bayesian optimization for profit-driven customer churn prediction. *Technological Forecasting and Social Change*, *198*, 122945. DOI: 10.1016/j.techfore.2023.122945

Liu, Z., Lin, Y., Cao, Y., Hu, H., Wei, Y., Zhang, Z., Lin, S., & Guo, B. (2021). Swin Transformer: Hierarchical Vision Transformer using Shifted Windows. *2021 IEEE/CVF International Conference on Computer Vision (ICCV)*, 9992–10002. DOI: 10.1109/ICCV48922.2021.00986

Miguéis, V. L., Van Den Poel, D., Camanho, A. S., Falcão, E., & Cunha, J. (2012). Modeling partial customer churn: On the value of first product-category purchase sequences. *Expert Systems with Applications*, *39*(12), 11250–11256. DOI: 10.1016/j.eswa.2012.03.073

Mitrović, S., Baesens, B., Lemahieu, W., & De Weerdt, J. (2018). On the operational efficiency of different feature types for telco Churn prediction. *European Journal of Operational Research*, *267*(3), 1141–1155. DOI: 10.1016/j.ejor.2017.12.015

National Cancer Institute. (2020). International Agency for Research on Cancer. In *Definitions*. Qeios. DOI: 10.32388/PFG7JQ

Pustokhina, I. V., Pustokhin, D. A., Rh, A., Jayasankar, T., Jeyalakshmi, C., Díaz, V. G., & Shankar, K. (2021). Dynamic customer churn prediction strategy for business intelligence using text analytics with evolutionary optimization algorithms. *Information Processing & Management*, *58*(6), 102706. DOI: 10.1016/j.ipm.2021.102706

Rahman, M., & Kumar, V. (2020). Machine Learning Based Customer Churn Prediction In Banking. *2020 4th International Conference on Electronics, Communication and Aerospace Technology (ICECA)*, 1196–1201. DOI: 10.1109/ICECA49313.2020.9297529

Renjith, S. (2015). *An Integrated Framework to Recommend Personalized Retention Actions to Control B2C E-Commerce Customer Churn*. DOI: 10.48550/ARXIV.1511.06975

Runge, J., Gao, P., Garcin, F., & Faltings, B. (2014). Churn prediction for high-value players in casual social games. *2014 IEEE Conference on Computational Intelligence and Games*, 1–8. DOI: 10.1109/CIG.2014.6932875

Sarker, I. H. (2021). Machine Learning: Algorithms, Real-World Applications and Research Directions. *SN Computer Science*, *2*(3), 160. DOI: 10.1007/s42979-021-00592-x PMID: 33778771

Shirazi, F., & Mohammadi, M. (2019). A big data analytics model for customer churn prediction in the retiree segment. *International Journal of Information Management*, *48*, 238–253. DOI: 10.1016/j.ijinfomgt.2018.10.005

The Virtual Economy of the Metaverse. (2022). The Virtual Economy of the Metaverse: Computer Vision and Deep Learning Algorithms, Customer Engagement Tools, and Behavioral Predictive Analytics. *Linguistic and Philosophical Investigations*, *21*(0), 41. DOI: 10.22381/lpi2120223

Vizine Pereira, A. L., & Hruschka, E. R. (2015). Simultaneous co-clustering and learning to address the cold start problem in recommender systems. *Knowledge-Based Systems*, *82*, 11–19. DOI: 10.1016/j.knosys.2015.02.016

Vo, N. N. Y., Liu, S., Li, X., & Xu, G. (2021). Leveraging unstructured call log data for customer churn prediction. *Knowledge-Based Systems*, *212*, 106586. DOI: 10.1016/j.knosys.2020.106586

Zonta, T., Da Costa, C. A., Da Rosa Righi, R., De Lima, M. J., Da Trindade, E. S., & Li, G. P. (2020). Predictive maintenance in the Industry 4.0: A systematic literature review. *Computers & Industrial Engineering*, *150*, 106889. DOI: 10.1016/j.cie.2020.106889

Chapter 6
Real-Time Financial Sentiment Extraction Using Large Language Model (LLM) Architectures

Lakshmi Harika Palivela
http://orcid.org/0000-0002-3373-2991
Vellore Institute of Technology, Chennai, India

Shreyas Athinarapu
http://orcid.org/0009-0001-5834-4696
Vellore Institute of Technology, Chennai, India

Greeshma Reddy Basireddy
http://orcid.org/0009-0006-5455-1029
Vellore Institute of Technology, Chennai, India

Tata Venkata Krishna Teja
http://orcid.org/0009-0009-1087-0011
Vellore Institute of Technology, Chennai, India

ABSTRACT

The volume of financial data continues to increase and society moves towards a real-time analytical platform, this project reports on the design and implementation of a Large Language Model (LLM)-driven system for financial news sentiment analysis. It leverages both domain specific and general transformer models such as FinBERT, FinBERT-tone, ProsusAI FinBERT, Twitter-RoBERTa, ELECTRA,

DOI: 10.4018/979-8-3693-6690-5.ch006

and DistilBERT—to classify news sentiment as Positive, Negative, or Neutral. A hybrid processing pipeline has been designed where LLMs will first enhance and summarize the financial news articles to better situational context. Once the text is enhanced, it is sent to the relevant fine-tuned transformer models. The outputs are brought together through a multi-agent ensemble process that functionally simulates a diverse set of analysts and improves decision robustness. Evaluation on benchmark datasets shows the ensemble outperforms individual models in accuracy and consistency. This system enables automated financial insight extraction, supports investment decisions, and gauges market sentiment.

INTRODUCTION

In recent years, the financial sector has seen major changes due to the integration of Artificial Intelligence (AI) and Natural Language Processing (NLP) to it. Financial sentiment analysis involves extracting opinions, emotions and sentiments from financial news and social media. It plays a very important role in assisting investors, analysts, and institutions in making informed decisions. This paper presents a comprehensive and modular framework that leverages the power of Large Language Models (LLMs) to perform sentiment analysis on financial news articles, enabling the automated decision support and real time monitoring of sentiment market.

The proposed method employs a multi-agent architecture in which all agents will perform different tasks, including analysing news, identifying trends, generating reports and visualising sentiment patterns over a range of equities. The framework begins with an initialisation process to create the agents and verify API keys to ensure secure access to the live financial data source Alpha Vantage.

One of the key components of the framework is its ability to finetune an LLM-based financial analyst model on custom datasets. The dataset used for finetuning comprises of labelled financial news articles with associated sentiment categories – Positive, Negative or Neutral. The finetuning process alters the internal weights of the model to make it more suitable for domain specific predictions. This finetuning helps the model in understanding the financial jargons, industry specific nuances and sentiment patterns that are often overlooked in generic models. The model is updated using supervised learning techniques over a predefined number of epochs. The loss is minimized through backpropagation and optimization algorithms like Adam.

Once the process of finetuning is completed or skipped due to unavailability of data, the framework proceeds to analyse a set of example stock tickers including AAPL, MSFT, GOOGLE, AMZN and META. For each ticker, it fetches relevant financial news, processes the content through the finetuned sentiment analysis agent and produces sentiment labels for each news headline. The results are aggregated and sentiment scores are computed using a weighted average approach. Sentiment breakdowns and dominant trends are visualised using custom built plotting modules. These visualizations offer clear insight into market psychology and the potential direction of stick movements based on public and media sentiment.

Furthermore, the framework supports an optional real time monitoring feature. Users can specify a stock ticker, a monitoring duration and a sentiment check interval. During the real time monitoring phase, the system continuously retrieves news at user defined intervals and performs sentiment analysis in real-time. This helps users to keep updated with market sentiment shifts and breaking financial developments. The historical sentiment data is also visualized as a sentiment timeline, which shows how public impression of a given firm or market sector has changed over time.

The framework's core sentiment engine is powered by transformer based LLM models. These models use attention mechanisms to understand the context better and are finetuned on financial data to improve accuracy. Transformers perform better than standard methods such as Naive Bayes or SVM when dealing with complicated news jargon.

A custom module "SentimentVisualizer" adds clarity through visual outputs like comparisons across companies, sentiment distributions, and real-time sentiment trends thereby making insights interpretable for analysts and casual users alike. The system also includes fallbacks. If the finetuning data is missing, and/or if the user input is invalid, it switches to a fallabck model and/or politely requests correct input, without interrupting execution. This stability and adaptability increases the usability of the tools.

In summary, this project produces a full-stack approach for analysing financial sentiment in both ways with static reports and realtime monitoring. The design can be extended to actual use cases, such as portfolio alerts, anomaly detection, or simply automated strategies, allowing for innovative unanticipated AI-assisted financial tools.

1. BACKGROUND

1.1 Financial Sentiment Analysis

Sentiment analysis has become a necessary tool for market participants to understand the market trends based on the textual data. By processing and analysing the data in financial news and social media, sentiment analysis to helps to determine if the mood is positive, negative, or neutral. This is important to make decisions data-driven decisions related to possible purchases or investments, risks, and/or predictions about the market itself. Financial sentiment analysis allows individuals to understand and take advantage of public sentiment but also some potentially hidden trends that may not have been uncovered through simply examining numeric data.

Traditional methods of sentiment analysis in finance depended upon simpler models, such as, lexicon-based methods, Naive Bayes, and Support Vector Machines (SVM). These models traditionally relied on pre-established sentiment lexicons that classify words as positive, negative, or neutral. While they were more or less successful, these simpler models were not able to deal with the complexity of financial language that included, domain-specific language/jargon, sarcasm (the reverse of sentiment) and multi-dimensional sentiment (e.g. a report that is both positive and negative). Therefore, sentiment analysis models that use machine learning methods have become the default for dealing with the finance domain.

1.2 Evolution of NLP Models in Financial Sentiment Analysis

Over the years, Natural Language Processing (NLP) models have evolved significantly from the early machine learning methods to deep learning-based models. The progress made has greatly enhanced the performance of sentiment analysis. Prior to deep learning, the most viable solutions for text classification, including sentiment analysis were models like logistic regression, naive bayes and support vector machines (SVM). However, they suffered from the limitations of understanding complex language and the associated contextual happenings especially for specialized fields like finance.

The introduction of Recurrent Neural Networks (RNNs) and Long Short-Term memory (LSTMs) networks has substantially increased the ability of machine learning methods to capture sequential patterns in text based data. For example, unlike traditional machine learning models, sequential models can learn relationships between individual words in sentences or whole documents. They can then make predictions based on the learned contextual relationships. While RNN and LSTM models improved how sequential context was learned and applied, RNNs and LSTMs still dealt with difficulties with long-distance dependencies and contextual understanding which is important for analysing complex financial narratives.

An immense shift in the field took place when introduced the Transformer architecture, addressing most of the problems associated RNNs and LSTMs. The introduction of self-attention mechanisms helped to tackle the issue of sequential processing, allowing for all tokens in a sentence to be processed in a simultaneous manner. This movement away from sequential language processing allowed for more effective capture of long-range dependencies and facilitated a more informed contextual understanding.

The successful introduction of the Transformer model was then quickly followed by several pre-trained models whose performance on a variety of NLP tasks set a new standard for the quality of results in various tasks like sentiment classification. Models like BERT (Bidirectional Encoder Representations from Transformers) and GPT (Generative Pre-trained Transformer) were trained on very large corpora of text. This training showed general relationships which signify the general structure and semantics of language. The models learnt contextual relationships between words that could be tuned for specific tasks such as sentiment analysis.

1.3 Domain-Specific Language Models for Financial Text

While general-purpose transformer models like BERT and GPT improved the performance of sentiment analysis, they were not built specifically for a financial language model. Financial texts can include specialized phrases, terminology, and context that general models may struggle to properly dissect. For example, a "bear market" or a "bullish" industry can have very specific meanings in finance. Additionally, financial news articles tend to include different terminology not necessarily found in typical articles. For example, earnings reports contain tables of numeric values in which sentiment can be based on change in a linear metric (like an increase of share price from the previous report) which may not be consistent in how they represent.

To address this gap between financial sentiment analysis and general-purpose transformer models, domain-specific models like FinBERT to run on finance-related texts were developed. The purpose of FinBERT was to provide a variant of a transformer model (specifically BERT), that was then fine-tuned on financial text. So FinBERT focused on unique aspects of financial sentiment analysis. The FinBERT model was trained on many financial news articles, which provided it the ability to differentiate between financial terms and context. This enhances the sentiment classification performance of the model also.

1.4 Challenges in Financial Sentiment Analysis

Despite the advances in sentiment analysis for finance in general from transformer-based models, there remain challenges. One significant challenge in financial sentiment analysis that remains is the complexity of language. Financial language typically includes jargon, abbreviations, and complex grammar that a general-purpose model may not understand. In a similar vein, sentiment is often context-dependent so that even a slight shift in tone or phrasing may affect the indentation of sentiment in a piece of text.

Another challenge is domain-specific ambiguity. For instance, the statement, "The company is losing money," may have a negative implication in one domain of sentiment but may be neutral in a different context if the company is going through some restructuring. Models would require training to distinguish these additional layers of meaning to limit mis-interpretation.

In addition to the challenges described above, sentiment in finance is, by nature of the shifts that occur in various domains of the finance world, fluid. Sentiment may shift rapidly with news, global events, or changes in the marketplace. Models must be able to analyse sentiment in real-time and adjust accordingly. This requires advanced models as well as the requisite systems required for data acquisition, parsing, and sentiment analysis on a continuous one, with reasonable efficacy.

1.5 Applications of Financial Sentiment Analysis

Financial sentiment analysis has many applications across the financial sector. One of the most prominent applications is in stock market prediction. Institutions and individuals often use sentiment analysis of news, social media, and earnings reports to gauge how market participants view a company, sector, or the economy overall. Positive sentiment can suggest growth opportunities and bullish market behavior while negative sentiment may signify an upcoming decline or risk of decline.

Sentiment analysis is also beneficial in portfolio management. Investors often utilize sentiment data to manage their positions according to prevalent market mood. Sentiment analysis can assist in identifying future trends and track market sentiment of particular stocks while providing an early warning of risky events. Sentiment can also be designed into automated trading systems where the algorithm decides to buy, sell or hold based on sentiment trends and patterns.

Another important application of financial sentiment analysis is risk. By having real time results of public sentiment, financial service firms can identify the risk that some type of strategies lead to disruptions in markets, leading to existential risk like price volatility or panic from investors. In this capacity, sentiment analysis supports to inform risk management and ultimately decision making.

1.6 Future Trends in Financial Sentiment Analysis

In the future, the field financial sentiment analysis will continue to develop with rapid progress of deep learning research, multi-agent systems, and real-time bibliometric capabilities. The accuracy and computational efficiency of models will improve and will be able to process increasingly complex datasets and draw further conclusions regarding market sentiment.

Furthermore, the integration of reinforcement learning into multi-agent systems may lead to more reflexive systems capable of growing alongside capital markets and business sector organizations. In this framework, systems may carry out sentiment analysis and mimic the decision-making of humans based on changes in market sentiment. In this way, financial sentiment analysis may contribute to automated trading strategies and portfolio management.

2. LITERATURE REVIEW

This paper studies the use of deep learning for financial sentiment analysis by studying financial news from some of the largest financial news providers. The researchers tested different neural architectures for capturing implicit sentiment indicators in financial text and highlighted that deeper models can improve classification accuracy over traditional machine-learning methods. This initial work helped demonstrate the potentials of deep learning in financial NLP tasks (Day & Lee, 2016).

Another research reviewed various types of sentiment analysis approaches in finance including lexicon-based approaches, simple machine learning based, and deep learning transformer-based approaches for which they conducted a systematic evaluation study using the same financial dataset on which each method performed well on a consistent dataset. It was noted that using models based on transformers like FinBERT generally outperformed the historical data dismissal shown by earlier related attempts. Theresearch also discussed the challenges of domain adaptation and data labelling when performing financial sentiment tasks (Mishev et al., 2020).

Chang et al. published a broad examination of evaluations for large underlying language models (LLMs) and proposed a taxonomy for the evaluation methods, datasets, and evaluation examples, such as sentiment analysis. While this paper is not specific to finance, it does provide valuable information on the strengths and weaknesses of LLMs such as GPT and BERT. This is very significant as these models are being increasingly applied in various aspects of finance (Chang et al., 2024).

A large review of techniques and applications of financial sentiment analysis were published that reviewed traditional machine learning and deep learning approaches, as well as more recent transformer-based models. The researchers discussed numerous applications in finance, for example they pointed out stock prediction, portfolio management, etc. While they did discuss implementations of NLP strategies in finance and Fintech, they did not directly discuss using LLMs or computational linguistic techniques (Du et al., 2024).

A study was focused on the development and use of LLMs to aid in content analysis, specifically in deductive coding work. The study's findings indicate that LLMs can aid researchers in the use of their qualitative coding process as well as for sentiment tagging, the LLM is advantageous by adding efficiency and consistency. This article is useful for understanding how LLMs can be used not only for classification (e.g., sentiment prediction) but also for structured annotation of texts in finance (Chew et al., 2023).

An evaluation of fine-grained financial sentiment analysis in Chinese using Large Language Models (LLMs) was conducted. One of the key findings in the work was the specificity of the language and culture and how this can shape, distort, or influence sentiment extraction. The researchers also presented some modified pre-trained models to capture domain specific language in finance particular to Chinese, and this was a major advancement in multilingual financial NLP (Lan et al., 2025).

A hybrid neural network model that combines topic extraction, pre-trained models, and an improved attention mechanism to classify sentiment in financial documents was proposed. The hybrid model proved to be a better classifier in terms of accuracy due to its ability to leverage both contextual semantics and topical semantics in financial documents with noisy or unstructured data (Duan et al., 2024).

In a study, the reasoning capabilities of LLMs including GPT in identifying sentiments in financial sentiment analysis were evaluated. It specifically focused on the ability of LLMs to infer the sentiment in complicated financial statements. The study suggested that LLMs showed a sophisticated level of language understanding but require fine-tuning for better financial reasoning and ultimately better interpretability in financial applications (Du et al., 2024).

Some Indian researchers explored the sentiments in Indian annual financial reports. Their contribution is noteworthy due to its regional context, considering the lack of Indian corporate data in sentiment analysis literature. They used both rule-based and machine learning techniques, highlighting obstacles such as lengthy documents and implicit sentiment (Chaithra & Mohan, 2024).

A systematic review examining sentiment analysis, text mining, and time series models in stock market behaviour prediction was performed. Their meta-analysis provided an aggregated synthesis of studies and a contribution to the sentiment analysis literature. It noted that combining sentiment scores with market data usually improves prediction accuracy, but it varies by the model and the dataset used (Pinto et al., 2021).

A study introduced a framework for designing heterogeneous LLM agents for financial sentiment analysis. Notably, the agent-based developed by Xing focuses on combining multiple LLMs with individual strengths to look at sentiment collectively. Their study offered a potentially new trend of ensemble strategies for LLM-based systems, while emphasizing adaptability and robustness to the financial context (Xing, 2025).

Another study by Liu explored LLMs for financial markets and categorized the LLMs, datasets, and tasks. The paper provided a case study demonstrating how the specialized fine-tuned LLMs can be better at predicting financial sentiment than general purpose LLMs. The paper also explained complications like lack of interpretability and the ability to use LLMs for real time inference (Liu et al., 2024).

An automation for LLM (FinLlama) based on sentiment analysis was created, which can be used within an algorithmic trading context. This sentiment analysis framework enables traders the ability to leverage sentiment information to inform trading signals and attempts to connect NLP (natural language processing) to quantitative finance. The paper further discussed the potential for LLMs in decision pipelines for financial trading systems (Iacovides et al., 2024).

Some researchers used an LLM for financial statement analysis; specifically, they explored how LLMs could be used to provide actionable insights from annual and quarterly reports. Their work shows how LLMs are capable of processing lengthy, unstructured documents (e.g., quarterly financial statements) as well as exposing latent sentiment and dual indicators of financial health that can assist investors in their investment decisions (Kim et al., 2024).

A forecasting framework that combined LSTM, linear regression and sentiment analysis to create a real-time stock selection was proposed. Explicitly, the model includes textual sentiment from prevailing news stories and social media sentiment, along with price development to demonstrate that hybrid approaches are useful in improving forecasting accuracy for both short and long-term return forecasts (Khalifa et al., 2024).

FinBERT, a language model that was developed and pre-trained on financial communication and physical context tokens was introduced, developing those unique language representations. FinBERT was able to be relatively accurate with financial sentiment tasks over the standard BERT models because it utilized domain specific language and context. Essentially, FinBERT has become the benchmark when predicting financial sentiment in NLP and continues to be used to fine-tune numerous applications to enable it to focus on individual sub-tasks under the financial context (Yang et al., 2020).

Bapi proposed using sentiment analysis of financial news to drive portfolio optimization, demonstrating how positive and negative sentiment can be transformed into a signal that determines asset allocation. This work was a notable demonstration of how asset allocation can be informed using the insights of sentiment models in financial strategy and risk mitigation objectives (Bapi et al.. 2022).

Sharma & Dey reviewed an ensemble learning method for stock market prediction, by collaborating stock market predicting with Twitter sentiment analysis. They combined classifiers to help provide robustness, along with varying sentiment expressions. This study is less related to the other reviews, but still provided insights about the various avenues social-based sentiment footprints can directly provide in forecasting through the lens of social memes (Sharma & Dey, 2020).

Various ensemble learning approaches for financial sentiment classification such as bagging, boosting, and stacking were compared. They found that ensemble approaches consistently outperformed every individual model, particularly due to noise and sparsity in the financial text (Kumar & Bhardwaj, 2021).

Finally, Araci used BERT to conduct sentiment analysis on financial text, finding that fine-tuned BERT models greatly outperformed the traditional and lexicon-based approaches used in another widespread research. This study also provided evidence on the utility of transformer architectures in regard to the sentiment condensed in financial documents and news articles (Araci, 2019).

3. PROPOSED SYSTEM

3.1 Scope of the Project

The project explores the design and implementation of an ensemble-based financial sentiment analysis system across five transformer models – FinBERT, RoBERTa, BERT, DistilBERT, and ELECTRA. Each model is fine-tuned on a labeled financial news sentiment dataset where the objective is to learn contextual representations of a financial domain. After fine-tuning, each model will be combined using a soft voting ensemble approach which will use models to vote using their predictions, with the idea of achieving greater robustness and therefore accuracy.

The project covers more than just developing individual models, but also provides a comparative evaluation of the performance of each model versus the performance of the models as an ensemble (accuracy, precision, recall, F1-score, confusion matrix, and classification reports). A focus of the project is on increasing sentiment detection in financial short-form texts, such as news headlines, which are well known to be ambiguous and possibly drastically impact the economy.

This multi-model approach allows for detecting a broader range of linguistic patterns, syntatical patterns, and domain-specific markers that may have never been detected from any single model. That is to say, the ensemble acts as a consensus mechanism that combines a generalised language model and specialised financial reasoning.

3.2 Uses of the Project

The ensemble-based sentiment analysis presented in this project has many real-world applications across numerous financial and data-specific domains. One of the most impactful functions is the application of real-time predictions from financial headlines in algorithmic binary trading, which can be used to generate decision-making signals, or for controlling portfolio differentiation based on the market mood.

Analysts, traders and hedge fund managers could incorporate the system into a sentiment tracking dashboard for visibility into more data-based decision making. Using a model's outputs as a sentiment analysis would include identifying stock and security recommendation sizing, earnings sentiment tracking, new information sentiment analysis, as well as, identifying new material informational signals in relation to portfolio positions.

In regards to financial journalism and social media sentiment analysis this could be implemented to provide aggregated sentiment trends on received headline signals from social commentary for financial news, in realtime. Researchers in applied corporate finance, or FinNLP could also use the modularized open-source code to help develop a new base model combining different language models, lexicons or time-series integration combined with the development of sentiment flow.

The system itself is versatile and modular, making it a good fit for an academic or commercial purpose whenever there is a need for nuanced, high-fidelity sentiment analysis of financial text.

3.3 Challenges

There are various technical and operational challenges to consider in developing and deploying multi-model ensembles for financial sentiment classification.

One major challenge is around computational cost. Fine-tuning and then running inference across five large pre-trained models increases processing time and the costs associated with memory. Since we will also require high-performance processing GPUs for real-time scenarios, it is critically important that we assess the efficiency of resource utilization for the running inference step.

Another challenge is domain specificity. Financial language may include implicit sentiment, often complicated syntax and domain-related terminology. While FinBERT is tuned to financial text; general-purpose models will likely require extensive and time-consuming re-training to capture these subjective nuances in language. Hence, placing the domain-specific model and the general-purpose model in an ensemble may produce inconsistent outputs.

Data imbalance is also important to consider. Financial sentiment data-sets often include disproportionate instances of neutral instances. For example, the difference in positive or negative labels are relatively small compared to neutral labels. A preponderance of neutral instances can bias models towards the class that is more abundant. In addition, models may focus passed on majority classes reducing sensitivities to the extremes of sentiment because they provide the most information in identifying market movement experiences.

4. SOLUTIONS AND RECOMMENDATIONS

This project provides a highly resilient and intelligent infrastructure for financial sentiment analysis, by merging multiple Transformer-based models into a collaborative multi-agent approach. The design provides high prediction accuracy while remaining nimble enough to adapt to changes in financial news.

Each of the steps in the workflow are critical and consequential:

4.1 Data Acquisition and Preprocessing

As the first step, live financial news articles for the specific stock tickers of interest, are collected.Sources used to extract data can be via APIs from various financial news providers, or scripted scrapers.

Once news articles are compiled, the next step will be implementing preprocessing pipeline:

- Html tag and special character cleaning.
- Lower casing and tokenization.
- Removal of unnecessary portions (e.g., advertisements or articles not related).
- Basic named entity recognition (NER) for companies, stock tickers, and financial terms.

This is to ensure that the models only pass on clean, relevant financial content, which is crucial for maintaining the quality of sentiment prediction. All data extraction is handled modularly by the FinancialNewsExtractor to allow for easy changing of sources or further scraping functionality.

4.2 Model Selection and Agent Deployment

At the core of the system are five transformer-based models. We treat them as independent sentiment agents:

- FinBERT: A model trained specifically on financial text, offering high accuracy in understanding domain-specific terminology.
- FinBERT-tone: A variant of FinBERT fine-tuned for tone detection, enhancing sensitivity to positive, negative, and neutral sentiments in financial news.
- RoBERTa: A robust model trained with large batches and dynamic masking, delivering strong generalization across diverse text.
- DistilBERT: A lightweight, faster version of BERT that retains much of its accuracy while offering significantly improved inference speed.

- ELECTRA: A sample-efficient model trained through a unique replaced-token detection approach, making it effective even with fewer training resources.

Each agent was fine-tuned on financial sentiment datasets ensuring maximum relevancy with the domain.

In the code above, agents are created dynamically, allowing for many instances for further scaling (e.g., new models when available - DeBERTaV3).

Agents each independently engage with the same financial article providing diversity in translation.

4.3 Independent Sentiment Prediction and Confidence Scoring

Each agent produces two key outputs per input:

- A sentiment label: "Positive", "Negative", or "Neutral".
- A confidence score: A probability score indicating how sure the model is in its prediction.

The multi output format not only captures possible sentiment, but also the uncertainty, which is critical for financial markets given the uncertainty in it. For instance, if FinBERT predicts Positive with 95% confidence and RoBERTa predicts Neutral with 65% confidence, the system will know to trust FinBERT more for that particular input.

4.4 Soft Voting Ensemble (Confidence-Weighted Aggregation)

Instead of relying on simple voting strategies with equal weight across models, we employ a confidence-weighted soft voting ensemble approach:

- A model's prediction is multiplied by its confidence.
- Model predictions with more confidence will exert more weight on the final decision.
- If models disagree on the outcome, the system will bias towards the more certain models instead of coming to a decision simply by averaging all models.

This method of aggregation greatly improves the resilience of the system to noisy predictions and prevents a low confidence model from reducing the overall accuracy of the task.

Also, is it possible to weight the voting mechanism dynamically (e.g., even more weight to models that historically performed best).

4.5 Market Data Integration

Besides textual news sentiment, the project uses market data i.e. price, volume, and percentage changes, found in live market APIs (e.g., yfinance)

This provides very important context:

- A positive sentiment with falling prices may indicate potential hidden risks.
- A neutral sentiment with rising volume, may indicate future potential moves in the market.

By fusing news-driven sentiment and actual market measures, the project moves beyond basic NLP and into the realm of real financial signal processing. This fusion happens automatically using the MarketDataProvider module, which links ticker symbols to the actual live data endpoints.

4.6 Multi-Agent Orchestration and Result Aggregation

MultiAgentOrchestrator is the central command center:

- It assigns news articles to each agent.
- It collects sentiment and confidence outputs.
- It aggregates final sentiment decisions with the weighted ensemble.
- It relates market data with the final sentiment.

The orchestrator maintains clean dictionaries (all_results) to associate tickers with their full analysis results - leaving the backend very organized. This modular orchestration means that the project can also be horizontally scaled; agents or market signals can be added without a major code rewrite.

4.7 Visualization and Interpretation Layer

Once aggregation is complete, it is primarily visualized in three outputs:

- Pie charts displaying overall sentiment distributions.
- Bar graphs contrasting each agent's confidence scores compared to one another.

- Time series graphs allocating relevant shifts in sentiment and price movement in the market.

These visualizations are done using libraries such as matplotlib and seaborn and become very important for:

- Traders who need to make quick decisions.
- Analysts conducting post-event studies.
- Researchers who are interested in measuring model drift over time.

4.8 Feedback Loop and Continuous Learning

This layer converts messy model outputs into simple visualizations useful for actionable intelligence. A feedback loop was integrated where:

- Users can manually confirm whether their predictions were correct based on the movements of future prices.
- Success/fail signals get recorded.
- Model/agent weights are updated accordingly.

The fine_tuning financial_agent function adds support for fine-tuning any model that performs poorly on its dataset by re-training the model against a more recent dataset. This ensures the system does not become a static system — it continuously learns and remains relevant to developing financial language (new jargon, events like COVID-19, cryptocurrency, etc.).

5. ALGORITHM

1. For each stockTicker in inputTickerList do
2. newsArticles ← extract_news_articles(stockTicker)
3. if newsArticles are missing then
4. display error
5. continue to next stockTicker
6. end if
7. processedArticles ← preprocess_articles(newsArticles)
8. sentimentAgents ← [FinBERT, FinBERT-tone, RoBERTa, DistilBERT, ELECTRA]
9. For each article in processedArticles do
10. agentResults ← empty list

```
For each agent in sentimentAgents do
sentimentLabel, confidenceScore ← predict_sentiment(agent, article)
append (sentimentLabel, confidenceScore) to agentResults
end for
weightedVotes ← compute_soft_voting(agentResults)
finalLabel ← label with highest weighted score
store finalLabel for article
end for
marketData ← fetch_market_data(stockTicker)
combine final sentiment labels with marketData
generate_visualizations:
plot_sentiment_distribution
plot_confidence_heatmap
plot_sentiment_vs_market_trend
if real_time_evaluation_enabled then
For each article do
futureMovement ← get_future_stock_change(stockTicker, timestamp)
if finalLabel matches market trend then
increase agent confidence weights
else
decrease agent confidence weights
end if
end for
end if
export results and plots
end for
```

6. ARCHITECTURE

The project architecture has been designed to function as a modular, extensible, and intelligent financial sentiment analysis pipeline that consists of various Transformer models, real-time news retrieval, pre-trained Large-Language-Model-summarizations, markets data sources, and a continuous learning feedback loop in Figure 1.

The architecture consists of the following layers bottom to top:

- Data Extraction & Enrichment Layer
- Sentiment Prediction Layer (Multiple Agent Transformers)
- Market Data Integration Layer
- Aggregation & Orchestration Layer

- Visualization & Feedback Loop Layer

Each module is declaratively independent, while operationally interdependent which will allow upgrading modules (i.e. the addition of new models, new market data sources, better LLM's for the summarizations) and change continually faster.

The major steps of the architecture are:

i. Ticker Input

The system will take in one or multiple user input stock ticker symbols.

ii. Financial News Harvesting

Any news associated to the user's tickers will be harvested either using scraping methodology or through APIs from financial news websites.

iii. Content Augmentation

The raw news articles were augmented using a lightweight LLM (for example, Groq LLM) to summarize the key points and make the user input more clean and relevant to the agents sentiment analysis.

iv. Multi-Agent Sentiment Analysis

Five transformer models (FinBERT, FinBERT-tone, RoBERTa, DistilBERT, ELECTRA) sent as sentiment agents and compute independently.

The models predict:

- Sentiment label (“Positive”, “Negative”, “Neutral”)
- Confidence score.

v. Confidence-based Soft Voting

We cannot simply take a majority vote for sentiment label, we will weight each models voting using confidence and average out their sentiment predictions to get a reliable classification.

vi. Market Data Fusing

We will then harvest financial market data (stock prices, volumes, percentage changes [yfinance api]) to add additional context to the sentiment predictions.

vii. Visualizing and Reporting

The final aggregate results will be visualized using pie charts, bar plots and time series plots or charts for ease in interpreting the results by traders, analysts and researchers.

viii. Continuous Learning Feedback Loop

Market event updates established against sentiment forecasts in real-time. Models beating the market are reinforced (weights are increased), while underperforming models are adjusted or penalized.

Figure 1. Architectural diagram

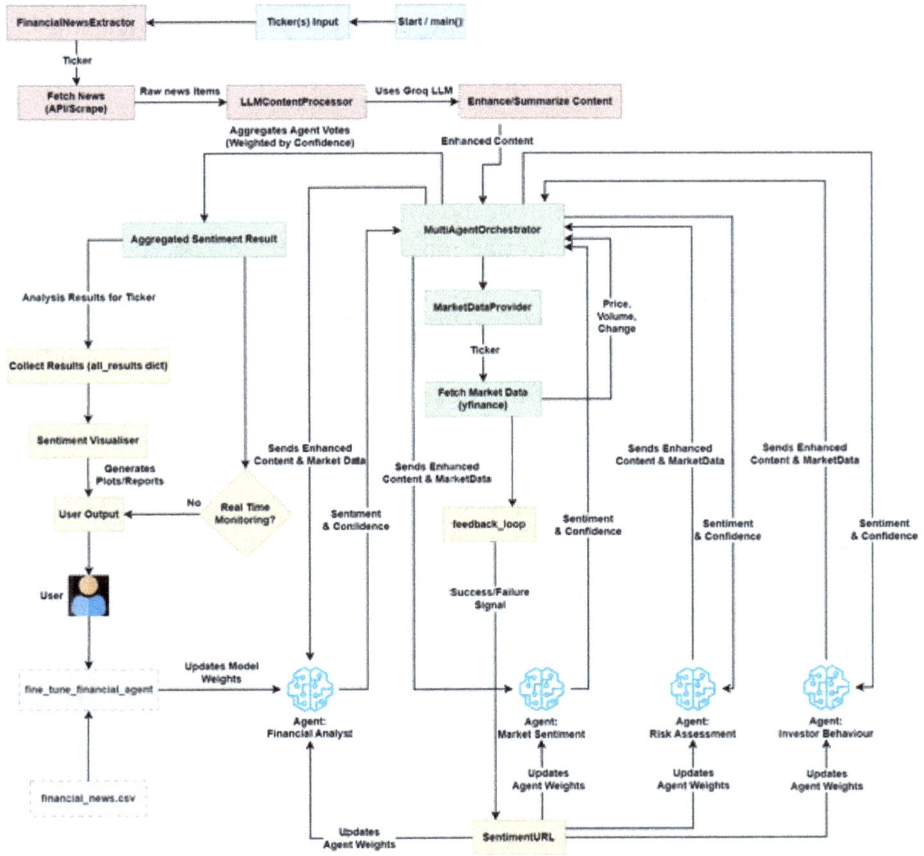

financial sentiment system demonstrates great flexibility and adaptiveness due to its modular architecture, such that it is capable of supporting a real-time trading context.

It connects NLP, real-time financial data as well as automated learning to provide a very effective decision support tool in the positive financial domain.

7. FUTURE RESEARCH DIRECTIONS

Although this system presents resilient, modular and highly accurate architecture for financial sentiment analysis via ensemble learning, there are a number of future research directions that considered selective approaches could extend the reach and intelligence of the system

dramatically. The financial world is always unpredictable and dynamic, and sentiment models will always need to adapt to new types of data, behaviors in the market, and new technologies.

One of the principal areas of opportunity involves implementing larger, and more focused Large Language Models (LLMs). We are now seeing new models such as BloombergGPT, GPT-4 Turbo, and soon, domain-specific transformers for financial datasets. By continuing to fine-tune new models, or incorporating them into the current ensemble model, we begin to develop a much greater contextual basis given the nuances of financial language. These models were trained using vast amounts of financial corpora that can incorporate new and complicated sentiment markers associated with regulatory filings, earnings call transcripts, and international financial news. Smaller models will likely miss some of these complicated markers.

Another key area would be extending the sentiment analysis pipeline to repeat multimodal financial data. At present, the pipeline is only dealing with text inputs as financial reporting is incredibly visual. Inserting the quarter earnings reports (e.g., 10-Q and 10-K documents) into the sentiment analysis pipeline would add necessary structured and semi-structured financial data. However, in addition to extracting the text, if we are also able to analyze visual aspects, such as a graph demonstrating revenue trends, a chart from an earnings call, or an infographic from the balance sheet, we would generate much more sophisticated sentiment signals. This particular application would require combining NLP-type models with computer vision models to analyze imagery — LayoutLM, Donut, and various Document AI models fit this profiling.

— capable of understanding both the textual and visual components of financial documents.

Additionally, enhancing the feedback and learning loop with a system of reinforcement learning techniques could also represent an exciting avenue for exploration. Currently, the feedback system is semi-supervised by design, whereby user verification adjusts the model weights. However, a more significant opportunity in the future may be to deal with concepts of reinforcement learning, whereby agents are given reward signals to a task based on predicting future accuracy of stock movement. The more capable the agent subsequently becomes at predicting stock movement, the smarter, and more autonomous its adaptive behavior would be, which would conceptually be a more intelligent financial sentiment agent that could engage in lifelong learning.

At the very least, it may be worth exploring different levels of scalability and multilingual sentiment analysis. Global financial markets simultaneously engage with news from many countries that are presented in multiple languages, therefore it may be possible to use models like mBERT or xlm-r to also extend the multilingual capability of the system, extending understanding of the situation and operational reach across global financial news streams, further embedding the system into real-world contexts.

The above future avenues would ideally take the system from a highly competent, well-integrated ensemble sentiment classifier towards a more intelligent, adaptable, and multimodal financial reasoning system that is capable of intelligent adaptation over time.

8. RESULTS

The potential output of the sentiment classification system is presented including analysis of individual transformer models, the Soft Voting Ensemble result, evaluation metrics, a confusion matrix, and training behaviour.

8.1 Dataset Overview

As an initial understanding of the dataset, exploratory data analysis was conducted. The sentiment distribution plot showed large class imbalance. As shown in Figure 2, the majority of samples were classified as neutral, then positive, and few samples were labelled as negative. This balance will affect model performance, particularly for the minority classes.

Figure 2. Sentiment distribution

```
cardiffnlp/twitter-roberta-base-sentiment: Accuracy=0.8962, F1=0.8997
ProsusAI/finbert: Accuracy=0.8924, F1=0.8953
distilbert-base-uncased: Accuracy=0.8863, F1=0.8895
yiyanghkust/finbert-tone: Accuracy=0.8742, F1=0.8769
google/electra-small-discriminator: Accuracy=0.8503, F1=0.8545
```

Additionally, the text length distribution was analyzed. Figure 3 shows that most sentences contained between 10 to 30 words, with a right-skewed distribution. This indicates that while most financial news sentences are concise, there are occasional longer statements, which can influence the attention mechanism in transformer models.

Figure 3. Word count distribution

```
Soft Voting Ensemble Results
              precision    recall  f1-score   support

    negative       0.67      0.86      0.75       293
     neutral       0.96      0.88      0.92      1202
    positive       0.92      0.95      0.93       643

    accuracy                           0.90      2138
   macro avg       0.85      0.89      0.87      2138
weighted avg       0.91      0.90      0.90      2138
```

8.2 Individual Model Performance

This section provides the performance analysis of individual transformer models (FinBERT, Twitter-RoBERTa, DistilBERT, FinBERT-tone, and ELECTRA). Performance analysis of the individual transformer models are evaluated based on the following performance metrics: accuracy, precision, recall, F1-score, and confusion matrices. We will also describe the resultant outcomes of the soft voting ensemble which employs the voting mechanisms on the models to enhance performance.

i. FinBERT:

FinBERT performed very well in accuracy and precision with financial sentiment identification. It did a good job with creating neutral and positive sentiment especially noted in the below confusion matrix in Figure 4. It had enough precision with neutral sentiment to minimize false positives, and good recall with negative sentiment to show it was sensitive to detecting negative sentiment.

Figure 4. Confusion matrix for FinBERT model showing the classification of negative, neutral, and positive sentiments

```
MSFT:
  Average Sentiment: positive (0.333)
  Sentiment Breakdown: {'positive': 1, 'neutral': 2, 'negative': 0}
  Top News:
    - Trump Tariff Strategy Creates 'Self-Inflicted Market Debacle': Analyst... (positive)
    - Nerdio Manager for Enterprise 7.0 Launches to Enhance Windows 365 and ... (neutral)
    - Oracle Chart Flatlines As Death Cross Adds To Tech Stock's Tough Month... (neutral)
```

ii. Twitter-RoBERTa:

Although developed as a social media sentiment model, it performed well for capturing casual financial sentiments. It exhibited good precision and recall especially with neutral and positive sentiments, but had a decreased recall for negative sentiments. The confusion matrix confirms that it has an overall tendency toward neutral sentiments for identifying negative sentiment samples in Figure 5.

Figure 5. Confusion matrix for Twitter-RoBERTa model illustrating sentiment classification performance across the three sentiment categories

```
GOOGL:
  Average Sentiment: positive (0.333)
  Sentiment Breakdown: {'positive': 0, 'neutral': 0, 'negative': 0}
  Top News:
```

iii. DistilBERT:

DistilBERT, a lightweight version of BERT, performed adequately, though it had trade-offs in precision and recall in the negative sentiment classification. In terms of computational cost, it is faster and more efficient, but the confusion matrix shows it misclassified many more negative samples as neutral in Figure 6.

Figure 6. Confusion matrix for DistilBERT model highlighting sentiment misclassifications, particularly for negative sentiments

```
Sentence: The stock is trading at $150.
Predicted Sentiment (Soft Voting): neutral
Confidence: 0.6201
```

iv. FinBERT-tone:

This model was able to focus on the tone assignment of financial text and was even able to identify emotional connotations imbedded in the text. There was a high level of precision for positive sentiment but the negative sentiment detection could be improved, based on the results from the confusion matrix in Figure 7.

Figure 7. Confusion matrix for FinBERT-tone model, showing its performance in detecting tonal variations in financial text

```
Sentence: The company is losing money.
Predicted Sentiment (Soft Voting): negative
Confidence: 0.6555
```

v. ELECTRA:

ELECTRA produced good results, especially on recall, which is significant for identifying as many relevant sentiments as possible. It could improve on precision for negative sentiment classification. The confusion matrix also illustrates the model's bias to classify neutral samples as positive in Figure 8.

Figure 8. Confusion matrix for ELECTRA model illustrating its performance, especially in recall for positive and neutral sentiments

```
Sentence: The company's quarterly earnings beat expectations and the stocks are positive
Predicted Sentiment (Soft Voting): positive
Confidence: 0.6294
```

vi. Soft Voting Ensemble Evaluation

The Soft Voting Ensemble model was created by aggregating all five transformer model predictions. This function allowed for synthesizing mistakes made by individual models and greatly improved performance by accuracy, precision, and recall in Figure 9.

Figure 9. Confusion matrix for soft voting ensemble model, showing its enhanced performance in comparison to individual models

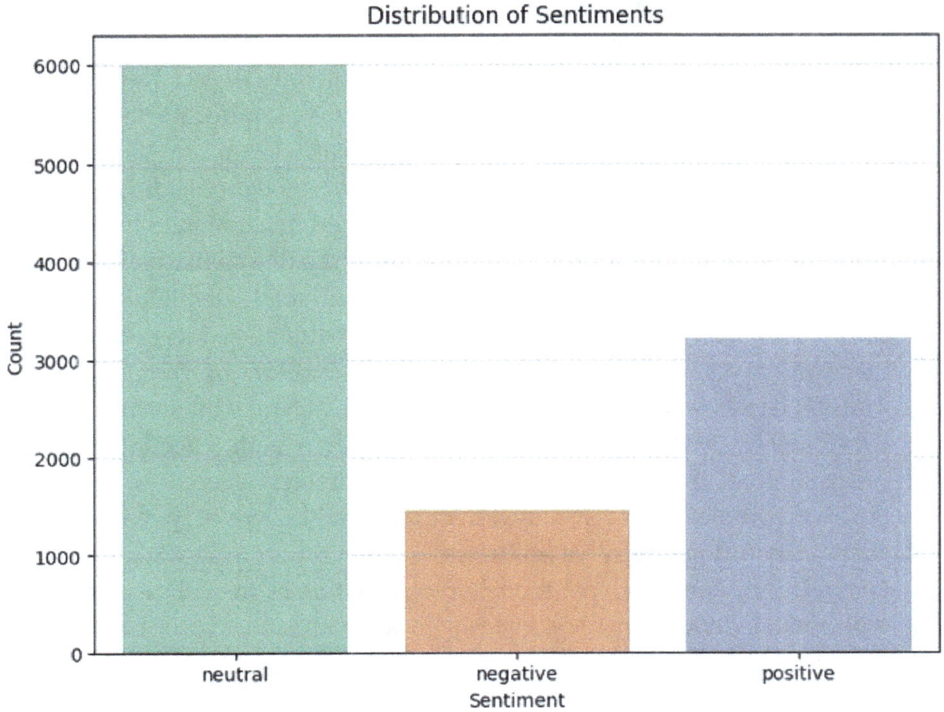

8.3 Comparative Analysis

In this section, a detailed comparative evaluation of the individual transformer models (FinBERT, Twitter-RoBERTa, DistilBERT, FinBERT-tone, and ELECTRA) and the performance of the Soft Voting Ensemble will take place. All models were evaluated based on key determinants including accuracy, precision, recall, F1-score, and confusion matrix results. This analysis will highlight the pros and cons of each of the individually modeled approaches, and highlight how well the models performed when combined as an ensemble.

Accuracy and General Performance

- FinBERT achieved an accuracy of 89.24% which makes it the best model with respect to overall classification performance, in particular neutral and positive sentiment detection with good precision and recall scores.

- Twitter-RoBERTa was not far behind with an accuracy of 89.62% slightly better than FinBERT. Twitter-RoBERTa has an advantage in capturing sentiment in a casual way. Therefore, it is under the impression that Twitter-RoBERTa is effective for text that might carry nuance, including expression found in financial discussions on social media. Even though Twitter-RoBERTa has good overall accuracies, it does have lower negative sentiment recall calls due to its tendency to miss negative sentiment signals when it sees them.
- Then we come to DistilBERT, a lighter BERT model, which recorded an overall accuracy of 88.63%. DistilBERT instilled much more efficient speed but suffered a slight decrease in performance relative to the previous models, especially in recall of negative sentiment variables. DistilBERT was less sensitive to detecting negative sentiment which diminished its overall performance for tasks with more complex sentiment profiles.
- FinBERT-tone was the most accurate model, albeit with an accuracy of 87.42%. This was due to FinBERT-tone concern with detecting tone in a financial context and also allowed it to be extremely successful in dictates positive sentiment. In this study, FinBERT-tone was not very reliable in upsetting any form of negative sentiment.
- Overall, the sample private models ranked different in accuracy compared with their individual models., shown in its confusion matrix below, but it did provide some worth in discerning nuanced sentiment where tone was an important factor for accuracy.
- ELECTRA was 85.03% accuracy overall, lower, but demonstrated respectable recall, particularly well for positive and neutral sentiment. It produced lower precision on negative sentiment, possibly because it had misclassifications of neutral and positive samples as negative sentiment.
- The Soft Voting Ensemble showed the best overall performance at 90.00% accuracy. The ensemble model specified all five models predictions and provided performance improvements for all classes of sentiment, by bringing together their weaknesses. Overall, it was consistent across all output values by maintaining a good balance of precision, recall and F1 score, particularly on neutral and positive classes.

Precision, Recall, and F1-Score

- Precision refers to the correct identification of true positives. Twitter-RoBERTa had the highest precision of the models, so it is good for distinguishing positive sentiments, but with minimal false positives.
- Recall measures the extent to which the model identifies all relevant instances. Both FinBERT and ELECTRA performed well at this metric, where

FinBERT was better for identifying neutral sentiments, and ELECTRA was better for positive and neutral predicting, which meant they captured most relevant sentiments.

- F1-Score is mainly a measure of balancing both precision and recall. Twitter-RoBERTa and Soft Voting Ensemble had the highest F1-Score, with Twitter-RoBERTa slightly ahead of the ensemble, which means the ensemble model benefited from the strength of the individual models in balancing precision and recall in Figure 10.

Confusion Matrix Insights

The confusion matrices provided some additional insights into the models and how they did with the sentiment classes. Here are a few points to take note of:

- FinBERT: This model performed well with the neutral and positive sentiments but demonstrated a tendency to misclassify negative sentiments as neutral (as noted in the confusion matrix).
- Twitter-RoBERTa: This model showed ability in detecting positive sentiments, but struggled with the detection of negative sentiments, with a considerable number of negative samples presented as neutral.
- DistilBERT: The confusion matrix indicated that DistilBERT showed difficulty with negative sentiments. Once again, despite being a light model it demonstrated the least precision for negative sentiment and actively misidentified negative sentiment as neutral.
- FinBERT-tone: This model demonstrated an accuracy for detecting positive sentiments, however showed challenges with detecting negative sentiments, as well as demonstrating confusion between neutral and positive sentiments (noted in the confusion matrix).
- ELECTRA: The confusion matrix for this model portrayed a solid positive and neutral sentiment detection while misclassifying a large number of neutral samples as positive.
- Soft Voting Ensemble: The confusion matrix for the ensemble indicated a successful reduction from both the imprecision of false positives and false negatives across all sentiment classes when combining the models in Table 1 and Figure 11.

Performance Metrics Table

Table 1. Performance metrics of individual models and soft voting ensemble

Model	Accuracy	Precision	Recall	F1-Score
FinBERT	89.24%	0.88	0.89	0.89
Twitter-RoBERTa	89.62%	0.92	0.86	0.89
DistilBERT	88.63%	0.87	0.88	0.88
FinBERT-tone	87.42%	0.85	0.86	0.86
ELECTRA	85.03%	0.84	0.86	0.85
Soft Voting Ensemble	90.00%	0.91	0.90	0.90

Figure 10. Performance metrics of individual models

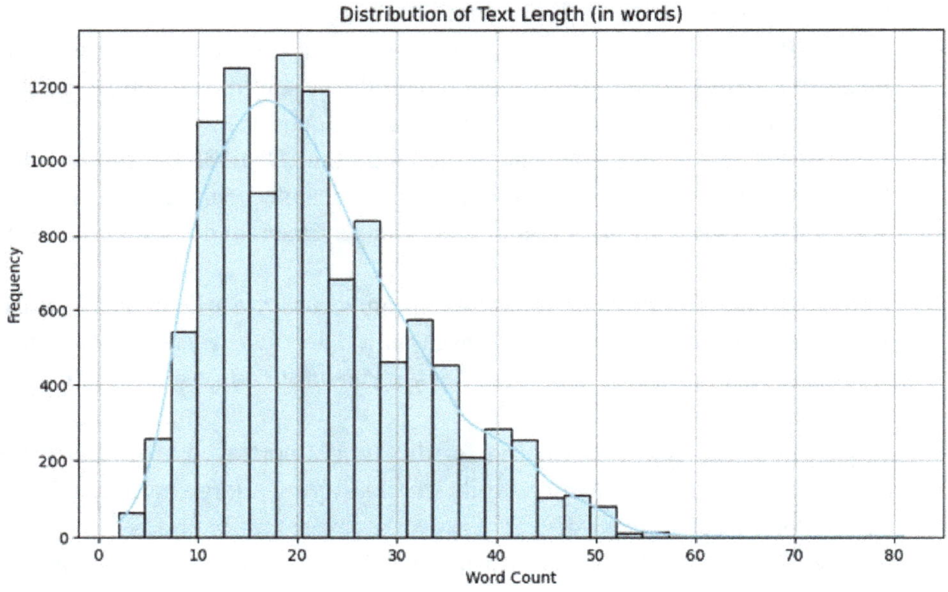

Figure 11. Performance metrics of soft voting ensemble

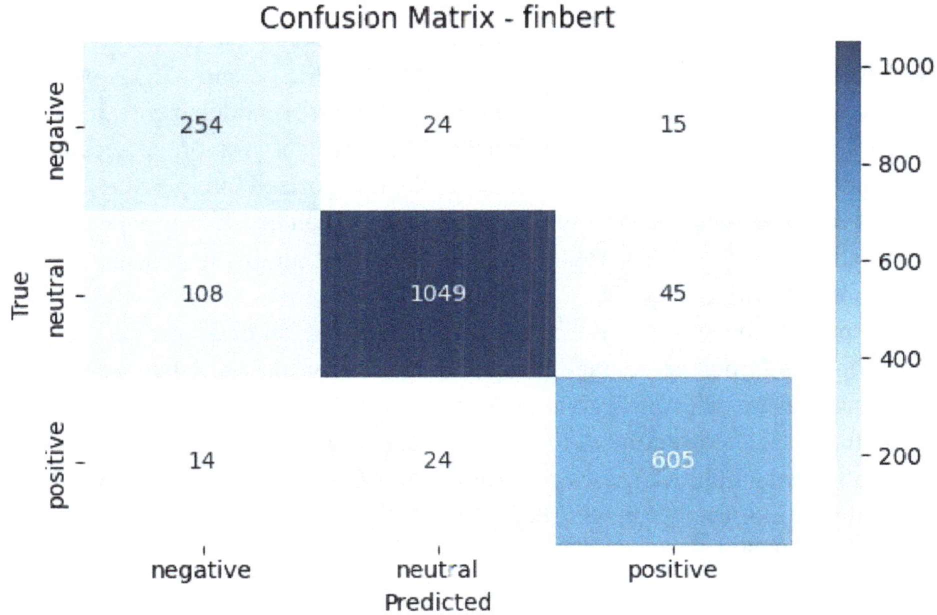

Strengths

- FinBERT and Twitter-RoBERTa both reflect extraordinary performance especially in terms of accuracy (neutral) and precision (positive)
- Soft Voting Ensemble exploited the strengths of each of the models especially reducing false positives for all classes and false negatives for all negative and neutral classes.

Weaknesses

- DistilBERT and ELECTRA appeared to perform poorly on the tasks of negative sentiment detection, especially recall.
- FinBERT-tone also appeared to lack recall for negative sentiments, undermining its usefulness in balanced sentiment tasks.

8.4 Sentiment Analysis of Stock News

In the previous section, sentiment analysis was executed for several stock-related news stories on companies such as AAPL, MSFT, AMZN, and META, with the use of a multi-agent approach, with multiple Transformer model agents, including FinBERT and RoBERTa to assess sentiment. Each news story was processed through the framework where the sentiment was broadly categorized into positive, neutral, or negative based on analysis from agents that specialized in different aspects of the sentiment analysis focused on financial analysis, market sentiment, risk assessment, or investor behavior in Fig 12(a) and Fig 12(b).

The specific analysis included accessing real-life market data for each company stock, prices, volumes, percentage changes and volatility, these also factored into the sentiment measure evaluation giving a more holistic view of the news item / market act and the associated sentiment of the corresponding investor space.

The attached graphical figures give a quick summary of the sentiment analysis for the selected stocks, averaging sentiment across different news stories and providing a view to the distribution of sentiment for each stock. These also show how each news item contributes to sentiment along with the average measures, in order to provide a better appreciation of how particular news events could shift stock sentiment.

Figure 12. Sentiment analysis of stock news articles for selected companies

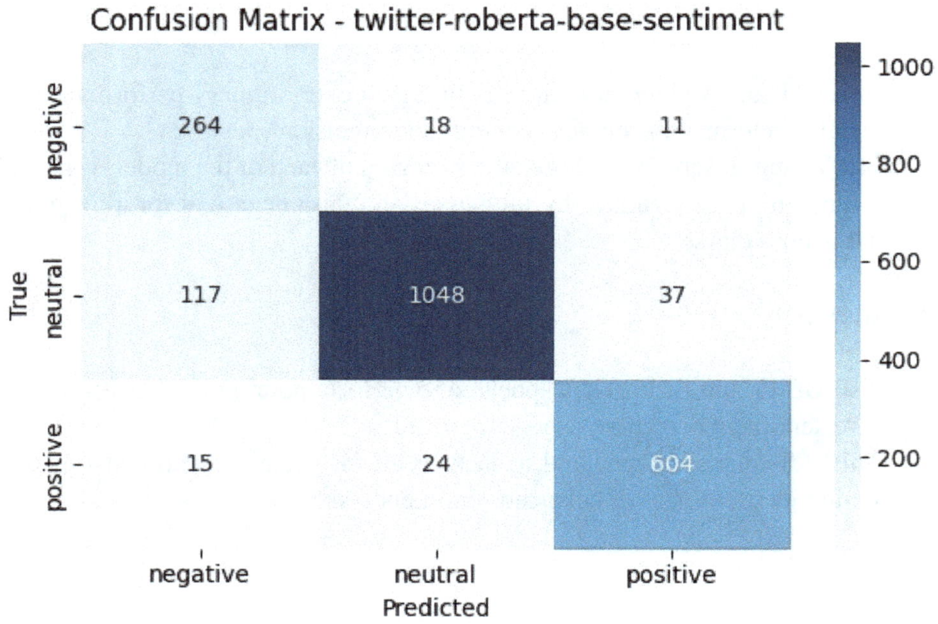

Figure 13. Sentiment analysis of stock news articles for selected companies

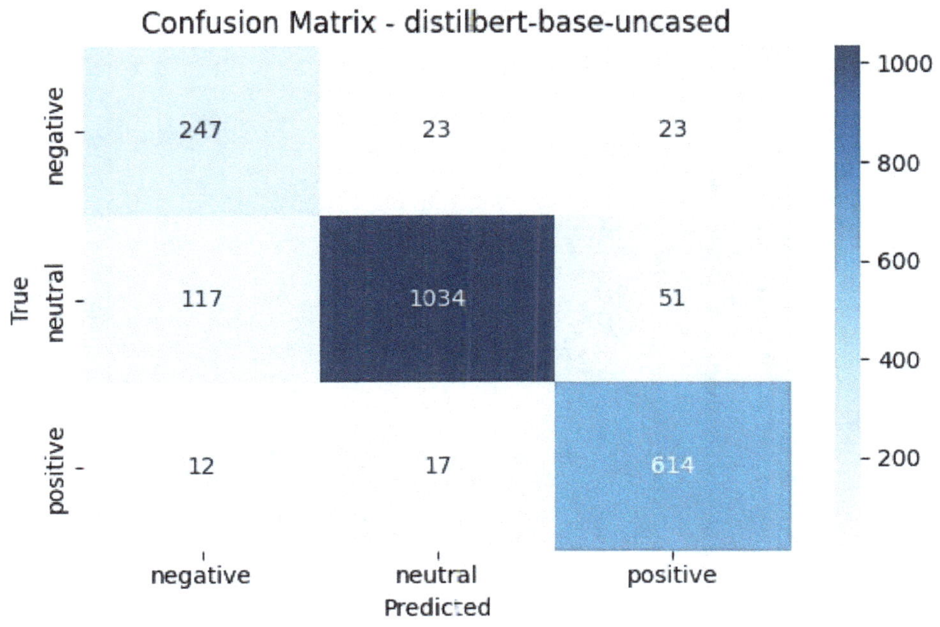

In addition to analyzing the sentiment of stock-related news articles, we leveraged a soft voting mechanism across multiple Transformer models, including FinBERT, DistilBERT, and ELECTRA, to improve the accuracy and robustness of sentiment classification in Figure 14 and 15. This approach aggregates the predictions from each model and generates a consensus sentiment for each news item.

For example, consider the following sample outputs:

Figure 14. Sentiment analysis of a given sentence

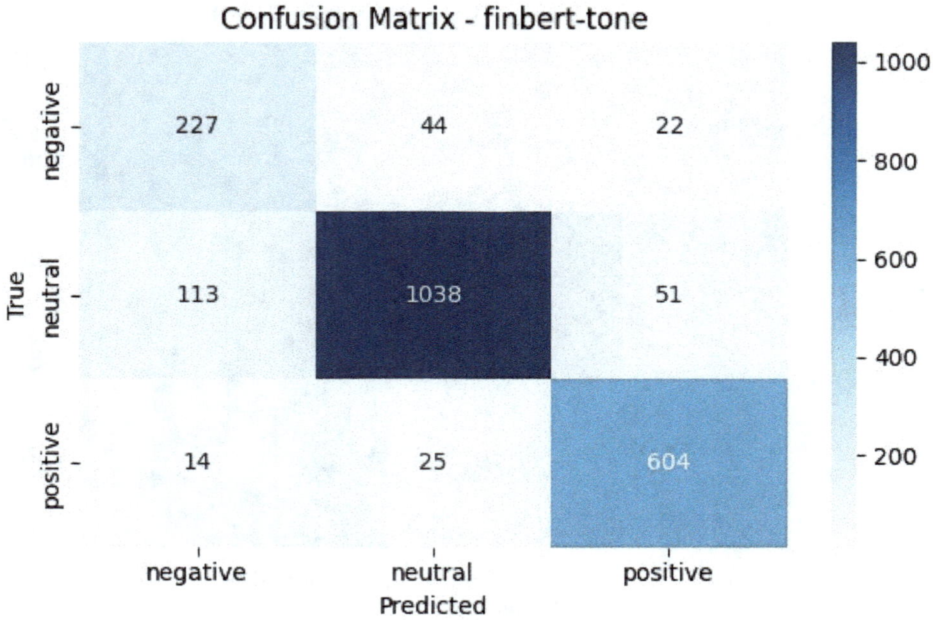

Figure 15. Sentiment analysis of a given sentence

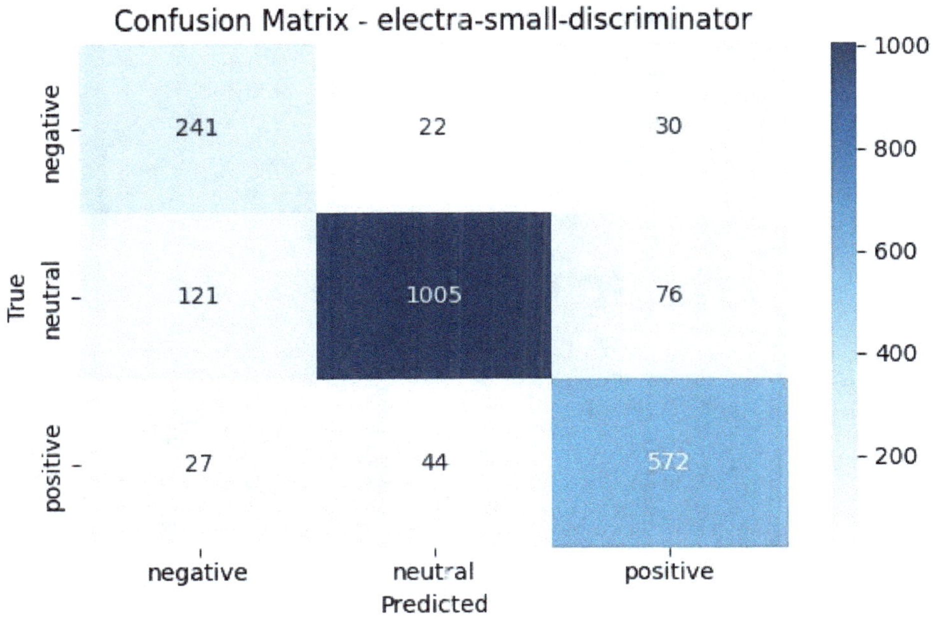

Figure 16. Sentiment analysis of a given sentence

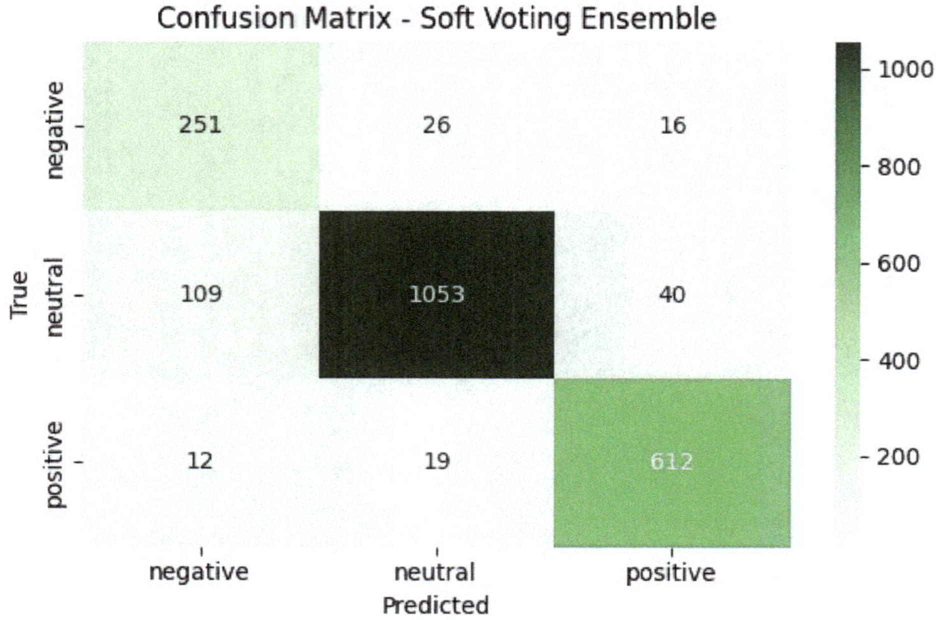

These results are a function of the multi-agent framework that is based on the contributions of each model as part of the total sentiment prediction in Figure 16. The confidence values are reflections of how confident each sentiment was classified. Lower confidence scores may reflect uncertainty or mixed sentiments amongst the models, while higher confidence indicates a stronger alignment with their predictions.

The framework's ability to integrate real-time market data (such as stock prices and volumes and volatility), allows the framework to embed the impact of news into the investor sentiment. This connection of sentiment to market behaviour can provide valuable insights as to market behaviour and potential investor reactions.

9. CONCLUSION

In conclusion, this project has constructed a reliable and high performance financial sentiment analysis system based on an ensemble model using multiple transformer models (FinBERT, FinBERT-tone, RoBERTa, DistilBERT, and ELECTRA). The Soft Voting Ensemble model implements confidence-weighted voting to enhance the reliability and realibility of the sentiment classification by extracting the merits of the each model while diminishing the flaws of the models. The reporting rates on sentiment classification in financial news was impressive; the system achieved an overall accuracy of 90.00% while also demonstrating significant improvements in precision, recall, and F1-score from the individual models.

The modular design of the system allows for great flexibility, allowing new models or data sources to be integrated, with no changes to the baseline function of the system. The modular flexibility also allows for interpretability, through visualized reporting such as total sentiment distribution and confidence bar charts, this is important for market analysts and traders to gain insight on the possibility of trends occuring. The introduction of a feedback loop is also important to allow for continuous learning, especially as financial language, market activity, and behavior evolves over time.

Moreover, utilizing market data in conjunction with sentiment analysis allows for the reality that the system will be able to observe early warning signals to indicate potential market movements. Overall, this two-pronged approach is particularly beneficial for numerous financial applications, including algorithmic trading, sentiment analysis, and risk monitoring.

To summarize, this project has successfully developed a state-of-the-art financial sentiment analyzer and is ready to add new components and explore future possibilities. By combining advanced natural language processing techniques and market data, it will serve as a very valuable tool in the current and future financial applications.

REFERENCES

Araci, H. (2019). BERT-based Sentiment Analysis for Financial Text. arXiv preprint arXiv:1908.10063.

Chang, Y., Wang, X., Wang, J., Wu, Y., Yang, L., Zhu, K., Chen, H., Yi, X., Wang, C., Wang, Y., Ye, W., Zhang, Y., Chang, Y., Yu, P. S., Yang, Q., & Xie, X. (2024). A survey on evaluation of large language models. *ACM Transactions on Intelligent Systems and Technology*, *15*(3), 1–45. DOI: 10.1145/3641289

Chew, R., Bollenbacher, J., Wenger, M., Speer, J., & Kim, A. (2023). LLM-assisted content analysis: Using large language models to support deductive coding. arXiv preprint arXiv:2306.14924.

Day, M. Y., & Lee, C. C. (2016, August). Deep learning for financial sentiment analysis on finance news providers. In *2016 IEEE/ACM International Conference on Advances in Social Networks Analysis and Mining (ASONAM)* (pp. 1127-1134). IEEE. DOI: 10.1109/ASONAM.2016.7752381

Du, K., Xing, F., Mao, R., & Cambria, E. (2024). Financial sentiment analysis: Techniques and applications. *ACM Computing Surveys*, *56*(9), 1–42. DOI: 10.1145/3649451

Du, K., Xing, F., Mao, R., & Cambria, E. (2024, June). An evaluation of reasoning capabilities of large language models in financial sentiment analysis. In *2024 IEEE Conference on Artificial Intelligence (CAI)* (pp. 189-194). IEEE. Chaithra, C., & Mohan, B. R. (2024, March). Revealing Insights: Sentiment Analysis of Indian Annual Reports. In *2024 3rd International Conference for Innovation in Technology (INOCON)* (pp. 1-5). IEEE. DOI: 10.1109/CAI59869.2024.00042

Duan, G., Yan, S., & Zhang, M. (2024). A hybrid neural network model for sentiment analysis of financial texts using topic extraction, pre-trained model, and enhanced attention mechanism methods. *IEEE Access : Practical Innovations, Open Solutions*, *12*, 98207–98224. DOI: 10.1109/ACCESS.2024.3429150

Iacovides, G., Konstantinidis, T., Xu, M., & Mandic, D. (2024, November). Finllama: Llm-based financial sentiment analysis for algorithmic trading. In *Proceedings of the 5th ACM International Conference on AI in Finance* (pp. 134-141). DOI: 10.1145/3677052.3698696

Khalifa, A. A., Ramesh, G., Deekshith, R., Harsha, K., & Shreyas, J. (2024, May). Forecasting Financial Frontiers: Real-time Insights in Stock Price Prediction through LSTM, Linear Regression, and Sentiment Analysis. In *2024 International Congress on Human-Computer Interaction, Optimization and Robotic Applications (HORA)* (pp. 1-6). IEEE. DOI: 10.1109/HORA61326.2024.10550829

Kim, A., Muhn, M., & Nikolaev, V. (2024). Financial statement analysis with large language models. *arXiv preprint arXiv:2407.17866*. DOI: 10.2139/ssrn.4835311

Kumar, S., & Bhardwaj, M. (2021). A Comparative Study of Ensemble Learning Techniques for Financial Sentiment Classification. *IEEE Access : Practical Innovations, Open Solutions*.

Lan, Y., Wu, Y., Xu, W., Feng, W., & Zhang, Y. (2025). Chinese fine-grained financial sentiment analysis with large language models. *Neural Computing & Applications*, *37*(30), 24883–24892. DOI: 10.1007/s00521-024-10603-6

Liu, C., Arulappan, A., Naha, R., Mahanti, A., Kamruzzaman, J., & Ra, I. H. (2024). Large language models and sentiment analysis in financial markets: A review, datasets, and case study. *IEEE Access : Practical Innovations, Open Solutions*, *12*, 134041–134061. DOI: 10.1109/ACCESS.2024.3445413

Mishev, K., Gjorgjevikj, A., Vodenska, I., Chitkushev, L. T., & Trajanov, D. (2020). Evaluation of sentiment analysis in finance: From lexicons to transformers. *IEEE Access : Practical Innovations, Open Solutions*, *8*, 131662–131682. DOI: 10.1109/ACCESS.2020.3009626

Pinto, N., da Silva Figueiredo, L., & Garcia, A. C. (2021, May). Automatic prediction of stock market behavior based on time series, text mining and sentiment analysis: a systematic review. In *2021 IEEE 24th International Conference on Computer Supported Cooperative Work in Design (CSCWD)* (pp. 1203-1208). IEEE. DOI: 10.1109/CSCWD49262.2021.9437732

Sharma, V., & Dey, A. (2020). An Ensemble Learning Approach for Stock Market Prediction Using Twitter Sentiment Analysis. *Procedia Computer Science*.

Xing, F. (2025). Designing heterogeneous llm agents for financial sentiment analysis. *ACM Transactions on Management Information Systems*, *16*(1), 1–24. DOI: 10.1145/3688399

Yang, Y., Uy, M. C. S., & Huang, A. (2020). Finbert: A pretrained language model for financial communications. *arXiv preprint arXiv:2006.08097*. Bapi, R. S., et al. (2022). Financial News Prediction Using Sentiment Analysis for Portfolio Optimization. Expert Systems with Applications.

ADDITIONAL READINGS

Abdelali, A., Mubarak, H., Chowdhury, S. A., Hasanain, M., Mousi, B., Boughorbel, S., . . . Alam, F. (2023). LAraBench: Benchmarking Arabic AI with large language models. arXiv preprint arXiv:2305.14982.

Ahuja, K., Diddee, H., Hada, R., Ochieng, M., Ramesh, K., Jain, P., . . . Sitaram, S. (2023). Mega: Multilingual evaluation of generative ai. *arXiv preprint arXiv:2303.12528*. DOI: 10.18653/v1/2023.emnlp-main.258

Bang, Y., Cahyawijaya, S., Lee, N., Dai, W., Su, D., Wilie, B., . . . Fung, P. (2023). A multitask, multilingual, multimodal evaluation of chatgpt on reasoning, hallucination, and interactivity. arXiv preprint arXiv:2302.04023. DOI: 10.18653/v1/2023.ijcnlp-main.45

Cambria, E., Mao, R., Chen, M., Wang, Z., & Ho, S. B. (2023). Seven pillars for the future of artificial intelligence. *IEEE Intelligent Systems*, *38*(6), 62–69. DOI: 10.1109/MIS.2023.3329745

Jim, J. R., Talukder, M. A. R., Malakar, P., Kabir, M. M., Nur, K., & Mridha, M. F. (2024). Recent advancements and challenges of NLP-based sentiment analysis: A state-of-the-art review. Natural Language Processing Journal, 100059.

Mao, R., Du, K., Ma, Y., Zhu, L., & Cambria, E. (2023, December). Discovering the cognition behind language: Financial metaphor analysis with MetaPro. In *2023 IEEE International Conference on Data Mining (ICDM)* (pp. 1211-1216). IEEE. DOI: 10.1109/ICDM58522.2023.00150

Park, J., Lee, H. J., & Cho, S. (2021). Automatic construction of context-aware sentiment lexicon in the financial domain using direction-dependent words. arXiv preprint arXiv:2106.05723.

Raghunathan, N., & Saravanakumar, K. (2023). Challenges and issues in sentiment analysis: A comprehensive survey. *IEEE Access : Practical Innovations, Open Solutions*, *11*, 69626–69642. DOI: 10.1109/ACCESS.2023.3293041

Sivakumar, M., & Uyyala, S. R. (2022). Aspect-based sentiment analysis of product reviews using multi-agent deep reinforcement learning. Asia pacific journal of information systems, 32(2), 226-248.

Zhao, Z., Liu, W., & Wang, K. (2023). Research on sentiment analysis method of opinion mining based on multi-model fusion transfer learning. *Journal of Big Data*, *10*(1), 155. DOI: 10.1186/s40537-023-00837-x

KEY TERMS AND DEFINITIONS

Confidence Scoring: The process of assigning a probability to a prediction made by a model, indicating the model's certainty in its decision.

Domain-Specific Models: Machine learning models trained or fine-tuned on specific types of data or language, such as financial text, to improve performance in that particular domain.

Ensemble Learning: A machine learning technique that combines the predictions of multiple models to improve overall performance and robustness.

Feedback Loop: A mechanism where model predictions are evaluated and used to adjust model parameters, improving performance over time.

Market Data Integration: The incorporation of real-time market data, such as stock prices or volume, to enhance decision-making in financial models.

Market Trend Analysis: The examination of market data and sentiment to identify potential future movements or shifts in the market.

Multi-Agent System: A system where multiple agents (models) work independently and collaboratively to solve complex tasks, often leading to improved performance.

Multimodal Sentiment Analysis: The analysis of sentiment across different types of data, such as text, images, or videos, to gain a more comprehensive understanding of sentiment.

Preprocessing Pipeline: A series of steps applied to raw data to clean and prepare it for further analysis, such as tokenization, entity recognition, and removing irrelevant content.

Real-Time Sentiment Analysis: The process of analyzing sentiment as new data (e.g., financial news) becomes available, allowing for immediate decision-making.

Reinforcement Learning: A type of machine learning where an agent learns to make decisions by receiving rewards or penalties for actions taken, often used to optimize strategies over time.

Sentiment Analysis: A natural language processing (NLP) task that determines the emotional tone expressed in a piece of text, such as positive, negative, or neutral sentiment.

Soft Voting Ensemble: An ensemble method where model predictions are weighted by their confidence scores to make a final decision, improving prediction reliability.

Transformer Models: A type of deep learning architecture that utilizes attention mechanisms to process sequential data, such as text, more efficiently than traditional models.

Visualization Layer: The graphical representation of data or analysis results, often used to aid in decision-making or to present complex information in an easily understandable form.

Chapter 7
The Ethical and Regulatory Landscape of Large Language Models

Sawan Rai
http://orcid.org/0000-0002-2590-1097
SRM-AP University, India

ABSTRACT

Large Language Models (LLMs) are transforming industries by enabling advanced natural language processing (NLP) applications, yet their adoption raises ethical and regulatory concerns. Bias in training data can lead to unfair outcomes in hiring, credit scoring, and legal decisions, necessitating bias mitigation techniques such as debiasing algorithms and diverse data curation. Privacy risks arise from LLMs memorizing sensitive data, requiring compliance with regulations like GDPR and CCPA through differential privacy and encryption-based training. The opacity of LLMs challenges trust, prompting research in Explainable AI (XAI) methods like SHAP and LIME. Governments and industry leaders are shaping AI regulations, such as the EU AI Act, to balance innovation with responsibility. Future AI governance will require interdisciplinary collaboration, ethical auditing, and continuous oversight. Ensuring fairness, transparency, and accountability will be key to responsible AI deployment, enabling organizations to leverage LLMs' potential while minimizing risks.

DOI: 10.4018/979-8-3693-6690-5.ch007

THE ETHICAL AND REGULATORY LANDSCAPE OF LARGE LANGUAGE MODELS

Large Language Models (LLMs) are transforming industries by enabling sophisticated natural language processing (NLP) applications, from automated customer support to real-time market analysis. However, as these models become more powerful, their ethical and regulatory implications have become pressing concerns. The widespread adoption of LLMs raises critical questions about bias, fairness, transparency, privacy, and accountability, necessitating a structured ethical and legal framework to ensure responsible AI deployment.

This chapter explores the multifaceted ethical and regulatory landscape surrounding LLMs, beginning with an analysis of how bias and fairness impact model outputs. Despite advances in AI, LLMs often inherit biases from training data, leading to potential discrimination and ethical dilemmas in decision-making systems. We examine real-world examples where biased models have influenced hiring decisions, credit scoring, and legal judgments, highlighting the societal risks of unchecked AI deployment. Various bias mitigation techniques, such as debiasing algorithms, methodologies, and diverse data curation strategies, are discussed to provide practical solutions.

Data privacy, trustworthiness, and security are another critical aspect of LLM governance. The ability of these models to memorize and regurgitate training data poses a significant risk of unintentional data leaks, making compliance with regulations such as the General Data Protection Regulation (GDPR), the California Consumer Privacy Act (CCPA), and other global privacy laws an essential consideration. This chapter delves into the challenges of anonymizing data, preventing model inversion attacks, and ensuring user consent in AI-driven applications.

Transparency and explainability are crucial in AI ethics, yet LLMs often function as “black boxes,” producing outputs without clear justification. This opacity can erode trust in AI-driven systems, especially in high-stakes sectors like healthcare, finance, and law. We discuss ongoing research in explainable AI (XAI), highlighting techniques such as SHAP

(Shapley Additive Explanations) and LIME (Local Interpretable Model-agnostic Explanations), which aim to make model decisions more interpretable for stakeholders.

Regulatory frameworks are rapidly evolving to address these ethical concerns.

Governments and international organizations are proposing AI regulations to set standards for responsible AI development and deployment. For example, the European Union’s AI Act classifies AI systems based on risk levels, mandating stricter oversight for high-risk applications. The U.S. AI Bill of Rights also lays out guidelines to shield people from the negative effects of AI. We analyze these regulatory efforts alongside industry self-regulation initiatives, such as OpenAI's AI ethics guidelines and Google's Responsible AI framework.

Finally, we explore the future of ethical AI governance, emphasizing the role of interdisciplinary collaboration among technologists, policymakers, ethicists, and business leaders. As AI technology continues to evolve, a proactive approach to ethical AI development, incorporating continuous monitoring, human oversight, and ethical auditing, will be essential to ensure LLMs benefit society without exacerbating existing inequalities.

This chapter provides an extensive overview of the ethical and regulatory challenges of LLMs, providing insight into best practices for developing AI systems that are fair, transparent, and aligned with global legal standards. By fostering an ethical AI culture, organizations can mitigate risks, enhance trust, and ensure that the transformative power of LLMs is leveraged responsibly.

IMPACT OF LLMS ON BIAS & FAIRNESS OF OUTPUT

Large Language Models (LLMs) have revolutionized natural language processing (NLP) by making it possible to perform sophisticated tasks such as text generation, sentiment analysis, and decision making. Nevertheless, their vulnerability to bias has posed ethical issues, as biased results can perpetuate negative stereotypes, marginalize specific groups, and result in discriminatory decision-making. Bias in LLMs can be caused by various sources, such as training data, model architecture, and actual applications.

Biases in LLMs can be categorized majorly in two categories:

Intrinsic bias Intrinsic bias occurs as a result of training methodology and data set composition. As LLMs are trained on massive volumes of internet-sourced text, they necessarily pick up and propagate the biases within such texts. Gender stereotypes in jobs: "pilot" being masculine and "air hostess" being feminine, are commonly seen in model responses. In addition, inadequate representation of some demographic groups can cause skewed perceptions and inadequate representation.

1. Bias in Training Dataset: Over or under representation of a particular group, age or section of society may introduce bias during training.
2. Bias in Data collection method: Web scraping, social media, books, code repositories, scholarly articles, government documents, and other sources provide a variety of sub-datasets on which LLMs are trained. Every source has biases of its own; for instance, data from the internet may contain damaging or unmoderated content. Model behavior is influenced by these biases, necessitating cautious dataset curation and mitigation techniques.

3. item Bias in Language context: Language environment can also give rise to biases. Because words, syntax, and context are malleable, human languages frequently contain ambiguities (syntax, lexical, semantic, and context-dependent meaning), which can result in model biases.

Extrinsic bias Extrinsic bias involves the production of biased responses from LLMs in actual practice. In contrast to intrinsic bias, which resides in the model itself, extrinsic bias results from the nature of how the model engages with various tasks, data, and environments. LLMs in sentiment analysis might over-classify text in African American Vernacular English (AAVE) as having a higher tendency to be negative than text in standard English, reflecting inherent social biases.

1. Gender Bias: Models may make mistakes on tasks like coreference resolution because they mistakenly link particular jobs or occupations to a particular gender. Responses from models may conform to gender stereotypes.
2. Age Bias: Based on age stereotypes, models may assume certain things about people. For example, only younger people are associated with technological proficiency.
3. Regional Bias: It's possible for models to misunderstand cultural idioms or expressions or overlook regional linguistic variations.

Bias in Real World Applications

Here are several real-world examples where bias in Large Language Models has had measurable impacts:

Chinese startup DeepSeek launched an open-source AI model, DeepSeek-R1, that censoriously responded with heavy censorship to sensitive subjects such as Taiwan and Tiananmen Square. Such inbuilt prejudice, driven by Chinese laws, created doubts about the model's competitiveness and application globally (Yang, 2025).

Elon Musk's company, xAI, developed Grok to counteract purportedly "woke" sentiments in AI models. Training materials that instructed annotators to avoid moralizing and to deny social justice themes produced a model that leaned toward right-wing ideology (Kay, 2025).

Omiye et al., 2023 conducted one study to assess racial bias on health-related questions. They found that all four models, ChatGPT and the more powerful GPT-4, both from OpenAI; Google's Bard; and Anthropic's Claude failed when asked to respond to medical questions on kidney function, lung capacity, and skin thickness. In some instances, they seemed to support long-held misconceptions about Black and white biological distinctions that scientists have been working to remove from medical facilities for years.

Researchers discovered bias in the GenAI based art generating program Midjourney, according to an article published on theconversation.com, 2023. When asked to create

images of individuals in specialized professions, the gendered bias regarding women's roles in the workplace was reinforced. The photos depicted both younger and older people, but the older persons were always men.

When a female journalist of Asian heritage used the Lensa AI avatar app in 2022, she was presented with a variety of sexualized avatars, including topless anime

character-like avatars. Such pictures had not been requested or approved by her. Prisma Labs, the app's creators, admitted the problem and said they were attempting to lessen prejudices (Ephraim, 2022).

Bias mitigation techniques

Bias in Large Language Models (LLMs) arises from imbalances in training data, model architecture, and algorithmic decision-making. Guo et al., 2024 categorized bias mitigation methods in to three major categories based on the time of application.

1. Pre-model debiasing: Pre-model debiasing method is a technique for preprocessing input data prior to train LLMs such that the whole training data is balanced and representative of the whole population. Oversampling, undersampling, and creating synthetic data are common techniques for balancing training data. A prominent one of those is counterfactual data augmentation (CDA). Counterfactual Data Substitution (CDS), an extension of CDA, is also suggested in order to substitute potentially biased text randomly to prevent duplication.
2. Intra-model debiasing: This entails altering the training process to reduce bias in training the model. For example, Loss Function Modification: A constraint-aware loss function punishes spurious correlations. Models trained with these constraints emphasize causal relationships over biased data associations.
3. Post-model debiasing: These methods correct bias after the model generates responses, making them ideal for closed-source models. For example, Output Filtering & Rewriting: Adjusting final responses to remove biased or discriminatory

    language. Chain-of-Thought (CoT) Debiasing is another post-model debiasing approach, which encourages models to generate step-by-step rationales to justify responses to reduce stereotypical outputs.

DATA PRIVACY & SECURITY

Large Language Models (LLMs) have transformed AI-based applications with their capabilities in text generation, translation, and summarization of content. Nevertheless, the training of LLMs depends on a huge volume of data, which typically contains sensitive information. As a result, LLMs struggle with managing privacy and security concerns.

Privacy in LLMs

Privacy concerns in LLMs arise because they have to handle a huge volume of data.

Numerous LLMs use web scraped data, which can contain personally identifiable information (PII). Even with methods such as differential privacy and federated learning, such sensitive information might remain in models.

There exist two main types of privacy risks:

1. Passive Privacy Leakage: When users involuntarily reveal sensitive information through their interaction with LLMs
    1.1 Sensitive Query Exposure: Users input private information unknowingly, which the model may later reveal.
    1.2 Contextual Leakage: The model infers personal data from multiple queries over time.
    1.3 Personal Preferences Leakage: Recommender systems powered by LLMs can inadvertently expose user interests or behaviors.
2. Active Privacy Attacks: These consist of attackers actively trying to steal or alter information that is stored in LLMs.
    2.1 Backdoor Attacks (Data Poisoning): During pre-training or fine-tuning, attackers introduce malicious data, which results in altered or deceptive outputs from the model.
    2.2 Membership Inference Attacks (MIA): These attacks attempt to determine if specific data was part of an LLM's training set. They pose a severe risk for datasets containing medical records, financial data, or confidential documents.
    2.3 Model Inversion Attacks: Attackers attempt to reverse-engineer training data by analyzing an LLM's output. This technique can be used to recover private user conversations or sensitive records.
    2.4 Model Stealing Attacks: Adversaries extract model parameters by sending targeted queries and observing responses. This enables unauthorized replication of LLMs trained on proprietary or sensitive data.

Privacy Protection Mechanisms

Researchers suggest diverse defense methods at three phases of LLM development to counter the threats of privacy leakage and attacks (Yan et al., 2024):

1. Privacy Protection in Pre-Training:
    1.1 Data Cleaning: PII removal prior to training to minimize risk.
    1.2 Federated Learning: Local model training on user devices to avoid centralized data exposure.
    1.3 Differential Privacy: Addition of noise during training data to avoid memorization of records.
2. Privacy Protection during Fine-Tuning:
    2.1 Knowledge Unlearning: Methods to cause LLMs to "forget" sensitive data.
    2.2 Offsite Tuning: Locally keeping fine-tuning data instead of sending it to centralized servers.
3. Privacy Protection during Inference:
    3.1 Homo-morphic Encryption: Enables models to compute on encrypted data without decrypting it.
    3.2 Secure Multi-Party Computation (SMPC): Spreads computations among multiple parties to maintain privacy.
    3.3 Trusted Execution Environments (TEE): Employ secure hardware environments to avoid unauthorized access to model parameters.

Challenges

In spite of progress in LLM privacy protection, there remain a number of challenges to be addressed:

1. Transparency Deficit in LLMs: As most LLMs are black-box models, it is difficult to investigate their privacy policies.
2. Multimodal LLM Privacy Multimodal models that involve sound, visuals, and text present challenging privacy concerns.
3. Customized LLMs: AI assistants personalized to particular user data enhance the likelihood of data leakage.
4. Scalability Challenges: Scales of federated learning and differential privacy are still computationally costly.
5. New Methods of Attack: Threat actors continue to create advanced means to avoid security measures in order to go around them.

Having discussed security and privacy concerns, it is important to investigate Explainable AI (XAI) and transparency since they play a significant part in preventing the hidden biases and weaknesses of AI models. Interpretability improvement helps ensure that LLMs

protect not only sensitive information but also offer responsible and reliable decision-making.

TRANSPARENCY & EXPLAINABLE AI

The goal of Explainable Artificial Intelligence (XAI), a branch of artificial intelligence, is to make machine learning models' decision-making processes easier for people to comprehend, decode, and explain.

Why we need XAI

As AI systems increase in sophistication, especially with the advent of deep learning and big language models, their internal workings tend to be opaque, operating as "black boxes" (de Carvalho Souza et al., 2025).

Concerns about trust, justice, and accountability arise from the inability to justify LLM decisions. A model making an erroneous or biased decision makes it challenging to pinpoint the source of the issue or to correct it. Moreover, without explainability, users cannot have confidence in the outputs, potentially hindering the adoption of LLMs in mission-critical applications. For instance, in healthcare, an LLM could suggest a specific treatment based on patterns that it learned from past data, yet without knowing the reasons why the model suggested that, physicians might be unwilling to act upon it.

The ability of XAI to close the gap between sophisticated algorithms and human explainability makes it significant. Transparency in AI systems is crucial in high-stakes industries like healthcare, banking, and law to prevent ethical dilemmas and mistrust. For instance, when an AI system makes a medical diagnosis or denies a loan request, stakeholders must know the rationale behind these decisions to ensure fairness, precision, and accountability.

Techniques

Because LLMs are so complex, several techniques have been developed to shed light their decision-making procedures in an effort to make them easier to understand and more transparent. These approaches fall into two general categories:

- Post-hoc explainability: These techniques are applicable after the response generated from the LLM.

– Attention Mechanism: Attention mechanisms point to which regions of the input text the model is concentrating on during prediction and exposing the token relationships within a sentence. Through the visualization attention weights, we can observe how much weight the model assigns to specific words or phrases when generating a response.
– Another powerful method is LIME (Local Interpretable Model-agnostic Explanations), which estimates the behavior of the sophisticated model with a less complex, interpretable model. By altering the input and tracking the changes in the model's predictions, it produces a local explanation that reveals the factors that influence the choice.
– SHAP (Shapley Additive Explanations) is one of the techniques in the post-hoc category which gives every feature a contribution score according to cooperative game theory. SHAP values can explain the effect that every input token has upon the model's output, providing both local and global interpretations.

- Intrinsic explainability: Intrinsic explainability refers to the inherent transparency of a model's decision-making process due to its interpretable structure.

For instance, rule-based systems or decision trees are more straightforward and less complex to explain than LLMs. While these models might not have the predictive capability of LLMs, they offer greater transparency into decision-making. Merging these less complex models with LLMs can provide a hybrid solution, where the LLM offers high precision, and the less complex model provides clarity.

Real life Examples of XAI

In actual applications, Large Language explainability Models (LLMs) play a crucial role to enhance transparency and accountability, particularly in sectors such as law,

healthcare, finance, and customer service. Following are some real-life examples where explainability has been successfully used in LLMs (Lai et al., 2024).

- AI is used more frequently to help judges make rulings and evaluating the risk of offending. For instance, in 2023, a court in Colombia utilized the ChatGPT decision-making outcome to guide judges for punishing a case involving medical insurance.
- Legal LLMs streamline repetitive tasks, enabling judges to focus on complex cases. Luminance AI, developed by a British start-up, automates document

processing and contract generation. This reduces time and labor costs, improving efficiency in legal workflows.

- LLMs recommend treatment plans based on patient records while attention mechanisms highlight key symptoms influencing decisions. This enhances transparency, allowing healthcare professionals to understand the model's reasoning. As a result, doctors can validate or adjust AI-driven suggestions effectively.
- LLMs are used in finance for market analysis, fraud detection, and credit scoring. When detecting fraud, SHAP values explain which factors (e.g., spending patterns, location) influenced the decision. This enhances transparency and ensures compliance with regulatory standards.
- Counterfactual explanations help analysts explore hypothetical scenarios where a transaction wouldn't be flagged as fraud. This reveals the model's decision boundaries, increasing transparency and trust in the system.

REGULATORY FRAMEWORKS

AI is now used in more important reasoning and decision-making tasks thanks to LLMs. For this reason, ethics-based audits play a central position in the quickly expanding fields of AI regulation and AI safety. Proponents of various regulatory approaches contend

that AI systems should be regulated similarly to nuclear weapons, which pose a catastrophic risk (particularly at the technological frontiers); consumer goods, which present a variety of risks to the user; pharmaceuticals, which necessitate a strong prerelease regulatory framework; and/or environmental pollution, to which the law responds with a range of instruments read.dukeupress.edu, 2024. Both, State and Private entities (who own LLMs) have acted upon regulating the LLMs. Few important regulatory frameworks have been discussed in brief in new two subsections.

Government based

- European Union's Artificial Intelligence Act (AI Act): AI act of EU is the first regulatory code for managing the development and operation of artificial intelligence (AI) in the EU. Passed on 1 August 2024, the AI Act seeks to provide that AI technologies are designed and used so as to be secure, clear, and compliant with essential rights. The AI Act covers all types and fields of AI with exceptions for those utilized solely for non-professional purposes, military affairs, national defense, and scientific research. This systemic solution guarantees that AI solutions in all sectors conform to the set standards, forging a harmonized regulatory framework within the EU. [1]

- The Blueprint for an AI Bill of Rights: It provides guidelines for the ethical advancement and application of artificial intelligence (AI) in the United States and was published by the White House in October 2022. It emphasizes protecting individuals from AI-related harms while promoting fairness, transparency, and accountability. The framework is built on five core principles: (1) Safe and Effective AI, (2) Algorithmic Discrimination Protections, (3) Data Privacy, (4) Notice and Explanation, and (5) Human Alternatives and Oversight. This blueprint serves as a non-binding policy recommendation, guiding government agencies, businesses, and AI

• In October 2019, Russian President Vladimir Putin approved the National Strategy for the Development of Artificial Intelligence (AI) up to 2030. The strategy outlines short-term goals to be achieved by 2024 and medium-term goals by 2030, aiming to position Russia as a leading AI power. Key objectives include enhancing scientific research in AI, improving access to information and computing resources, and advancing personnel training in the field. The strategy mandates the integration of AI development into national programs like the "Digital Economy of the Russian Federation" and requires annual progress reports to the President. [3]

• NITI Aayog of India released National Strategy for Artificial Intelligence in 2018, outlines India's vision to harness AI for inclusive growth and position itself as a global leader in the field. Key points on which India is working are: (1) A need to bolster AI research capabilities and cultivate a skilled workforce. (2) Ensuring the availability of quality data while maintaining privacy and security. (3) Addressing issues related to awareness, infrastructure, and funding to promote AI integration across sectors. (4) Ethical AI Development: Formulating guidelines to ensure AI systems are transparent, unbiased, and secure.

Industry wise self-regulations

- OpenAI: In order to guarantee that the technology preserves principles like liberty, equity, and respect for human rights, OpenAI highlights the significance of democratic leadership in AI development. The group backs the U.S. National Security Memorandum on Artificial Intelligence, which emphasizes the need for resources like

data center capacity and semiconductor chip and promotes the proper application of AI in national security. OpenAI works with the U.S. Agency for International

Development to use AI to expedite administrative tasks and with organizations such as DARPA to improve cybersecurity. The business upholds stringent usage guidelines that forbid the production of weapons or other detrimental uses of its technology. To ensure compliance with ethical norms, OpenAI's Product Policy and National Security teams formally evaluate potential national security agreements. 5

- Meta: The company's dedication to the ethical advancement of AI is demonstrated by Meta's Responsible AI Connect 2024. Among its primary projects is the Llama Responsible Use Guide, which offers developers best practices for implementing large language models (LLMs) in a way that makes them safe and beneficial for users. Additionally, Meta introduced the Llama Social Impact Grant Program to support initiatives that apply AI for societal benefit. By encouraging equity, openness, and accountability in the application of AI, these programs show Meta's dedication to integrating ethical AI principles throughout all stages of product development. [6]
- Google: Google's "A Policy Agenda for Responsible Progress in Artificial Intelligence" outlines a strategic framework to harness AI's potential while addressing associated challenges. Its major motive is to building trust in AI systems. This involves implementing standards, best practices, and regulations, such as expert risk assessments for high-risk AI applications to ensure ethical development and deployment. AI's role in global security necessitates measures to prevent its malicious use. Collaboration among governments, academia, industry, and civil society is vital to align AI advancements with human values and address safety implications.[7]

In addition to this, all renowned AI Tech giants are actively working on making responsible AI product in sync with AI regulations of various governing bodies.

FUTURE OF GLOBAL AI GOVERNANCE

With artificial intelligence (AI) transforming industries and societies at an accelerating pace, the necessity of a solid and concerted worldwide AI governance framework grows ever more pressing. The earlier discussion about AI regulations concentrated on national and institutional frameworks, identifying the various regulatory strategies across jurisdictions.

However, because AI transcends national boundaries, its administration necessitates a more cohesive worldwide strategy that balances innovation with societal protection and guarantees ethical, legal, and technical monitoring. Establishing mechanisms that support security, accountability, and transparency in AI deployment while reducing economic rivalry and geopolitical conflicts is the goal of global AI governance Zaidan and Ibrahim, 2024.

BARRIERS TO STRONG GLOBAL AI GOVERNANCE

Several challenges hinder the establishment of an effective global AI governance system:

- AI governance attempts are hampered by conflicting national interests, as some nations give precedence to innovation while others aim for tight control through regulation. The geopolitical context generates competition over cooperation, rendering it challenging to create a commonly accepted governance structure.
- Various regulatory agencies, such as the UN, OECD, and EU, suggest AI governance standards. But the absence of harmonization between these institutions leads to overlapping, and in some cases conflicting, regulations.
- Most AI governance debates are fueled by high-income nations, excluding low-income countries that might not have the capacity and expertise to engage meaningfully.

  Such exclusion can result in governance frameworks that fail to meet the needs of all countries.
- Although legal and governance frameworks take years to develop and put into place, AI technologies develop rapidly. Before appropriate monitoring mechanisms are put in place, this regulatory lag creates a gap that allows AI systems to be exploited.
- Enforcement and Compliance Challenges: Even if international agreements are made, state compliance is challenging to enforce. In the absence of enforcement or legal compliance, states may choose to exempt themselves from obeying international AI governance norms.

PATHWAYS FORWARD FOR GLOBAL AI GOVERNANCE

- Multilateral institutions like UN, G20, and regional organizations can be used to create AI governance to bridge the gaps between national policies. The Global Digital Compact and UN Common Agenda are some of the initiatives that focus on such international cooperation.
- A mix of legally enforceable rules (hard law) and non-binding guidelines (soft law) can offer regulatory stability and flexibility. This model has been

proposed for AI regulation to allow for varying national interests while maintaining minimum ethical and safety standards.

- In order to establish AI governance frameworks that promote responsible innovation while averting detrimental AI applications, governments and AI-driven businesses must work together.
- A more equitable AI governance framework can be established by giving underrepresented countries financial and technical support. A governance structure that benefits exclusively technologically advanced countries can be avoided by guaranteeing fair access to AI technologies.

RECOMMENDATIONS FOR FUTURE AI GOVERNANCE

- Establish a Global Authority to Regulate AI An independent AI regulatory agency can establish and implement international AI standards, much like the International Atomic Energy Agency (IAEA) does for nuclear control.
- Adopt Governance Frameworks for AI Using Current Models Frameworks like the Council of Europe's AI Convention and the EU AI Act can serve as models for AI governance, which can then be modified for worldwide use.
- Create global guidelines for AI safety and risk assessment. Creating international risk assessment guidelines will aid in reducing the negative effects of AI applications, especially in crucial fields like mass surveillance, deepfake technology, and autonomous weaponry.
- Strengthen Ethical AI Standards: To guarantee that AI benefits mankind fairly, it is important to promote AI ethics research and incorporate fairness, transparency, and human right principles into AI governance.

Because of competing national interests, fragmented regulations, and enforcement constraints, global AI governance continues to be a difficult task. Nonetheless, a strong governance framework may be created by encouraging multilateral cooperation, using hybrid regulatory approaches, and guaranteeing equitable representation of all countries. To guarantee AI's responsible and advantageous application globally, future AI governance initiatives should prioritize openness, responsibility, and international cooperation.

REFERENCES

de Carvalho Souza, M. E., Souza, M. E. D. C., & Weigang, L. (2025). Unveiling the black box: The significance of xai in making llms transparent. *Authorea Preprints*.

Ephraim. (2022). The viral ai avatar app lensa undressed me without my consent [https://www.technologyreview.com/2022/12/12/1064751/the-viral-ai- avatar-app-lensa-undressed-me-without-my-consent/ [Accessed: (15-march-2025)]].

Guo, Y., Guo, M., Su, J., Yang, Z., Zhu, M., Li, H., Qiu, M., & Liu, S. S. (2024). Bias in large language models: Origin, evaluation, and mitigation. arXiv preprint arXiv:2411.10915.

Kay, G. (2025, February 28). Inside Grok's war on "woke." Business Insider. https://www.businessinsider.com/xai-grok-training-bias-woke-idealogy-2025-02

Lai, J., Gan, W., Wu, J., Qi, Z., & Philip, S. Y. (2024). *Large language models in law: A survey*. AI Open.

Omiye, J. A., Lester, J. C., Spichak, S., Rotemberg, V., & Daneshjou, R. (2023). Large language models propagate race-based medicine. *NPJ Digital Medicine*, *6*(1), 195.

read.dukeupress.edu. (2024). Regulatory analogies, llms, and generative ai [https://read.dukeupress.edu/critical-ai/article-abstract/doi/10.1215/2834703X-11205238 [Accessed: (17-march-2025)]].

theconversation.com. (2023). Ageism, sexism, classism and more: 7 examples of bias in ai-generated images [https://theconversation.com/ageism-sexism-classism -and- more-7-examples-of-bias-in-ai-generated-images-208748 [Accessed:(15-march-2025)]].

Yan, B., Li, K., Xu, M., Dong, Y., Zhang, Y., Ren, Z., & Cheng, X. (2024). On protecting the data privacy of large language models (llms): A survey. arXiv preprint arXiv:2403.05156.

Yang, Z. (2025, January 31). Here's How DeepSeek Censorship Actually Works—and How to Get Around It. WIRED. https://www.wired.com/story/deepseek-censorship/

Zaidan, E., & Ibrahim, I. A. (2024). Ai governance in a complex and rapidly changing regulatory landscape: A global perspective. *Humanities & Social Sciences Communications*, *11*(1), 1–18.

Chapter 8
Transforming Financial Decision-Making:
The Role of Large Language Models in Risk Management and Fraud Detection

Puneett Bhatnagr
http://orcid.org/0000-0002-9281-1809
Amity University, India

ABSTRACT

This chapter investigates the knowledge gained through the transformational role of Large Language Models (LLMs) in financial risk management and fraud detection, especially as it relates to modern financial decision-making. Conventional approaches to financial analysis have introduced machine learning techniques to handle vast and complex datasets. Specifically, LLMs, from OpenAI's GPT series to Bloomberg's GPT, are a significant change because they represent the ability of institutions to process and understand structurally as well as unstructured financial data. This chapter illustrates how LLMs improve risk assessment by deriving the context and integrating sentiment analysis from regulated documents and market trends to provide nuanced insights. In the case of fraud detection, LLMs outperform others in terms of their ability to detect anomalies, identity theft prevention, and document validation based on real-time upcoming transactions and communication patterns.

DOI: 10.4018/979-8-3693-6690-5.ch008

1. INTRODUCTION

Over the past decades, there has been a shift in financial decision-making practices from manual paper-based systems to fully automation-oriented facilities (Yang, 2022). During the modern digital era, no other alternatives existed for actions such as making investment decisions except for human judgment augmented with commonly used statistical methods and standard computing tools to assess risks and detect fraud (Chaquet-Ulldemolins et al., 2022). Previous early decision-making procedures worked well until they hit their limits after dealing with very large and complicated datasets (Ionescu & Diaconita, 2023). The breakthrough came in 2002 when machine learning and artificial intelligence started flooding the market, leading to the machine production of high-end predictive models and automated systems for faster data processing; however, this has brought inequality to the market. There is now a clear divide between those who did not invest in machine learning and artificial intelligence systems are now behind (Schmitt, 2022). Large Language Models have caused the financial industry to reach a turning point in decisive decision-making transformation (Khan et al., 2024).

However, a rapid transformation of the financial industry has been observed because of the increasing adoption of AI technologies in areas such as risk management and fraud detection (Tian et al., 2024). The most important one is the growing investment in AI-driven risk management solutions because financial institutions realise that, in the wake of increasingly complex and changing risk landscapes, they need an advanced cognitive tool to better assess the variety of risks they face (Nallakaruppan et al., 2024). According to the latest industry reports, global AI spending on financial services is expected to reach $40 billion by 2025, with a large chunk of it being for improving risk management and detection of fraud (Reite et al., 2024).

Today, GPT series from OpenAI or Bloomberg GPT are on the frontier of creating AI which has myriads of data pointed at them, which is not limited to structured financial data but rather extremely vast, unstructured information (Fernandez et al., 2023). These models are vital for a clearer understanding of and the ability to create human-readable texts (Bhatnagr et al., 2024), as they can parse and comprehend complex financial records, earnings announcements, government filings, news reports, social voices, and internal communications (Delgadillo et al., 2024). This has allowed financial institutions to uncover new opportunities for insight that were just not available or were simply too labour-intensive to process (Trummer, 2022). Using sentiment analysis, LLMs can predict how the market will move based on articles and posts in news and social media, extract critical pieces of information from lengthy financial statements, and even discover any process that might indicate fraud or expose risks (Shobayo et al., 2024).

LLM's ability to perform well beyond the capacity to handle big data is attributable to contextual understanding and adaptivity (Suri et al., 2023). For example, LLMs such as GPT-3 can be generalised across many tasks and hence can be very useful for any type of financial decision (Balkus & Yan, 2023). It is seamlessly integrated with existing risk management frameworks and helps in making real-time decisions with the right set of timely and accurate insights while also improving fraud-detection systems (Delgadillo et al., 2024). Moreover, these models allow more banks to use them, as they are grown more efficiently and more easily (Fernandez et al., 2023).

The appearance of LLMs marks a tipping point in the change in financial decisions from data to intelligence (Trummer, 2022). Financial institutions and the organisations with which they work have thus redefined risk management, fraud detection, and strategic planning since organisations can process and understand complex, unstructured data at scale (Shobayo et al., 2024). With the increase in complexity and data-driven nature of the financial landscape, LLM will keep its place intact and grow bigger to exploit the sector's unprecedented possibilities of innovation and efficiency (Delgadillo et al., 2024).

2. THEORETICAL FOUNDATIONS OF LLMS IN FINANCIAL RISK MANAGEMENT

The architecture and capability of large language models (LLMs) provide a theoretical basis for applications in financial risk management (Denecke et al., 2024). Transformer architecture leads to LLMs, which is a breakthrough in deep learning in the field of natural language processing (NLP) (Sahoo et al., 2024). Self-attention and multihead attention are mechanisms used by transformers to capture contextual relationships and dependencies (i.e. sequence to sequence) in a given data sequence (Muller et al., 2024). Using this architecture, LLMs can discern complex patterns in text and numerical data, and thus understand individual data points as well as their interrelationships across all documents (Zhou et al., 2024). Recognising these nuances and understanding the interplay between different types of data is critical in the realm of finance, where language is nuanced and the interplay between different data types defines the problem (Pan et al., 2024). Documents such as balance sheets, regulatory filings, and market reports are complex and intricate; hence, they can be disseminated by LLMs to pick out subtle cues and other relations that more traditional models might fail to identify (Cheng, 2024).

One such powerful use of LLM in financial risk management is its ability to integrate structured and unstructured data, providing a balanced picture of financial landscapes. It provides quantitative insights from structured data in the form of transaction records, the use of various financial ratios, and the price of equities

(Tripathi et al., 2024). However, they represent only half of the picture. News articles, analysts' opinions, social media, and internal mail are qualitative sources whose content plays a major role in estimating risks and market projections (Sezgin, 2024). The ability to synthesise all the different sources of data comes with the job of LLM (Bhatnagr & Rajesh, 2024), and the net result of this is that it provides LLM with a balanced perspective on risks and opportunities (Li et al., 2023). For instance, LLM could peruse the company's financial record, latest regulations, and market sentiment and offer a more enriched decision-making picture (Sahoo et al., 2024).

Additionally, when LLMs are incorporated into traditional financial models, the accuracy of the prediction and pedigrees of risk increases exponentially (Delgadillo et al., 2024). Standard models, such as credit scoring systems, are based on historical financial data and predefined criteria and, hence, may overlook some nuances of risk indicators. By incorporating LLM, these systems can assess behavioural patterns, market sentiment, and external factors, in addition to analysing data (Roumeliotis et al., 2024). Thus, an LLM could read not only the financial statements of a borrower but also news coverage of the borrower's company and other context-sensitive information (Bhatnagr et al., 2024a), such as reviews of the borrower as a customer and their social media sentiment, to make a better assessment of the borrower's creditworthiness (Fazlija & Harder, 2022). Similarly, LLMs can support the traditional quantitative models used for market risk analysis by including real-time news sentiments and geopolitical events, providing a more dynamic and reactive approach (Liu et al., 2024). LLMs have been theoretically established as revolutionising factors in financial risk management (Jung & Jang, 2024). It has an advanced architecture for providing contextualisation at depth and can handle a variety of data variations to reach decisions with greater and more accurate knowledge (Fu & Zhang, 2024). When combined with conventional models in the financial world, LLMs provide better predictive accuracy and further dimensions of insight to navigate the global financial market, as it is today (Jeong, 2024).

3. APPLICATIONS OF LLMS IN RISK MANAGEMENT

Large Language Models (LLMs) applied in risk management reconsider how financial institutions evaluate, forecast, and control risks at various scales (Fernandez et al., 2023). The use of LLMs in credit risk assessment advances beyond traditional scoring methods, as LLMs integrate structured and unstructured data to create a score (Zhang et al., 2023). Traditional credit evaluation is usually based on numerical data such as credit scores, income statements, and debt-income ratios. This is valuable, but it overlooks important qualitative factors that affect a borrower's creditworthiness (Li et al., 2024). Although no types of information are evaluated by LLMs, they utilise numerical data as well as textual information such as customer reviews, news sentiment, and social media discourse (Xing, 2024). For instance, if a small business applies for a loan and has stable financials but has recently been covered with negative news or customer complaints (Bhatnagr et al., 2024c), an LLM can use that qualitative data to score risk (Preiksaitis et al., 2024). Combining these two methods results in more sophisticated and comprehensive credit evaluations that are less prone to default and score an applicant who would otherwise be overlooked in traditional models.

In market risk analysis, LLMs are leading the way in processing real-time data from various sources, aiding the forecasting of market trends, and identifying looming risks in advance (Delgadillo et al., 2024). Unlike typical market analysis models, which are based to a great extent on historic price movements and statistical parameters, LLMs are in a position to use real-time news articles, earnings, analysts' opinions, and political events to derive a real-time, multifaceted image of market situations (Liu et al., 2024). For example, during market volatility, an LLM can evaluate breaking news, sentiments from social networks, and investor opinions to identify emerging risks and forecast future market movements (Abolghasemi et al., 2023). This real-time, data-driven perception assists the investor and risk manager in making decisions based on facts, adjusting the course of investments, and implementing hedging strategies in advance, minimising the effect of adverse market situations (Jeong, 2024).

Operational risk monitoring is another domain in which LLMs are extremely useful. Operational risks, such as internal fraud, compliance breaches, and errors by people, are normally embedded in the vast amounts of unstructured data generated by an organisation, such as internal documents, emails, incident reports, and communication histories (Balsiger et al., 2024). Operational risks are easily scanned by the LLM from the above sources, and patterns and anomalies are selected, possibly suggesting risks (Xing, 2024). For example, an LLM can scan employee communication to identify signs of insider dealing, conflicts of interest, and violation of company codes (Li et al., 2024). It can also scan compliance reporting to monitor compliance with regulations and flag issues to be investigated (Fernandez et al., 2023). This type of scrutiny is important to assist an organisation in realising and assessing operational risks before they become major challenges and thus ensure its integrity and compliance (Baum, 2024).

The partnership between Tiger Brokers and DeepSeek provided DeepSeek-R1's AI model for use by the developer of the trading assistant chatbot TigerGPT. Within its descriptive application, LLMs help enhance market evaluations to make timely trading decisions (Delgadillo et al., 2024). TigerGPT utilises DeepSeek-R1 to assess complex market patterns, together with news sentiment and user input, to deliver personalised investment counselling and guidance (Xing, 2024). Platform users receive a dynamic market analysis and discover investment prospects and risk assessment capabilities from the AI-based assistance system (Liu et al., 2024). The implementation of LLMs for risk analysis automation separates market investigations into two categories, consumer-friendly and expert-level knowledge delivery, while also enhancing user participation (Jeong, 2024).

4. APPLICATIONS OF LLMS IN FRAUD DETECTION

Thus, LLMs use many advanced approaches to discover fraud from multiple perspectives (Sinha et al., 2024). The ability of LLM to scan enormous amounts of transaction-based data to detect transaction anomalies, indicating possible fraud, has proven to be one of the most powerful applications of LLM (Patsakis et al., 2024). Unlike other, more common, purely numerical-based mechanisms, LLM leverages contextual factors, such as the sequence of recent transactions (among other things), their geographical location, and temporal patterns to discover previously invisible anomalies. Imagine, for instance, that an LLM detects a large transaction from a location that is out of the ordinary at an out-of-ordinary time if the pattern is too far removed from the common pattern.

Fraud detection using multiple angles is one of the main techniques utilised by LLMs (Selim et al., 2024). It is among the most powerful applications in which LLM observes enormous amounts of transaction-based data searching for anomalies, possibly putative fraud (Martínez et al., 2024). In contrast to traditional numerical threshold-based methods, LLM uses contextual factors -- what has happened in the past, the individual's location, and the timing–to identify subtle anomalies (Patsakis et al., 2024). For example, if a pattern involves a pattern that would flag a large transaction from an abnormal location at an abnormal time, LLMs may catch an attempted identity theft. Using LLMs to analyse various sets of information such as login times, the pace at which users are typing, information about the devices, location, and much more, they can discern patterns such as identity theft or takeover. For example, if a customer who logs into his account from New York suddenly logs into a different location or third country on a different device, the LLM would be able to detect this activity and ask for further security questions. With pattern-based inspection, the verification of credentials does not end with the ROC point, and it provides additional protection from identity theft.

LLM capabilities also significantly helped in document fraud analysis. Billions of loan applications, contracts, and invoices are made into financial institutions every day (Bhatnagr & Rajesh, 2024a). These documents can then be reviewed by LLMs to identify inconsistencies and cross-reference them in the databases for authentication (Li et al., 2024). For instance, if the application is for a loan, an LLM can check whether the facts in the job match PCs or private fact bases and alert discrepancies, possibly indicating falsified documents or false promises (Deng et al., 2024).

By monitoring fraud in real-time, LLM offers one of the major benefits of using it to detect fraud (Sinha et al., 2024). The ability to track transactions and communication enables the real-time monitoring and detection of suspicious activities and prompt responses to them. LLM helps process streams of data in real-time with real-time processing, aiding in the screening, in real-time, of data streams in such a way that fraud may be caught in real-time and interventions made (Selim et al., 2024). It aids in eliminating monetary losses and minimising fraud.

The use of cutting-edge LLMs for Fraud Protection in the case of JPMorgan is a notable point where LLMs have been proven to detect fraud. JPMorgan has introduced LLMs into its infrastructure to enable real-time monitoring through fraud detection of the transactional activity of many millions of accounts (Patsakis et al., 2024). Since then, LLMs have been scanning intricate patterns of users' activity and patterns of those flows between them as well as external sources to accurately identify the risks of fraud (Li et al., 2024). In this case, this anticipatory strategy dramatically lowered the rate of false positives, improving the speed of fraud detection and allowing the bank to stop the fraud well before the customer's accounts are damaged (Deng et al., 2024).

5. BENEFITS AND CHALLENGES OF IMPLEMENTING LLMS

The transformative benefits of the implementation of Large Language Models (LLMs) in financial risk management and fraud detection are many, although they are also accompanied by a series of challenges that institutions should deal with very carefully (Li et al., 2024). A great benefit of LLMs is that they tend to be more accurate in evaluating the much more complex datasets used for risk assessment and fraud detection (Delgadillo et al., 2024). LLMs can do this by integrating structured and unstructured data from several different sources, such as transaction records, market reports, customer communications, and social media sentiments, to look beyond the obvious and create a more sophisticated and complete view of potential risk and anomalous behaviours (Balsiger et al., 2024). This ability for contextual awareness and language intricacy helps them detect subtle patterns and correlates that the traditional system might miss, making risk models better and fraud detection mechanisms better (Xing, 2024).

Real-time analysis is another major benefit that allows financial institutions to act on the risks and incidents of fraud as well as when they happen (Fernandez et al., 2023). However, traditional systems latent the identification of emerging threats based on batch processing and retrospective analyses (Tripathi et al., 2024). On the other hand, LLMs can receive vast flows of data in real-time and yield timely alerts and actionable insights (Guo et al., 2024). The ability to know it all in real time is important to prevent fraud, control market runs, and comply with fast-evolving regulations (Derner et al., 2024), which ultimately enable more proactive decision making (Denecke et al., 2024).

The scalability of LLMs attracts all financial institutions. The models are efficient in handling enormous quantities of data (Pilny et al., 2024) and, consequently, are suitable for use by multinational banks and other small-scale financial institutions (Telenti et al., 2024). The scalability of the models to fit the increasing demands, as the generation of data continues to surge at an exponential rate, means that the institution continues to offer quality risk and fraud control, regardless of the size and complexity of the data they are handling (Zhou et al., 2024).

However, despite the wonderful benefits, the employment of LLM also raises some challenges to be addressed by financial institutions. Customer data privacy concerns are among the most significant concerns (Kshetri, 2023). The employment of LLM normally calls for the employment of enormous amounts of customer financial information, which raises enormous concerns about security and privacy (Kalaw & Baxter, 2024). Adherence to rigorous data protection laws and regulations, such as the GDPR, CCPA, and respective industry-specific laws, is necessary (Zhui et al., 2024) . The institution must establish effective encryption practices, anonymisation techniques, and tight control mechanisms to ensure customer data protection and compliance.

Another significant issue comes in the area of model interpretability (Head et al., 2023). Deep neural network-based LLMs are, in most situations, black boxes' whose internal working mechanisms are unknown to users (Cheng, 2024). This decision-making and prediction opacity in the event of applications in the area of financial risk control and fraud prediction, in situations where transparency is required to ensure compliance and trust from stakeholders, is problematic (Wang et al., 2023). The only solution to this issue comes in the form of developing explainable AI (XAI) frameworks to offer transparency into the decision-making mechanisms in the event of LLMs.

Computational resource constraints also pose a challenge for the mass adoption of LLM. The deployment and training of LLM require huge computational horsepower, in the form of high-end GPUs and cloud-scale infrastructure, and are, in some cases, expensive. The demands could be prohibitive to the availability and use by less significant financial institutions, and so the advantage of the use of LLM could be denied to them. Mitigating this challenge is a possible solution to the use of pre-trained models, model architecture efficiency, and cloud-based AI services.

Finally, ethical issues are at the root of LLM use. The models are trained on enormous datasets, and the datasets may also have embedded bias, resulting in biased and discriminatory decisions in the event of the evaluation of risks, such as fraud monitoring, if the issue is not checked. Therefore, biased datasets could result in some segments being disproportionately labelled high-risk or subjected to disproportionate scrutiny in the event of fraud. Fair decision-making and accountability are ensured through the use of LLMs by proper curation of the datasets used to train the models, regular bias audits, and fairness-aware algorithms to remove risks.

6. BENEFITS AND CHALLENGES OF IMPLEMENTING LLMS

Financial risk management and fraud detection in financial institutions can be transformed using Large Language Models. However, this results in cost, and it is rife with ethical and regulatory implications regarding data privacy and algorithmic bias. These issues need to be addressed to ensure that LLM deployment is compliant with the legal framework and promises the fair use of financial decisions. Algorithmic bias in AI systems used for financial services can cause discriminatory practices and negatively affect the way services are conducted. We provide several real-world examples of such bias.

- **Racial bias:** Research has shown that mortgage-underwriting AI systems can have racial prejudice. According to one study, black applicants denied home loans far more often than white applicants, with comparable financial profiles. This difference illustrates the possibility that existing prejudices from historical lending data are unwittingly continued by AI models and produce discriminatory results.
- **Amazon's development of gender-biased AI-based recruitment tools** shows one such instance (Gender Bias in Recruitment Tools). The purpose of the system was to make hiring a more efficient process; however, it systematically disadvantaged female applicants. The AI model has been trained on resumes for over a decade, most of them submitted by men, which has led to a bias that favours male candidates and penalises resumes, which mention words related to women.
- **An internal assessment of the UK's Department for Work and Pensions (DWP)** found that the DWP's AI system for detecting welfare fraud is biased based on age, disability, marital status, and nationality. There were concerns that the system disproportionately targeted certain groups for fraud investigations and vulnerable populations were subject to unjust scrutiny.

These cases underscore the necessity for rigorous evaluation and mitigation strategies to address biases in AI systems and ensure equitable treatment across all demographics.

Regulatory Frameworks and Compliance

The deployment of LLMs in financial services must adhere to stringent data-protection regulations designed to safeguard individual privacy and ensure ethical data usage. Key regulatory frameworks include the following.

- **General Data Protection Regulation (GDPR):** GDPR is the regulations enforced in the European Union, which require organisations 'to process' personal data to ensure adequate protection of individual privacy rights. This means that, when it comes to LLMs, an organisation must preserve data minimisation, have explicit consent to use data, and allow individuals to exercise their right to be forgotten or have personal data deleted at request. Noncompliance can cost a hefty penny; therefore, it is important to adopt GDPR principles in the design of the AI system and best practices for handling data.
- **California Consumer Privacy Act (CCPA):** The CCPA is applicable in California, USA, where consumers have the right to access, delete, and share personal information obtained from businesses. LLMs operate under the necessity of compliance with data practice transparency, allowing consumers to choose not to sell data and solid data security measures to prevent unauthorised access. They also have to be ready to publicise the categories of collected personal information and the use of these data.

To align with these regulations, financial institutions should implement the following practices.

- **Data anonymisation and minimisation:** anonymises personal data before the training of LLMs to avoid the identification of individuals. Collecting only the data as per the needs of various purposes also reduces the exposure to breaches of data and data minimisation compliance principles.
- **Most Platforms Conduct Regular Audits and Impact Assessments:** By conducting a DPIA, companies can identify and minimise the risks inherent to the data processing carried out while using LLMs. Audits regularly serve to keep the organisation compliant and notice any deviation from ordinary data protection policies.

- **Transparency and Consent Mechanisms:** This will make users aware of how their data will be used and obtain explicit consent from them which ensures transparency. The mechanisms must be easy for individuals to use to express their data preferences, incite trust, and comply with regulations.

By proactively addressing ethical considerations and adhering to regulatory frameworks, financial institutions can harness the benefits of LLMs, while upholding the principles of fairness, accountability, and respect for individual privacy.

7. BEST PRACTICES FOR INTEGRATING LLMS IN FINANCIAL INSTITUTIONS

To make LLMs successful in the financial institution context, best practices to achieve accuracy, compliance, and efficiency across the deployment phases should be adhered to (Fernandez et al., 2023). Data management is a first-order approach, and its importance determines the quality and reliability of the model outputs. However, for LLMs, although large and diverse datasets keep them running, the effectiveness of these models is exacerbated by the integrity and quality of the data they consume (Li et al., 2024). Rigorous data cleaning and preprocessing are necessary for financial data, as they are frequently complex, heterogeneous, and inconsistent. It ranges from removing duplicate records, handling missing values, properly formatting unstructured data (emails, reports, socially active parties' data, etc.), and standing data in one format throughout the pipeline to structured data (transaction records, account balances, etc.). In addition, accurate data labelling and annotation are also necessary and crucial when training LLMs to perform a specific task such as fraud detection or risk assessment; errors in the initial labelling stage can propagate to errors in the predictions made by the model (Jeong, 2024).

The next two important steps in the integration process are model training and validation. Having LLMs trained on various datasets and then refreshed at regular intervals to adapt to new trends and behaviours is crucial because of the ever-changing nature of financial markets and fraud techniques (Xing, 2024). You train an LLM by fine-tuning pre-trained models on various domain-specific data to increase their importance and how contextual they are in the financial environment. However, this is not sufficient, and we need to continuously validate our models, as their accuracy and reliability degrade over time. This involves testing the predictive power of the model using cross-validation, back-testing, and performance benchmarking. Furthermore, model validation relies on accuracy metrics and demonstrates that the model can withstand biases, false positives, and other points of vulnerability in decision making. The LLM is re-trained through a series of re-training cycles and regular updates so that it remains sharp in the most up-to-date state of affairs, information development, and regulatory changes to remain effective over the long run.

Another block to the optimal practice of deploying LLM in financial institutions is continuous monitoring. Real applications of trained and validated models are still subject to unforeseen issues such as data drift, shifts in the patterns of fraud, or regulation changes that affect model performance. LLM uses effective feedback mechanisms to adjust shifts. Continuous monitoring involves monitoring the model response that begins in real-time, locating anomalies, and monitoring performance metrics to monitor the degradation of precision and relevance. For instance, a sudden spike in false positive and false negative rate metrics can serve as an indicator that a fraud detection model requires new training or where a new parameter should stand. In addition to the feedback mechanisms, it also explores a mechanism to incorporate fresh data and insights into the model to learn from errors and profit from experience to ensure the long-term performance and reliability of the model.

A collaborative approach is essential for integrating LLM with its ongoing management. These complex models do not deploy in a financial environment solely by themselves; they are products of cross-functional teams. This involves all forms of data scientists, risk analysts, compliance officers, legal experts, and IT professionals working together to lead the implementation process holistically. Technical expertise in model building and optimisation comes from data scientists and machine learning engineers, while risk analysts understand the domain specifics that may fine-tune the model to work in practice, for example, credit risk assessment or market analysis. In this case, compliance officers ensure that the integration process is aligned with regulatory standards and protect the organisation from legal and ethical risks, particularly with data privacy and fairness regulation. The multidisciplinary nature of this collaboration guarantees that LLM results can be technically sound and coherent with business objectives, regulatory requirements, and measures.

8. FUTURE DIRECTIONS AND INNOVATIONS

Fast advancements in LLMs will be set in the future in financial risk management and fraud detection by architectural innovations of LLMs, integration of developing technologies, alterations in the regulatory landscape, and personalisation. The development of LLM architectures is one of the most promising areas of development: in this context, the birth of more efficient, and adaptive, like "liquid" neural networks, is promising. Liquid neural networks are dynamic; that is, they can adjust their parameters in real time based on new data and are thus highly effective in highly volatile environments, such as financial markets. First, these models not only provide improved predictive accuracy but also significantly reduce computational demands;

thus, they are more easily used by institutions possessing scarce resources. With this, we have an architectural advancement that would democratise LLMS use to a broader spectrum of financial institutions, even firms which might not have the resources and capacity to procure a server infrastructure to host their LLM.

Another critical future trajectory lies in the integration of LLMs into other leading-edge technologies, most significantly, blockchain. The combination of blockchain and LLMs can redefine the domain of financial risk management by ensuring the security, transparency, and track record of the transactions. The transactional data of blockchain networks can be reviewed by LLMs to identify anomalies, money laundering, or compliance breaches in real time, and the impossibility of editing the blockchain ensures the integrity of the information. This integration is most effective in applications such as anti-money-laundering (AML) and know-your-customer (KYC) processes, in which the synergy between the employment of LLM-driven examination and blockchain's impenetrable record can simplify the verification processes and increase the rate of fraud discoveries. The integration of LLMs into IoT devices and real-time streams could also enhance the breadth of what they can provide, making them carry out integrated risks based on a variety of constantly varying parameters.

As LLMs become increasingly prevalent in the financial world, regulation to develop and deploy them is crucial. AI in the finance world is beginning to attract the attention of regulators, including data protection, algorithm transparency, and ethical decisions based on AI. New regulations are starting to guarantee the high standards of fairness, accountability, and interpretability of LLM and other AI models that are central to them. Finally, the demand for model interpretability, bias reduction, and operational flexibility in the deployment of LLMs is necessary in the future. The attendance of auditing mechanisms and compliance tests on AI will become the norm, and effective and compliant LLMs can be deployed along the lines of ethical and legal requirements.

Another exciting area in the future of LLM applications in the finance world lies in the progression of personalised financial services. LLMs are good at processing individual customer information; through this, financial institutions can provide extremely customised products and services based on each client's unique needs and preferences. From customised portfolios and risk profiling to custom-loan proposals and budget recommendations, vast quantities of personal and behavioural data are easily processed by the LLM to provide appropriate, real-time recommendations. This kind of personalisation promotes customer engagement, happiness, and loyalty, and also helps the institution spot opportunities in terms of cross-selling and up-selling. In wealth management, LLM can assess a person's expenditure patterns, income patterns, and long-term objectives to provide custom-designed strategies, promoting client-oriented advice in the area of money.

LLMs have the opportunity to play a role in future financial risk management and fraud detection. New model architectures of liquid neural networks could offer superior performance improvements at lower resource demands, bringing LLM to a greater number of institutions. Keeping this in mind and working with technologies such as blockchain and IoT, their applications can be maximally built upon for further development in terms of increasingly more secure, complete risk analysis. Financial institutions must strike a balance between innovation and compliance in terms of the ethical and transparent use of LLMs, whereas regulatory frameworks must adapt to solve challenges when they apply to AI as a whole. Finally, the growing development of more personalised financial services will empower LLMs to enrich their relationship with customers by delivering personalised data and inspiration, based on customers' requirements, – these LLMs are more important in the transition of the financial industry.

9. CONCLUSION

Large-language models integrated into the domain of financial risk management and fraud detection are a paradigm shift by financial institutions when deciding. By leveraging the computing power of LLM, the institution can provide a more specific kind of risk evaluation, better recognise fraudulent actions, and generally improve its efficiency in actions. As the nature of the market is dynamic and the strategies of fraudsters are continuously evolving, the latest available technologies must be allowed to be used periodically. Compared with traditional methodologies, LLMs can handle large amounts of structured and unstructured data with a high level of capacity. In the new world of finance, they have inalienable tools in the form of real-time processing, contextualisation, and learning.

Nevertheless, there are numerous challenges in the use of LLMs. However, thoughtful consideration and planning are required for challenging areas in data privacy, model interpretability, and computational requirements. People handling data in financial institutions are using new technology, and therefore, it is necessary to incorporate the latest in data handling, build models, and monitor their proper and optimal use. The future holds great promise for the use of LLMs in finance. The capabilities and uses of the models will increase with improved model architectures, the coupling of models with other supportive technologies, including blockchain, and the development of regulation regimes. Moreover, the use of even the smallest financial institutions is possible as models become more efficient and accessible. Ultimately, the revolution in LLMs is not only for fraud detection and financial risk management, but more generally, calls for adapting to these technologies. Organisations within financial services that lead to the adoption of using the use of LLMs in day-to-day operations will increase their decision-making capacity, and will also be at a huge competitive advantage in an ever-changing market.

REFERENCES

Abolghasemi, M., Ganbold, O., & Rotaru, K. (2023). Humans vs Large Language Models: Judgmental Forecasting in an Era of Advanced AI. *arXiv (Cornell University)*. https://doi.org//arxiv.2312.06941DOI: 10.48550

Balkus, S. V., & Yan, D. (2023). Improving short text classification with augmented data using GPT-3. *Natural Language Engineering*, *30*(5), 943–972. DOI: 10.1017/S1351324923000438

Balsiger, D., Dimmler, H., Egger-Horstmann, S., & Hanne, T. (2024). Assessing Large Language Models Used for Extracting Table Information from Annual Financial Reports. *Computers*, *13*(10), 257. DOI: 10.3390/computers13100257

Baum, S. D. (2024). Assessing the risk of takeover catastrophe from large language models. *Risk Analysis : An Official Publication of the Society for Risk Analysis*. Advance online publication. DOI: 10.1111/risa.14353 PMID: 38945529

Bhatnagr, P., & Rajesh, A. (2024a). Online customer experience in Indian digital banks impacting continuous intention usage: Generation Y and Z perspective. *Journal of Financial Reporting & Accounting*. DOI: 10.1108/JFRA-11-2023-0638

Bhatnagr, P., & Rajesh, A. (2024b). Artificial intelligence features and expectation confirmation theory in digital banking apps: Gen Y and Z perspective. *Management Decision*. Advance online publication. DOI: 10.1108/MD-07-2023-1145

Bhatnagr, P., Rajesh, A., & Misra, R. (2024a). A study on driving factors for enhancing financial performance and customer-centricity through digital banking. *International Journal of Quality and Service Sciences*, *16*(2), 218–250. DOI: 10.1108/IJQSS-09-2023-0141

Bhatnagr, P., Rajesh, A., & Misra, R. (2024b). Continuous intention usage of artificial intelligence enabled digital banks: A review of expectation confirmation model. *Journal of Enterprise Information Management*, *37*(6), 1763–1787. DOI: 10.1108/JEIM-11-2023-0617

Bhatnagr, P., Rajesh, A., & Misra, R. (2024c). The impact of Fintech innovations on digital currency adoption: a blockchain-based study in India. *International Journal of Accounting and Information Management*. DOI: 10.1108/IJAIM-11-2023-0275

Chaquet-Ulldemolins, J., Gimeno-Blanes, F., Moral-Rubio, S., Muñoz-Romero, S., & Rojo-Álvarez, J. (2022). On the Black-Box Challenge for Fraud Detection Using Machine Learning (II): Nonlinear Analysis through Interpretable Autoencoders. *Applied Sciences (Basel, Switzerland)*, *12*(8), 3856. DOI: 10.3390/app12083856

Cheng, J. (2024). Applications of large language models in pathology. *Bioengineering (Basel, Switzerland)*, *11*(4), 342. DOI: 10.3390/bioengineering11040342 PMID: 38671764

Delgadillo, J., Kinyua, J., & Mutigwe, C. (2024). FinSoSent: Advancing Financial Market Sentiment Analysis through Pretrained Large Language Models. *Big Data and Cognitive Computing*, *8*(8), 87. DOI: 10.3390/bdcc8080087

Denecke, K., May, R., & Romero, O. R. (2024). Potential of large language models in health care: Delphi study. *Journal of Medical Internet Research*, *26*, e52399. DOI: 10.2196/52399 PMID: 38739445

Deng, D., Zhang, C., Zheng, H., Pu, Y., Ji, S., & Wu, Y. (2024). AdversaFlow: Visual Red Teaming for Large Language Models with Multi-Level Adversarial Flow. *IEEE Transactions on Visualization and Computer Graphics*, •••, 1–11. DOI: 10.1109/TVCG.2024.3456150 PMID: 39283796

Derner, E., Batistič, K., Zahálka, J., & Babuška, R. (2024). A Security Risk Taxonomy for Prompt-Based Interaction with Large Language Models. *IEEE Access : Practical Innovations, Open Solutions*, *12*, 126176–126187. DOI: 10.1109/ACCESS.2024.3450388

Fazlija, B., & Harder, P. (2022). Using financial news sentiment for stock price direction prediction. *Mathematics*, *10*(13), 2156. DOI: 10.3390/math10132156

Fernandez, R. C., Elmore, A. J., Franklin, M. J., Krishnan, S., & Tan, C. (2023). How large language models will disrupt data management. *Proceedings of the VLDB Endowment International Conference on Very Large Data Bases*, *16*(11), 3302–3309. DOI: 10.14778/3611479.3611527

Fu, K., & Zhang, Y. (2024). Incorporating Multi-Source market sentiment and price data for stock price prediction. *Mathematics*, *12*(10), 1572. DOI: 10.3390/math12101572

Guo, Z., Lai, A., Thygesen, J. H., Farrington, J., Keen, T., & Li, K. (2024). Large Language Models for Mental Health Applications: A Systematic Review (Preprint). *JMIR Mental Health*, *11*, e57400. DOI: 10.2196/57400 PMID: 39423368

Head, C. B., Jasper, P., McConnachie, M., Raftree, L., & Higdon, G. (2023). Large language model applications for evaluation: Opportunities and ethical implications. *New Directions for Evaluation*, *2023*(178–179), 33–46. DOI: 10.1002/ev.20556

Ionescu, S., & Diaconita, V. (2023). Transforming Financial Decision-Making: The interplay of AI, cloud computing and advanced data management technologies. *International Journal of Computers, Communications & Control, 18*(6). Advance online publication. DOI: 10.15837/ijccc.2023.6.5735

Jeong, C. (2024). Domain-specialized LLM: Financial fine-tuning and utilization method using Mistral 7B. *Journal of Intelligent Information Systems, 30*(1), 93–120. DOI: 10.13088/jiis.2024.30.1.093

Jung, H. D., & Jang, B. (2024). Enhancing financial sentiment analysis ability of language model via targeted Numerical Change-Related masking. *IEEE Access : Practical Innovations, Open Solutions, 12*, 50809–50820. DOI: 10.1109/ACCESS.2024.3385855

Kalaw, F. G. P., & Baxter, S. L. (2024). Ethical considerations for large language models in ophthalmology. *Current Opinion in Ophthalmology, 35*(6), 438–446. Advance online publication. DOI: 10.1097/ICU.0000000000001083 PMID: 39259616

Khan, M. A., Alhumoudi, H., Alakkas, A., Minhaj, S. M., & Alhashem, M. (2024). The present scenario of artificial intelligence and machine learning in financial services: An empirical study. *Journal of Infrastructure Policy and Development, 8*(11), 8818. DOI: 10.24294/jipd.v8i11.8818

Kshetri, N. (2023). Cybercrime and privacy threats of large language models. *IT Professional, 25*(3), 9–13. DOI: 10.1109/MITP.2023.3275489

Li, Q., Hong, J., Xie, C., Tan, J., Xin, R., Hou, J., Yin, X., Wang, Z., Hendrycks, D., Wang, Z., Li, B., He, B., & Song, D. (2024). LLM-PBE: Assessing Data Privacy in Large Language Models. *Proceedings of the VLDB Endowment International Conference on Very Large Data Bases, 17*(11), 3201–3214. DOI: 10.14778/3681954.3681994

Li, W., Manley, M., Read, J., Kaul, A., Bakir, M. S., & Yu, S. (2023). H3DATTEN: Heterogeneous 3-D integrated Hybrid analog and Digital Compute-in-Memory accelerator for Vision transformer Self-Attention. *IEEE Transactions on Very Large Scale Integration (VLSI). IEEE Transactions on Very Large Scale Integration (VLSI) Systems, 31*(10), 1592–1602. DOI: 10.1109/TVLSI.2023.3299509

Liu, C., Arulappan, A., Naha, R., Mahanti, A., Kamruzzaman, J., & Ra, I. (2024). Large Language Models and Sentiment Analysis in Financial Markets: A review, datasets and case study. *IEEE Access : Practical Innovations, Open Solutions, 12*, 134041–134061. DOI: 10.1109/ACCESS.2024.3445413

Martínez, P. A., Bernabé, G., & García, J. M. (2024). Code detection for hardware acceleration using large language models. *IEEE Access : Practical Innovations, Open Solutions*, *12*, 35271–35281. DOI: 10.1109/ACCESS.2024.3372853

Muller, L., Churchland, P. S., & Sejnowski, T. J. (2024). Transformers and Cortical Waves: encoders for pulling in context across time. *arXiv (Cornell University)*. https://doi.org//arxiv.2401.14267DOI: 10.48550

Nallakaruppan, M. K., Chaturvedi, H., Grover, V., Balusamy, B., Jaraut, P., Bahadur, J., Meena, V. P., & Hameed, I. A. (2024). Credit risk assessment and financial decision support using explainable artificial intelligence. *Risks*, *12*(10), 164. DOI: 10.3390/risks12100164

Pan, S., Zheng, Y., & Liu, Y. (2024). Integrating graphs with large language models: Methods and prospects. *IEEE Intelligent Systems*, *39*(1), 64–68. DOI: 10.1109/MIS.2023.3332242

Patsakis, C., Casino, F., & Lykousas, N. (2024). Assessing LLMs in malicious code deobfuscation of real-world malware campaigns. *arXiv (Cornell University)*. https://doi.org//arxiv.2404.19715DOI: 10.48550

Pilny, A., McAninch, K., Slone, A., & Moore, K. (2024). From manual to machine: Assessing the efficacy of large language models in content analysis. *Communication Research Reports*, *41*(2), 61–70. DOI: 10.1080/08824096.2024.2327547

Preiksaitis, C., Ashenburg, N., Bunney, G., Chu, A., Kabeer, R., Riley, F., Ribeira, R., & Rose, C. (2024). The Role of large language Models in Transforming Emergency Medicine: Scoping review. *JMIR Medical Informatics*, *12*, e53787. DOI: 10.2196/53787 PMID: 38728687

Reite, E. J., Karlsen, J., & Westgaard, E. G. (2024). Improving client risk classification with machine learning to increase anti-money laundering detection efficiency. *Journal of Money Laundering Control*. DOI: 10.1108/JMLC-03-2024-0040

Roumeliotis, K. I., Tselikas, N. D., & Nasiopoulos, D. K. (2024). LLMS and NLP Models in Cryptocurrency Sentiment Analysis: A Comparative Classification Study. *Big Data and Cognitive Computing*, *8*(6), 63. DOI: 10.3390/bdcc8060063

Sahoo, S. S., Plasek, J. M., Xu, H., Uzuner, Ö., Cohen, T., Yetisgen, M., Liu, H., Meystre, S., & Wang, Y. (2024). Large language models for biomedicine: Foundations, opportunities, challenges, and best practices. *Journal of the American Medical Informatics Association : JAMIA*, *31*(9), 2114–2124. DOI: 10.1093/jamia/ocae074 PMID: 38657567

Schmitt, M. (2022). Automated machine learning: AI-driven decision making in business analytics. *arXiv (Cornell University)*. https://doi.org//arxiv.2205.10538DOI: 10.48550

Selim, A., Zhao, J., & Yang, B. (2024). Large language model for smart inverter Cyber-Attack detection via textual analysis of Volt/VAR commands. *IEEE Transactions on Smart Grid*, *1*(6), 6179–6182. Advance online publication. DOI: 10.1109/TSG.2024.3453648

Sezgin, E. (2024). Redefining virtual Assistants in Health care: The future with large language models. *Journal of Medical Internet Research*, *26*, e53225. DOI: 10.2196/53225 PMID: 38241074

Shobayo, O., Adeyemi-Longe, S., Popoola, O., & Ogunleye, B. (2024). Innovative sentiment analysis and prediction of stock price using FINBERT, GPT-4 and Logistic Regression: A Data-Driven Approach. *Big Data and Cognitive Computing*, *8*(11), 143. DOI: 10.3390/bdcc8110143

Sinha, R., Elhafsi, A., Agia, C., Foutter, M., Schmerling, E., & Pavone, M. (2024). Real-Time Anomaly Detection and Reactive Planning with Large Language Models. *arXiv (Cornell University)*. /arxiv.2407.08735DOI: 10.15607/RSS.2024.XX.114

Suri, G., Slater, L. R., Ziaee, A., & Nguyen, M. (2023). Do large language models show decision heuristics similar to humans? A case study using GPT-3.5. *arXiv (Cornell University)*. https://doi.org//arxiv.2305.04400DOI: 10.48550

Telenti, A., Auli, M., Hie, B. L., Maher, C., Saria, S., & Ioannidis, J. P. A. (2024). Large language models for science and medicine. *European Journal of Clinical Investigation*, *54*(6), e14183. Advance online publication. DOI: 10.1111/eci.14183 PMID: 38381530

Tian, X., Tian, Z., Khatib, S. F. A., & Wang, Y. (2024). Machine learning in internet financial risk management: A systematic literature review. *PLoS One*, *19*(4), e0300195. DOI: 10.1371/journal.pone.0300195 PMID: 38625972

Tripathi, S., Sukumaran, R., & Cook, T. S. (2024). Efficient healthcare with large language models: Optimizing clinical workflow and enhancing patient care. *Journal of the American Medical Informatics Association : JAMIA*, *31*(6), 1436–1440. DOI: 10.1093/jamia/ocad258 PMID: 38273739

Trummer, I. (2022). From BERT to GPT-3 codex. *Proceedings of the VLDB Endowment International Conference on Very Large Data Bases*, *15*(12), 3770–3773. DOI: 10.14778/3554821.3554896

Wang, X., Li, X., Yin, Z., Wu, Y., & Liu, J. (2023). Emotional intelligence of Large Language Models. *Journal of Pacific Rim Psychology*, *17*, 18344909231213958. Advance online publication. DOI: 10.1177/18344909231213958

Xing, F. (2024). Designing heterogeneous LLM agents for financial sentiment analysis. *ACM Transactions on Management Information Systems*. Advance online publication. DOI: 10.1145/3688399

Yang, N. (2022). Financial big Data Management and control and Artificial intelligence analysis method based on data mining technology. *Wireless Communications and Mobile Computing*, *2022*(1), 1–13. DOI: 10.1155/2022/7596094

Zhang, L., Yu, Q., Zhou, B., Zhang, Y., & Hu, Z. (2023). Incorporating feature interactions and contrastive learning for credit prediction. *IEEE Access : Practical Innovations, Open Solutions*, *11*, 111944–111955. DOI: 10.1109/ACCESS.2023.3322429

Zhou, S., Zhou, Z., Wang, C., Liang, Y., Wang, L., Zhang, J., Zhang, J., & Lv, C. (2024). A User-Centered framework for data privacy protection using large language models and attention mechanisms. *Applied Sciences (Basel, Switzerland)*, *14*(15), 6824. DOI: 10.3390/app14156824

Zhui, L., Fenghe, L., Xuehu, W., Qining, F., & Wei, R. (2024). Ethical Considerations and Fundamental Principles of large language models in medical Education: Viewpoint. *Journal of Medical Internet Research*, *26*, e60083. DOI: 10.2196/60083 PMID: 38971715

Chapter 9

The Ethical and Regulatory Landscape of Large Language Models

Sawan Rai
http://orcid.org/0000-0002-2590-1097
SRM-AP University, India

ABSTRACT

Large Language Models (LLMs) are transforming industries by enabling advanced natural language processing (NLP) applications, yet their adoption raises ethical and regulatory concerns. Bias in training data can lead to unfair outcomes in hiring, credit scoring, and legal decisions, necessitating bias mitigation techniques such as debiasing algorithms and diverse data curation. Privacy risks arise from LLMs memorizing sensitive data, requiring compliance with regulations like GDPR and CCPA through differential privacy and encryption-based training. The opacity of LLMs challenges trust, prompting research in Explainable AI (XAI) methods like SHAP and LIME. Governments and industry leaders are shaping AI regulations, such as the EU AI Act, to balance innovation with responsibility. Future AI governance will require interdisciplinary collaboration, ethical auditing, and continuous oversight. Ensuring fairness, transparency, and accountability will be key to responsible AI deployment, enabling organizations to leverage LLMs' potential while minimizing risks.

DOI: 10.4018/979-8-3693-6690-5.ch009

THE ETHICAL AND REGULATORY LANDSCAPE OF LARGE LANGUAGE MODELS

Large Language Models (LLMs) are transforming industries by enabling sophisticated natural language processing (NLP) applications, from automated customer support to real-time market analysis. However, as these models become more powerful, their ethical and regulatory implications have become pressing concerns. The widespread adoption of LLMs raises critical questions about bias, fairness, transparency, privacy, and accountability, necessitating a structured ethical and legal framework to ensure responsible AI deployment.

This chapter explores the multifaceted ethical and regulatory landscape surrounding LLMs, beginning with an analysis of how bias and fairness impact model outputs. Despite advances in AI, LLMs often inherit biases from training data, leading to potential discrimination and ethical dilemmas in decision-making systems. We examine real-world examples where biased models have influenced hiring decisions, credit scoring, and legal judgments, highlighting the societal risks of unchecked AI deployment. Various bias mitigation techniques, such as debiasing algorithms, methodologies, and diverse data curation strategies, are discussed to provide practical solutions.

Data privacy, trustworthiness, and security are another critical aspect of LLM governance. The ability of these models to memorize and regurgitate training data poses a significant risk of unintentional data leaks, making compliance with regulations such as the General Data Protection Regulation (GDPR), the California Consumer Privacy Act (CCPA), and other global privacy laws an essential consideration. This chapter delves into the challenges of anonymizing data, preventing model inversion attacks, and ensuring user consent in AI-driven applications.

Transparency and explainability are crucial in AI ethics, yet LLMs often function as "black boxes," producing outputs without clear justification. This opacity can erode trust in AI-driven systems, especially in high-stakes sectors like healthcare, finance, and law. We discuss ongoing research in explainable AI (XAI), highlighting techniques such as SHAP

(Shapley Additive Explanations) and LIME (Local Interpretable Model-agnostic Explanations), which aim to make model decisions more interpretable for stakeholders.

Regulatory frameworks are rapidly evolving to address these ethical concerns.

Governments and international organizations are proposing AI regulations to set standards for responsible AI development and deployment. For example, the European Union's AI Act classifies AI systems based on risk levels, mandating stricter oversight for high-risk applications. The U.S. AI Bill of Rights also lays out guidelines to shield people from the negative effects of AI. We analyze these regulatory efforts alongside industry self-regulation initiatives, such as OpenAI's AI ethics guidelines and Google's Responsible AI framework.

Finally, we explore the future of ethical AI governance, emphasizing the role of interdisciplinary collaboration among technologists, policymakers, ethicists, and business leaders. As AI technology continues to evolve, a proactive approach to ethical AI development, incorporating continuous monitoring, human oversight, and ethical auditing, will be essential to ensure LLMs benefit society without exacerbating existing inequalities.

This chapter provides an extensive overview of the ethical and regulatory challenges of LLMs, providing insight into best practices for developing AI systems that are fair, transparent, and aligned with global legal standards. By fostering an ethical AI culture, organizations can mitigate risks, enhance trust, and ensure that the transformative power of LLMs is leveraged responsibly.

IMPACT OF LLMS ON BIAS & FAIRNESS OF OUTPUT

Large Language Models (LLMs) have revolutionized natural language processing (NLP) by making it possible to perform sophisticated tasks such as text generation, sentiment analysis, and decision making. Nevertheless, their vulnerability to bias has posed ethical issues, as biased results can perpetuate negative stereotypes, marginalize specific groups, and result in discriminatory decision-making. Bias in LLMs can be caused by various sources, such as training data, model architecture, and actual applications.

Biases in LLMs can be categorized majorly in two categories:

Intrinsic bias Intrinsic bias occurs as a result of training methodology and data set composition. As LLMs are trained on massive volumes of internet-sourced text, they necessarily pick up and propagate the biases within such texts. Gender stereotypes in jobs: "pilot" being masculine and "air hostess" being feminine, are commonly seen in model responses. In addition, inadequate representation of some demographic groups can cause skewed perceptions and inadequate representation.

1. Bias in Training Dataset: Over or under representation of a particular group, age or section of society may introduce bias during training.
2. Bias in Data collection method: Web scraping, social media, books, code repositories, scholarly articles, government documents, and other sources provide a variety of sub-datasets on which LLMs are trained. Every source has biases of its own; for instance, data from the internet may contain damaging or unmoderated content. Model behavior is influenced by these biases, necessitating cautious dataset curation and mitigation techniques.

3. item Bias in Language context: Language environment can also give rise to biases. Because words, syntax, and context are malleable, human languages frequently contain ambiguities (syntax, lexical, semantic, and context-dependent meaning), which can result in model biases.

Extrinsic bias Extrinsic bias involves the production of biased responses from LLMs in actual practice. In contrast to intrinsic bias, which resides in the model itself, extrinsic bias results from the nature of how the model engages with various tasks, data, and environments. LLMs in sentiment analysis might over-classify text in African American Vernacular English (AAVE) as having a higher tendency to be negative than text in standard English, reflecting inherent social biases.

1. Gender Bias: Models may make mistakes on tasks like coreference resolution because they mistakenly link particular jobs or occupations to a particular gender. Responses from models may conform to gender stereotypes.
2. Age Bias: Based on age stereotypes, models may assume certain things about people. For example, only younger people are associated with technological proficiency.
3. Regional Bias: It's possible for models to misunderstand cultural idioms or expressions or overlook regional linguistic variations.

Bias in Real World Applications

Here are several real-world examples where bias in Large Language Models has had measurable impacts:

Chinese startup DeepSeek launched an open-source AI model, DeepSeek-R1, that censoriously responded with heavy censorship to sensitive subjects such as Taiwan and Tiananmen Square. Such inbuilt prejudice, driven by Chinese laws, created doubts about the model's competitiveness and application globally (Yang, 2025).

Elon Musk's company, xAI, developed Grok to counteract purportedly "woke" sentiments in AI models. Training materials that instructed annotators to avoid moralizing and to deny social justice themes produced a model that leaned toward right-wing ideology (Kay, 2025).

Omiye et al., 2023 conducted one study to assess racial bias on health-related questions. They found that all four models, ChatGPT and the more powerful GPT-4, both from OpenAI; Google's Bard; and Anthropic's Claude failed when asked to respond to medical questions on kidney function, lung capacity, and skin thickness. In some instances, they seemed to support long-held misconceptions about Black and white biological distinctions that scientists have been working to remove from medical facilities for years.

Researchers discovered bias in the GenAI based art generating program Midjourney, according to an article published on theconversation.com, 2023. When asked to create

images of individuals in specialized professions, the gendered bias regarding women's roles in the workplace was reinforced. The photos depicted both younger and older people, but the older persons were always men.

When a female journalist of Asian heritage used the Lensa AI avatar app in 2022, she was presented with a variety of sexualized avatars, including topless anime

character-like avatars. Such pictures had not been requested or approved by her. Prisma Labs, the app's creators, admitted the problem and said they were attempting to lessen prejudices (Ephraim, 2022).

Bias mitigation techniques

Bias in Large Language Models (LLMs) arises from imbalances in training data, model architecture, and algorithmic decision-making. Guo et al., 2024 categorized bias mitigation methods in to three major categories based on the time of application.

1. Pre-model debiasing: Pre-model debiasing method is a technique for preprocessing input data prior to train LLMs such that the whole training data is balanced and representative of the whole population. Oversampling, undersampling, and creating synthetic data are common techniques for balancing training data. A prominent one of those is counterfactual data augmentation (CDA). Counterfactual Data Substitution (CDS), an extension of CDA, is also suggested in order to substitute potentially biased text randomly to prevent duplication.
2. Intra-model debiasing: This entails altering the training process to reduce bias in training the model. For example, Loss Function Modification: A constraint-aware loss function punishes spurious correlations. Models trained with these constraints emphasize causal relationships over biased data associations.
3. Post-model debiasing: These methods correct bias after the model generates responses, making them ideal for closed-source models. For example, Output Filtering & Rewriting: Adjusting final responses to remove biased or discriminatory

    language. Chain-of-Thought (CoT) Debiasing is another post-model debiasing approach, which encourages models to generate step-by-step rationales to justify responses to reduce stereotypical outputs.

DATA PRIVACY & SECURITY

Large Language Models (LLMs) have transformed AI-based applications with their capabilities in text generation, translation, and summarization of content. Nevertheless, the training of LLMs depends on a huge volume of data, which typically contains sensitive information. As a result, LLMs struggle with managing privacy and security concerns.

Privacy in LLMs

Privacy concerns in LLMs arise because they have to handle a huge volume of data.

Numerous LLMs use web scraped data, which can contain personally identifiable information (PII). Even with methods such as differential privacy and federated learning, such sensitive information might remain in models.

There exist two main types of privacy risks:

1. Passive Privacy Leakage: When users involuntarily reveal sensitive information through their interaction with LLMs
    - 1.1 Sensitive Query Exposure: Users input private information unknowingly, which the model may later reveal.
    - 1.2 Contextual Leakage: The model infers personal data from multiple queries over time.
    - 1.3 Personal Preferences Leakage: Recommender systems powered by LLMs can inadvertently expose user interests or behaviors.
2. Active Privacy Attacks: These consist of attackers actively trying to steal or alter information that is stored in LLMs.
    - 2.1 Backdoor Attacks (Data Poisoning): During pre-training or fine-tuning, attackers introduce malicious data, which results in altered or deceptive outputs from the model.
    - 2.2 Membership Inference Attacks (MIA): These attacks attempt to determine if specific data was part of an LLM's training set. They pose a severe risk for datasets containing medical records, financial data, or confidential documents.
    - 2.3 Model Inversion Attacks: Attackers attempt to reverse-engineer training data by analyzing an LLM's output. This technique can be used to recover private user conversations or sensitive records.
    - 2.4 Model Stealing Attacks: Adversaries extract model parameters by sending targeted queries and observing responses. This enables unauthorized replication of LLMs trained on proprietary or sensitive data.

Privacy Protection Mechanisms

Researchers suggest diverse defense methods at three phases of LLM development to counter the threats of privacy leakage and attacks (Yan et al., 2024):

1. Privacy Protection in Pre-Training:
   1.1 Data Cleaning: PII removal prior to training to minimize risk.
   1.2 Federated Learning: Local model training on user devices to avoid centralized data exposure.
   1.3 Differential Privacy: Addition of noise during training data to avoid memorization of records.
2. Privacy Protection during Fine-Tuning:
   2.1 Knowledge Unlearning: Methods to cause LLMs to "forget" sensitive data.
   2.2 Offsite Tuning: Locally keeping fine-tuning data instead of sending it to centralized servers.
3. Privacy Protection during Inference:
   3.1 Homo-morphic Encryption: Enables models to compute on encrypted data without decrypting it.
   3.2 Secure Multi-Party Computation (SMPC): Spreads computations among multiple parties to maintain privacy.
   3.3 Trusted Execution Environments (TEE): Employ secure hardware environments to avoid unauthorized access to model parameters.

Challenges

In spite of progress in LLM privacy protection, there remain a number of challenges to be addressed:

1. Transparency Deficit in LLMs: As most LLMs are black-box models, it is difficult to investigate their privacy policies.
2. Multimodal LLM Privacy Multimodal models that involve sound, visuals, and text present challenging privacy concerns.
3. Customized LLMs: AI assistants personalized to particular user data enhance the likelihood of data leakage.
4. Scalability Challenges: Scales of federated learning and differential privacy are still computationally costly.
5. New Methods of Attack: Threat actors continue to create advanced means to avoid security measures in order to go around them.

Having discussed security and privacy concerns, it is important to investigate Explainable AI (XAI) and transparency since they play a significant part in preventing the hidden biases and weaknesses of AI models. Interpretability improvement helps ensure that LLMs

protect not only sensitive information but also offer responsible and reliable decision-making.

TRANSPARENCY & EXPLAINABLE AI

The goal of Explainable Artificial Intelligence (XAI), a branch of artificial intelligence, is to make machine learning models' decision-making processes easier for people to comprehend, decode, and explain.

Why we need XAI

As AI systems increase in sophistication, especially with the advent of deep learning and big language models, their internal workings tend to be opaque, operating as "black boxes" (de Carvalho Souza et al., 2025).

Concerns about trust, justice, and accountability arise from the inability to justify LLM decisions. A model making an erroneous or biased decision makes it challenging to pinpoint the source of the issue or to correct it. Moreover, without explainability, users cannot have confidence in the outputs, potentially hindering the adoption of LLMs in mission-critical applications. For instance, in healthcare, an LLM could suggest a specific treatment based on patterns that it learned from past data, yet without knowing the reasons why the model suggested that, physicians might be unwilling to act upon it.

The ability of XAI to close the gap between sophisticated algorithms and human explainability makes it significant. Transparency in AI systems is crucial in high-stakes industries like healthcare, banking, and law to prevent ethical dilemmas and mistrust. For instance, when an AI system makes a medical diagnosis or denies a loan request, stakeholders must know the rationale behind these decisions to ensure fairness, precision, and accountability.

Techniques

Because LLMs are so complex, several techniques have been developed to shed light their decision-making procedures in an effort to make them easier to understand and more transparent. These approaches fall into two general categories:

- Post-hoc explainability: These techniques are applicable after the response generated from the LLM.

– Attention Mechanism: Attention mechanisms point to which regions of the input text the model is concentrating on during prediction and exposing the token relationships within a sentence. Through the visualization attention weights, we can observe how much weight the model assigns to specific words or phrases when generating a response.
– Another powerful method is LIME (Local Interpretable Model-agnostic Explanations), which estimates the behavior of the sophisticated model with a less complex, interpretable model. By altering the input and tracking the changes in the model's predictions, it produces a local explanation that reveals the factors that influence the choice.
– SHAP (Shapley Additive Explanations) is one of the techniques in the post-hoc category which gives every feature a contribution score according to cooperative game theory. SHAP values can explain the effect that every input token has upon the model's output, providing both local and global interpretations.

- Intrinsic explainability: Intrinsic explainability refers to the inherent transparency of a model's decision-making process due to its interpretable structure.

For instance, rule-based systems or decision trees are more straightforward and less complex to explain than LLMs. While these models might not have the predictive capability of LLMs, they offer greater transparency into decision-making. Merging these less complex models with LLMs can provide a hybrid solution, where the LLM offers high precision, and the less complex model provides clarity.

Real life Examples of XAI

In actual applications, Large Language explainability Models (LLMs) play a crucial role to enhance transparency and accountability, particularly in sectors such as law,

healthcare, finance, and customer service. Following are some real-life examples where explainability has been successfully used in LLMs (Lai et al., 2024).

- AI is used more frequently to help judges make rulings and evaluating the risk of offending. For instance, in 2023, a court in Colombia utilized the ChatGPT decision-making outcome to guide judges for punishing a case involving medical insurance.
- Legal LLMs streamline repetitive tasks, enabling judges to focus on complex cases. Luminance AI, developed by a British start-up, automates document

processing and contract generation. This reduces time and labor costs, improving efficiency in legal workflows.

- LLMs recommend treatment plans based on patient records while attention mechanisms highlight key symptoms influencing decisions. This enhances transparency, allowing healthcare professionals to understand the model's reasoning. As a result, doctors can validate or adjust AI-driven suggestions effectively.
- LLMs are used in finance for market analysis, fraud detection, and credit scoring. When detecting fraud, SHAP values explain which factors (e.g., spending patterns, location) influenced the decision. This enhances transparency and ensures compliance with regulatory standards.
- Counterfactual explanations help analysts explore hypothetical scenarios where a transaction wouldn't be flagged as fraud. This reveals the model's decision boundaries, increasing transparency and trust in the system.

REGULATORY FRAMEWORKS

AI is now used in more important reasoning and decision-making tasks thanks to LLMs. For this reason, ethics-based audits play a central position in the quickly expanding fields of AI regulation and AI safety. Proponents of various regulatory approaches contend

that AI systems should be regulated similarly to nuclear weapons, which pose a catastrophic risk (particularly at the technological frontiers); consumer goods, which present a variety of risks to the user; pharmaceuticals, which necessitate a strong prerelease regulatory framework; and/or environmental pollution, to which the law responds with a range of instruments read.dukeupress.edu, 2024. Both, State and Private entities (who own LLMs) have acted upon regulating the LLMs. Few important regulatory frameworks have been discussed in brief in new two subsections.

Government based

- European Union's Artificial Intelligence Act (AI Act): AI act of EU is the first regulatory code for managing the development and operation of artificial intelligence (AI) in the EU. Passed on 1 August 2024, the AI Act seeks to provide that AI technologies are designed and used so as to be secure, clear, and compliant with essential rights. The AI Act covers all types and fields of AI with exceptions for those utilized solely for non-professional purposes, military affairs, national defense, and scientific research. This systemic solution guarantees that AI solutions in all sectors conform to the set standards, forging a harmonized regulatory framework within the EU. [1]

- The Blueprint for an AI Bill of Rights: It provides guidelines for the ethical advancement and application of artificial intelligence (AI) in the United States and was published by the White House in October 2022. It emphasizes protecting individuals from AI-related harms while promoting fairness, transparency, and accountability. The framework is built on five core principles: (1) Safe and Effective AI, (2) Algorithmic Discrimination Protections, (3) Data Privacy, (4) Notice and Explanation, and (5) Human Alternatives and Oversight. This blueprint serves as a non-binding policy recommendation, guiding government agencies, businesses, and AI

- In October 2019, Russian President Vladimir Putin approved the National Strategy for the Development of Artificial Intelligence (AI) up to 2030. The strategy outlines short-term goals to be achieved by 2024 and medium-term goals by 2030, aiming to position Russia as a leading AI power. Key objectives include enhancing scientific research in AI, improving access to information and computing resources, and advancing personnel training in the field. The strategy mandates the integration of AI development into national programs like the "Digital Economy of the Russian Federation" and requires annual progress reports to the President. [3]
- NITI Aayog of India released National Strategy for Artificial Intelligence in 2018, outlines India's vision to harness AI for inclusive growth and position itself as a global leader in the field. Key points on which India is working are: (1) A need to bolster AI research capabilities and cultivate a skilled workforce. (2) Ensuring the availability of quality data while maintaining privacy and security. (3) Addressing issues related to awareness, infrastructure, and funding to promote AI integration across sectors. (4) Ethical AI Development: Formulating guidelines to ensure AI systems are transparent, unbiased, and secure.

Industry wise self-regulations

- OpenAI: In order to guarantee that the technology preserves principles like liberty, equity, and respect for human rights, OpenAI highlights the significance of democratic leadership in AI development. The group backs the U.S. National Security Memorandum on Artificial Intelligence, which emphasizes the need for resources like

data center capacity and semiconductor chip and promotes the proper application of AI in national security. OpenAI works with the U.S. Agency for International

Development to use AI to expedite administrative tasks and with organizations such as DARPA to improve cybersecurity. The business upholds stringent usage guidelines that forbid the production of weapons or other detrimental uses of its technology. To ensure compliance with ethical norms, OpenAI's Product Policy and National Security teams formally evaluate potential national security agreements. 5

- Meta: The company's dedication to the ethical advancement of AI is demonstrated by Meta's Responsible AI Connect 2024. Among its primary projects is the Llama Responsible Use Guide, which offers developers best practices for implementing large language models (LLMs) in a way that makes them safe and beneficial for users. Additionally, Meta introduced the Llama Social Impact Grant Program to support initiatives that apply AI for societal benefit. By encouraging equity, openness, and accountability in the application of AI, these programs show Meta's dedication to integrating ethical AI principles throughout all stages of product development. [6]
- Google: Google's "A Policy Agenda for Responsible Progress in Artificial Intelligence" outlines a strategic framework to harness AI's potential while addressing associated challenges. Its major motive is to building trust in AI systems. This involves implementing standards, best practices, and regulations, such as expert risk assessments for high-risk AI applications to ensure ethical development and deployment. AI's role in global security necessitates measures to prevent its malicious use. Collaboration among governments, academia, industry, and civil society is vital to align AI advancements with human values and address safety implications.[7]

In addition to this, all renowned AI Tech giants are actively working on making responsible AI product in sync with AI regulations of various governing bodies.

FUTURE OF GLOBAL AI GOVERNANCE

With artificial intelligence (AI) transforming industries and societies at an accelerating pace, the necessity of a solid and concerted worldwide AI governance framework grows ever more pressing. The earlier discussion about AI regulations concentrated on national and institutional frameworks, identifying the various regulatory strategies across jurisdictions.

However, because AI transcends national boundaries, its administration necessitates a more cohesive worldwide strategy that balances innovation with societal protection and guarantees ethical, legal, and technical monitoring. Establishing mechanisms that support security, accountability, and transparency in AI deployment while reducing economic rivalry and geopolitical conflicts is the goal of global AI governance Zaidan and Ibrahim, 2024.

BARRIERS TO STRONG GLOBAL AI GOVERNANCE

Several challenges hinder the establishment of an effective global AI governance system:

- AI governance attempts are hampered by conflicting national interests, as some nations give precedence to innovation while others aim for tight control through regulation. The geopolitical context generates competition over cooperation, rendering it challenging to create a commonly accepted governance structure.
- Various regulatory agencies, such as the UN, OECD, and EU, suggest AI governance standards. But the absence of harmonization between these institutions leads to overlapping, and in some cases conflicting, regulations.
- Most AI governance debates are fueled by high-income nations, excluding low-income countries that might not have the capacity and expertise to engage meaningfully.

    Such exclusion can result in governance frameworks that fail to meet the needs of all countries.
- Although legal and governance frameworks take years to develop and put into place, AI technologies develop rapidly. Before appropriate monitoring mechanisms are put in place, this regulatory lag creates a gap that allows AI systems to be exploited.
- Enforcement and Compliance Challenges: Even if international agreements are made, state compliance is challenging to enforce. In the absence of enforcement or legal compliance, states may choose to exempt themselves from obeying international AI governance norms.

PATHWAYS FORWARD FOR GLOBAL AI GOVERNANCE

- Multilateral institutions like UN, G20, and regional organizations can be used to create AI governance to bridge the gaps between national policies. The Global Digital Compact and UN Common Agenda are some of the initiatives that focus on such international cooperation.
- A mix of legally enforceable rules (hard law) and non-binding guidelines (soft law) can offer regulatory stability and flexibility. This model has been

proposed for AI regulation to allow for varying national interests while maintaining minimum ethical and safety standards.

- In order to establish AI governance frameworks that promote responsible innovation while averting detrimental AI applications, governments and AI-driven businesses must work together.
- A more equitable AI governance framework can be established by giving underrepresented countries financial and technical support. A governance structure that benefits exclusively technologically advanced countries can be avoided by guaranteeing fair access to AI technologies.

RECOMMENDATIONS FOR FUTURE AI GOVERNANCE

- Establish a Global Authority to Regulate AI An independent AI regulatory agency can establish and implement international AI standards, much like the International Atomic Energy Agency (IAEA) does for nuclear control.
- Adopt Governance Frameworks for AI Using Current Models Frameworks like the Council of Europe's AI Convention and the EU AI Act can serve as models for AI governance, which can then be modified for worldwide use.
- Create global guidelines for AI safety and risk assessment. Creating international risk assessment guidelines will aid in reducing the negative effects of AI applications, especially in crucial fields like mass surveillance, deepfake technology, and autonomous weaponry.
- Strengthen Ethical AI Standards: To guarantee that AI benefits mankind fairly, it is important to promote AI ethics research and incorporate fairness, transparency, and human right principles into AI governance.

Because of competing national interests, fragmented regulations, and enforcement constraints, global AI governance continues to be a difficult task. Nonetheless, a strong governance framework may be created by encouraging multilateral cooperation, using hybrid regulatory approaches, and guaranteeing equitable representation of all countries. To guarantee AI's responsible and advantageous application globally, future AI governance initiatives should prioritize openness, responsibility, and international cooperation.

REFERENCES

de Carvalho Souza, M. E., Souza, M. E. D. C., & Weigang, L. (2025). Unveiling the black box: The significance of xai in making llms transparent. *Authorea Preprints.*

Ephraim. (2022). The viral ai avatar app lensa undressed me without my consent [https://www.technologyreview.com/2022/12/12/1064751/the-viral-ai- avatar-app-lensa-undressed-me-without-my-consent/ [Accessed: (15-march-2025)]].

Guo, Y., Guo, M., Su, J., Yang, Z., Zhu, M., Li, H., Qiu, M., & Liu, S. S. (2024). Bias in large language models: Origin, evaluation, and mitigation. arXiv preprint arXiv:2411.10915.

Kay, G. (2025, February 28). Inside Grok's war on "woke." Business Insider. https://www.businessinsider.com/xai-grok-training-bias-woke-idealogy-2025-02

Lai, J., Gan, W., Wu, J., Qi, Z., & Philip, S. Y. (2024). *Large language models in law: A survey.* AI Open.

Omiye, J. A., Lester, J. C., Spichak, S., Rotemberg, V., & Daneshjou, R. (2023). Large language models propagate race-based medicine. *NPJ Digital Medicine*, *6*(1), 195.

read.dukeupress.edu. (2024). Regulatory analogies, llms, and generative ai [https://read.dukeupress.edu/critical-ai/article-abstract/doi/10.1215/2834703X-11205238 [Accessed: (17-march-2025)]].

theconversation.com. (2023). Ageism, sexism, classism and more: 7 examples of bias in ai-generated images [https://theconversation.com/ageism-sexism-classism -and- more-7-examples-of-bias-in-ai-generated-images-208748 [Accessed:(15-march-2025)]].

Yan, B., Li, K., Xu, M., Dong, Y., Zhang, Y., Ren, Z., & Cheng, X. (2024). On protecting the data privacy of large language models (llms): A survey. arXiv preprint arXiv:2403.05156.

Yang, Z. (2025, January 31). Here's How DeepSeek Censorship Actually Works—and How to Get Around It. WIRED. https://www.wired.com/story/deepseek-censorship/

Zaidan, E., & Ibrahim, I. A. (2024). Ai governance in a complex and rapidly changing regulatory landscape: A global perspective. *Humanities & Social Sciences Communications*, *11*(1), 1–18.

Chapter 10
Transforming Financial Decision-Making:
The Role of Large Language Models in Risk Management and Fraud Detection

Puneett Bhatnagr
http://orcid.org/0000-0002-9281-1809
Amity University, India

ABSTRACT

This chapter investigates the knowledge gained through the transformational role of Large Language Models (LLMs) in financial risk management and fraud detection, especially as it relates to modern financial decision-making. Conventional approaches to financial analysis have introduced machine learning techniques to handle vast and complex datasets. Specifically, LLMs, from OpenAI's GPT series to Bloomberg's GPT, are a significant change because they represent the ability of institutions to process and understand structurally as well as unstructured financial data. This chapter illustrates how LLMs improve risk assessment by deriving the context and integrating sentiment analysis from regulated documents and market trends to provide nuanced insights. In the case of fraud detection, LLMs outperform others in terms of their ability to detect anomalies, identity theft prevention, and document validation based on real-time upcoming transactions and communication patterns.

DOI: 10.4018/979-8-3693-6690-5.ch010

1. INTRODUCTION

Over the past decades, there has been a shift in financial decision-making practices from manual paper-based systems to fully automation-oriented facilities (Yang, 2022). During the modern digital era, no other alternatives existed for actions such as making investment decisions except for human judgment augmented with commonly used statistical methods and standard computing tools to assess risks and detect fraud (Chaquet-Ulldemolins et al., 2022). Previous early decision-making procedures worked well until they hit their limits after dealing with very large and complicated datasets (Ionescu & Diaconita, 2023). The breakthrough came in 2002 when machine learning and artificial intelligence started flooding the market, leading to the machine production of high-end predictive models and automated systems for faster data processing; however, this has brought inequality to the market. There is now a clear divide between those who did not invest in machine learning and artificial intelligence systems are now behind (Schmitt, 2022). Large Language Models have caused the financial industry to reach a turning point in decisive decision-making transformation (Khan et al., 2024).

However, a rapid transformation of the financial industry has been observed because of the increasing adoption of AI technologies in areas such as risk management and fraud detection (Tian et al., 2024). The most important one is the growing investment in AI-driven risk management solutions because financial institutions realise that, in the wake of increasingly complex and changing risk landscapes, they need an advanced cognitive tool to better assess the variety of risks they face (Nallakaruppan et al., 2024). According to the latest industry reports, global AI spending on financial services is expected to reach $40 billion by 2025, with a large chunk of it being for improving risk management and detection of fraud (Reite et al., 2024).

Today, GPT series from OpenAI or Bloomberg GPT are on the frontier of creating AI which has myriads of data pointed at them, which is not limited to structured financial data but rather extremely vast, unstructured information (Fernandez et al., 2023). These models are vital for a clearer understanding of and the ability to create human-readable texts (Bhatnagr et al., 2024), as they can parse and comprehend complex financial records, earnings announcements, government filings, news reports, social voices, and internal communications (Delgadillo et al., 2024). This has allowed financial institutions to uncover new opportunities for insight that were just not available or were simply too labour-intensive to process (Trummer, 2022). Using sentiment analysis, LLMs can predict how the market will move based on articles and posts in news and social media, extract critical pieces of information from lengthy financial statements, and even discover any process that might indicate fraud or expose risks (Shobayo et al., 2024).

LLM's ability to perform well beyond the capacity to handle big data is attributable to contextual understanding and adaptivity (Suri et al., 2023). For example, LLMs such as GPT-3 can be generalised across many tasks and hence can be very useful for any type of financial decision (Balkus & Yan, 2023). It is seamlessly integrated with existing risk management frameworks and helps in making real-time decisions with the right set of timely and accurate insights while also improving fraud-detection systems (Delgadillo et al., 2024). Moreover, these models allow more banks to use them, as they are grown more efficiently and more easily (Fernandez et al., 2023).

The appearance of LLMs marks a tipping point in the change in financial decisions from data to intelligence (Trummer, 2022). Financial institutions and the organisations with which they work have thus redefined risk management, fraud detection, and strategic planning since organisations can process and understand complex, unstructured data at scale (Shobayo et al., 2024). With the increase in complexity and data-driven nature of the financial landscape, LLM will keep its place intact and grow bigger to exploit the sector's unprecedented possibilities of innovation and efficiency (Delgadillo et al., 2024).

2. THEORETICAL FOUNDATIONS OF LLMS IN FINANCIAL RISK MANAGEMENT

The architecture and capability of large language models (LLMs) provide a theoretical basis for applications in financial risk management (Denecke et al., 2024). Transformer architecture leads to LLMs, which is a breakthrough in deep learning in the field of natural language processing (NLP) (Sahoo et al., 2024). Self-attention and multihead attention are mechanisms used by transformers to capture contextual relationships and dependencies (i.e. sequence to sequence) in a given data sequence (Muller et al., 2024). Using this architecture, LLMs can discern complex patterns in text and numerical data, and thus understand individual data points as well as their interrelationships across all documents (Zhou et al., 2024). Recognising these nuances and understanding the interplay between different types of data is critical in the realm of finance, where language is nuanced and the interplay between different data types defines the problem (Pan et al., 2024). Documents such as balance sheets, regulatory filings, and market reports are complex and intricate; hence, they can be disseminated by LLMs to pick out subtle cues and other relations that more traditional models might fail to identify (Cheng, 2024).

One such powerful use of LLM in financial risk management is its ability to integrate structured and unstructured data, providing a balanced picture of financial landscapes. It provides quantitative insights from structured data in the form of transaction records, the use of various financial ratios, and the price of equities

(Tripathi et al., 2024). However, they represent only half of the picture. News articles, analysts' opinions, social media, and internal mail are qualitative sources whose content plays a major role in estimating risks and market projections (Sezgin, 2024). The ability to synthesise all the different sources of data comes with the job of LLM (Bhatnagr & Rajesh, 2024), and the net result of this is that it provides LLM with a balanced perspective on risks and opportunities (Li et al., 2023). For instance, LLM could peruse the company's financial record, latest regulations, and market sentiment and offer a more enriched decision-making picture (Sahoo et al., 2024).

Additionally, when LLMs are incorporated into traditional financial models, the accuracy of the prediction and pedigrees of risk increases exponentially (Delgadillo et al., 2024). Standard models, such as credit scoring systems, are based on historical financial data and predefined criteria and, hence, may overlook some nuances of risk indicators. By incorporating LLM, these systems can assess behavioural patterns, market sentiment, and external factors, in addition to analysing data (Roumeliotis et al., 2024). Thus, an LLM could read not only the financial statements of a borrower but also news coverage of the borrower's company and other context-sensitive information (Bhatnagr et al., 2024a), such as reviews of the borrower as a customer and their social media sentiment, to make a better assessment of the borrower's creditworthiness (Fazlija & Harder, 2022). Similarly, LLMs can support the traditional quantitative models used for market risk analysis by including real-time news sentiments and geopolitical events, providing a more dynamic and reactive approach (Liu et al., 2024). LLMs have been theoretically established as revolutionising factors in financial risk management (Jung & Jang, 2024). It has an advanced architecture for providing contextualisation at depth and can handle a variety of data variations to reach decisions with greater and more accurate knowledge (Fu & Zhang, 2024). When combined with conventional models in the financial world, LLMs provide better predictive accuracy and further dimensions of insight to navigate the global financial market, as it is today (Jeong, 2024).

3. APPLICATIONS OF LLMS IN RISK MANAGEMENT

Large Language Models (LLMs) applied in risk management reconsider how financial institutions evaluate, forecast, and control risks at various scales (Fernandez et al., 2023). The use of LLMs in credit risk assessment advances beyond traditional scoring methods, as LLMs integrate structured and unstructured data to create a score (Zhang et al., 2023). Traditional credit evaluation is usually based on numerical data such as credit scores, income statements, and debt-income ratios. This is valuable, but it overlooks important qualitative factors that affect a borrower's creditworthiness (Li et al., 2024). Although no types of information are evaluated by LLMs, they utilise numerical data as well as textual information such as customer reviews, news sentiment, and social media discourse (Xing, 2024). For instance, if a small business applies for a loan and has stable financials but has recently been covered with negative news or customer complaints (Bhatnagr et al., 2024c), an LLM can use that qualitative data to score risk (Preiksaitis et al., 2024). Combining these two methods results in more sophisticated and comprehensive credit evaluations that are less prone to default and score an applicant who would otherwise be overlooked in traditional models.

In market risk analysis, LLMs are leading the way in processing real-time data from various sources, aiding the forecasting of market trends, and identifying looming risks in advance (Delgadillo et al., 2024). Unlike typical market analysis models, which are based to a great extent on historic price movements and statistical parameters, LLMs are in a position to use real-time news articles, earnings, analysts' opinions, and political events to derive a real-time, multifaceted image of market situations (Liu et al., 2024). For example, during market volatility, an LLM can evaluate breaking news, sentiments from social networks, and investor opinions to identify emerging risks and forecast future market movements (Abolghasemi et al., 2023). This real-time, data-driven perception assists the investor and risk manager in making decisions based on facts, adjusting the course of investments, and implementing hedging strategies in advance, minimising the effect of adverse market situations (Jeong, 2024).

Operational risk monitoring is another domain in which LLMs are extremely useful. Operational risks, such as internal fraud, compliance breaches, and errors by people, are normally embedded in the vast amounts of unstructured data generated by an organisation, such as internal documents, emails, incident reports, and communication histories (Balsiger et al., 2024). Operational risks are easily scanned by the LLM from the above sources, and patterns and anomalies are selected, possibly suggesting risks (Xing, 2024). For example, an LLM can scan employee communication to identify signs of insider dealing, conflicts of interest, and violation of company codes (Li et al., 2024). It can also scan compliance reporting to monitor compliance with regulations and flag issues to be investigated (Fernandez et al., 2023). This type of scrutiny is important to assist an organisation in realising and assessing operational risks before they become major challenges and thus ensure its integrity and compliance (Baum, 2024).

The partnership between Tiger Brokers and DeepSeek provided DeepSeek-R1's AI model for use by the developer of the trading assistant chatbot TigerGPT. Within its descriptive application, LLMs help enhance market evaluations to make timely trading decisions (Delgadillo et al., 2024). TigerGPT utilises DeepSeek-R1 to assess complex market patterns, together with news sentiment and user input, to deliver personalised investment counselling and guidance (Xing, 2024). Platform users receive a dynamic market analysis and discover investment prospects and risk assessment capabilities from the AI-based assistance system (Liu et al., 2024). The implementation of LLMs for risk analysis automation separates market investigations into two categories, consumer-friendly and expert-level knowledge delivery, while also enhancing user participation (Jeong, 2024).

4. APPLICATIONS OF LLMS IN FRAUD DETECTION

Thus, LLMs use many advanced approaches to discover fraud from multiple perspectives (Sinha et al., 2024). The ability of LLM to scan enormous amounts of transaction-based data to detect transaction anomalies, indicating possible fraud, has proven to be one of the most powerful applications of LLM (Patsakis et al., 2024). Unlike other, more common, purely numerical-based mechanisms, LLM leverages contextual factors, such as the sequence of recent transactions (among other things), their geographical location, and temporal patterns to discover previously invisible anomalies. Imagine, for instance, that an LLM detects a large transaction from a location that is out of the ordinary at an out-of-ordinary time if the pattern is too far removed from the common pattern.

Fraud detection using multiple angles is one of the main techniques utilised by LLMs (Selim et al., 2024). It is among the most powerful applications in which LLM observes enormous amounts of transaction-based data searching for anomalies, possibly putative fraud (Martínez et al., 2024). In contrast to traditional numerical threshold-based methods, LLM uses contextual factors -- what has happened in the past, the individual's location, and the timing–to identify subtle anomalies (Patsakis et al., 2024). For example, if a pattern involves a pattern that would flag a large transaction from an abnormal location at an abnormal time, LLMs may catch an attempted identity theft. Using LLMs to analyse various sets of information such as login times, the pace at which users are typing, information about the devices, location, and much more, they can discern patterns such as identity theft or takeover. For example, if a customer who logs into his account from New York suddenly logs into a different location or third country on a different device, the LLM would be able to detect this activity and ask for further security questions. With pattern-based inspection, the verification of credentials does not end with the ROC point, and it provides additional protection from identity theft.

LLM capabilities also significantly helped in document fraud analysis. Billions of loan applications, contracts, and invoices are made into financial institutions every day (Bhatnagr & Rajesh, 2024a). These documents can then be reviewed by LLMs to identify inconsistencies and cross-reference them in the databases for authentication (Li et al., 2024). For instance, if the application is for a loan, an LLM can check whether the facts in the job match PCs or private fact bases and alert discrepancies, possibly indicating falsified documents or false promises (Deng et al., 2024).

By monitoring fraud in real-time, LLM offers one of the major benefits of using it to detect fraud (Sinha et al., 2024). The ability to track transactions and communication enables the real-time monitoring and detection of suspicious activities and prompt responses to them. LLM helps process streams of data in real-time with real-time processing, aiding in the screening, in real-time, of data streams in such a way that fraud may be caught in real-time and interventions made (Selim et al., 2024). It aids in eliminating monetary losses and minimising fraud.

The use of cutting-edge LLMs for Fraud Protection in the case of JPMorgan is a notable point where LLMs have been proven to detect fraud. JPMorgan has introduced LLMs into its infrastructure to enable real-time monitoring through fraud detection of the transactional activity of many millions of accounts (Patsakis et al., 2024). Since then, LLMs have been scanning intricate patterns of users' activity and patterns of those flows between them as well as external sources to accurately identify the risks of fraud (Li et al., 2024). In this case, this anticipatory strategy dramatically lowered the rate of false positives, improving the speed of fraud detection and allowing the bank to stop the fraud well before the customer's accounts are damaged (Deng et al., 2024).

5. BENEFITS AND CHALLENGES OF IMPLEMENTING LLMS

The transformative benefits of the implementation of Large Language Models (LLMs) in financial risk management and fraud detection are many, although they are also accompanied by a series of challenges that institutions should deal with very carefully (Li et al., 2024). A great benefit of LLMs is that they tend to be more accurate in evaluating the much more complex datasets used for risk assessment and fraud detection (Delgadillo et al., 2024). LLMs can do this by integrating structured and unstructured data from several different sources, such as transaction records, market reports, customer communications, and social media sentiments, to look beyond the obvious and create a more sophisticated and complete view of potential risk and anomalous behaviours (Balsiger et al., 2024). This ability for contextual awareness and language intricacy helps them detect subtle patterns and correlates that the traditional system might miss, making risk models better and fraud detection mechanisms better (Xing, 2024).

Real-time analysis is another major benefit that allows financial institutions to act on the risks and incidents of fraud as well as when they happen (Fernandez et al., 2023). However, traditional systems latent the identification of emerging threats based on batch processing and retrospective analyses (Tripathi et al., 2024). On the other hand, LLMs can receive vast flows of data in real-time and yield timely alerts and actionable insights (Guo et al., 2024). The ability to know it all in real time is important to prevent fraud, control market runs, and comply with fast-evolving regulations (Derner et al., 2024), which ultimately enable more proactive decision making (Denecke et al., 2024).

The scalability of LLMs attracts all financial institutions. The models are efficient in handling enormous quantities of data (Pilny et al., 2024) and, consequently, are suitable for use by multinational banks and other small-scale financial institutions (Telenti et al., 2024). The scalability of the models to fit the increasing demands, as the generation of data continues to surge at an exponential rate, means that the institution continues to offer quality risk and fraud control, regardless of the size and complexity of the data they are handling (Zhou et al., 2024).

However, despite the wonderful benefits, the employment of LLM also raises some challenges to be addressed by financial institutions. Customer data privacy concerns are among the most significant concerns (Kshetri, 2023). The employment of LLM normally calls for the employment of enormous amounts of customer financial information, which raises enormous concerns about security and privacy (Kalaw & Baxter, 2024). Adherence to rigorous data protection laws and regulations, such as the GDPR, CCPA, and respective industry-specific laws, is necessary (Zhui et al., 2024) . The institution must establish effective encryption practices, anonymisation techniques, and tight control mechanisms to ensure customer data protection and compliance.

Another significant issue comes in the area of model interpretability (Head et al., 2023). Deep neural network-based LLMs are, in most situations, black boxes' whose internal working mechanisms are unknown to users (Cheng, 2024). This decision-making and prediction opacity in the event of applications in the area of financial risk control and fraud prediction, in situations where transparency is required to ensure compliance and trust from stakeholders, is problematic (Wang et al., 2023). The only solution to this issue comes in the form of developing explainable AI (XAI) frameworks to offer transparency into the decision-making mechanisms in the event of LLMs.

Computational resource constraints also pose a challenge for the mass adoption of LLM. The deployment and training of LLM require huge computational horsepower, in the form of high-end GPUs and cloud-scale infrastructure, and are, in some cases, expensive. The demands could be prohibitive to the availability and use by less significant financial institutions, and so the advantage of the use of LLM could be denied to them. Mitigating this challenge is a possible solution to the use of pre-trained models, model architecture efficiency, and cloud-based AI services.

Finally, ethical issues are at the root of LLM use. The models are trained on enormous datasets, and the datasets may also have embedded bias, resulting in biased and discriminatory decisions in the event of the evaluation of risks, such as fraud monitoring, if the issue is not checked. Therefore, biased datasets could result in some segments being disproportionately labelled high-risk or subjected to disproportionate scrutiny in the event of fraud. Fair decision-making and accountability are ensured through the use of LLMs by proper curation of the datasets used to train the models, regular bias audits, and fairness-aware algorithms to remove risks.

6. BENEFITS AND CHALLENGES OF IMPLEMENTING LLMS

Financial risk management and fraud detection in financial institutions can be transformed using Large Language Models. However, this results in cost, and it is rife with ethical and regulatory implications regarding data privacy and algorithmic bias. These issues need to be addressed to ensure that LLM deployment is compliant with the legal framework and promises the fair use of financial decisions. Algorithmic bias in AI systems used for financial services can cause discriminatory practices and negatively affect the way services are conducted. We provide several real-world examples of such bias.

- **Racial bias:** Research has shown that mortgage-underwriting AI systems can have racial prejudice. According to one study, black applicants denied home loans far more often than white applicants, with comparable financial profiles. This difference illustrates the possibility that existing prejudices from historical lending data are unwittingly continued by AI models and produce discriminatory results.
- **Amazon's development of gender-biased AI-based recruitment tools** shows one such instance (Gender Bias in Recruitment Tools). The purpose of the system was to make hiring a more efficient process; however, it systematically disadvantaged female applicants. The AI model has been trained on resumes for over a decade, most of them submitted by men, which has led to a bias that favours male candidates and penalises resumes, which mention words related to women.
- **An internal assessment of the UK's Department for Work and Pensions (DWP)** found that the DWP's AI system for detecting welfare fraud is biased based on age, disability, marital status, and nationality. There were concerns that the system disproportionately targeted certain groups for fraud investigations and vulnerable populations were subject to unjust scrutiny.

These cases underscore the necessity for rigorous evaluation and mitigation strategies to address biases in AI systems and ensure equitable treatment across all demographics.

Regulatory Frameworks and Compliance

The deployment of LLMs in financial services must adhere to stringent data-protection regulations designed to safeguard individual privacy and ensure ethical data usage. Key regulatory frameworks include the following.

- **General Data Protection Regulation (GDPR):** GDPR is the regulations enforced in the European Union, which require organisations 'to process' personal data to ensure adequate protection of individual privacy rights. This means that, when it comes to LLMs, an organisation must preserve data minimisation, have explicit consent to use data, and allow individuals to exercise their right to be forgotten or have personal data deleted at request. Noncompliance can cost a hefty penny; therefore, it is important to adopt GDPR principles in the design of the AI system and best practices for handling data.
- **California Consumer Privacy Act (CCPA):** The CCPA is applicable in California, USA, where consumers have the right to access, delete, and share personal information obtained from businesses. LLMs operate under the necessity of compliance with data practice transparency, allowing consumers to choose not to sell data and solid data security measures to prevent unauthorised access. They also have to be ready to publicise the categories of collected personal information and the use of these data.

To align with these regulations, financial institutions should implement the following practices.

- **Data anonymisation and minimisation:** anonymises personal data before the training of LLMs to avoid the identification of individuals. Collecting only the data as per the needs of various purposes also reduces the exposure to breaches of data and data minimisation compliance principles.
- **Most Platforms Conduct Regular Audits and Impact Assessments:** By conducting a DPIA, companies can identify and minimise the risks inherent to the data processing carried out while using LLMs. Audits regularly serve to keep the organisation compliant and notice any deviation from ordinary data protection policies.

- **Transparency and Consent Mechanisms:** This will make users aware of how their data will be used and obtain explicit consent from them which ensures transparency. The mechanisms must be easy for individuals to use to express their data preferences, incite trust, and comply with regulations.

By proactively addressing ethical considerations and adhering to regulatory frameworks, financial institutions can harness the benefits of LLMs, while upholding the principles of fairness, accountability, and respect for individual privacy.

7. BEST PRACTICES FOR INTEGRATING LLMS IN FINANCIAL INSTITUTIONS

To make LLMs successful in the financial institution context, best practices to achieve accuracy, compliance, and efficiency across the deployment phases should be adhered to (Fernandez et al., 2023). Data management is a first-order approach, and its importance determines the quality and reliability of the model outputs. However, for LLMs, although large and diverse datasets keep them running, the effectiveness of these models is exacerbated by the integrity and quality of the data they consume (Li et al., 2024). Rigorous data cleaning and preprocessing are necessary for financial data, as they are frequently complex, heterogeneous, and inconsistent. It ranges from removing duplicate records, handling missing values, properly formatting unstructured data (emails, reports, socially active parties' data, etc.), and standing data in one format throughout the pipeline to structured data (transaction records, account balances, etc.). In addition, accurate data labelling and annotation are also necessary and crucial when training LLMs to perform a specific task such as fraud detection or risk assessment; errors in the initial labelling stage can propagate to errors in the predictions made by the model (Jeong, 2024).

The next two important steps in the integration process are model training and validation. Having LLMs trained on various datasets and then refreshed at regular intervals to adapt to new trends and behaviours is crucial because of the ever-changing nature of financial markets and fraud techniques (Xing, 2024). You train an LLM by fine-tuning pre-trained models on various domain-specific data to increase their importance and how contextual they are in the financial environment. However, this is not sufficient, and we need to continuously validate our models, as their accuracy and reliability degrade over time. This involves testing the predictive power of the model using cross-validation, back-testing, and performance benchmarking. Furthermore, model validation relies on accuracy metrics and demonstrates that the model can withstand biases, false positives, and other points of vulnerability in decision making. The LLM is re-trained through a series of re-training cycles and regular updates so that it remains sharp in the most up-to-date state of affairs, information development, and regulatory changes to remain effective over the long run.

Another block to the optimal practice of deploying LLM in financial institutions is continuous monitoring. Real applications of trained and validated models are still subject to unforeseen issues such as data drift, shifts in the patterns of fraud, or regulation changes that affect model performance. LLM uses effective feedback mechanisms to adjust shifts. Continuous monitoring involves monitoring the model response that begins in real-time, locating anomalies, and monitoring performance metrics to monitor the degradation of precision and relevance. For instance, a sudden spike in false positive and false negative rate metrics can serve as an indicator that a fraud detection model requires new training or where a new parameter should stand. In addition to the feedback mechanisms, it also explores a mechanism to incorporate fresh data and insights into the model to learn from errors and profit from experience to ensure the long-term performance and reliability of the model.

A collaborative approach is essential for integrating LLM with its ongoing management. These complex models do not deploy in a financial environment solely by themselves; they are products of cross-functional teams. This involves all forms of data scientists, risk analysts, compliance officers, legal experts, and IT professionals working together to lead the implementation process holistically. Technical expertise in model building and optimisation comes from data scientists and machine learning engineers, while risk analysts understand the domain specifics that may fine-tune the model to work in practice, for example, credit risk assessment or market analysis. In this case, compliance officers ensure that the integration process is aligned with regulatory standards and protect the organisation from legal and ethical risks, particularly with data privacy and fairness regulation. The multidisciplinary nature of this collaboration guarantees that LLM results can be technically sound and coherent with business objectives, regulatory requirements, and measures.

8. FUTURE DIRECTIONS AND INNOVATIONS

Fast advancements in LLMs will be set in the future in financial risk management and fraud detection by architectural innovations of LLMs, integration of developing technologies, alterations in the regulatory landscape, and personalisation. The development of LLM architectures is one of the most promising areas of development: in this context, the birth of more efficient, and adaptive, like "liquid" neural networks, is promising. Liquid neural networks are dynamic; that is, they can adjust their parameters in real time based on new data and are thus highly effective in highly volatile environments, such as financial markets. First, these models not only provide improved predictive accuracy but also significantly reduce computational demands;

thus, they are more easily used by institutions possessing scarce resources. With this, we have an architectural advancement that would democratise LLMS use to a broader spectrum of financial institutions, even firms which might not have the resources and capacity to procure a server infrastructure to host their LLM.

Another critical future trajectory lies in the integration of LLMs into other leading-edge technologies, most significantly, blockchain. The combination of blockchain and LLMs can redefine the domain of financial risk management by ensuring the security, transparency, and track record of the transactions. The transactional data of blockchain networks can be reviewed by LLMs to identify anomalies, money laundering, or compliance breaches in real time, and the impossibility of editing the blockchain ensures the integrity of the information. This integration is most effective in applications such as anti-money-laundering (AML) and know-your-customer (KYC) processes, in which the synergy between the employment of LLM-driven examination and blockchain's impenetrable record can simplify the verification processes and increase the rate of fraud discoveries. The integration of LLMs into IoT devices and real-time streams could also enhance the breadth of what they can provide, making them carry out integrated risks based on a variety of constantly varying parameters.

As LLMs become increasingly prevalent in the financial world, regulation to develop and deploy them is crucial. AI in the finance world is beginning to attract the attention of regulators, including data protection, algorithm transparency, and ethical decisions based on AI. New regulations are starting to guarantee the high standards of fairness, accountability, and interpretability of LLM and other AI models that are central to them. Finally, the demand for model interpretability, bias reduction, and operational flexibility in the deployment of LLMs is necessary in the future. The attendance of auditing mechanisms and compliance tests on AI will become the norm, and effective and compliant LLMs can be deployed along the lines of ethical and legal requirements.

Another exciting area in the future of LLM applications in the finance world lies in the progression of personalised financial services. LLMs are good at processing individual customer information; through this, financial institutions can provide extremely customised products and services based on each client's unique needs and preferences. From customised portfolios and risk profiling to custom-loan proposals and budget recommendations, vast quantities of personal and behavioural data are easily processed by the LLM to provide appropriate, real-time recommendations. This kind of personalisation promotes customer engagement, happiness, and loyalty, and also helps the institution spot opportunities in terms of cross-selling and up-selling. In wealth management, LLM can assess a person's expenditure patterns, income patterns, and long-term objectives to provide custom-designed strategies, promoting client-oriented advice in the area of money.

LLMs have the opportunity to play a role in future financial risk management and fraud detection. New model architectures of liquid neural networks could offer superior performance improvements at lower resource demands, bringing LLM to a greater number of institutions. Keeping this in mind and working with technologies such as blockchain and IoT, their applications can be maximally built upon for further development in terms of increasingly more secure, complete risk analysis. Financial institutions must strike a balance between innovation and compliance in terms of the ethical and transparent use of LLMs, whereas regulatory frameworks must adapt to solve challenges when they apply to AI as a whole. Finally, the growing development of more personalised financial services will empower LLMs to enrich their relationship with customers by delivering personalised data and inspiration, based on customers' requirements, – these LLMs are more important in the transition of the financial industry.

9. CONCLUSION

Large-language models integrated into the domain of financial risk management and fraud detection are a paradigm shift by financial institutions when deciding. By leveraging the computing power of LLM, the institution can provide a more specific kind of risk evaluation, better recognise fraudulent actions, and generally improve its efficiency in actions. As the nature of the market is dynamic and the strategies of fraudsters are continuously evolving, the latest available technologies must be allowed to be used periodically. Compared with traditional methodologies, LLMs can handle large amounts of structured and unstructured data with a high level of capacity. In the new world of finance, they have inalienable tools in the form of real-time processing, contextualisation, and learning.

Nevertheless, there are numerous challenges in the use of LLMs. However, thoughtful consideration and planning are required for challenging areas in data privacy, model interpretability, and computational requirements. People handling data in financial institutions are using new technology, and therefore, it is necessary to incorporate the latest in data handling, build models, and monitor their proper and optimal use. The future holds great promise for the use of LLMs in finance. The capabilities and uses of the models will increase with improved model architectures, the coupling of models with other supportive technologies, including blockchain, and the development of regulation regimes. Moreover, the use of even the smallest financial institutions is possible as models become more efficient and accessible. Ultimately, the revolution in LLMs is not only for fraud detection and financial risk management, but more generally, calls for adapting to these technologies. Organisations within financial services that lead to the adoption of using the use of LLMs in day-to-day operations will increase their decision-making capacity, and will also be at a huge competitive advantage in an ever-changing market.

REFERENCES

Abolghasemi, M., Ganbold, O., & Rotaru, K. (2023). Humans vs Large Language Models: Judgmental Forecasting in an Era of Advanced AI. *arXiv (Cornell University)*. https://doi.org//arxiv.2312.06941DOI: 10.48550

Balkus, S. V., & Yan, D. (2023). Improving short text classification with augmented data using GPT-3. *Natural Language Engineering*, *30*(5), 943–972. DOI: 10.1017/S1351324923000438

Balsiger, D., Dimmler, H., Egger-Horstmann, S., & Hanne, T. (2024). Assessing Large Language Models Used for Extracting Table Information from Annual Financial Reports. *Computers*, *13*(10), 257. DOI: 10.3390/computers13100257

Baum, S. D. (2024). Assessing the risk of takeover catastrophe from large language models. *Risk Analysis : An Official Publication of the Society for Risk Analysis*. Advance online publication. DOI: 10.1111/risa.14353 PMID: 38945529

Bhatnagr, P., & Rajesh, A. (2024a). Online customer experience in Indian digital banks impacting continuous intention usage: Generation Y and Z perspective. *Journal of Financial Reporting & Accounting*. DOI: 10.1108/JFRA-11-2023-0638

Bhatnagr, P., & Rajesh, A. (2024b). Artificial intelligence features and expectation confirmation theory in digital banking apps: Gen Y and Z perspective. *Management Decision*. Advance online publication. DOI: 10.1108/MD-07-2023-1145

Bhatnagr, P., Rajesh, A., & Misra, R. (2024a). A study on driving factors for enhancing financial performance and customer-centricity through digital banking. *International Journal of Quality and Service Sciences*, *16*(2), 218–250. DOI: 10.1108/IJQSS-09-2023-0141

Bhatnagr, P., Rajesh, A., & Misra, R. (2024b). Continuous intention usage of artificial intelligence enabled digital banks: A review of expectation confirmation model. *Journal of Enterprise Information Management*, *37*(6), 1763–1787. DOI: 10.1108/JEIM-11-2023-0617

Bhatnagr, P., Rajesh, A., & Misra, R. (2024c). The impact of Fintech innovations on digital currency adoption: a blockchain-based study in India. *International Journal of Accounting and Information Management*. DOI: 10.1108/IJAIM-11-2023-0275

Chaquet-Ulldemolins, J., Gimeno-Blanes, F., Moral-Rubio, S., Muñoz-Romero, S., & Rojo-Álvarez, J. (2022). On the Black-Box Challenge for Fraud Detection Using Machine Learning (II): Nonlinear Analysis through Interpretable Autoencoders. *Applied Sciences (Basel, Switzerland)*, *12*(8), 3856. DOI: 10.3390/app12083856

Cheng, J. (2024). Applications of large language models in pathology. *Bioengineering (Basel, Switzerland), 11*(4), 342. DOI: 10.3390/bioengineering11040342 PMID: 38671764

Delgadillo, J., Kinyua, J., & Mutigwe, C. (2024). FinSoSent: Advancing Financial Market Sentiment Analysis through Pretrained Large Language Models. *Big Data and Cognitive Computing*, *8*(8), 87. DOI: 10.3390/bdcc8080087

Denecke, K., May, R., & Romero, O. R. (2024). Potential of large language models in health care: Delphi study. *Journal of Medical Internet Research*, *26*, e52399. DOI: 10.2196/52399 PMID: 38739445

Deng, D., Zhang, C., Zheng, H., Pu, Y., Ji, S., & Wu, Y. (2024). AdversaFlow: Visual Red Teaming for Large Language Models with Multi-Level Adversarial Flow. *IEEE Transactions on Visualization and Computer Graphics*, •••, 1–11. DOI: 10.1109/TVCG.2024.3456150 PMID: 39283796

Derner, E., Batistič, K., Zahálka, J., & Babuška, R. (2024). A Security Risk Taxonomy for Prompt-Based Interaction with Large Language Models. *IEEE Access : Practical Innovations, Open Solutions*, *12*, 126176–126187. DOI: 10.1109/ACCESS.2024.3450388

Fazlija, B., & Harder, P. (2022). Using financial news sentiment for stock price direction prediction. *Mathematics*, *10*(13), 2156. DOI: 10.3390/math10132156

Fernandez, R. C., Elmore, A. J., Franklin, M. J., Krishnan, S., & Tan, C. (2023). How large language models will disrupt data management. *Proceedings of the VLDB Endowment International Conference on Very Large Data Bases*, *16*(11), 3302–3309. DOI: 10.14778/3611479.3611527

Fu, K., & Zhang, Y. (2024). Incorporating Multi-Source market sentiment and price data for stock price prediction. *Mathematics*, *12*(10), 1572. DOI: 10.3390/math12101572

Guo, Z., Lai, A., Thygesen, J. H., Farrington, J., Keen, T., & Li, K. (2024). Large Language Models for Mental Health Applications: A Systematic Review (Preprint). *JMIR Mental Health*, *11*, e57400. DOI: 10.2196/57400 PMID: 39423368

Head, C. B., Jasper, P., McConnachie, M., Raftree, L., & Higdon, G. (2023). Large language model applications for evaluation: Opportunities and ethical implications. *New Directions for Evaluation*, *2023*(178–179), 33–46. DOI: 10.1002/ev.20556

Ionescu, S., & Diaconita, V. (2023). Transforming Financial Decision-Making: The interplay of AI, cloud computing and advanced data management technologies. *International Journal of Computers, Communications & Control, 18*(6). Advance online publication. DOI: 10.15837/ijccc.2023.6.5735

Jeong, C. (2024). Domain-specialized LLM: Financial fine-tuning and utilization method using Mistral 7B. *Journal of Intelligent Information Systems, 30*(1), 93–120. DOI: 10.13088/jiis.2024.30.1.093

Jung, H. D., & Jang, B. (2024). Enhancing financial sentiment analysis ability of language model via targeted Numerical Change-Related masking. *IEEE Access : Practical Innovations, Open Solutions, 12*, 50809–50820. DOI: 10.1109/ACCESS.2024.3385855

Kalaw, F. G. P., & Baxter, S. L. (2024). Ethical considerations for large language models in ophthalmology. *Current Opinion in Ophthalmology, 35*(6), 438–446. Advance online publication. DOI: 10.1097/ICU.0000000000001083 PMID: 39259616

Khan, M. A., Alhumoudi, H., Alakkas, A., Minhaj, S. M., & Alhashem, M. (2024). The present scenario of artificial intelligence and machine learning in financial services: An empirical study. *Journal of Infrastructure Policy and Development, 8*(11), 8818. DOI: 10.24294/jipd.v8i11.8818

Kshetri, N. (2023). Cybercrime and privacy threats of large language models. *IT Professional, 25*(3), 9–13. DOI: 10.1109/MITP.2023.3275489

Li, Q., Hong, J., Xie, C., Tan, J., Xin, R., Hou, J., Yin, X., Wang, Z., Hendrycks, D., Wang, Z., Li, B., He, B., & Song, D. (2024). LLM-PBE: Assessing Data Privacy in Large Language Models. *Proceedings of the VLDB Endowment International Conference on Very Large Data Bases, 17*(11), 3201–3214. DOI: 10.14778/3681954.3681994

Li, W., Manley, M., Read, J., Kaul, A., Bakir, M. S., & Yu, S. (2023). H3DATTEN: Heterogeneous 3-D integrated Hybrid analog and Digital Compute-in-Memory accelerator for Vision transformer Self-Attention. *IEEE Transactions on Very Large Scale Integration (VLSI). IEEE Transactions on Very Large Scale Integration (VLSI) Systems, 31*(10), 1592–1602. DOI: 10.1109/TVLSI.2023.3299509

Liu, C., Arulappan, A., Naha, R., Mahanti, A., Kamruzzaman, J., & Ra, I. (2024). Large Language Models and Sentiment Analysis in Financial Markets: A review, datasets and case study. *IEEE Access : Practical Innovations, Open Solutions, 12*, 134041–134061. DOI: 10.1109/ACCESS.2024.3445413

Martínez, P. A., Bernabé, G., & García, J. M. (2024). Code detection for hardware acceleration using large language models. *IEEE Access : Practical Innovations, Open Solutions*, *12*, 35271–35281. DOI: 10.1109/ACCESS.2024.3372853

Muller, L., Churchland, P. S., & Sejnowski, T. J. (2024). Transformers and Cortical Waves: encoders for pulling in context across time. *arXiv (Cornell University)*. https://doi.org//arxiv.2401.14267DOI: 10.48550

Nallakaruppan, M. K., Chaturvedi, H., Grover, V., Balusamy, B., Jaraut, P., Bahadur, J., Meena, V. P., & Hameed, I. A. (2024). Credit risk assessment and financial decision support using explainable artificial intelligence. *Risks*, *12*(10), 164. DOI: 10.3390/risks12100164

Pan, S., Zheng, Y., & Liu, Y. (2024). Integrating graphs with large language models: Methods and prospects. *IEEE Intelligent Systems*, *39*(1), 64–68. DOI: 10.1109/MIS.2023.3332242

Patsakis, C., Casino, F., & Lykousas, N. (2024). Assessing LLMs in malicious code deobfuscation of real-world malware campaigns. *arXiv (Cornell University)*. https://doi.org//arxiv.2404.19715DOI: 10.48550

Pilny, A., McAninch, K., Slone, A., & Moore, K. (2024). From manual to machine: Assessing the efficacy of large language models in content analysis. *Communication Research Reports*, *41*(2), 61–70. DOI: 10.1080/08824096.2024.2327547

Preiksaitis, C., Ashenburg, N., Bunney, G., Chu, A., Kabeer, R., Riley, F., Ribeira, R., & Rose, C. (2024). The Role of large language Models in Transforming Emergency Medicine: Scoping review. *JMIR Medical Informatics*, *12*, e53787. DOI: 10.2196/53787 PMID: 38728687

Reite, E. J., Karlsen, J., & Westgaard, E. G. (2024). Improving client risk classification with machine learning to increase anti-money laundering detection efficiency. *Journal of Money Laundering Control*. DOI: 10.1108/JMLC-03-2024-0040

Roumeliotis, K. I., Tselikas, N. D., & Nasiopoulos, D. K. (2024). LLMS and NLP Models in Cryptocurrency Sentiment Analysis: A Comparative Classification Study. *Big Data and Cognitive Computing*, *8*(6), 63. DOI: 10.3390/bdcc8060063

Sahoo, S. S., Plasek, J. M., Xu, H., Uzuner, Ö., Cohen, T., Yetisgen, M., Liu, H., Meystre, S., & Wang, Y. (2024). Large language models for biomedicine: Foundations, opportunities, challenges, and best practices. *Journal of the American Medical Informatics Association : JAMIA*, *31*(9), 2114–2124. DOI: 10.1093/jamia/ocae074 PMID: 38657567

Schmitt, M. (2022). Automated machine learning: AI-driven decision making in business analytics. *arXiv (Cornell University)*. https://doi.org//arxiv.2205.10538DOI: 10.48550

Selim, A., Zhao, J., & Yang, B. (2024). Large language model for smart inverter Cyber-Attack detection via textual analysis of Volt/VAR commands. *IEEE Transactions on Smart Grid*, *1*(6), 6179–6182. Advance online publication. DOI: 10.1109/TSG.2024.3453648

Sezgin, E. (2024). Redefining virtual Assistants in Health care: The future with large language models. *Journal of Medical Internet Research*, *26*, e53225. DOI: 10.2196/53225 PMID: 38241074

Shobayo, O., Adeyemi-Longe, S., Popoola, O., & Ogunleye, B. (2024). Innovative sentiment analysis and prediction of stock price using FINBERT, GPT-4 and Logistic Regression: A Data-Driven Approach. *Big Data and Cognitive Computing*, *8*(11), 143. DOI: 10.3390/bdcc8110143

Sinha, R., Elhafsi, A., Agia, C., Foutter, M., Schmerling, E., & Pavone, M. (2024). Real-Time Anomaly Detection and Reactive Planning with Large Language Models. *arXiv (Cornell University)*. /arxiv.2407.08735DOI: 10.15607/RSS.2024.XX.114

Suri, G., Slater, L. R., Ziaee, A., & Nguyen, M. (2023). Do large language models show decision heuristics similar to humans? A case study using GPT-3.5. *arXiv (Cornell University)*. https://doi.org//arxiv.2305.04400DOI: 10.48550

Telenti, A., Auli, M., Hie, B. L., Maher, C., Saria, S., & Ioannidis, J. P. A. (2024). Large language models for science and medicine. *European Journal of Clinical Investigation*, *54*(6), e14183. Advance online publication. DOI: 10.1111/eci.14183 PMID: 38381530

Tian, X., Tian, Z., Khatib, S. F. A., & Wang, Y. (2024). Machine learning in internet financial risk management: A systematic literature review. *PLoS One*, *19*(4), e0300195. DOI: 10.1371/journal.pone.0300195 PMID: 38625972

Tripathi, S., Sukumaran, R., & Cook, T. S. (2024). Efficient healthcare with large language models: Optimizing clinical workflow and enhancing patient care. *Journal of the American Medical Informatics Association : JAMIA*, *31*(6), 1436–1440. DOI: 10.1093/jamia/ocad258 PMID: 38273739

Trummer, I. (2022). From BERT to GPT-3 codex. *Proceedings of the VLDB Endowment International Conference on Very Large Data Bases*, *15*(12), 3770–3773. DOI: 10.14778/3554821.3554896

Wang, X., Li, X., Yin, Z., Wu, Y., & Liu, J. (2023). Emotional intelligence of Large Language Models. *Journal of Pacific Rim Psychology*, *17*, 18344909231213958. Advance online publication. DOI: 10.1177/18344909231213958

Xing, F. (2024). Designing heterogeneous LLM agents for financial sentiment analysis. *ACM Transactions on Management Information Systems*. Advance online publication. DOI: 10.1145/3688399

Yang, N. (2022). Financial big Data Management and control and Artificial intelligence analysis method based on data mining technology. *Wireless Communications and Mobile Computing*, *2022*(1), 1–13. DOI: 10.1155/2022/7596094

Zhang, L., Yu, Q., Zhou, B., Zhang, Y., & Hu, Z. (2023). Incorporating feature interactions and contrastive learning for credit prediction. *IEEE Access : Practical Innovations, Open Solutions*, *11*, 111944–111955. DOI: 10.1109/ACCESS.2023.3322429

Zhou, S., Zhou, Z., Wang, C., Liang, Y., Wang, L., Zhang, J., Zhang, J., & Lv, C. (2024). A User-Centered framework for data privacy protection using large language models and attention mechanisms. *Applied Sciences (Basel, Switzerland)*, *14*(15), 6824. DOI: 10.3390/app14156824

Zhui, L., Fenghe, L., Xuehu, W., Qining, F., & Wei, R. (2024). Ethical Considerations and Fundamental Principles of large language models in medical Education: Viewpoint. *Journal of Medical Internet Research*, *26*, e60083. DOI: 10.2196/60083 PMID: 38971715

Compilation of References

Abbasi, A., Lau, R. Y. K., & Brown, D. E. (2015). Predicting behavior. *IEEE Intelligent Systems*, *30*(3), 35–43. DOI: 10.1109/MIS.2015.19

Abel, J. (2024). *Generative AI Could Revolutionize Business Analytics*. AI Business.

Agarwal, R., Vieillard, N., Stanczyk, P., Ramos, S., Geist, M., & Bachem, O. (2023). Gkd: Generalized knowledge distillation for auto-regressive sequence models. *ArXiv Preprint ArXiv:2306.13649, 12*.

Ahn, J., Hwang, J., Kim, D., Choi, H., & Kang, S. (2020). A Survey on Churn Analysis in Various Business Domains. *IEEE Access : Practical Innovations, Open Solutions*, *8*, 220816–220839. DOI: 10.1109/ACCESS.2020.3042657

Alberti, C., Lee, K., & Collins, M. (2019). *A BERT Baseline for the Natural Questions*. https://arxiv.org/abs/1901.08634v3

Alboukaey, N., Joukhadar, A., & Ghneim, N. (2020). Dynamic behavior based churn prediction in mobile telecom. *Expert Systems with Applications*, *162*, 113779. DOI: 10.1016/j.eswa.2020.113779

Allen, T. (2025). *Manifesting the Promise of Generative AI for Business Intelligence*.

Alparslan, A. (2025). The Role of Accuracy and Validation Effectiveness in Conversational Business Analytics. *IEEE Access : Practical Innovations, Open Solutions*, *13*, 1–25. DOI: 10.1109/ACCESS.2025.3540975

Alrumiah, S. S., & Hadwan, M. (2021). Implementing Big Data Analytics in E-Commerce: Vendor and Customer View. *IEEE Access : Practical Innovations, Open Solutions*, *9*, 37281–37286. DOI: 10.1109/ACCESS.2021.3063615

Anthropic. (2024). The Claude 3 model family: Opus, Sonnet, Haiku [Technical report]. https://www-cdn.anthropic.com/de8ba9b01c9ab7cbabf5c33b80b7bbc618857627/Model_Card_Claude_3.pdf

Araci, H. (2019). BERT-based Sentiment Analysis for Financial Text. arXiv preprint arXiv:1908.10063.

Balkus, S. V., & Yan, D. (2023). Improving short text classification with augmented data using GPT-3. *Natural Language Engineering*, *30*(5), 943–972. DOI: 10.1017/S1351324923000438

Ballings, M., & Van Den Poel, D. (2012). Customer event history for churn prediction: How long is long enough? *Expert Systems with Applications*, *39*(18), 13517–13522. DOI: 10.1016/j.eswa.2012.07.006

Balsiger, D., Dimmler, H., Egger-Horstmann, S., & Hanne, T. (2024). Assessing Large Language Models Used for Extracting Table Information from Annual Financial Reports. *Computers*, *13*(10), 257. DOI: 10.3390/computers13100257

Bao, Y., Shah, A. P., Narang, N., Rivers, J., Maksey, R., Guan, L., Barrere, L. N., Evenson, S., Basole, R., Miao, C., Mehta, A., Boulay, F., Park, S. M., Pearson, N. E., Joy, E., He, T., Thakur, S., Ghosal, K., On, J., … Wei, W. (2024). *Harnessing Business and Media Insights with Large Language Models*. 1–21.

Bao, Y., Shah, A. P., Narang, N., Rivers, J., Maksey, R., Guan, L., Barrere, L. N., Evenson, S., Basole, R., Miao, C., Mehta, A., Boulay, F., Park, S. M., Pearson, N. E., Joy, E., He, T., Thakur, S., Ghosal, K., On, J., & Wei, W. (2024). *Harnessing Business and Media Insights with Large Language Models*. https://arxiv.org/abs/2406.06559v1

Baum, S. D. (2024). Assessing the risk of takeover catastrophe from large language models. *Risk Analysis : An Official Publication of the Society for Risk Analysis*. Advance online publication. DOI: 10.1111/risa.14353 PMID: 38945529

Belani, G. (2024). *3 Examples of LLM Use in Business Intelligence Why Use LLMs for Business Intelligence*.

Bender, E. M., Gebru, T., McMillan-Major, A., & Shmitchell, S. (2021). On the dangers of stochastic parrots: Can language models be too big? *FAccT 2021 - Proceedings of the 2021 ACM Conference on Fairness, Accountability, and Transparency*, 610–623. DOI: 10.1145/3442188.3445922

Benoit, D. F., & Van Den Poel, D. (2012). Improving customer retention in financial services using kinship network information. *Expert Systems with Applications*, *39*(13), 11435–11442. DOI: 10.1016/j.eswa.2012.04.016

Berengueres, J., & Sandell, M. (2023). Applying Standards to Advance Upstream &Downstream Ethics in Large Language Models. *ArXiv Preprint ArXiv:2306.03503*, 1–8.

Bharadwaj, C. (2024). *NLP applications and their use cases for modern enterprises.*

Bhatnagr, P., & Rajesh, A. (2024a). Online customer experience in Indian digital banks impacting continuous intention usage: Generation Y and Z perspective. *Journal of Financial Reporting & Accounting*. DOI: 10.1108/JFRA-11-2023-0638

Bhatnagr, P., Rajesh, A., & Misra, R. (2024c). The impact of Fintech innovations on digital currency adoption: a blockchain-based study in India. *International Journal of Accounting and Information Management*. DOI: 10.1108/IJAIM-11-2023-0275

Bhatnagr, P., & Rajesh, A. (2024b). Artificial intelligence features and expectation confirmation theory in digital banking apps: Gen Y and Z perspective. *Management Decision*. Advance online publication. DOI: 10.1108/MD-07-2023-1145

Bhatnagr, P., Rajesh, A., & Misra, R. (2024a). A study on driving factors for enhancing financial performance and customer-centricity through digital banking. *International Journal of Quality and Service Sciences*, *16*(2), 218–250. DOI: 10.1108/IJQSS-09-2023-0141

Bhatnagr, P., Rajesh, A., & Misra, R. (2024b). Continuous intention usage of artificial intelligence enabled digital banks: A review of expectation confirmation model. *Journal of Enterprise Information Management*, *37*(6), 1763–1787. DOI: 10.1108/JEIM-11-2023-0617

Bommasani, R., Klyman, K., Longpre, S., Kapoor, S., Maslej, N., Xiong, B., Zhang, D., & Liang, P. (2023). The foundation model transparency index. arXiv preprint arXiv:2310.12941. https://arxiv.org/abs/2310.12941

Busany, N., Hadar, E., Hadad, H., Rosenblum, G., Maszlanka, Z., Akhigbe, O., & Amyot, D. (2024). *Automating Business Intelligence Requirements with Generative AI and Semantic Search.*

Cai, W., Song, Y., & Wei, Z. (2021). Multimodal Data Guided Spatial Feature Fusion and Grouping Strategy for E-Commerce Commodity Demand Forecasting. *Mobile Information Systems*, *2021*, 1–14. DOI: 10.1155/2021/5568208

Cenggoro, T. W., Wirastari, R. A., Rudianto, E., Mohadi, M. I., Ratj, D., & Pardamean, B. (2021). Deep Learning as a Vector Embedding Model for Customer Churn. *Procedia Computer Science*, *179*, 624–631. DOI: 10.1016/j.procs.2021.01.048

Chang, Y., Wang, X., Wang, J., Wu, Y., Yang, L., Zhu, K., Chen, H., Yi, X., Wang, C., Wang, Y., Ye, W., Zhang, Y., Chang, Y., Yu, P. S., Yang, Q., & Xie, X. (2024). A survey on evaluation of large language models. *ACM Transactions on Intelligent Systems and Technology*, *15*(3), 1–45. DOI: 10.1145/3641289

Chaquet-Ulldemolins, J., Gimeno-Blanes, F., Moral-Rubio, S., Muñoz-Romero, S., & Rojo-Álvarez, J. (2022). On the Black-Box Challenge for Fraud Detection Using Machine Learning (II): Nonlinear Analysis through Interpretable Autoencoders. *Applied Sciences (Basel, Switzerland)*, *12*(8), 3856. DOI: 10.3390/app12083856

Chawla, C., Chatterjee, S., Gadadinni, S. S., Verma, P., & Banerjee, S. (2024). Agentic AI: The building blocks of sophisticated AI business applications. *Journal of AI. Robotics & Workplace Automation*, *3*(3), 196. DOI: 10.69554/XEHZ1946

Chen, K., Fei, C., Bi, Z., Liu, J., Peng, B., Zhang, S., Pan, X., Xu, J., Wang, J., Yin, C. H., & Associates. (2024). Deep Learning and Machine Learning—Natural Language Processing: From Theory to Application. *ArXiv Preprint ArXiv:2411.05026.*

Chen, C.-C., Huang, H.-H., & Chen, H.-H. (2020). *NLP in FinTech Applications: Past.* Present and Future.

Cheng, J. (2024). Applications of large language models in pathology. *Bioengineering (Basel, Switzerland)*, *11*(4), 342. DOI: 10.3390/bioengineering11040342 PMID: 38671764

Cheung, M. (2024). *A Reality check of the benefits of LLM in business*. 1–20.

Chew, R., Bollenbacher, J., Wenger, M., Speer, J., & Kim, A. (2023). LLM-assisted content analysis: Using large language models to support deductive coding. arXiv preprint arXiv:2306.14924.

Chu, D. (2024). *What are the Challenges of Using LLM in Data Visualization.*

Chung, H. W., Hou, L., Longpre, S., Zoph, B., Tay, Y., Fedus, W., Li, Y., Wang, X., Dehghani, M., Brahma, S., Webson, A., Gu, S. S., Dai, Z., Suzgun, M., Chen, X., Chowdhery, A., Castro-Ros, A., Pellat, M., Robinson, K., & Wei, J. (2022). *Scaling Instruction-Finetuned Language Models.* https://arxiv.org/abs/2210.11416v5

Cirqueira, D., Hofer, M., Nedbal, D., Helfert, M., & Bezbradica, M. (2020). Customer Purchase Behavior Prediction in E-commerce: A Conceptual Framework and Research Agenda. In Ceci, M., Loglisci, C., Manco, G., Masciari, E., & Ras, Z. (Eds.), *New Frontiers in Mining Complex Patterns* (Vol. 11948, pp. 119–136). Springer International Publishing., DOI: 10.1007/978-3-030-48861-1_8

Collins, M. (2011). *Statistical machine translation: IBM models 1 and 2*. Columbia Columbia Univ.

Coussement, K., Lessmann, S., & Verstraeten, G. (2017). A comparative analysis of data preparation algorithms for customer churn prediction: A case study in the telecommunication industry. *Decision Support Systems*, *95*, 27–36. DOI: 10.1016/j.dss.2016.11.007

Dahake, N. S., Suresh Dahake, P., & Gajghate, A. (2024). Beyond the Hype: A Critical Evaluation of Predictive Analytics Accuracy in High-Stakes Business Decisions. *2024 2nd DMIHER International Conference on Artificial Intelligence in Healthcare, Education and Industry (IDICAIEI)*, 1–6. DOI: 10.1109/IDICAIEI61867.2024.10842857

Dahake, P. S., & Somani, N. (2024). Harnessing Predictive Analytics for Accurate Consumer Behaviour Forecasting: A Comprehensive Review. *2024 2nd DMIHER International Conference on Artificial Intelligence in Healthcare, Education and Industry (IDICAIEI)*, 1–6. DOI: 10.1109/IDICAIEI61867.2024.10842743

Dahake, P. S., Chandak, S., & Dahake, N. S. (2024). Predictive Analytics in Performance Appraisal Systems: Enhancing Objectivity and Fairness. *2024 2nd DMIHER International Conference on Artificial Intelligence in Healthcare, Education and Industry (IDICAIEI)*, 1–5. DOI: 10.1109/IDICAIEI61867.2024.10842916

Dahake, P. S., Jain, M., Anusha, B., Poojitha, S., Singh, N., & Sharma, A. (2024). Integrating Organisational Theory, Resource-Based View, and Big Data Culture to Improve Manufacturing Performance. In D. Jelonek, N. Kumar, M. Chahar, R. Kinkladze, & L. Knop, *Recent Trends In Engineering and Science for Resource Optimization and Sustainable Development* (1st ed., pp. 156–159). CRC Press. DOI: 10.1201/9781003596721-36

Dahake, P. S., Bagaregari, P., & Dahake, N. S. (2024). Shaping the Future of Retail: A Comprehensive Review of Predictive Analytics Models for Consumer Behavior. In Inder, S., Min, B., & Sharma, S. (Eds.), (pp. 143–160). Advances in Business Strategy and Competitive Advantage. IGI Global., DOI: 10.4018/979-8-3693-1734-1.ch011

Dahake, P. S., Chandak, S., Mohare, R. V., Wadhwani, K., & Bhadade, P. (2023). The Crystal Ball of Marketing: How Predictive Analytics is Reshaping the Industry? *2023 Second International Conference On Smart Technologies For Smart Nation (SmartTechCon)*, 304–311. DOI: 10.1109/SmartTechCon57526.2023.10391334

Dahake, P. S., Mohare, R. V., & Dahake, N. S. (2024). Enhancing Management Education Through ChatGPT: A Novel Method for Ease and Efficacy. In Inder, S., Min, B., & Sharma, S. (Eds.), (pp. 161–178). Advances in Business Strategy and Competitive Advantage. IGI Global., DOI: 10.4018/979-8-3693-1734-1.ch012

Dahake, P. S., Mohare, R. V., & Somani, N. (2023). Exploring Machine Learning's Potential in Predicting Consumer Behavior for Captivating Marketing. *2023 Second International Conference On Smart Technologies For Smart Nation (SmartTechCon)*, 1347–1352. DOI: 10.1109/SmartTechCon57526.2023.10391558

DataChat. (2025). *The Hidden Risks of Using Large Language Models for Business Data Analytics*.

Day, M. Y., & Lee, C. C. (2016, August). Deep learning for financial sentiment analysis on finance news providers. In *2016 IEEE/ACM International Conference on Advances in Social Networks Analysis and Mining (ASONAM)* (pp. 1127-1134). IEEE. DOI: 10.1109/ASONAM.2016.7752381

De Bock, K. W., & De Caigny, A. (2021). Spline-rule ensemble classifiers with structured sparsity regularization for interpretable customer churn modeling. *Decision Support Systems*, *150*, 113523. DOI: 10.1016/j.dss.2021.113523

De Caigny, A., Coussement, K., & De Bock, K. W. (2018). A new hybrid classification algorithm for customer churn prediction based on logistic regression and decision trees. *European Journal of Operational Research*, *269*(2), 760–772. DOI: 10.1016/j.ejor.2018.02.009

de Carvalho Souza, M. E., Souza, M. E. D. C., & Weigang, L. (2025). Unveiling the black box: The significance of xai in making llms transparent. *Authorea Preprints*.

Delgadillo, J., Kinyua, J., & Mutigwe, C. (2024). FinSoSent: Advancing Financial Market Sentiment Analysis through Pretrained Large Language Models. *Big Data and Cognitive Computing*, *8*(8), 87. DOI: 10.3390/bdcc8080087

Demo. (2025). *Guide to AI in Business analytics*.

Denecke, K., May, R., & Romero, O. R. (2024). Potential of large language models in health care: Delphi study. *Journal of Medical Internet Research*, *26*, e52399. DOI: 10.2196/52399 PMID: 38739445

Deng, D., Zhang, C., Zheng, H., Pu, Y., Ji, S., & Wu, Y. (2024). AdversaFlow: Visual Red Teaming for Large Language Models with Multi-Level Adversarial Flow. *IEEE Transactions on Visualization and Computer Graphics*, •••, 1–11. DOI: 10.1109/TVCG.2024.3456150 PMID: 39283796

Derner, E., Batistič, K., Zahálka, J., & Babuška, R. (2024). A Security Risk Taxonomy for Prompt-Based Interaction with Large Language Models. *IEEE Access : Practical Innovations, Open Solutions*, *12*, 126176–126187. DOI: 10.1109/ACCESS.2024.3450388

Devlin, J., Chang, M. W., Lee, K., & Toutanova, K. (2019). BERT: Pre-training of deep bidirectional transformers for language understanding. *NAACL HLT 2019 - 2019 Conference of the North American Chapter of the Association for Computational Linguistics: Human Language Technologies - Proceedings of the Conference*.

Devriendt, F., Berrevoets, J., & Verbeke, W. (2021). Why you should stop predicting customer churn and start using uplift models. *Information Sciences*, *548*, 497–515. DOI: 10.1016/j.ins.2019.12.075

Dholariya, F. (2024). *How Large Language Models (LLMs) are transforming Business intelligece (BI) and Analytics*.

Du, K., Xing, F., Mao, R., & Cambria, E. (2024, June). An evaluation of reasoning capabilities of large language models in financial sentiment analysis. In *2024 IEEE Conference on Artificial Intelligence (CAI)* (pp. 189-194). IEEE. Chaithra, C., & Mohan, B. R. (2024, March). Revealing Insights: Sentiment Analysis of Indian Annual Reports. In *2024 3rd International Conference for Innovation in Technology (INOCON)* (pp. 1-5). IEEE. DOI: 10.1109/CAI59869.2024.00042

Duan, G., Yan, S., & Zhang, M. (2024). A hybrid neural network model for sentiment analysis of financial texts using topic extraction, pre-trained model, and enhanced attention mechanism methods. *IEEE Access : Practical Innovations, Open Solutions*, *12*, 98207–98224. DOI: 10.1109/ACCESS.2024.3429150

Dubey, A., Jauhri, A., Pandey, A., Kadian, A., Al-Dahle, A., Letman, A., Mathur, A., Schelten, A., Vaughan, A., Yang, A., Fan, A., Goyal, A., Hartshorn, A., Yang, A., Mitra, A., Sravankumar, A., Korenev, A., Hinsvark, A., Rao, A., . . . Zhang, A. (2024). The Llama 3 herd of models [Technical report]. arXiv. https://doi.org//arXiv .2407.21783DOI: 10.48550

Du, K., Xing, F., Mao, R., & Cambria, E. (2024). Financial sentiment analysis: Techniques and applications. *ACM Computing Surveys*, *56*(9), 1–42. DOI: 10.1145/3649451

Ephraim. (2022). The viral ai avatar app lensa undressed me without my consent [https://www.technologyreview.com/2022/12/12/1064751/the-viral-ai- avatar-app-lensa-undressed-me-without-my-consent/ [Accessed: (15-march-2025)]].

Fazlija, B., & Harder, P. (2022). Using financial news sentiment for stock price direction prediction. *Mathematics*, *10*(13), 2156. DOI: 10.3390/math10132156

Ferdaus, M. M., Abdelguerfi, M., Ioup, E., Niles, K. N., Pathak, K., & Sloan, S. (2024). Towards Trustworthy AI: A Review of Ethical and Robust Large Language Models. *ArXiv*, 1–27.

Fernandez, R. C., Elmore, A. J., Franklin, M. J., Krishnan, S., & Tan, C. (2023). How large language models will disrupt data management. *Proceedings of the VLDB Endowment International Conference on Very Large Data Bases, 16*(11), 3302–3309. DOI: 10.14778/3611479.3611527

Floridi, L., & Chiriatti, M. (2020). GPT-3: Its Nature, Scope, Limits, and Consequences. *Minds and Machines, 30*(4), 681–694. DOI: 10.1007/s11023-020-09548-1

Fu, K., & Zhang, Y. (2024). Incorporating Multi-Source market sentiment and price data for stock price prediction. *Mathematics, 12*(10), 1572. DOI: 10.3390/math12101572

Gao, Y., Xiong, Y., Gao, X., Jia, K., Pan, J., Bi, Y., Dai, Y., Sun, J., Wang, M., & Wang, H. (2023). *Retrieval-Augmented Generation for Large Language Models: A Survey*. https://arxiv.org/abs/2312.10997v5

Getting started with Perplexity. (n.d.). Retrieved March 20, 2025, from https://www.perplexity.ai/hub/blog/getting-started-with-perplexity

Grohs, M., Abb, L., Elsayed, N., & Rehse, J. R. (2024). Large Language Models Can Accomplish Business Process Management Tasks. *Lecture Notes in Business Information Processing, 492*, 453–465. Advance online publication. DOI: 10.1007/978-3-031-50974-2_34

Guo, Y., Guo, M., Su, J., Yang, Z., Zhu, M., Li, H., Qiu, M., & Liu, S. S. (2024). Bias in large language models: Origin, evaluation, and mitigation. arXiv preprint arXiv:2411.10915.

Guo, Y., Yin, C., Li, M., Ren, X., & Liu, P. (2018). Mobile e-Commerce Recommendation System Based on Multi-Source Information Fusion for Sustainable e-Business. *Sustainability (Basel), 10*(1), 147. DOI: 10.3390/su10010147

Guo, Z., Lai, A., Thygesen, J. H., Farrington, J., Keen, T., & Li, K. (2024). Large Language Models for Mental Health Applications: A Systematic Review (Preprint). *JMIR Mental Health, 11*, e57400. DOI: 10.2196/57400 PMID: 39423368

Gupta, J., Sharma, A., Singhania, S., & Abidi, A. I. (2025b). Legal Assist AI: Leveraging Transformer-Based Model for Effective Legal Assistance. arXiv preprint arXiv:2505.22003. https://arxiv.org/abs/2505.22003

Gupta, J., Sharma, A., Singhania, S., Adnan, M., Deo, S., Abidi, A. I., & Gupta, K. (2025a). Large Language Models Acing Chartered Accountancy. *SN Computer Science, 6*(957), 957. Advance online publication. DOI: 10.1007/s42979-025-04497-x

Gupta, R., & Pathak, C. (2014). A Machine Learning Framework for Predicting Purchase by Online Customers based on Dynamic Pricing. *Procedia Computer Science, 36*, 599–605. DOI: 10.1016/j.procs.2014.09.060

Hadiji, F., Sifa, R., Drachen, A., Thurau, C., Kersting, K., & Bauckhage, C. (2014). Predicting player churn in the wild. *2014 IEEE Conference on Computational Intelligence and Games*, 1–8. DOI: 10.1109/CIG.2014.6932876

Head, C. B., Jasper, P., McConnachie, M., Raftree, L., & Higdon, G. (2023). Large language model applications for evaluation: Opportunities and ethical implications. *New Directions for Evaluation, 2023*(178–179), 33–46. DOI: 10.1002/ev.20556

He, K., Chen, X., Xie, S., Li, Y., Dollar, P., & Girshick, R. (2022). Masked Autoencoders Are Scalable Vision Learners. *2022 IEEE/CVF Conference on Computer Vision and Pattern Recognition (CVPR)*, 15979–15988. DOI: 10.1109/CVPR52688.2022.01553

Hilditch, A., Webb, D., & Baˇ, J. (2023). *Natural language processing on customer note data.*

Hsieh, C. Y., Li, C. L., Yeh, C. K., Nakhost, H., Fujii, Y., Ratner, A., Krishna, R., Lee, C. Y., & Pfister, T. (2023). Distilling Step-by-Step! Outperforming Larger Language Models with Less Training Data and Smaller Model Sizes. *Proceedings of the Annual Meeting of the Association for Computational Linguistics*, 8003–8017. DOI: 10.18653/v1/2023.findings-acl.507

Hu, E., Shen, Y., Wallis, P., Allen-Zhu, Z., Li, Y., Wang, S., Wang, L., & Chen, W. (2021). LoRA: Low-Rank Adaptation of Large Language Models. *ICLR 2022 - 10th International Conference on Learning Representations*. https://arxiv.org/abs/2106.09685v2

Iacovides, G., Konstantinidis, T., Xu, M., & Mandic, D. (2024, November). Finllama: Llm-based financial sentiment analysis for algorithmic trading. In *Proceedings of the 5th ACM International Conference on AI in Finance* (pp. 134-141). DOI: 10.1145/3677052.3698696

Introducing Microsoft 365 Copilot – your copilot for work - The Official Microsoft Blog. (n.d.). Retrieved March 20, 2025, from https://blogs.microsoft.com/blog/2023/03/16/introducing-microsoft-365-copilot-your-copilot-for-work/

Ionescu, S., & Diaconita, V. (2023). Transforming Financial Decision-Making: The interplay of AI, cloud computing and advanced data management technologies. *International Journal of Computers, Communications & Control, 18*(6). Advance online publication. DOI: 10.15837/ijccc.2023.6.5735

Jacob, B., Kligys, S., Chen, B., Zhu, M., Tang, M., Howard, A., Adam, H., & Kalenichenko, D. (2017). Quantization and Training of Neural Networks for Efficient Integer-Arithmetic-Only Inference. *Proceedings of the IEEE Computer Society Conference on Computer Vision and Pattern Recognition*, 2704–2713. DOI: 10.1109/CVPR.2018.00286

Jeong, C. (2023). *A Study on the Implementation of Generative AI Services Using an Enterprise Data-Based LLM Application Architecture*. Advances in Artificial Intelligence and Machine Learning., DOI: 10.54364/AAIML.2023.1191

Jeong, C. (2024). Domain-specialized LLM: Financial fine-tuning and utilization method using Mistral 7B. *Journal of Intelligent Information Systems*, *30*(1), 93–120. DOI: 10.13088/jiis.2024.30.1.093

Jiang, J., Xie, H., Shen, Y., Zhang, Z., Lei, M., Zheng, Y., Fang, Y., Li, C., Huang, D., Zhang, W., Li, Y., Yang, X., Cui, B., & Chen, P. (2024). *SiriusBI: Building End-to-End Business Intelligence Enhanced by Large Language Models*.

Jiao, J., Afroogh, S., Xu, Y., Atkinson, D., & Phillips, C. (2024). Navigating LLM Ethics: Advancements, Challenges, and Future Directions. *ArXiv.Org*.

Jung, H. D., & Jang, B. (2024). Enhancing financial sentiment analysis ability of language model via targeted Numerical Change-Related masking. *IEEE Access : Practical Innovations, Open Solutions*, *12*, 50809–50820. DOI: 10.1109/ACCESS.2024.3385855

Kalaw, F. G. P., & Baxter, S. L. (2024). Ethical considerations for large language models in ophthalmology. *Current Opinion in Ophthalmology*, *35*(6), 438–446. Advance online publication. DOI: 10.1097/ICU.0000000000001083 PMID: 39259616

Kampik, T., Warmuth, C., Rebmann, A., Agam, R., Egger, L. N. P., Gerber, A., Hoffart, J., Kolk, J., Herzig, P., Decker, G., van der Aa, H., Polyvyanyy, A., Rinderle-Ma, S., Weber, I., & Weidlich, M. (2024). Large Process Models: A Vision for Business Process Management in the Age of Generative AI. *KI -. Künstliche Intelligenz*. Advance online publication. DOI: 10.1007/s13218-024-00863-8

Kapania, S., Wang, R., Li, T. J.-J., Li, T., & Shen, H. (2024). *"I'm categorizing LLM as a productivity tool": Examining ethics of LLM use in HCI research practices*. 1–23.

Kay, G. (2025, February 28). Inside Grok's war on "woke." Business Insider. https://www.businessinsider.com/xai-grok-training-bias-woke-idealogy-2025-02

Kerem, G. (2024). *The impact of AI in Business Analytics: Challenges and Opportunities*.

Khalifa, A. A., Ramesh, G., Deekshith, R., Harsha, K., & Shreyas, J. (2024, May). Forecasting Financial Frontiers: Real-time Insights in Stock Price Prediction through LSTM, Linear Regression, and Sentiment Analysis. In *2024 International Congress on Human-Computer Interaction, Optimization and Robotic Applications (HORA)* (pp. 1-6). IEEE. DOI: 10.1109/HORA61326.2024.10550829

Khan, M. A., Alhumoudi, H., Alakkas, A., Minhaj, S. M., & Alhashem, M. (2024). The present scenario of artificial intelligence and machine learning in financial services: An empirical study. *Journal of Infrastructure Policy and Development, 8*(11), 8818. DOI: 10.24294/jipd.v8i11.8818

Kim, A., Muhn, M., & Nikolaev, V. (2024). Financial statement analysis with large language models. *arXiv preprint arXiv:2407.17866*. DOI: 10.2139/ssrn.4835311

Klarna. (2024, February 27). Klarna AI assistant handles two-thirds of customer service chats in its first month. Klarna Press Release. https://www.klarna.com/international/press/klarna-ai-assistant-handles-two-thirds-of-customer-service-chats-in-its-first-month/

Kohl, O. (2024). *Why generative AI is the next big thing in business intelligence*. Pyramid.

Kshetri, N. (2023). Cybercrime and privacy threats of large language models. *IT Professional, 25*(3), 9–13. DOI: 10.1109/MITP.2023.3275489

Kumar, N. (2022). *Evolution of Natural Language Processing*. Linkdin. https://doi.org/https://www.linkedin.com/pulse/evolution-natural-language-processing-nitish-kumar/

Kumar, S., & Bhardwaj, M. (2021). A Comparative Study of Ensemble Learning Techniques for Financial Sentiment Classification. *IEEE Access : Practical Innovations, Open Solutions*.

Lai, J., Gan, W., Wu, J., Qi, Z., & Philip, S. Y. (2024). *Large language models in law: A survey*. AI Open.

Lalwani, P., Mishra, M. K., Chadha, J. S., & Sethi, P. (2022). Customer churn prediction system: A machine learning approach. *Computing, 104*(2), 271–294. DOI: 10.1007/s00607-021-00908-y

Lan, Y., Wu, Y., Xu, W., Feng, W., & Zhang, Y. (2025). Chinese fine-grained financial sentiment analysis with large language models. *Neural Computing & Applications, 37*(30), 24883–24892. DOI: 10.1007/s00521-024-10603-6

Leidner, J. L., Stevenson, M., & Court, R. (2018). *Challenges and Opportunities of NLP for HR Applications: A Discussion Paper.*

Le, P., & Zuidema, W. (2016). Quantifying the vanishing gradient and long distance dependency problem in recursive neural networks and recursive LSTMs. *Proceedings of the Annual Meeting of the Association for Computational Linguistics*, 87–93. DOI: 10.18653/v1/W16-1610

Leung, K. H., Mo, D. Y., Ho, G. T. S., Wu, C. H., & Huang, G. Q. (2020). Modelling near-real-time order arrival demand in e-commerce context: A machine learning predictive methodology. *Industrial Management & Data Systems*, *120*(6), 1149–1174. DOI: 10.1108/IMDS-12-2019-0646

Lin, C.-Y. (2004). ROUGE: A Package for Automatic Evaluation of Summaries. *Text Summarization Branches Out*, 74–81. https://aclanthology.org/W04-1013/

Li, Q., Hong, J., Xie, C., Tan, J., Xin, R., Hou, J., Yin, X., Wang, Z., Hendrycks, D., Wang, Z., Li, B., He, B., & Song, D. (2024). LLM-PBE: Assessing Data Privacy in Large Language Models. *Proceedings of the VLDB Endowment International Conference on Very Large Data Bases*, *17*(11), 3201–3214. DOI: 10.14778/3681954.3681994

Liu, S., Liu, G., Zhu, B., Luo, Y., Wu, L., & Wang, R. (2024). Balancing Innovation and Privacy: Data Security Strategies in Natural Language Processing Applications. *2024 5th International Conference on Machine Learning and Computer Application (ICMLCA)*, 609–613.

Liu, Y., Yao, Y., Ton, J.-F., Zhang, X., Guo, R., Cheng, H., Klochkov, Y., Taufiq, M. F., & Li, H. (2023). *Trustworthy LLMs: a Survey and Guideline for Evaluating Large Language Models' Alignment.* 1–81.

Liu, C., Arulappan, A., Naha, R., Mahanti, A., Kamruzzaman, J., & Ra, I. H. (2024). Large language models and sentiment analysis in financial markets: A review, datasets, and case study. *IEEE Access : Practical Innovations, Open Solutions*, *12*, 134041–134061. DOI: 10.1109/ACCESS.2024.3445413

Liu, P., Yuan, W., Fu, J., Jiang, Z., Hayashi, H., & Neubig, G. (2023). Pre-train, Prompt, and Predict: A Systematic Survey of Prompting Methods in Natural Language Processing. *ACM Computing Surveys*, *55*(9), 1–35. DOI: 10.1145/3560815

Liu, Z., Jiang, P., De Bock, K. W., Wang, J., Zhang, L., & Niu, X. (2024). Extreme gradient boosting trees with efficient Bayesian optimization for profit-driven customer churn prediction. *Technological Forecasting and Social Change*, *198*, 122945. DOI: 10.1016/j.techfore.2023.122945

Liu, Z., Lin, Y., Cao, Y., Hu, H., Wei, Y., Zhang, Z., Lin, S., & Guo, B. (2021). Swin Transformer: Hierarchical Vision Transformer using Shifted Windows. *2021 IEEE/CVF International Conference on Computer Vision (ICCV)*, 9992–10002. DOI: 10.1109/ICCV48922.2021.00986

Li, W., Manley, M., Read, J., Kaul, A., Bakir, M. S., & Yu, S. (2023). H3DATTEN: Heterogeneous 3-D integrated Hybrid analog and Digital Compute-in-Memory accelerator for Vision transformer Self-Attention. *IEEE Transactions on Very Large Scale Integration (VLSI). IEEE Transactions on Very Large Scale Integration (VLSI) Systems*, *31*(10), 1592–1602. DOI: 10.1109/TVLSI.2023.3299509

Luo, Y., Yang, Z., Meng, F., Li, Y., Zhou, J., & Zhang, Y. (2023). *An Empirical Study of Catastrophic Forgetting in Large Language Models During Continual Fine-tuning*. https://arxiv.org/abs/2308.08747v5

Martínez, P. A., Bernabé, G., & García, J. M. (2024). Code detection for hardware acceleration using large language models. *IEEE Access : Practical Innovations, Open Solutions*, *12*, 35271–35281. DOI: 10.1109/ACCESS.2024.3372853

Marvin, G., Hellen, N., Jjingo, D., & Nakatumba-Nabende, J. (2024). *Prompt Engineering in Large Language Models*. 387–402. DOI: 10.1007/978-981-99-7962-2_30

Mashaabi, M., Alotaibi, A., Qudaih, H., Alnashwan, R., & Al-Khalifa, H. (2022). Natural Language Processing in Customer Service: A Systematic Review. *ArXiv*.

Microsoft. (2024). Phi-4 technical report [Technical report]. arXiv. https://arxiv.org/abs/2412.08905

Miguéis, V. L., Van Den Poel, D., Camanho, A. S., Falcão, E., & Cunha, J. (2012). Modeling partial customer churn: On the value of first product-category purchase sequences. *Expert Systems with Applications*, *39*(12), 11250–11256. DOI: 10.1016/j.eswa.2012.03.073

Mikolov, T., Chen, K., Corrado, G., & Dean, J. (2013). Efficient Estimation of Word Representations in Vector Space. *1st International Conference on Learning Representations, ICLR 2013 - Workshop Track Proceedings*. https://arxiv.org/abs/1301.3781v3

Mishev, K., Gjorgjevikj, A., Vodenska, I., Chitkushev, L. T., & Trajanov, D. (2020). Evaluation of sentiment analysis in finance: From lexicons to transformers. *IEEE Access : Practical Innovations, Open Solutions*, *8*, 131662–131682. DOI: 10.1109/ACCESS.2020.3009626

Mitrović, S., Baesens, B., Lemahieu, W., & De Weerdt, J. (2018). On the operational efficiency of different feature types for telco Churn prediction. *European Journal of Operational Research, 267*(3), 1141–1155. DOI: 10.1016/j.ejor.2017.12.015

Mohamadi, S., Mujtaba, G., Le, N., Doretto, G., & Adjeroh, D. A. (2023). *ChatGPT in the Age of Generative AI and Large Language Models: A Concise Survey*. 1–60.

Mutually Human. (2025). *The Future of Data Analytics: How AI is reshaping the Landscape*.

Nallakaruppan, M. K., Chaturvedi, H., Grover, V., Balusamy, B., Jaraut, P., Bahadur, J., Meena, V. P., & Hameed, I. A. (2024). Credit risk assessment and financial decision support using explainable artificial intelligence. *Risks, 12*(10), 164. DOI: 10.3390/risks12100164

Nasseri, M., Brandtner, P., Zimmermann, R., Falatouri, T., Darbanian, F., & Obinwanne, T. (2023). Applications of Large Language Models (LLMs) in Business Analytics – Exemplary Use Cases in Data Preparation Tasks. *Lecture Notes in Computer Science (Including Subseries Lecture Notes in Artificial Intelligence and Lecture Notes in Bioinformatics), 14059 LNCS*, 182–198. DOI: 10.1007/978-3-031-48057-7_12

National Cancer Institute. (2020). International Agency for Research on Cancer. In *Definitions*. Qeios. DOI: 10.32388/PFG7JQ

Naveed, H., Khan, A. U., Qiu, S., Saqib, M., Anwar, S., Usman, M., Akhtar, N., Barnes, N., & Mian, A. (2023). *A Comprehensive Overview of Large Language Models*. https://arxiv.org/abs/2307.06435v10

Omiye, J. A., Lester, J. C., Spichak, S., Rotemberg, V., & Daneshjou, R. (2023). Large language models propagate race-based medicine. *NPJ Digital Medicine, 6*(1), 195.

Open, A. I. (2023). GPT-4 Technical Report. arXiv preprint arXiv:2303.08774. from https://arxiv.org/abs/2303.08774

Organisation for Economic Co-operation and Development. (2024). AI principles overview. OECD.AI. https://oecd.ai/en/ai-principles

Orza, P. (2024). *11 Real-Life Examples of NLP in Action*. Made in Webflow.

Pan, S., Zheng, Y., & Liu, Y. (2024). Integrating graphs with large language models: Methods and prospects. *IEEE Intelligent Systems, 39*(1), 64–68. DOI: 10.1109/MIS.2023.3332242

Perełkiewicz, M., & Po'swiata, R. P. (2024). *A Review of the Challenges with Massive Web-mined Corpora Used in Large Language Models Pre-Training*. https://arxiv.org/abs/2407.07630v1

Pestov, I. (2018, December). *"A History of Machine Translation from the Cold War... - Google Scholar*. Freecodecamp. Org.

Pilny, A., McAninch, K., Slone, A., & Moore, K. (2024). From manual to machine: Assessing the efficacy of large language models in content analysis. *Communication Research Reports*, *41*(2), 61–70. DOI: 10.1080/08824096.2024.2327547

Pinto, N., da Silva Figueiredo, L., & Garcia, A. C. (2021, May). Automatic prediction of stock market behavior based on time series, text mining and sentiment analysis: a systematic review. In *2021 IEEE 24th International Conference on Computer Supported Cooperative Work in Design (CSCWD)* (pp. 1203-1208). IEEE. DOI: 10.1109/CSCWD49262.2021.9437732

Preiksaitis, C., Ashenburg, N., Bunney, G., Chu, A., Kabeer, R., Riley, F., Ribeira, R., & Rose, C. (2024). The Role of large language Models in Transforming Emergency Medicine: Scoping review. *JMIR Medical Informatics*, *12*, e53787. DOI: 10.2196/53787 PMID: 38728687

Pustokhina, I. V., Pustokhin, D. A., Rh, A., Jayasankar, T., Jeyalakshmi, C., Díaz, V. G., & Shankar, K. (2021). Dynamic customer churn prediction strategy for business intelligence using text analytics with evolutionary optimization algorithms. *Information Processing & Management*, *58*(6), 102706. DOI: 10.1016/j.ipm.2021.102706

Raffel, C., Shazeer, N., Roberts, A., Lee, K., Narang, S., Matena, M., Zhou, Y., Li, W., & Liu, P. J. (2019). Exploring the Limits of Transfer Learning with a Unified Text-to-Text Transformer. *Journal of Machine Learning Research*, *21*, 1–67. https://arxiv.org/abs/1910.10683v4

Rahman, M., & Kumar, V. (2020). Machine Learning Based Customer Churn Prediction In Banking. *2020 4th International Conference on Electronics, Communication and Aerospace Technology (ICECA)*, 1196–1201. DOI: 10.1109/ICECA49313.2020.9297529

Raza, S., Bamgbose, O., Ghuge, S., Tavakol, F., Reji, D. J., & Bashir, S. R. (2024). *Developing Safe and Responsible Large Language Model : Can We Balance Bias Reduction and Language Understanding in Large Language Models?* 1–39.

read.dukeupress.edu. (2024). Regulatory analogies, llms, and generative ai [https://read.dukeupress.edu/critical-ai/article-abstract/doi/10.1215/2834703X-11205238 [Accessed: (17-march-2025)]].

Reite, E. J., Karlsen, J., & Westgaard, E. G. (2024). Improving client risk classification with machine learning to increase anti-money laundering detection efficiency. *Journal of Money Laundering Control*. DOI: 10.1108/JMLC-03-2024-0040

Renjith, S. (2015). *An Integrated Framework to Recommend Personalized Retention Actions to Control B2C E-Commerce Customer Churn*. DOI: 10.48550/ARXIV.1511.06975

Reznikov, B. R., & Member, F. C. (2023). *How Natural Language Processing Is Revolutionizing Business Operations*. Forbes Technology Council.

Roumeliotis, K. I., Tselikas, N. D., & Nasiopoulos, D. K. (2024). LLMS and NLP Models in Cryptocurrency Sentiment Analysis: A Comparative Classification Study. *Big Data and Cognitive Computing*, *8*(6), 63. DOI: 10.3390/bdcc8060063

Runge, J., Gao, P., Garcin, F., & Faltings, B. (2014). Churn prediction for high-value players in casual social games. *2014 IEEE Conference on Computational Intelligence and Games*, 1–8. DOI: 10.1109/CIG.2014.6932875

Sahoo, S., & Dutta, K. (2024). *THE SHIFTING PARADIGM IN AI : WHY Generative Artificial Intelligence IS THE NEW ECONOMIC VARIABLE.*

Sahoo, P., Singh, A. K., Saha, S., Jain, V., Mondal, S., & Chadha, A. (2024). *A Systematic Survey of Prompt Engineering in Large Language Models: Techniques and Applications*. https://arxiv.org/abs/2402.07927v2

Sahoo, S. S., Plasek, J. M., Xu, H., Uzuner, Ö., Cohen, T., Yetisgen, M., Liu, H., Meystre, S., & Wang, Y. (2024). Large language models for biomedicine: Foundations, opportunities, challenges, and best practices. *Journal of the American Medical Informatics Association : JAMIA*, *31*(9), 2114–2124. DOI: 10.1093/jamia/ocae074 PMID: 38657567

Sarker, I. H. (2021). Machine Learning: Algorithms, Real-World Applications and Research Directions. *SN Computer Science*, *2*(3), 160. DOI: 10.1007/s42979-021-00592-x PMID: 33778771

Selim, A., Zhao, J., & Yang, B. (2024). Large language model for smart inverter Cyber-Attack detection via textual analysis of Volt/VAR commands. *IEEE Transactions on Smart Grid*, *1*(6), 6179–6182. Advance online publication. DOI: 10.1109/TSG.2024.3453648

Sezgin, E. (2024). Redefining virtual Assistants in Health care: The future with large language models. *Journal of Medical Internet Research*, *26*, e53225. DOI: 10.2196/53225 PMID: 38241074

Shah, V. (2024). *The impact of AI in business analytics: A complete guide*. Thoughtspot.

Sharma, V., & Dey, A. (2020). An Ensemble Learning Approach for Stock Market Prediction Using Twitter Sentiment Analysis. *Procedia Computer Science*.

Shirazi, F., & Mohammadi, M. (2019). A big data analytics model for customer churn prediction in the retiree segment. *International Journal of Information Management, 48*, 238–253. DOI: 10.1016/j.ijinfomgt.2018.10.005

Shobayo, O., Adeyemi-Longe, S., Popoola, O., & Ogunleye, B. (2024). Innovative sentiment analysis and prediction of stock price using FINBERT, GPT-4 and Logistic Regression: A Data-Driven Approach. *Big Data and Cognitive Computing, 8*(11), 143. DOI: 10.3390/bdcc8110143

Sinha, R., Elhafsi, A., Agia, C., Foutter, M., Schmerling, E., & Pavone, M. (2024). Real-Time Anomaly Detection and Reactive Planning with Large Language Models. *arXiv (Cornell University)*. /arxiv.2407.08735DOI: 10.15607/RSS.2024.XX.114

Strubell, E., Ganesh, A., & McCallum, A. (2019). Energy and Policy Considerations for Deep Learning in NLP. *Proceedings of the 57th Annual Meeting of the Association for Computational Linguistics*. DOI: 10.18653/v1/P19-1355

Sutskever, I., Vinyals, O., & Le, Q. V. (2014). Sequence to Sequence Learning with Neural Networks. *Advances in Neural Information Processing Systems, 4*(January), 3104–3112. https://arxiv.org/abs/1409.3215v3

Team, G., Anil, R., Borgeaud, S., Alayrac, J.-B., Yu, J., Soricut, R., Schalkwyk, J., Dai, A. M., Hauth, A., Millican, K., Silver, D., Johnson, M., Antonoglou, I., Schrittwieser, J., Glaese, A., Chen, J., Pitler, E., Lillicrap, T., Lazaridou, A., & Vinyals, O. (2023). *Gemini: A Family of Highly Capable Multimodal Models*. https://arxiv.org/abs/2312.11805v4

Telenti, A., Auli, M., Hie, B. L., Maher, C., Saria, S., & Ioannidis, J. P. A. (2024). Large language models for science and medicine. *European Journal of Clinical Investigation, 54*(6), e14183. Advance online publication. DOI: 10.1111/eci.14183 PMID: 38381530

The Virtual Economy of the Metaverse. (2022). The Virtual Economy of the Metaverse: Computer Vision and Deep Learning Algorithms, Customer Engagement Tools, and Behavioral Predictive Analytics. *Linguistic and Philosophical Investigations, 21*(0), 41. DOI: 10.22381/lpi2120223 theconversation.com. (2023). Ageism, sexism, classism and more: 7 examples of bias in ai-generated images [https://theconversation.com/ageism-sexism-classism -and- more-7-examples-of-bias-in-ai-generated-images-208748 [Accessed:(15-march-2025)]].

Tian, X., Tian, Z., Khatib, S. F. A., & Wang, Y. (2024). Machine learning in internet financial risk management: A systematic literature review. *PLoS One*, *19*(4), e0300195. DOI: 10.1371/journal.pone.0300195 PMID: 38625972

Tlaie, A. (2024). *Exploring and steering the moral compass of Large Language Models. 6*, 1–12.

Touvron, H., Lavril, T., Izacard, G., Martinet, X., Lachaux, M.-A., Lacroix, T., Rozière, B., Goyal, N., Hambro, E., Azhar, F., Rodriguez, A., Joulin, A., Grave, E., & Lample, G. (2023). *LLaMA: Open and Efficient Foundation Language Models*. https://arxiv.org/abs/2302.13971v1

Tripathi, S., Sukumaran, R., & Cook, T. S. (2024). Efficient healthcare with large language models: Optimizing clinical workflow and enhancing patient care. *Journal of the American Medical Informatics Association : JAMIA*, *31*(6), 1436–1440. DOI: 10.1093/jamia/ocad258 PMID: 38273739

Trummer, I. (2022). From BERT to GPT-3 codex. *Proceedings of the VLDB Endowment International Conference on Very Large Data Bases*, *15*(12), 3770–3773. DOI: 10.14778/3554821.3554896

Ungless, E. L., Vitsakis, N., Garforth, J., Ross, B., & Birch, A. (2024). *E THICS W HITEPAPER : Whitepaper on Ethical Research into Large Language Models*. 1–47.

Vaswani, A., Shazeer, N., Parmar, N., Uszkoreit, J., Jones, L., Gomez, A. N., Kaiser, Ł., & Polosukhin, I. (2017). Attention Is All You Need. *Advances in Neural Information Processing Systems, 2017-December*, 5999–6009. https://arxiv.org/abs/1706.03762v7

Vaswani, A., Shazeer, N., Parmar, N., Uszkoreit, J., Jones, L., Gomez, A. N., Kaiser, Ł., & Polosukhin, I. (2017). Attention is all you need. *Advances in Neural Information Processing Systems*.

Vertsel, A., & Rumiantsau, M. (2024). *Hybrid LLM/Rule-based Approaches to Business Insights Generation from Structured Data*.

Vizine Pereira, A. L., & Hruschka, E. R. (2015). Simultaneous co-clustering and learning to address the cold start problem in recommender systems. *Knowledge-Based Systems*, *82*, 11–19. DOI: 10.1016/j.knosys.2015.02.016

Vo, N. N. Y., Liu, S., Li, X., & Xu, G. (2021). Leveraging unstructured call log data for customer churn prediction. *Knowledge-Based Systems, 212*, 106586. DOI: 10.1016/j.knosys.2020.106586

Wang, L., Cheng, Y., Xiang, A., Zhang, J., & Yang, H. (2024). Application of natural language processing in financial risk detection. *ArXiv Preprint ArXiv:2406.09765*.

Wang, X., Li, X., Yin, Z., Wu, Y., & Liu, J. (2023). Emotional intelligence of Large Language Models. *Journal of Pacific Rim Psychology, 17*, 18344909231213958. Advance online publication. DOI: 10.1177/18344909231213958

Wasserkrug, S., Boussioux, L., Hertog, D. den, & Greenland, A. (2024). *Using Large Language Models to Create Analytics Solutions*.

Weizenbaum, J. (1966). ELIZA-A computer program for the study of natural language communication between man and machine. *Communications of the ACM, 9*(1), 36–45. DOI: 10.1145/365153.365168

Woensel, W. Van, & Motie, S. (2024). *NLP4PBM : A Systematic Review on Process Extraction using Natural Language Processing with Rule-based, Machine and Deep Learning Methods*. 1–50.

Wood, T. (2024). *Business uses of natural language processing - the 2024 capabilities of NLP*.

Wu, S., Irsoy, O., Lu, S., Dabravolski, V., Dredze, M., Gehrmann, S., . . . Mann, G. (2023). BloombergGPT: A Large Language Model for Finance. arXiv preprint arXiv:2303.17564. https://arxiv.org/abs/2303.17564

Xing, F. (2025). Designing heterogeneous llm agents for financial sentiment analysis. *ACM Transactions on Management Information Systems, 16*(1), 1–24. DOI: 10.1145/3688399

Yan, B., Li, K., Xu, M., Dong, Y., Zhang, Y., Ren, Z., & Cheng, X. (2024). On protecting the data privacy of large language models (llms): A survey. arXiv preprint arXiv:2403.05156.

Yang, J., Wang, Z., Lin, Y., & Zhao, Z. (2024a). Global Data Constraints: Ethical and Effectiveness Challenges in Large Language Model. *ArXiv E-Prints*, arXiv--2406.

Yang, J., Wang, Z., Lin, Y., & Zhao, Z. (2024b). *Large Language Model Tokenizer Bias: A Case Study and Solution on GPT-4o*. 1–6.

Yang, Y., Uy, M. C. S., & Huang, A. (2020). Finbert: A pretrained language model for financial communications. *arXiv preprint arXiv:2006.08097*. Bapi, R. S., et al. (2022). Financial News Prediction Using Sentiment Analysis for Portfolio Optimization. Expert Systems with Applications.

Yang, Z. (2025, January 31). Here's How DeepSeek Censorship Actually Works—and How to Get Around It. WIRED. https://www.wired.com/story/deepseek-censorship/

Yang, N. (2022). Financial big Data Management and control and Artificial intelligence analysis method based on data mining technology. *Wireless Communications and Mobile Computing*, *2022*(1), 1–13. DOI: 10.1155/2022/7596094

Zaidan, E., & Ibrahim, I. A. (2024). Ai governance in a complex and rapidly changing regulatory landscape: A global perspective. *Humanities & Social Sciences Communications*, *11*(1), 1–18.

Zhang, B., Nagesh, A., & Knight, K. (2020). Parallel Corpus Filtering via Pretrained Language Models. *Proceedings of the Annual Meeting of the Association for Computational Linguistics*, 8545–8554. DOI: 10.18653/v1/2020.acl-main.756

Zhang, L., Yu, Q., Zhou, B., Zhang, Y., & Hu, Z. (2023). Incorporating feature interactions and contrastive learning for credit prediction. *IEEE Access : Practical Innovations, Open Solutions*, *11*, 111944–111955. DOI: 10.1109/ACCESS.2023.3322429

Zhao, H., Wu, L., Shan, Y., Jin, Z., Sui, Y., Liu, Z., Feng, N., Li, M., & Zhang, W. (2015). *A Comprehensive Survey of Large Language Models in Management: Applications, Challenges, and Opportunities*. DOI: 10.2139/ssrn.4932769

Zhou, S., Zhou, Z., Wang, C., Liang, Y., Wang, L., Zhang, J., Zhang, J., & Lv, C. (2024). A User-Centered framework for data privacy protection using large language models and attention mechanisms. *Applied Sciences (Basel, Switzerland)*, *14*(15), 6824. DOI: 10.3390/app14156824

Zhui, L., Fenghe, L., Xuehu, W., Qining, F., & Wei, R. (2024). Ethical Considerations and Fundamental Principles of large language models in medical Education: Viewpoint. *Journal of Medical Internet Research*, *26*, e60083. DOI: 10.2196/60083 PMID: 38971715

Zonta, T., Da Costa, C. A., Da Rosa Righi, R., De Lima, M. J., Da Trindade, E. S., & Li, G. P. (2020). Predictive maintenance in the Industry 4.0: A systematic literature review. *Computers & Industrial Engineering*, *150*, 106889. DOI: 10.1016/j.cie.2020.106889

About the Contributors

Ali Imam Abidi is an academic expert in Large Language Models, Data Science, Computer Vision, Visual Data Analytics, and Deformable Image Registration, with a Ph.D. from IIT (BHU) Varanasi. His initial research focused on thoracic CT image registration, addressing breathing-induced deformations. Since then, he has widened his research avenues to a broader range of computer vision applications. Currently an Associate Professor at Sharda University, he has 9 years of experience in academia and industry, including roles at Infosys and the National Institute of Design. Dr. Abidi has published widely in reputable journals, contributed to conferences, and holds patents in image processing and AI-driven technologies. He is also active in academic administration and Ph.D. supervision, emphasizing hands-on learning.

Shreyas Athinarapu is pursuing Bachelor of Technology in Vellore Institute of Technology, Chennai, India. He has developed significant interests in natural language processing, computer vision, and intelligent systems during his studies. His current research involves large language models, real-time data analysis and document intelligence in different fields such as healthcare, finance and insurance. Shreyas has been involved with projects covering medical imaging, and automated document processing. He hopes to connect the gap between academic research and practical applications by designing scalable, AI-driven systems that can facilitate decision making. Upon graduation, he plans to further his research in applied artificial intelligence through advanced studies and industry collaboration.

Parihar Suresh Dahake is working as an Assistant Professor at Ramdeobaba University,Nagpur in the School of Management. He received his BTech, MBA. and Ph.D. from the Rashtrasant Tukdoji Maharaj Nagpur University and PGDIBO, M.Com from Indira Gandhi National Open University (IGNOU). Dr.Parihar dahake has Qualified SET(Commerce) and SET (Management). He has 15 Years of Teaching Experience and 13 years of Research Experience. His areas of expertise are Consumer behavior, Organizational Behaviour, Marketing management, and IMC

Nihar Suresh Dahake is currently working as an Assistant Professor at Dr. Ambedkar Institute of Management Studies and Research. He holds B.Com., M.Com., and MBA degrees from Rashtrasant Tukadoji Maharaj Nagpur University and obtained his Ph.D. from Sant Gadge Baba Amravati University. Dr. Dahake has qualified SET in both Commerce and Management. He possesses 14 years of teaching experience and 8 years of research experience. His academic and research interests include Financial Accounting, Consumer Behaviour, Marketing Management, and Financial Management.

Krishna Gandhi is a Technology Leader in AI, Automation, and Quality Assurance (QA) with deep expertise in Artificial Intelligence (AI), Machine Learning (ML), and Generative AI. She specializes in Geographic Information Systems (GIS), software quality assurance, and application development across the Energy, Mobile Applications, and Network domains, leveraging AI-driven automation to enhance system reliability, data accuracy, and operational efficiency. With extensive experience in cloud computing (Azure, AWS, GCP), and big data analytics, Krishna has led the development and deployment of AI-powered automation tools and frameworks in energy sector. Her work focuses on optimizing geospatial data processing, ensuring data integrity, and improving decision-making through AI-driven insights. As an expert in software development and testing, Krishna drives innovation by integrating AI and automated quality assurance solutions into complex enterprise applications. She is passionate about bridging AI, GIS, and automation to deliver scalable, high-performance solutions for the Energy sector while ensuring compliance, security, and efficiency in AI-driven applications.

Pawan Kr. Goel is an accomplished academician and researcher with 19.5 years of experience, is an Associate Professor at Raj Kumar Goel Institute of Technology, Ghaziabad. He holds a Ph.D. in Computer Science Engineering and is UGC NET qualified. His expertise spans various domains, including wireless sensor networks, cloud computing, and artificial intelligence. Dr. Goel has published extensively in prestigious journals and conferences, with notable papers on topics such as cybersecurity, IoT, and machine learning. He is an active member of numerous professional bodies, including the IEEE, Computer Society of India and the International Association of Engineers. Recognized for his contributions, he has received several awards and certificates of appreciation. Dr. Goel is dedicated to fostering industry-academia collaborations and has organized numerous workshops and seminars. He is also involved in various training programs, MOOCs, and NPTEL certifications, contributing significantly to the advancement of education and research in his field.

Jatin Gupta is an undergraduate student at Sharda University, Greater Noida, with a specialization in Data Science & Analytics. His research interests include deep learning in CNNs and natural language processing, particularly large language models (LLMs). He is currently working on CA-ThinkFlow—a project focused on developing a large language model for the finance sector—and has led research in Legal Assist AI and digital image tampering detection. He also interned at Infosys, where he contributed to enhancing demand forecasting models. Additionally, he has written book chapters on Challenges in Current Health Information Systems is in progress. His work spans diverse areas, including demand forecasting, real-time translation for the deaf and mute, and innovative cybersecurity measures, with multiple publications set to be published and several research articles in progress.

Lakshmi Harika Palivela completed her B.Tech in Computer Science and Engineering from Jawaharlal Nehru Technological University Kakinada in 2009, M.Tech in Computer Science and Engineering from Jawaharlal Nehru Technological University Kakinada in 2011, and Ph.D. in the faculty of Information and Communication Engineering MIT Campus, Anna University, Chennai in 2020. She is currently working as an Assistant Professor (Sr.) at Vellore Institute of Technology, Chennai. Her research interests include Machine Learning, Distributed systems, Image processing, Data Analytics and Video Analytics

Akhil Sharma is a senior-year university student at Sharda University in Knowledge Park III, Greater Noida, with a focus on data analysis and visualization. His research interests include data analysis, machine learning, and large language models. He is currently working on CA-ThinkFlow and has previously undertaken projects such as Legal Assist AI and Digital Image Tampering Detection and Task Analysis. He has gained practical experience through internships at Halonix Technologies and Terre Armée, and has contributed to publications including Legal Assist AI: Leveraging Transformers for Legal Assistance, Indian Sign Language Detection using Machine Learning, and Challenges in Health Information Systems.

Pankaj Verma is a Senior Data Scientist and AI practitioner with over 13 years of expertise in machine learning, deep learning, computer vision, and Generative AI. He holds an MBA in Operations Management, Finance, and Data Analytics, along with a Bachelor's in Electronics and Communication Engineering. His research spans multiple industries, including Oil & Gas, Renewable Energy, Power transmission, where he focuses on AI-driven solutions to optimize operations, enhance decision-making, and improve efficiency. With a strong foundation in statistical inference, predictive modelling, and causal analysis, Pankaj specializes in time series forecasting, anomaly detection, causal analysis and large-scale MLOps frameworks for AI deployment. His expertise includes causal inference for root cause analysis and unsupervised learning techniques for anomaly detection and predictive maintenance. His recent work explores Retrieval-Augmented Generation (RAG) and transformer-based architectures to enhance AI-driven decision-making in complex environments. As a data science enthusiast, Pankaj is passionate about bridging the gap between theoretical research and industrial applications, leveraging AI-powered solutions to drive efficiency, reduce risks, and create tangible business impact.

Index

A

AI Governance 74, 255, 257, 266, 267, 268, 269, 293, 295, 304, 305, 306, 307
Algorithmic Bias 2, 133, 134, 178, 279, 317

B

Bias 1, 2, 5, 6, 15, 16, 17, 18, 19, 35, 39, 41, 43, 56, 62, 63, 66, 73, 85, 87, 90, 97, 117, 118, 120, 130, 133, 134, 143, 145, 161, 162, 165, 166, 178, 180, 186, 225, 227, 238, 255, 256, 257, 258, 259, 269, 278, 279, 283, 293, 294, 295, 296, 297, 307, 316, 317, 321
Business Analytics 1, 2, 3, 6, 41, 45, 46, 48, 50, 52, 54, 57, 59, 72, 75, 76, 77, 78, 81, 85, 86, 87, 88, 89, 90, 93, 96, 97, 113, 115, 116, 117, 118, 119, 120, 121, 124, 125, 126, 127, 129, 130, 131, 132, 290, 328
Business Applications 49, 52, 79, 146, 184, 190

C

Chatbots 4, 30, 48, 70, 71, 105, 113, 121, 122, 123, 133, 150, 151, 153, 154, 173, 178, 183, 184
Churn Prediction 190, 191, 194, 195, 196, 197, 198, 203, 206, 207, 208, 210, 212, 213, 214
Customer Retention 105, 175, 189, 190, 191, 195, 196, 197, 202, 203, 205, 206, 207, 208, 209, 210, 212

D

Data Privacy 1, 5, 9, 33, 41, 72, 85, 87, 90, 97, 117, 122, 127, 128, 133, 134, 170, 177, 186, 256, 260, 265, 269, 278, 279, 282, 284, 288, 291, 294, 298, 303, 307, 316, 317, 320, 322, 326, 329
Deep Learning 46, 47, 49, 56, 82, 88, 92, 101, 102, 133, 134, 135, 138, 142, 145, 149, 179, 187, 188, 190, 202, 203, 208, 210, 214, 218, 220, 221, 250, 253, 262, 273, 300, 311

E

E-Commerce 32, 53, 120, 121, 125, 134, 153, 174, 183, 189, 190, 191, 192, 193, 195, 196, 197, 198, 202, 203, 204, 205, 206, 207, 208, 209, 210, 212, 213
Ethics 1, 3, 4, 5, 6, 7, 11, 34, 37, 38, 39, 40, 41, 42, 43, 256, 257, 264, 268, 294, 295, 302, 306
Explainability 1, 77, 118, 202, 256, 262, 263, 294, 300, 301
Explainable AI 97, 118, 129, 255, 256, 262, 278, 293, 294, 300, 316

F

Fairness 6, 15, 18, 32, 33, 41, 63, 73, 79, 97, 127, 130, 145, 161, 165, 178, 185, 204, 211, 255, 256, 257, 262, 265, 268, 279, 281, 282, 283, 293, 294, 295, 300, 303, 306, 317, 319, 320, 321
Financial Sentiment Analysis 216, 217, 218, 219, 220, 221, 222, 224, 226, 230, 233, 248, 250, 251, 288, 291, 326, 329
Fine-Tuning 49, 64, 65, 66, 68, 76, 81, 85, 86, 88, 90, 99, 102, 119, 127, 129, 144, 145, 148, 149, 222, 224, 225, 229, 260, 261, 281, 288, 298, 299, 319, 326
Fraud Detection 107, 108, 133, 166, 167, 168, 264, 271, 272, 273, 276, 277, 279, 281, 282, 284, 286, 302, 309, 310, 311, 314, 315, 317, 319, 320, 322, 324

G

Generative AI 128, 131, 132, 252, 269, 307
Governance Frameworks 178, 267, 268, 305, 306

L

Large Language Models 1, 2, 7, 15, 22, 29, 34, 41, 43, 45, 46, 47, 48, 50, 52, 57, 63, 64, 66, 69, 72, 73, 74, 76, 77, 78, 79, 80, 81, 82, 83, 85, 86, 87, 88, 90, 93, 107, 110, 120, 122, 128, 130, 131, 132, 133, 135, 143, 154, 179, 184, 187, 216, 222, 234, 250, 251, 252, 255, 256, 257, 258, 259, 260, 266, 269, 271, 272, 273, 274, 277, 279, 286, 287, 288, 289, 290, 291, 293, 294, 295, 296, 297, 298, 304, 307, 309, 310, 311, 312, 315, 317, 324, 325, 326, 327, 328, 329
law 20, 22, 33, 53, 73, 125, 185, 256, 262, 263, 264, 267, 269, 294, 300, 301, 302, 305, 307
LLM 1, 2, 3, 5, 6, 7, 8, 9, 10, 11, 13, 14, 15, 17, 20, 21, 22, 23, 25, 26, 27, 28, 29, 32, 34, 35, 36, 37, 38, 39, 40, 41, 43, 48, 49, 52, 53, 54, 55, 56, 61, 62, 64, 65, 66, 67, 68, 69, 70, 71, 72, 74, 75, 86, 87, 88, 89, 90, 94, 95, 96, 97, 98, 99, 100, 101, 102, 103, 104, 105, 106, 107, 108, 109, 110, 111, 112, 113, 114, 115, 116, 117, 118, 119, 120, 121, 122, 123, 124, 125, 126, 127, 128, 129, 130, 131, 132, 134, 144, 145, 154, 187, 188, 215, 216, 217, 221, 222, 223, 231, 250, 251, 256, 260, 261, 262, 263, 273, 274, 275, 276, 277, 278, 279, 281, 282, 283, 284, 288, 291, 294, 298, 299, 300, 301, 311, 312, 313, 314, 315, 316, 317, 319, 320, 321, 322, 326, 329
LLMOps 45, 49, 72, 78

M

Machine Learning 13, 31, 34, 82, 88, 90, 91, 131, 135, 139, 150, 163, 187, 189, 191, 194, 195, 196, 202, 203, 204, 205, 206, 211, 212, 213, 214, 218, 221, 222, 253, 262, 271, 272, 282, 286, 288, 289, 290, 300, 309, 310, 320, 324, 326, 327, 328
Machine Learning Models 139, 189, 196, 202, 218, 253, 262, 300
Model Transparency 55, 79

N

Nagpur 189, 192, 193, 195, 196, 202, 204, 206, 207, 209
Natural Language Processing 46, 47, 49, 52, 56, 57, 91, 100, 132, 133, 134, 138, 155, 185, 187, 188, 194, 213, 216, 218, 223, 249, 252, 253, 255, 256, 257, 273, 293, 294, 295, 311

O

OpenAI's GPT 271, 309

P

Predictive Analytics 76, 91, 128, 189, 190, 191, 196, 197, 199, 202, 203, 204, 206, 207, 211, 214
Prompt Engineering 22, 52, 66, 81, 82, 119, 129

R

Regulatory Compliance 1, 2, 41, 77, 107, 117, 123, 124, 153, 166, 168
Reinforcement Learning 66, 67, 77, 125, 220, 234, 252, 253
Risk Management 35, 90, 107, 109, 120, 122, 130, 169, 186, 220, 271, 272, 273, 274, 277, 279, 282, 283, 284, 290, 309, 310, 311, 312, 315, 317, 320, 321, 322, 328
Rule-Based Systems 47, 49, 118, 133, 134, 135, 136, 137, 138, 139, 263, 301

S

Security Risks 73
Sentiment Analysis 2, 3, 49, 85, 87, 91, 94, 106, 114, 116, 133, 139, 140, 145, 146, 150, 157, 164, 169, 170, 178, 180, 215, 216, 217, 218, 219, 220, 221,

222, 223, 224, 225, 226, 230, 231, 233, 234, 244, 248, 249, 250, 251, 252, 253, 257, 258, 271, 272, 287, 288, 289, 290, 291, 295, 296, 309, 310, 325, 326, 327, 328, 329

T

Text Preprocessing 134, 145
Transformer Architecture 57, 88, 143, 218, 273, 311
Transformer Models 56, 134, 135, 149, 215, 216, 219, 224, 230, 231, 235, 236, 239, 245, 248, 253

www.ingramcontent.com/pod-product-compliance
Lightning Source LLC
LaVergne TN
LVHW060004031026
849161LV00025B/1412